Genocide

A Critical Bibliographic Review

Edited by *Israel W. Charny*

Contributing Editors

ALAN L. BERGER

FRANK CHALK

ISRAEL W. CHARNY

WILLIAM C. GAY

DAVID R. HAWK

RICHARD G. HOVANNISIAN

KURT JONASSOHN

LEO KUPER

JAMES E. MACE

RONALD E. SANTONI

SAMUEL TOTTEN

Facts On File Publications
New York, New York

Genocide: A Critical Bibliographic Review

copyright © 1988 by the Institute of the International Conference on the Holocaust and Genocide, P.O. Box 10311, Jerusalem 93624, Israel

Published in the United States of America by Facts on File, Inc.
460 Park Avenue South, New York, N.Y. 10016

First published in Great Britain by Mansell Publishing Limited
6 All Saints Street, London N1 9RL

Library of Congress Cataloging-in-Publication Data

Genocide: a critical bibliographic review.

  Bibliography: p.
  1. Genocide—Bibliography. I. Charny, Israel W.
Z7164.G45G45 1988 [HV6542]   016.3641'51 87–33215
ISBN 0-8160-1903-7

A publication of the
Institute of the International Conference
on the Holocaust and Genocide

Printed in Great Britain
10 9 8 7 6 5 4 3 2 1

Contents

iii

Foreword

Genocide pervades the contemporary imagination and well it might, for over 50 million persons have fallen victim to genocide since 1900; since 1945 alone there had been major examples in Bangladesh, Cambodia, Burundi, and elsewhere. Yet with all this politically sanctioned death and human suffering, both the origin and the meaning of this form of human destructiveness are still problematic. What is genocide? What is its history? How, if at all, is it related to specific forms of government? To types of economic organization? Is there a basic structure to genocide? Or perhaps a logic, though irrational, that underlies various examples of genocide? Do present attempts to explain genocide actually succeed? What conditions must be met if genocide is to be averted? Why do some intended victims resist and others not? Does resistance save lives or only lead to more massive destruction?

Only recently have scholars begun to explore these issues with the care they deserve and there is much still to be done. To focus on issues of the sort posed may help save lives; it will certainly deepen our understanding of what man is capable of, of the nature of society, and the sources of human conflict.

ROGER W. SMITH
Department of Government
College of William and Mary

Introduction

Each chapter of *Genocide: A Critical Bibliographic Review* is intended to present an authoritative, encyclopedia-like statement of the knowledge base in a given field or area of study of genocide, and an annotated critical bibliography which represents, in the judgment of the Contributing Editor, a significant compilation of definitive and meaningful literature in the area of study.

To which professions or fields of study should we turn to understand genocide? Perhaps *history* is the first to spring to mind. The conventional historical record tends to be a bleak story of unending losses of life of many peoples, almost with a refrain that this is the way it is in the history of mankind and so it will forever be: mass killers will reign in many eras, and over and over again innocent peoples will pay the ultimate price. Historians, moreover, are often so involved in the recording and documentation of specific events that they do not do enough tracing of the broad patterns of sequences, causes, and effects of genocide at a level of abstraction that would set the stage for increased recognition of dangers and the likelihood of new events of mass death in the *future*.

Shall we turn to *psychology* to understand the nature of genocide? There certainly is progress in our understanding of the psychology of individuals who are responsible for mass murder, and there is substantial progress in our understanding of the psychology of the collective group and its powerful mechanisms of ideological legitimation, routinization and authorization, mob intoxication and euphoria, diffusion of values and responsibility, and more. Yet how often are the insights and theories available to modern-day psychology realistically applicable to and at all usable for intervention in the processes of *realpolitik* of governments, leaders and peoples? Moreover, psychologists too often tend to overemphasize an almost naïve psychologization of life and are reluctant to acknowledge and integrate psychological insight with historical, political, and other important contexts for understanding major human events.

Move from one field of study to another and the same picture emerges: each yields significant insights into the nature of genocide, and none is sufficient in itself to offer an interpretation of events like the "brilliant" organization of the Holocaust by the advanced German culture, the Cambodian regime's slaughter of its own people, or the Turkish devotion not only to ridding Anatolia of the Armenians but to this day, seventy and more years later, to denying there ever was a genocide. *Sociology* offers important interpretations of categories of events and patterns of societies, but generally generates little appreciation of the passions and dynamics of the actors in these societal events. *Literature* and *the arts* penetrate deeply into the interior of a given event with moving characterizations of the real human actors as well as the dramas of meanings and sequences that unfold, yet rarely go beyond the artist's gift to produce systematic concepts and categories and methods of collection of data that can make possible systematic efforts to identify and confront pre-genocidal warnings in the future. The field of *political science* would appear to be in a singular position to represent the actions of government leaders and the workings of state bureaucracies that execute genocidal policy, yet seems unable to grasp the mysteries of national and ethnic cultural styles, and the historical markers that shed light on the readiness of a people in any given era and place in history to undertake genocidal policies. And so on—philosophy and values and religious thought; education; the fields of communication and information systems; law, human rights, and international relations; and still others all are very relevant to our understanding of genocide and the possibilities of its prevention in the future, yet none in its own right can encompass the sources and dynamics that sustain the process wherein a whole society devotes itself, at so many different levels of action, to the mass annihilation of a target people or peoples.

This volume is designed to organize the state-of-the-art knowledge in various fields of the study of genocide and its prevention. Would that it were already possible to integrate information and concepts from scholars in different fields in a single encompassing model of genocide! It is our judgment that this task is beyond us, but that it is prudent and appropriate at this point to assemble parallel insights from different fields. A series of uniform guidelines was submitted to all of the Contributing Editors who agreed to act as spokesmen for their respective fields of study, but each chapter has been left in the language of concepts and jargon of its respective field as well as to the idiomatic treatment of the Contributing Editor.

An interesting exception and hopeful harbinger of future integrations of knowledge from different fields is represented by those works that are, in fact, cited in more than one disciplinary treatment. At first, we considered restricting the annotation of a given item to its most appropriate context, and cross-referencing to that annotation if the editors of other chapters wished to refer to the same work. However, it became clear that the annotation of an item represented an important part of the tapestry of the chapter in which it was submitted, and that there are interesting nuances in the way the same work is treated by different editors representing different disciplines. In the end, it was decided to allow for multiple entries except in a number of instances in which the editorial judgment was that the repetition was superfluous. No doubt readers will enjoy tracking which works were awarded the honor of being cited on different occasions by scholars of different fields.

The Contributing Editors were each asked to summarize what it is that we know today in their discipline about the Holocaust and other genocides, what are the key questions that require further scholarship in their field, and what are the prospects for achieving significant development of information in and understanding of these questions in the foreseeable future. On reading the various chapters, one also gains the impression that in many cases it is simply too early in the history of serious scholarly study of genocide to attempt definitive and critical formulations. One reason is that we simply know too little about the phenomenon of genocide in virtually every field. Another reason is that each discipline soon runs up against the limits of understanding possible when one is restricted to working only in the language of that single discipline, and to summarize the state of the art and knowledge in a given field about genocide is not fully possible without access to vital pieces of information that become available only when the knowledge it provides is integrated with that from other disciplines.

This volume begins with an introduction and overview of the emerging study of genocide—for all practical purposes a new concept that is beginning to come into its own as a distinct focus of scholarship. A second chapter reviews the development of concepts and even a few beginning real-world projects and efforts at prevention of genocide. These chapters reflect well enough, I think, some of the excitement of the inventiveness and courage of early efforts to study genocide, and dream of the eventual prevention of mass death along with the sober knowledge that so much tragedy lies ahead until our knowledge and skills catch up with the need.

Both of these chapters were written by myself with a good deal of assistance from various colleagues, but in particular I will acknowledge here the collaboration of the eminent scholar of genocide, Leo Kuper, in the preparation of the chapter on the prevention of genocide, an area of thought and enterprise in which he has braved a unique and outstanding trail of leadership as a responsible scholar and courageous doer.

The history and sociology of genocide are treated in a series of chapters, beginning with a probing look at the long series of mass murders from the dawn of recorded history and through all the ages, and culminating in the large-scale instances in our "enlightened" and "civilized" century: the Holocaust, the Armenian genocide, the Cambodian autogenocide, as well as a variety of other mass killings.

Historian Frank Chalk and sociologist Kurt Jonassohn of Concordia

University in Montreal collaborate on presenting a picture of the overall history and sociology of genocidal killings beginning with antiquity, using a different classification or typology of genocide around which they organize their tracking of genocide through the ages up to and including the new variants produced by the twentieth century.

Alan Berger, Chairman of the Jewish Studies Program at Syracuse University and editor of a series entitled "Post-Holocaust Jewish Thought" published by Syracuse University Press, identifies how the Holocaust represents a fundamental rupture with all previous civilization. In his treatment of the Holocaust, Professor Berger remains sensitive and faithful to its uniqueness, but at the same time spotlights its universality for all human beings.

Richard Hovannisian, holder of a Chair of Armenian Studies at the University of California in Los Angeles and beloved doyen of scholarship on the Armenian genocide, interprets that event and its sequelae, and encounters the painful and poignant question of how a people who no longer enjoy sovereign status can place their claim before the world for heinous evil most damnably done them. The literature of the Armenian genocide also brings into special focus patterns of "rationalization, revision, and denial": efforts to revise history to wipe out the traces of recorded events of mass murder that characterize what has been called "the last stage of genocide."

David Hawk, former Director of Amnesty International America, U.S. Section, and now Director of the Cambodia Documentation Commission (which is seeking to bring charges of genocide against the still-vested Khmer Rouge government of Democratic Kampuchea), assembles the record of the incredible "Cambodian autogenocide," where the full brunt of a ruling clique's ideological extremism and the intoxicating cult of power and death were brought to bear with insane vengeance on its own people. (Note that the relative differentiation of two target groups among the victims—the Buddhist priesthood and the Cham, a Muslim minority—provides scholars of genocide with a "legitimate" excuse for bringing charges of genocide against the Cambodian government under the existing limited definitions of the United Nations Convention of Genocide, which does not allow for "political genocide" or mass murder of one's own people, utilizing instead definitions based on extermination of *other* groups.)

James Mace, formerly at the Ukrainian Research Institute of Harvard University, and now Director of the United States Commission on the Ukraine Famine in Washington, D.C., brings together the information base for the much less well known genocidal murders in the U.S.S.R. under the leadership of Stalin. Estimates of the scale of the killings range well into the twenty and more millions of dead, including the induced famine (genocide by starvation) in the Ukraine in 1932–33, and the deportation of whole nations during and immediately after World War II.

Leo Kuper undertakes the selection and integration of information about a variety of other lesser-known cases of genocide and genocidal massacres, and organizes them from the point of view of a typology of genocide. The typology used by Kuper includes genocides of indigenous groups, genocides of hostage groups, genocides and struggles for power or against discrimination or for self-determination, and genocides in the course of war. (It is only right to note that the editor's instructions to Professor Kuper led unfairly to his writing a shorter encyclopedic statement than is found in other chapters, and apologies are due him for this misdirection. For further details about the typology of genocide, readers are referred to other publications of Kuper, especially his 1981 book and 1982 pamphlet, which will be found annotated in Chapter 1, as well as to his chapter in the anthology edited by me (1984), *Toward the Under-standing and Prevention of Genocide*, which is also annotated in Chapter 1.) The cases selected by Kuper include that of the Hereroes, the Aztecs and Incas, Indians in Brazil, Paraguay, and North America, the aboriginal inhabitants of Australia and the Caribbean, the peoples of East Timor and Tibet, the Baha'is (an instance of threatened genocide), peoples or groups in Bangladesh, Burundi, Equatorial Guinea, Guatemala, Nigeria, and Uganda, Ukrainians (in addition to the coverage by Mace previously noted) and other population groups in the U.S.S.R, and the American War in Vietnam.

The psychology of genocide is treated by myself. As in all matters of psychology at this point in evolution, there is reason to say that we psychologists make too much ado with the relatively limited understanding we have at this point of how the human mind works, individually and collectively. Yet for those of us who see and appreciate the enormous progress that is taking place in this "soft science," the steps we are now able to take towards unraveling the mystery of how human beings gravitate towards committing genocide are exciting. In fact, it begins to appear that bridging between understanding the mind and creating real-life tools for intervention and prevention of genocide will soon no longer be out of reach.

Philosophers William Gay of the University of North Carolina at Charlotte, and Ronald Santoni from Denison University in Ohio, in effect undertake two tasks in a single chapter devoted to philosophical thought and genocide: a review of philosophical thought on genocide, and a review especially of the contemporary and future faces of multiple genocide and nuclear destruction. It is certainly not inappropriate that it is the "mother discipline" of philosophy that takes on itself to warn us of the overwhelming menace of nuclear and other modern means of destruction that threaten not only single peoples but many peoples at a time, if not all of planetary civilization.

Finally, the volume concludes with three sterling chapters by peace researcher and educator Samuel Totten of the University of Arkansas, first on the literature, art, and film of the Holocaust, then the literature, art, and film of genocide in general, and finally—in a probe of the future through the eyes and heart of the artist—the literature, art, and film of nuclear and other futuristic destruction. Totten's descriptions of the works of art he has indefatigably collated are in themselves a moving experience. He, too, responsibly concludes that literature and art have not necessarily been catalysts for change in the thinking of humanity to an extent that we can point to the increasing probability of our future safety, but perhaps in some mysterious way these expressions of man's wisdom and creative spirit will influence our futures for the better.

Some significant topics are *not* covered in this volume. They include the development of a body of legal conventions and tools for the punishment of genocide and its prevention, and humanitarian approaches to law that provide a possible basis for intervention in ongoing and threatening cases of genocide; the nature of available and needed information systems for dealing with genocide; the roles of various professions and professionals in response to past histories of genocide and what roles the professions might play in the future of civilization to stop mass killing; and the nature and meaning of denials of genocides long since past (as in the case of the Armenian genocide). Hopefully many of these will be treated in a subsequent volume.

The reader should not expect to find a uniformity of definition of genocide in the various chapters. Thus for example the typology of genocide used by Kuper differs from the one proposed by Chalk and Jonassohn. Also, some Contributing Editors have touched on events that they regard as genocidal while others do not. One example is the question of whether both or one of the atomic bombings of Hiroshima and Nagasaki by the United States constitute genocidal killings. There are issues that are not developed but which some Contributing Editors recommended be taken up: the problems of famine in the world, and problems of destruction of the environment (for example, the poisoning of rivers and the contamination of atmospheres). Even within the writing of a single Contributing Editor, the definition of genocide suffers from alternations between working from the accepted legal definition of genocide under the present U.N. Convention, and various proposals for expansion of the Convention such as are called for by the Whitaker Report (*see* especially Chapter 1). There are some scholars who will be critical of the failure to introduce and hold to a more precise definition of genocide, but ultimately the position I take is that there is a simple commonsense definition that caring people sense intuitively: that, unless clearcut self-defense can be reasonably proven, whenever a large number of people are put to death by other people, it constitutes genocide. The fact that international law lags behind this self-evident truth, or that scholars are forever splitting their argumentative heads over definitions, cannot stop us from speaking in a commonsense language.

I should like to think that ultimately what I have called a *humanistic definition of genocide* will prevail even over understandable efforts to identify genocide as the attempt to exterminate the identity of a specifically targeted ethnic or national or religious or other group, which I would consider an important subgrouping of genocide. The larger issue, I believe, is the valuing of all human life, and I should like to see the previous concept of genocide achieve a larger meaning as the willful, unnecessary (for self-defense) destruction of a large number or group of human beings.

Perhaps some years from now the time will be right to attempt an integration of the scholarly statements of the different editors from different disciplines in a single, multilevel, branching typology along with a single cumulative annotated bibliography of genocide. It will be nice to think that this volume will have contributed toward the possibility of such an integration. At this point, this volume is an effort to represent responsibly the state of knowledge including differences of conceptualization on the part of reputable scholars. It is our strong hope that the encyclopedic statements and annotated bibliographies presented here will prove to be an indispensable aid to future scholarship in the study of genocide and its prevention.

Needless to say, a variety of thanks and appreciations are in order. An enormous amount of work goes into creating a volume such as this.

I want first of all to express my appreciations to each of the Contributing Editors, many of them today dear friends and certainly esteemed colleagues with whom I look forward to many future collaborative efforts in our mutual commitment to greater understanding of genocide. Professor Roger Smith of the Department of Government at the College of William and Mary, a serious critic and thinker in scholarship of genocide, has been kind enough to offer a thoughtful foreword to this work (and I also look forward to enjoying more of the fruits of his scholarship in his own contribution to an eventual future volume).

A special vote of thanks is due Marc I. Sherman, M.L.S., for his thoughtful critical review of the entire manuscript as well as knowledgeable technical copyediting of the manuscript. Sherman is Director of Information Systems for the Research Authority of Tel Aviv University, and recent coauthor with Julian R. Friedman of *Human Rights: An International and Comparative Law Bibliography* (1985), published by Greenwood Press, Westport, Connecticut.

Encouragement of this undertaking has come from many sources including the staff of Mansell Publishing Limited in London, who have conveyed a steady interest and provided helpful counsel through the long gestation of this book. Thanks are also due Lynne Rienner, Lynne Rienner Publishers Inc., Boulder, Colorado, my editor for three previous books on nonviolence and genocide that I published with Westview Press, who encouraged the development of this project and made the introductions to Mansell Publishing.

Appreciations are also due Bamberger-Rosenheim Ltd., of Tel Aviv, not simply for the Lanier word processing equipment that has been acquired through them, nor only for their programming consultation and reliable service, but for a consistent financial helpfulness to the Institute of the International Conference on the Holocaust and Genocide which often makes the difference in our ability to undertake projects that would otherwise be beyond our financial means.

Acknowledgment and warm appreciations are due all the secretarial and computer technical staff who participated in creating this volume, especially to Pauline Cooper, Managing Editor of the *Internet on the Holocaust and*

Genocide, who has been mainly responsible for the assembly of this manuscript.

Finally, in all that I am grateful for being able to do at this time in my life, I enjoy the wonderful love-friendship and encouragement of Judy Charny, my wife.

Thus, the conclusion of yet another project of thinkers and writers, and dare we admit that even work in the terrible area of genocide scholarship is actually *fun* for those of us who normally enjoy such tasks of gathering knowledge and interpreting it in new forms. Nonetheless, it has to be clear that the real purpose of this project, in a field which is uniquely dreadful, is to contribute one more small inspiration to the long-range knowledge process that is needed if we are to save human life as we know it from mass destruction.

Lechayim! (In Hebrew: To Life!)

ISRAEL W. CHARNY
Jerusalem

1

The Study of Genocide

Israel W. Charny

Like many catastrophic natural events and incurable terminal illnesses, genocide for many years has simply been an event that happened, with little to no warning, for reasons unknown. Even many of the peoples who themselves suffered genocide did not seek much beyond a "Bad Man" or prejudice-discrimination explanation of how an enemy did them in.

Today, however, one can look with some satisfaction on the increasing emergence of scholarship and scientific study of genocide as a process whose origins and lawful development can be tracked with some measure of understanding and also predictability, and therefore one may also dare begin to think of possibilities for some day preventing genocide. Well-regarded studies of genocide as a process include works by Leo Kuper (1981, 1985), Helen Fein (1979, 1984), Irving Horowitz (1980), Ben Whitaker (1985), and Israel Charny (1982, 1984).

The word *genocide* was first coined by a Polish Jewish jurist, Raphael Lemkin, who crusaded relentlessly for an international legal standard to outlaw the purposeful extermination of peoples such as the Jews or the Armenians. Almost singlehandedly he brought about the adoption of the United Nations Convention against Genocide.

It has been emphasized that the actual definition of genocide as illegal had been achieved *before* the adoption of the United Nations Convention on Genocide. The charter for the international military tribune which tried the major war criminals at Nuremberg specified three types of crime (Kuper, 1985, p. 5):

1. Crimes against peace—including the waging of a war of aggression.
2. War crimes such as the murder of civilian populations, killing of hostages, wanton destruction of cities, towns, or villages.

3. Crimes against humanity, which were specified as "murder, extermination, enslavement, deportation and other inhumane acts committed against any civilian population, before or during the war, or persecutions on political, racial or religious grounds . . ."

The indictment of 8 October 1945 of major German war criminals charged that the defendants had "conducted deliberate and systematic genocide, viz., the extermination of racial and national groups, against the civilian population of certain occupied territories in order to destroy particular races and classes of people and national, racial or religious groups" (Whitaker, 1985, 8:22).

Nonetheless, the U.N. Convention on Genocide today constitutes the key statement in international law about the crime of genocide.

The Definition of Genocide

Lemkin (1944, p. 79) saw genocide as the effort to destroy the "essential foundations of the life of national groups" whose objectives "would be the disintegration of the political and social institutions of culture, language, national feelings, religion, and the economic existence of national groups, and the destruction of the personal security, liberty, health, dignity, and even the lives of the individuals belonging to such groups."

Notwithstanding the above emphasis on the elimination of the continuity of a people even more than the fact of mass murder itself, for most lay people the central, immediately understood meaning of genocide is mass destruction of any target people. However, many legal and political authorities continue to insist on a definition of genocide as deriving from a distinct intention to obliterate the continuity of an ethnic, racial or religious group, in whole or in part. This definition would mean that even an overwhelming event of mass murder which did not aim to destroy the identity of the victim people would *not* be considered genocide. Thus, the atom-bombing of Nagasaki by the U.S.A. would not be considered genocide—even if it were agreed that military needs did not justify dropping the second bomb, and even if it were agreed that insufficient warnings were given the victims—not only because it was an act of "war," but *because* the U.S.A. did not intend to exterminate the Japanese people as such. Of course, it cannot be emphasized too much that whatever one's opinions about the U.S. atomic bombings of Japan, it is clear that nuclear weapons figure prominently in the potential for even more terrible mass murders in the future (*see* remarks later in this chapter on the future dangers of "nuclear genocide" and "omnicide").

The U.N. Convention on Genocide confirmed that genocide was a crime under international law. It defined the crime to include the killing of members of any national, ethnic, racial or religious entity. Conspicuously omitted, as a result of political pressures at the time of the formulation of the Convention, are instances of killing political enemies, and there is also no coverage of the mass murder of a country's own nationals. The case of Stalin's murders of "enemies" of the Soviet regime is a good example of both exclusions; the case of Pol Pot's regime in Cambodia murder of 1 to 3 million of its own nationals is another instance. [If only to mitigate the absurdity and injustice that such events do not qualify as genocide, scholars seek nonetheless to prove that among the target population there were distinct national or religious entities earmarked for extermination because of their identity, hence some of these mass killings would also constitute genocide. *See* Letgers (1984) on the case of Stalin's killing of 20 million Soviets, and Hawk's (1984, also Chapter 7 in this book) research of the mass murder of Cambodians.]

Genocide may also take the form of an artificial introduction of famine or the deliberate withholding of aid to famine-ridden areas. During 1932–33, the Soviet Union created a famine in the Ukraine with as many as 6 million people reported dead. From the point of view of definitional issues, Mace (1984) and Conquest (1970) argue that this famine was intended not only to crush the peasants' resistance to collectivization, but also to undermine Ukrainian nationalism—which would qualify the killing as genocidal.

Helen Fein (1984, p. 4) has proposed an all-encompassing definition of genocide: "I believe one underlying explanation can encompass all types. Genocide is the calculated murder of a segment or all of a group defined outside the universe of obligation of the perpetrator by a government, elite, staff or crowd representing the perpetrator in response to a crisis or opportunity perceived to be caused by or impeded by the victim."

Fein has distinguished between four overall categories of genocide: *developmental genocide*, where the perpetrators clear the way for their colonization of an area inhabited by an indigenous people; *despotic genocide*, where the perpetrators clear away the opposition to their power as for example in a political revolution; *retributive genocide*, where peoples are locked into ethnic and other stratifications of order and dominance–submission struggles; and *ideological genocide*. She has created an outstanding teaching as well as research tool by projecting these types of genocide in a series of "fictional" scenarios where she removes the actual identifying names and places of actual events of genocide in the past, and thus creates a series of templates for possible situations in which genocides can be expected in the future.

Most major scholars of genocide have called for a broadening of the definition. Leo Kuper (1985) makes the point that "political affiliation can be as permanent and as immutable as racial origin" (p. 16), and further emphasizes that in many cases "it is impossible to disentangle the political component from the ethnic, racial or religious" (p. 100). Others also call for inclusion of sexual groups, such as homosexuals—the objects of Nazi extermination in the Holocaust (Porter, 1982)—or any other real group, such as the retarded and mentally ill, who were executed by the Nazis, or city dwellers, who were killed by the Cambodians, and even a "pseudo-group" such as "demonic enemies" or witches or enemies of the people according to whichever ruler's definition

(Chalk and Jonassohn in Chapter 3 of this book).

Some authors suggest using closely related terms like "genocidal massacres" (Kuper, 1981) or "genocidal killing" (Chalk and Jonassohn in this book) to cover instances that do not qualify technically as genocide under the existing Convention. Charny (1985) has proposed what he calls a *humanistic* definition of genocide, namely "the *wanton* murder of human beings on the basis of any identity whatsoever that they share—national, ethnic, racial, religious, political, geographical, ideological." He argues: "I reject out of hand that there can ever be any identity process that in itself will justify the murder of men, women and children 'because' they are 'anti' some 'ism' or because their physical characteristics are high- or low-cheekboned, short- or long-eared, or green- or orange-colored" (p. 448).

An authoritative U.N. study on genocide submitted by Special Rapporteur Ben Whitaker in 1985 seeks to maintain the gravity of the concept of genocide and calls for consideration of both the proportionate scale and the total number of victims in deciding what constitutes genocide. At the same time, the report calls for an extension of the definition under the Convention to include genocide of one's own group, and sexual groups, and also points to the desirability of including political genocide. Furthermore, the report (p. 13) also recommends further study of the possibilities of including cultural genocide or "ethnocide," as well as "ecocide."

When Does Genocide Take Place?

Although genocide is omnipresent in human history, it nonetheless occurs with a certain regularity under predictable conditions. Porter (1982) noted that genocide is most prevalent in times of war, colonization, and tribal conflict. Kuper (1981, 1985) provides a classification of genocide which is similar to that of Fein, and specifies some of the conditions under which genocide is more frequent:

1. Genocide against indigenous peoples (e.g. the murder of Indians in South American countries such as Paraguay).
2. Genocide following decolonization of a two-tier structure of domination (e.g. the Hutu in genocidal massacres by the Tutsi in Rwanda and Burundi).
3. Genocide in the process of struggles for power by ethnic or racial or religious groups, or struggles for greater autonomy or for secession (e.g. Bangladesh in 1971).
4. Genocide against hostage or scapegoat groups (e.g. the Armenians by the Turks in 1915, and the persecution of the Jews by the Nazis in the Holocaust).

Kuper further notes that "domestic" genocides, that is, genocides which arise on the basis of cleavages within a society, are a phenomenon of plural societies, in which there are sharp cleavages between ethnic, racial or religious groups. They arise under a variety of circumstances: struggles for power, consolidations of despotic regimes, annihilation of hostage groups in situations of crisis for host societies, economic expansion into areas inhabited by hunting and gathering groups, and under the facilitating conditions of international war.

Sociologist Horowitz (1980; *see* Horowitz, 1976) places emphasis on defining the nature of societies in which genocide takes place. Genocide is not a random or sporadic event, but a special sort of mass destruction that requires the approval of the State, which uses genocide as a technique for national solidarity. He proposes an analytical framework of eight types of society:

1. Genocidal societies—the State takes the lives of people who are deviant or people whose behaviour is dissident.
2. Deportation or incarceration societies—the State removes certain individuals or prevents them from interacting with a larger body politic.
3. Torture societies—peoples are victimized short of death and returned as living evidence of the risks of deviance.
4. Harassment societies—people are constantly picked up, searched, seized and held.
5. Traditional-shame societies—participation and collective will is generated through instilling a sense of disapproval and isolation.
6. Guilt societies—these internalize a sense of wrongdoing in the individual in addition to the shame mechanism previously described.
7. Tolerant societies—norms are well articulated and well understood; deviance is not celebrated, but it is not destroyed.
8. Permissive societies—norms are questioned and the community defines the normative rather than the State.

Porter (1982) undertook to formulate the clustering of characteristics that predict the occurrence of genocide, and also the contrasting convergence of characteristics that predict the reduced likelihood of genocide (Table 1).

Table 1. Genocide Prediction

Predict genocide	Predict genocide unlikely
Minority group is considered an outsider	Pervasive tolerance for minorities
Racist ideology	Strong minority with ready access to legal and human rights
Strong dependence on military	Temperate attitude to military
Power exclusion of political parties	Democratic political structure
Leadership has strong territorial ambitions	Weak territorial and imperial ambitions
Power of the State has been reduced by defeat and war or internal strife	No such precipitant events
Possibility of retaliation for genocide from some source is at minimum	Possibility of retaliation or interference by outside nations is considerable

Fein (1984) has also especially emphasized the objective powerlessness of the victim. She notes the following facilitating conditions of genocide:

1. Lack of visibility of the genocidal action.
2. Inability of the bystanders and third parties to apprehend the pattern of the crime.
3. Objective powerlessness of the victims and/or their stigmatization as not so innocent.
4. Inability of the victims to prosecute their victimizers.
5. Lack of sanctions by third parties and/or lack of will of other states to use their sanctions.

Fein also notes that once genocide has taken place, the most common way for the perpetrator to account for genocide is to deny that it ever happened. Another way is to declare that the actions were justified as defensive responses to attacks by the victims on the perpetrator.

Charny (1982), together with his collaborator Rapaport, propose that we look at how societies are organized both around forces that promote human life and forces that move towards the destruction of life long before an actual genocide event emerges. They suggest that all societies are characterized by both types of process, and under certain circumstances, which they believe can be analyzed and eventually taken as a basis for prediction of genocidal dangers, the balance is tilted in favor of societal processes that authorize mass destruction of another people. Charny and Rapaport's analytic schema is a unique effort to relate macrosocietal processes that culminate in genocide to the principles of psychology of the individual, and the behaviors of individuals in the family, groups, and society. Their analysis generates what they call a series of *genocide early warning processes*, which are systematic exaggerations and distortions of what are originally normal life experience processes. They suggest that looking at the unfolding process of genocide in this way gives us new possibilities for understanding how, some day, genocide can be prevented insofar as human beings, as individuals and as societal groups, can learn to cope with normal life experience processes more constructively and not allow violence to gain the upper hand.

They too note that once genocide has taken place, there are a considerable number of "experience-denying mechanisms" that are intended to make it possible to deny the very facts of the brutal murders that are being or have been committed—denials on the level of the individuals in the murdering society that enable them to go on with their everyday lives as if nothing untoward has taken place, as well as denials on the larger governmental and collective cultural level that are intended first to conceal and then cynically to wipe out the record of the murders.

The Proliferation of Genocide and Future Dangers of Nuclear Genocide and "Omnicide"

Our twentieth century has been called "the century of genocide" and some say that genocide has occurred more frequently in this century than ever before. Given the many indications that mass murder of peoples have been going on since time immemorial, and that many peoples have disappeared from the face of the earth, it is not clear whether mass killings in our own times are "simply" large-scale continuations of age-old patterns which as yet have not shown an evolutionary change. On the other hand, there are reasons to argue that the purposefulness, uncommon devotion and ingenuity committed to mass murder reached a new zenith in the Holocaust in our twentieth century, and that this development is reason enough to characterize ours as the age of mass murder.

It is generally considered that three outstanding examples of genocide in our century are the Holocaust, the massacre of the Armenians by the Turks, and the Cambodian "autogenocide." Other examples of genocide in this century are cited in the United Nations report by Ben Whitaker (1985): the German massacre of the Hereros in 1904 (the Hereros were reduced from a population of 80,000 to 15,000 starving refugees); the Ukrainian pogrom of Jews in 1919 (between 100,000 to 250,000 Jews were killed in 2,000 pogroms); the Tutsi massacre of Hutu in Burundi in 1965 and 1972 (between 100,000 and 300,000 Huti); the Paraguayan massacre of Aché Indians prior to 1974 (although they were a small tribe, their enslavement, torture and massacre is representative of genocidal events undergone by other indigenous peoples); and the contemporary Iranian killing of Baha'is—a process which in numbers is still small, but which is a classic example of a prejudicial relationship of a majority to a religious minority in its midst which presages the possibility of more serious genocide taking form.

Although by all definitions genocide represents the *purposeful* destruction of a people, it would be inhumane not to note the tremendous toll of death owing to hunger and deprivation and poor health conditions in many third world countries. Kuper (1985) notes that between 20 and 25 million (*sic*) children below the age of five die every year in developing countries. One-third of these deaths are from polluted water. Our profound indignation at the purposeful extermination of a people through genocide should not blind us to conditions of neglect and governmental and ecological abuses that lead to the senseless deaths of millions of human beings in more passive ways. On the other hand, there are long-standing traditions on the part of many humanitarians, environmentalists and peace researchers who are concerned with improving the lot of under-developed peoples and nations, but who have been virtually silent and strangely unimpassioned in response to purposeful genocidal killings, as if they could blithely continue with plans to distribute foods and medicines to the needy without having to confront the rampant evils of willful killers.

In any case, there are many who fear that today our world is moving resolutely towards the destruction of greater numbers of people than ever before, the desolation of life over vast geographical areas, conceivably even the destruction of all human life on planet Earth, and possibly the destruction of the planet itself. The new weapons of the atomic era portend future instances of "nuclear genocide," "multiple genocide" (where several different peoples can be annihilated at one and the same time—(Santoni, 1984), "omnicide" (the broad destruction of many people and sections of the earth) and "ecocide" (adverse alterations of the environment, often irremediable, perhaps through nuclear explosions, chemical weapons, and so forth).

The study of the process of genocide cannot be considered complete without reference also to a major constituency of people who *stand by* while the genocidal process takes place. While they do not play an active role in its determination, they represent—as individuals and groups, societies and governments—the *bystanders* to genocide (*see* Sheleff, 1978).

Professional and Organizational Initiatives

A few professional and organizational initiatives stand out in recent years concerned with the study of genocide as a process and an accompanying conception of the possibilities of prevention of some events of genocide in the future.

The International Conference on the Holocaust and Genocide in Tel Aviv in 1982 represented a pioneering effort to bring together many different peoples, such as Jews and Armenians, who normally are involved in the memorial of their own history of genocide, and to bring together many different professions in the interdisciplinary study of genocide as a process. Not incidentally the conference ran into considerable political pressures to close it down (Charny and Davidson, 1983), beginning with Turkish threats against certain Jews if the Armenians were allowed to participate, followed by Israeli government pressures to close the conference down because of its interpretation of its responsibility to protect Jewish lives. It has been suggested by some that any effort to create public events on the subject of genocide will inevitably evoke various forms of resistance from the very people who otherwise legitimize genocide. A certain measure of courage and political will to withstand hate groups and political forces would seem to be a requirement of scholarly and professional activities aiming at the prevention of genocide.

The 1982 conference was followed by the establishment of the Institute of the International Conference on the Holocaust and Genocide in Jerusalem by Israel Charny, Shamai Davidson and Elie Wiesel. The Institute publishes the *Internet on the Holocaust and Genocide*, an international newsletter devoted to bringing the news of activities and projects on the study of genocide and its prevention to a multiethnic and multidisciplinary readership. The Institute has also undertaken a variety of other projects, such as publication of this volume, and looks forward to the possibility of launching A World Human Rights and Genocide Early Warning Center.

In 1985, a new worldwide organization was launched, International Alert, whose purpose is to respond promptly on a political level to news of and indications of probable genocide, mass murder and massacres (*see* the further discussion in Chapter 2).

Another major development has been the submission of the Whitaker Report on genocide to the United Nations in 1985 (Whitaker, 1985; *see also* the special issue of the *Internet on the Holocaust and Genocide* devoted to this report). Critics will correctly point out that the report was subject to the usual cynical demagoguery and political neutralization we have come to expect from the U.N. system (Kuper, 1985). Nonetheless, the broad sweep of conceptualization in this report, and the record of what are ultimately feasible recommendations to expand the scope of the U.N. Convention on Genocide, develop a machinery for its implementation, and initiate major prevention initiatives, mark this document as an intellectual milestone in the study of genocide as a process.

One should also note the stretching of previously more secular efforts by ethnic peoples to commemorate their own genocide towards a more universal conception of genocide as the concern of all peoples. A new scholarly journal entitled *Holocaust and Genocide Studies* (Pergamon Press) made its appearance in 1986 under the chairmanship of Elie Wiesel, Chairman of the U.S. Holocaust Memorial Council, and edited by the Israeli Holocaust scholar Yehuda Bauer and the American Holocaust scholar Harry Cargas. A 1985 conference by the National Association for Armenian Studies and Research dedicated to the seventieth anniversary of the Armenian genocide was also devoted to the broad study of genocide to other peoples. Now that the conceptual direction has been established, it can be expected that there will be a growing number of organizations and professionals around the world who will address genocide as a universal problem.

Conclusion

In sum, the catastrophic events known as genocide are today seen by most authorities as the willful extermination of large numbers of a target group for whatever reasons justify their removal in the ideology of the perpetrators. The buildup towards genocidal events can be studied from several points of view of how nations and societies are organized and commit themselves both to supporting human life and to violent destruction of human life. The actual buildup of genocide takes place most frequently in certain contexts of war and other stresses on a society, and is also triggered by certain crucial symbolic events that justify a society's perception of another people as threatening its survival. Often this definition is contrived and unrealistic, and the enemy is in fact a pseudo-enemy, but so great is the power of the collective human imagination to treat fantasies as real that there is no stopping the death machine that comes into play to rid the ostensibly beleaguered people of this threat.

Charny (1982) has suggested that the process of genocide might be compared to a cancer in that a subunit of a living organism takes over and begins killing other parts of its own self relentlessly; and its ultimate success brings about not only the destruction of its victims but of the organism of which it itself is a part. The analogy continues in that there are forces in a society that can protect against the development of such a cancer, just as there are immunological forces in a person that can resist and fight back against an illness which threatens or begins to take hold. However, there are also many failures of the immunological process which permit the illness to run rampant.

Today we are somewhat beyond the unknowingness and impotence that characterized responses to genocide barely a few years ago. On the other hand, the study of genocide as a process has only recently begun, and there are many years before us before we can expect to see real fruits of such work. The ultimate irony is that there may no longer be a civilization on planet Earth at the time when we might have been ready to prevent genocidal murders.

Bibliography

Arendt, Hannah (1969). *Eichmann in Jerusalem*. New York: Viking Press.

Arendt, Hannah (1973). *The Origins of Totalitarianism*. New York: Harcourt Brace Jovanovich. 527 pp.
    This and the above are classic works by a European sociologist who succeeded in arousing great intellectual ferment in the Western world about totalitarianism in general and the Holocaust in particular, but also drew bitter fire for her seeming indifference or condescension to the victims. In perspective, many of Arendt's analyses, such as of "the banality of evil," and the readiness of people—including victims—to conform to authority and mass-crowd behaviors, stand the test of time. At the same time, she can be faulted for a kind of dispassionate elite-observer stance in which she failed to express sufficient empathy, sensitivity and identification with the victims. Moreover, Arendt did not at all respect the extent to which the demonic sequence of persecution measures naturally sapped the strength and wherewithal of Jews to fight back.

Arens, Richard (Ed.) (1976). *Genocide in Paraguay*. Philadelphia: Temple University Press. 171 pp.
    Eyewitness reports of genocidal measures against a small indigenous Indian tribe, the Aché. This book became significant not only because of its specific report of the elimination of this tribe, but as a reminder of the fact that other indigenous Indian tribes in South America were being subject to genocidal policies of colonization.

Charny, Israel W. (1982). *How Can We Commit the Unthinkable?: Genocide, The Human Cancer*. In collaboration with Chanan Rapaport. Foreword by Elie Wiesel. Boulder, CO: Westview Press. 430 pp. Republished in paperback by Hearst Books [Wm. Morrow] in 1983 under the title *Genocide, The Human Cancer*.
    An innovative probe of the psychology of human beings' availability to commit genocide, as individuals and in groups. Develops a proposal for a Genocide Early Warning System that has been hailed by critics as brilliant and potentially life-saving.

Charny, Israel W. (Ed.) (1984). *Toward the Understanding and Prevention of Genocide: Proceedings of the International Conference on the Holocaust and Genocide*. Boulder, CO, and London: Westview Press. 396 pp.

A selection of presentations at the historic 1982 conference. The featured chapter by Helen Fein presents scenarios of genocide past and future. The book includes case studies, analyses of the dynamics of genocide, papers on the arts, religion and education and genocide, intervention and prevention, and an epilogue of keynote addresses and round-table discussions.

Charny, Israel W. (1985). Genocide, the ultimate human rights problem. *Social Education: Special Issue on Human Rights*, 49(6), 448–452.
An introduction and review of the problem of genocide for social science teachers that begins with a brief fictional scenario of the roundup of teachers in a hypothetical country. The article discusses various definitions of genocide, the dynamics of the genocidal process, and the possibilities of prevention. Includes brief examples of genocide in our century and examples of "early warning" situations in our time. A useful teaching tool.

Charny, Israel W. and Davidson, Shamai (1983). *The Book of the International Conference on the Holocaust and Genocide: The Conference Program and Crisis*. Tel Aviv: Institute of the International Conference on the Holocaust and Genocide. 348 pp.
This album-like book of photocopies records the final program of the historic International Conference on the Holocaust and Genocide in Tel Aviv in 1982; responses from participants; reactions in the Israeli and world press; the abstracts of all papers accepted for the program, including those that were not delivered; and includes the detailed story of the crisis that attended the conference when Turkey made threats against Jews if the Armenians were to be "allowed" to participate.

Christie, Nils (1976). Definition of violent behaviour. In International Course of Criminology: *The Faces of Violence*, Vol. 1. Universidad del Zulia, Maracaibo, Venezuela, pp. 25–34.
A study of Norwegian concentration-camp guards under the Nazis, a significant number of whom engaged in torture and killed. "A very large number of people—I believe most people—would do the most horrible things to other people provided the situation became especially extreme."

Conquest, Robert (1970). *The Nation Killers*. New York: Macmillan. 222 pp.
An important account of a major genocidal epoch that to this day is not sufficiently recognized in the West: the extermination of nations in the U.S.S.R. The Crimean Tatars were given fifteen minutes, sometimes less, to collect what belongings they could carry. The Karachai were deported when most of the men were serving in the Red Army. Deportation by cattle truck and freight cars to "special settlement" in Siberia and elsewhere is reminiscent of the Nazis. Maps and other official documents were changed in a process Conquest describes as "the memory hole."

Dadrian, Vahakn N. (1975). A typology of genocide. *International Review of Modern Sociology*, 5(2), 201–212.
An early effort at conceptualizing types of genocide by a penetrating Armenian-American scholar.

Fein, Helen (1979). *Accounting for Genocide: National Responses and Jewish Victimization during the Holocaust*. New York: Free Press. 468 pp.
An award-winning, highly innovative sociological study of the Holocaust, and the differences in the fates of Jews in different countries occupied by the Nazis. Fein argues that the Holocaust was a "rational event": the destruction of the Jews was taken to its extreme whenever there was no opposition or "cost" to the Nazis, but was

appreciably retarded when peoples stood in the way of the Nazis. This book achieves an important level of empirical scholarship, as well as providing scholarly support for the ethical imperative that it pays to resist genocidal killers and governments.

Fein, Helen (1984). Scenarios of genocide: models of genocide and critical responses. In Charny (1984), pp. 3–31.

The author of *Accounting for Genocide* develops a remarkable series of fictional scenarios or scripts depicting both familiar and potential new patterns of genocide under different conditions of historical, political and social organization. These "templates" of future events of mass murder are gripping reading for both scholars and world leaders, and an exceptional teaching tool. In a concluding section on "critical responses to genocide," Fein also discusses strategies for aborting or reversing "deadly endings."

Garse, Yvan Van (1970). *A Bibliography of Genocide, Crimes against Humanity and War Crimes*. Sint Niklaas Waas, Studiecentrum voor Kriminologie en Gerechtelijke Geneeskunde, Belgium.

An early major bibliography of genocide.

Hawk, David (1982). The killing of Cambodia: was it genocide? A report on Pol Pot's brutalities. *New Republic*, 187, 15 Nov. 17–21.

The author is today Director of the Cambodian Documentation Commission, which has been compiling the evidential base for submitting a legal brief against the Cambodian government, which was responsible for murdering between 1 and 3 million of its six million citizens. David Hawk (*see* Chapter 7 of this book) has been an intrepid investigator and documentor of the nightmare of the "Cambodian autogenocide."

Hawk, David (1984). Pol Pot's Cambodia: was it genocide? In Charny (1984), pp. 51–59.

Even under a restricted definition of genocide, the mass murders in Cambodia qualify as such, since there were target groups such as the Chams (an Islamic minority) and the Buddhist monks. Were it not for political cynicism and indifference, Cambodia, which ratified the Genocide Convention, *could* be an instructive instance of enforcement of the Convention.

Holocaust and Genocide: Studies (first issue, May 1986). Editor-in-Chief, Yehudah Bauer; Associate Editor, Harry Cargas; Chairman of the Editorial Board, Elie Wiesel. Published by Pergamon Press Journals, Headington Hill Hall, Oxford OX3 0BW, England.

A scholarly journal that examines the Holocaust and related forms of genocide in their multidisciplinary aspects.

Horowitz, Irving Louis (1976). *Genocide: State Power and Mass Murder*. New Brunswick, NJ: Transaction. Revised edition (1980) under the title *Taking Lives*. 199 pp.

An important sociological analysis of relationships between the state and its citizens. Genocide is effected almost without exception by states, emphasizes Horowitz. The possibilities of programs of mass murder derive from the underlying model or philosophy of the society with regard to deviants. Horowitz identifies the following types: genocidal societies, deportation or incarceration societies, torture societies, harassment societies, traditional shame societies, guilt societies, tolerant societies, permissive societies.

Housepian, Marjorie (1966). The unremembered genocide. *Commentary*, September 1966. Reprinted as a pamphlet.

Possibly the first article on the Armenian genocide to appear in a national American publication since before 1930. An informative, moving account of the genocide that shocked many readers who had no idea that a pre-Hitler precedent for genocide existed.

Housepian, Marjorie (1972). *Smyrna, 1922: The Destruction of a City*. London: Faber & Faber. 275 pp.

A powerful, almost eye-witness but carefully researched and documented account of the burning of Smyrna by the Turks after their massacre of the entire Armenian and much of the Greek population. A careful reading of this book will reveal not only the particulars of this important specific tragedy, but a series of events which can be translated into general paradigms that recur so familiarly in one historical context after another.

Housepian-Dobkin, Marjorie (1984). What genocide? what holocaust? News from Turkey, 1915-23: a case study. In Charny (1984), pp. 100-112.

The evidence of the Turkish extermination of the Armenians "alas, is irrefutable," said Alan Dulles, then Chief of Staff to the American High Commissioner in Constantinople. But before too many years passed, the American press was often treating the "two sides" of the story even-handedly. "Denying the crime of genocide can only encourage and indeed *ensure* the repetition of genocide."

Hovannisian, Richard G. (1984). Genocide and denial: the Armenian case. In Charny (1984), pp. 84-99.

The denial of the Armenian genocide by Turkey is an effort to avoid responsibility and the moral, material, and political consequences of admission. Turkish writers and scholars are unable to deal with their national past honestly and are drawn into wheels of falsification and rationalization. *See also* this author's chapter (Chapter 5) in the present book.

International Conference on the Holocaust and Genocide (1984a). Round-table discussion following briefing on the conference crisis. In Charny (1984), pp. 364-373.

These are excerpts from the dramatic opening discussion that followed a briefing of participants on the crisis that had threatened to bring about cancellation of the historic conference in Tel Aviv in 1982. It includes remarks by some participants who asked to explain why they could not participate.

International Conference on the Holocaust and Genocide (1984b). Conference summation panel and round table. In Charny (1984), pp. 373-388.

Summaries of the conference proceedings by the major Track Leaders—John Felstiner (co-chairman with Sidra Ezrachi), Franklin Littell, John Somerville, Leo Kuper, and Shamai Davidson—followed by a moving round-table discussion from the floor of the meaning, impact and shortcomings of the conference process.

Internet on the Holocaust and Genocide (January–February 1985). *Special Double Issue on the Whitaker Report to the U.N.*, No. 3-4, 14 pp.

This special issue presents a précis of the Whitaker Report (*see* Whitaker, 1985), interpretive articles and editorial comment, as well as feature stories surrounding the preparation and submission of this major review of the status of the U.N. Convention on Genocide and the field of genocide prevention in general.

Internet on the Holocaust and Genocide (first issue, April 1985). An international information resource exchange. Published by the Institute of the International Conference on the Holocaust and Genocide, PO Box 10311, Jerusalem 93624, Israel.

    A newsletter devoted to news of professional activities, projects, conferences, publications, and other initiatives in the area of Holocaust studies and studies of genocide and its prevention. Began (irregular) publication in 1985, on a voluntary subscription and contribution basis.

Kaldi, Leita (1984). Gypsies and Jews: chosen people. In Charny (1984), pp. 113–118.

    Like the Jews, the Gypsies were the objects of genocide by the Nazis. A touching description of the Gypsy people—at once a lusty "outdoor people . . . who resist temptations of power," and a people who "live in the shadows of our societies, shrouded in fear, suspicion and secrecy."

Kenrick, Donald, and Puxon, Gratton (1972). *The Destiny of Europe's Gypsies*. New York: Basic Books. 256 pp.

    The definitive study of the destruction of the Gypsies in the Holocaust. A total of 219,000 deaths are reported or estimated in eighteen countries including 36,000 in Romania (out of a population of 300,000) and 35,000 in Poland (out of 50,000). In some countries the entire Gypsy population was destroyed. "These figures do not represent the full measure of Gypsy suffering," the authors add. According to Kaldi, the figures have since been found to be conservative.

Knight, Gerald (1982). A Genocide Bureau [Editor's title]. Text of talk delivered at the Symposium on Genocide, London, 20 March (originated by a group that later created the organization International Alert). Mimeographed, 14 pp. Available from the Baha'i International Community, 866 United Nations Plaza, New York, NY 10017.

    In the first part of this address, Knight presents the history, tradition and current embattled status of the Baha'is, a worldwide religious group that originated in Iran and which is committed to peace and the universality of man. It has been subjected to persecution and murder by the Khomeini regime.

    In the second part, Knight proposes the establishment of a "Genocide Bureau" that is very similar to Charny's proposal for a Genocide Early Warning System, the work of International Alert (*see* Kuper, 1985), and Kutner's World Genocide Tribunal. "At the moment, there is no . . . central clearing house for cases of genocide . . . the very existence of such a body would alert the world."

Kren, George, and Rappoport, Leon (1980). *The Holocaust and the Crisis of Human Behavior*. New York: Holmes & Meier. 176 pp.

    The joint work of an historian and a psychologist, this book is a thoughtful and inspiring analysis of the significance of the Holocaust for *all* areas of civilization as we have known them. No profession or scholarly discipline remains untouched by the Holocaust, for now we must contend with knowledge of the destructive nature of man and of human societal organization.

Kuper, Leo (1981). *Genocide: Its Political Use in the Twentieth Century*. London: Penguin Books; New Haven, CT: Yale University Press. 255 pp.

    Widely acclaimed, this excellent book describes various major incidents of genocide in our century. The details of each case are presented factually and clearly, and a conceptual typology is developed of types of genocide, and the characteristic conditions under which each takes place: against indigenous peoples; following decolonization of a two-tier structure of domination; in the process of struggle for power by ethnic, racial or religious groups, or struggles for autonomy or secession;

against hostage or scapegoat groups; and mass murder of political groups. Kuper writes in the correct and restrained manner of the scholar but also in an insistent ethical refrain that human beings, and the governmental organizations men create, must put a stop to senseless slaughter.

Kuper, Leo (1982). *International Action against Genocide*. London: Minority Rights Group. Pamphlet. 17 pp.
Adapted from *Genocide: Its Political Use in the Twentieth Century*, and published by an outstanding organization devoted to the protection of minorities around the world, this is an attractively prepared pamphlet. An excellent teaching tool. *See* the entry for the Minority Rights Group.

Kuper, Leo (1985). *The Prevention of Genocide*. New Haven, CT, and London: Yale University Press. 256 pp.
The doyen of scholars of genocide in the world today has summed up, in his characteristically scrupulous and understated style, both the record of international action against genocide to date and the requirements and possibilities of more generous and effective actions in the future. Kuper concludes, it seems reluctantly, that the record to date is with few exceptions a very sorry one, but he refuses to yield on his hopes and optimism about the future. There are possibilities for more meaningful international action against genocide within the framework of the U.N., as for example the appointment of a U.N. High Commissioner, and the establishment of an International Court to enforce the Genocide Convention. Outside the U.N., there are possible strategies through nongovernmental organizations, an early warning system, the media, religious leaders, and public campaigns. Kuper reports on the establishment of a new organization, International Alert, that is intended to seek urgent action in cases of emergent genocide. An indispensable reference.

Lapid, Pinchas (1974). The dress rehearsal for the Holocaust. *Bar Ilan University Bulletin*, Summer, 14–20. (In Hebrew)
An important interpretation of the Armenian genocide at the hands of the Turkish government in 1915–17. The government decision to execute the victims as a state policy; utilization of a series of deceptions and calculated denials of eye-witness reports; accusations that the minority constituted a grave danger to the regime; the complicity of foreign governments that could have helped hinder or arrest the process (in this case the German government, foreshadowing a later German government's role as key perpetrator of the Holocaust) are all recognizable aspects in this genocide and in another genocide yet to come.

Lemkin, Raphael (1944). *Axis Rule in Occupied Europe*. Washington, DC: Carnegie Endowment for World Peace. 674 pp.
A classic. By the man who originated the word "genocide," and is credited with having fought almost singlehandedly for the adoption of the Genocide Convention by the United Nations.

Letgers, Lyman H. (1984). The Soviet Gulag: is it genocide? In Charny (1984), pp. 60–66.
Genocide is a specific type of crime and does not embrace *all* forms of mass murder. Nonetheless, if the Soviet slaughter of 15 million peasants is omitted, it will "weaken and even trivialize the judicial concept of genocide."

Mace, James E. (1984). The man-made famine of 1933 in the Soviet Ukraine: what happened and why? In Charny (1984), pp. 67–83.

Between 5 and 7 million Ukrainians died in a man-made famine whose purpose was "to destroy the Ukrainian nation as a political factor and social organism." Churchill reported that Stalin, who otherwise disclaimed reports of the starving dead as fairy tales, admitted in a conversation with him to 10 million dead. *See* the author's chapter in this book (Chapter 6).

Minority Rights Group [29 Craven Street, London WC2N 5NT]
The Minority Rights Group (MRG) is devoted to the myriad ethnic, political, religious, and racial minority groups around the planet. It issues excellent studies of such groups as well as studies of the overall legal, political and social science issues that relate to the survival and welfare of minority groups. The following are illustrative MRG pamphlets. (*See also* the entry under Kuper, Leo, *International Action against Genocide*.)

Cooper, Roger (1982). *The Baha'is of Iran*.
Fawcett, James (1979). *The International Protection of Minorities*.
Lang, David Marshall, and Walker, Christopher (1981). *The Armenians*.
Mullin, Chris (1981). *The Tibetans*.
O'Shaughnessy, Hugh, and Corry, Stephen (1977). *What Future for the Amerindians of South America?*
Palley, Claire (1978). *Constitutional Law and Minorities*.
Suter, Keith (1981). *West Iran, East Timor and Indonesia*.

Morse, Arthur (1968). *While Six Million Died: A Chronicle of American Apathy*. New York: Random House.
This outstanding book shocked the American public and world opinion with its record of overwhelming American government indifference, cynicism, and even blatant anti-Semitism as the information poured in about the Holocaust and the desperate straits of Jews in Europe. President Franklin D. Roosevelt is among those revealed to be more concerned with his own political considerations than with the fates of the hapless Jews. A chronicle of many tragic and infuriating incidents such as the turning away of the *St. Louis* and its shipload of refugees from the shores of the U.S.A., and the State Department's refusing to acknowledge and act on "alleged" reports of the death camps.

Payne, Robert (1973). *Massacre*. New York: Macmillan. 168 pp.
Three million Bengalis were killed by Pakistan following the birth of Bangladesh in 1971. Payne describes the sequence of events of the massacre, and proposes a schema of such massacres in general. (1) The victims are lulled into a sense of security; (2) The death blow; (3) The victims recover from their paralysis; (4) The military mounts a second massacre; (5) The victims begin to organize; (6) The military mounts a third massacre; (7) "The victim bites off the enemy's hands and feet"; (8) The final massacre. "Massacre is an art, not a science, and it is carried out by men possessing recognizable qualities. Among these qualities is an overwhelming contempt for humanity, which extends not only to the victims, but to the soldiers ordered to massacre them."

Pilisuk, Marc, and Ober, Lyn. (1976). Torture and genocide as public health problems. *American Journal of Orthopsychiatry*, 46(3), 388–392.
The authors make the "obvious" point that genocide is in fact Public Health Problem No. 1, since more human beings lose their lives unnaturally at the hands of their fellow man than to any other illness or condition that terminates human lives prematurely.

Porter, Jack Nusan (1982a). What is genocide? Notes toward a definition. In Porter, Jack Nusan (Ed.), *Genocide and Human Rights: A Global Anthology*. Washington, DC: University Press of America, pp. 2–33.
A comprehensive, thoughtful review of the subject of genocide and its definition. Porter concludes that genocide is the deliberate destruction, in whole or part, of any minority, through mass murder or any other means, and that it involves three major components: ideology, technology, and bureaucracy/organization. Includes a discussion of the prediction of genocide: under what conditions the likelihood grows, and under what conditions the probability of genocide is reduced. With charts of major factors in genocide, examples of nineteenth- and twentieth-century genocide, and a bibliography.

Porter, Jack Nusan (Ed.) (1982b). *Genocide and Human Rights: A Global Anthology*. Washington, DC: University Press of America. 353 pp.
A very fine anthology. The conceptual paper by editor Porter, listed immediately above, is in itself an outstanding effort to define genocide and to summarize the conditions that facilitate its occurrence, and conditions which work against genocide taking place.

Rubenstein, Richard L. (1983). *The Age of Triage*. Boston: Beacon Press. 312 pp.
A thought-provoking, at times profound, yet strange and disturbing book by a former rabbi who in recent years has played a senior role in a foundation devoted to world peace created and sponsored by the Unification Church ("Moonies"). Rubenstein seems to recognize the naturalness of elimination of certain groups of huge numbers of human beings in nature's irreverent press towards selection of the fittest, albeit the mechanism is the deliberate annihilation of people deemed surplus by those in power. This study has been commended by Leo Kuper as innovative.

Santoni, Ronald E. (1984). Nuclear insanity and multiple genocide. In Charny (1984), pp. 147–153.
According to ordinary usage and dictionary meanings, the nuclear arms race is indeed "insane" and "mad." "Preoccupation with nuclear war, with utter destruction, is an illness, a form of extreme irrationality . . . it will eventually lead to multiple genocide or—its logical extension—*omnicide*."

Segev, Tom (1981). From Dachau to Bergen–Belsen: the commanders of the concentration camps. *Zmanim*, 6, 68–81, Tel Aviv University and Zmorah, Bitan and Modan Publishers. (In Hebrew)
The definitive study of the commanders of the Nazi concentration camps, which concludes that they were not inherently monsters, yet they became and were so in their roles.

Sereny, Gitta (1974). *Into That Darkness: From Mercy Killing to Mass Murder*. London: André Deutsch. 380 pp.
The story of Walter Stangl, commander of the Treblinka death camp, based on interviews of Stangl in his post-war jail by the author. The interviews and the reporting are extraordinarily skillful. The conclusion appears to be (as is also reported by most other investigators of the monsters of Nazi Germany) that this arch-administrator of a death factory was *not* a madman and not a sadist, but an ambitious and obedient executive, who rose in the ranks and held his position by doing his job "well" and remaining beyond criticism of his superiors. An important primary document of the insidious workings of the demonic inside us human beings.

Sheleff, Leon Shaskolsky (1978). *The Bystander: Behavior, Law, Ethics*. Lexington, MA: Lexington Books. 223 pp.

An outstanding summary of the subject of the bystander: what is known about the dynamics of the behavior and how and why people choose to be bystanders to another's despair; the legal status of the bystander as well as of the "Good Samaritan" who does come to his aid and may suffer disastrous responsibility for the outcome of the victim; and a thoughtful probing of the ethical meanings of the choice of whether to be a bystander or to take responsibility for assisting others. Sheleff is both an attorney and sociologist, and he writes with the passion of a concerned human being.

Wangyal, Phuntsog (1984). Tibet: a case of eradication of religion leading to genocide. In Charny (1984), pp. 119–126.

The author claims that the genocidal killings of the Tibetans are on a scale that may match those of Pol Pot. In a poignant statement he concludes that it is likely that Tibetans "will finally vanish as an ethnic group . . . The Tibetan people now undergoing genocide would like to hope that their suffering could contribute to the prevention of similar human suffering."

Wiesel, Elie (1973). *The Oath*. New York: Random House. 286 pp.

Wiesel, a child-survivor of the Holocaust, has been for many "the prophet of the Holocaust," at once witness, conscience, and spiritual leader to a world that must come to grips with human evil before it is too late and we are all destroyed. Awarded the Nobel Prize for Peace in 1986, and nominated many times for the Literature prize as well, Wiesel has been the first Chair of the U.S. government agency created to commemorate the Holocaust—and thereby to give watchful testimony to the dangers of new inhumanity to masses of human beings.

Wiesel is a gifted writer, and some of his works already constitute a classical literature of the Holocaust. Several of these are cited in Totten's chapter on the literature and art of the Holocaust (Chapter 11) in this book. Although a fictional work, *The Oath* is cited here because it is a contribution to our understanding of the generic process of genocide. It is the story of the building of a pogrom against Jews in a small European town, but in its microcosm it is symbolic of the macro-process of the unfolding of the Holocaust on the European continent.

Whitaker, Ben (1985). Revised and Updated Report on the Question of the Prevention and Punishment of the Crime of Genocide. 62 pp. (E/CN.4/Sub.2/1985/6, 2 July 1985)

This is a very significant report. It was submitted to the United Nations Sub-Commission on Prevention of Discrimination and Protection of Minorities of the Commission on Human Rights of the United Nations Economic and Social Council in Geneva in July 1985. The report is the first on genocide in many years, and only the second study called for by the United Nations since the original adoption of the U.N. Convention on Genocide in 1948.

The report calls for an enlarging of the definition of genocide, expanding legal jurisdiction to make it possible to punish genocide, and for new international structures such as a scientific early warning information system and a committee or tribunal on genocide that would respond directly to reports of mass murder.

From the point of view of the political process at the U.N., the appointment of Ben Whitaker, long-time head of the Minority Rights Group in London, as Special Rapporteur in itself promised a significant and meaningful report. Whitaker's report "named names" and identified explicitly various cases of genocide in the twentieth century, including that of the Armenians. Passage of the report, that is, its acceptance by the Sub-Commission, thus righted the incredible history of censorship of the

Armenian genocide in an earlier U.N. report (*see* Ruhashyankiko, 1978, listed in the next chapter). The report also makes many important recommendations for putting teeth into the Genocide Convention by enlarging the definition and implementing legal structures for prosecution of genocide.

Beyond its purpose as a working document in the U.N. political process, the report constitutes a comprehensive overview of knowledge and scholarly thinking about genocide and its prevention at the time of its preparation.

Wiesenthal, Simon (1967). *The Murderers among Us*. New York: McGraw-Hill. 340 pp.
A survivor of the Holocaust, Simon Wiesenthal has devoted his life to tracking down Nazi killers who went into hiding. Over the years, he has also become an impressive, powerful voice speaking for other embattled peoples, including the Gypsies, whose terrible fate in the Holocaust has often been overlooked and minimized in the comparative context of the persecution of the Jews. Among the unforgettable observations in this book are Wiesenthal's report of Nazis who would write home after killing Jewish children mercilessly to inquire solicitously about the health of their sick child, or how SS mathematicians calculated the size of a crater left by an Allied bomb on an airstrip and then the number of Jewish bodies that would be needed to fill the crater.

2

Intervention and Prevention of Genocide

Israel W. Charny

The title of this chapter clearly spells out a hope rather than an existing reality in the history of humankind, but the fact that the idea of doing something about genocide—intervening in an ongoing eruption of mass killing and seeking to prevent potential genocide—has become the subject of serious study is to be celebrated.

Assuming the world is not destroyed in immediately succeeding generations, there is reason to believe that meaningful efforts to prevent genocidal killings will develop in the legal, political, and communications fields, and by way of education and a more active public sentiment against mass murder. At present, there is a fatalism about genocide, a widely held view that virtually nothing can be done to eradicate the crime. Certainly, the contemporary record is bleak, notwithstanding the adoption of the Genocide Convention of 1948. Though Article IX of the Convention does provide for preventive action against genocide by one of the Contracting Parties, in the form of a submission to the International Court of Justice, it has never been invoked. Yet there have been many genocides in recent years, and there is probably an increasing threat of genocide, given the great pressure of population on resources and the ready availability of highly destructive weapons.

Two major documents regarding the possibilities of prevention of genocide to date are the 1985 United Nations report on genocide by Special Rapporteur Ben Whitaker of the United Kingdom, and *The Prevention of Genocide* by Leo Kuper of the University of California, published in 1985 by Yale University Press in the United States and U.K. Both publications bespeak the great contradictions that exist between stated hopes for intervention and prevention of genocide and the realities of *realpolitik* in our world.

As we shall see, the United Nations report organizes a series of entirely

20

rational, and in that sense quite realistic, proposals that, if undertaken, could contribute to the reduction of genocide. However, U.N. responses to the Whitaker study do not presage in the immediate future adoption of very many proposals, or, even if adopted, the will to give them authentic operational forms. The deliberations of the Sub-Commission on Discrimination and Protection of Minorities and the Commission on Human Rights of the United Nations Economic and Social Council in Geneva, to which the report was submitted, included demonstrations of demagoguery, cynicism and hatred, characteristic of the prejudicial and genocidal processes the report intends to condemn (*see* the special issue of the *Internet on the Holocaust and Genocide*.)

Kuper's "The Prevention of Genocide"

Leo Kuper's book *The Prevention of Genocide* is an anthem of hope for the possibilities of growth in the United Nations system, but at the same time, Kuper concludes reluctantly, that the U.N. record has been dismal "I assume that realistically, only a small contribution can be expected from the United Nations, at any rate in the immediate future" (p. 21). Or again: "The performance of the United Nations in response to genocide is as negative as its performance on charges of political mass murder. There are the same evasions of responsibility and protection of offending governments and the same overriding concern for state interests and preoccupation with ideological and regional alliances" (p. 160).

In its response to then-emerging events in Cambodia or Kampuchea under the Khmer Rouge, the Human Rights Commission deferred consideration of the massacres for a whole year. In 1978, three years after the forced evacuation of Phnom Penh, the Commission deliberated for the first time, and even then in true committee fashion delayed arriving at conclusions until a whole year later, a period during which innumerable people continued to die while the bungling bureaucratic machinery went about its work. Notwithstanding the commission's subsequent conclusion in 1979 that the situation represented "nothing less than autogenocide," and that the events were "the most serious that had occurred anywhere in the world since Nazism" (Kuper, p. 135), there then followed a series of the most cynical political maneuverings on the part of various governments. Among these the United States, erstwhile champion of human rights, stands fully indicted for its continuing recognition of Pol Pot, the ousted leader of the Khmer Rouge government, as the legitimate representative of Cambodia in the United Nations—lest the alternative of recognition of the North Vietnam-sponsored regime in Cambodia were to mean the confirmation of an historic communist enemy of the United States. An analogous situation would have been the United States continuing to support Adolf Hitler, had he lived, as the legitimate representative of the German government following World War II, in an effort to avoid acceptance of a communist leader who might have been installed in Germany by the Soviet Union.

Nonetheless, Kuper concludes that there are possibilities for preventive action within the United Nations. He draws attention to recent developments for protection against violations of human rights and some movement from the elaboration of norms to concern for implementation. The establishment of standing Working Groups on Slavery, on Enforced or Involuntary Disappearances, and on Indigenous Populations, provides a ready channel for drawing international attention to threatening situations. Similar functions are served by a variety of ad hoc groups. Moreover, there is an increasing readiness in the United Nations to exert pressure on governments guilty of gross violations of human rights.

Strategies for prevention of genocide must be related to the type of genocide. As reported in the previous chapter, Kuper distinguishes the following forms of domestic genocide (that is, genocides arising on the basis of internal divisions within a society):

1. Genocide against indigenous groups, including genocide against hunting and gathering groups in the interests of economic development (e.g. the Aché Indians in Paraguay).
2. Genocide following decolonization of a two-tier structure of domination (e.g. of Hutu in Burundi and of Tutsi in Rwanda).
3. Genocide in the process of struggles for power between ethnic or racial or religious groups; or for self-determination or against discrimination (e.g. Bangladesh).
4. Genocide against hostage or scapegoat groups (e.g. of Jews by the Nazis in the Holocaust).

Genocides rarely erupt without preliminary warning, and in particular, conflicts between racial, ethnic, and religious groups are likely to be protracted. These constitute the major source of domestic genocides, and often follow a predictable course, with many gross violations of human rights preceding the major catastrophe. Moreover, societies at risk of mass killings can usually be identified. Preventive action is therefore possible by alerting various agencies of the United Nations to gross violations of human rights in the societies at risk— such violations, for example, as arrest without trial, torture, extrajudicial executions and disappearances.

A more permissive approach to self-determination, short of secession, could contribute to the defusing of many of these conflicts (Kuper, 1985, pp. 215–217), and Buchheit (1978, Chapter 4) argues that under certain specified conditions, even secession should be entertained.

Pressure may also be exerted in appropriate specialized agencies of the United Nations, and in regional and other intergovernmental organizations (*see* Wiseberg and Scoble, 1982). However, it is essential that nongovernmental organizations take the initiative in activating the intergovernmental organizations, and by way of independent action—alerting international public opinion, making representations to governments, and organizing demonstrations and campaigns.

The Whitaker Report

The Whitaker Report emphasizes that genocide today is also a danger to civilization itself. Genocide has grown rather than receded in extent in history, and the logical conclusion of genocide in our era of nuclear weapons is likely to be more total "omnicide."

An important aspect of possible prevention of genocide some day is the enunciation of the anthem of the Genocide Convention that genocide is a crime which must be fought. In the words of the Whitaker Report, genocide is "the ultimate crime and the greatest violation of human rights it is possible to commit" (5:14). There needs to be a growing consensus on the part of human beings and organized society that penetrates the very basis of human culture that mass killing is unacceptable to civilized peoples, otherwise the prevailing momentum of historical experience will continue to confirm for generation after generation that genocide is a phenomenon of nature, like other disasters, and this view of the inevitability of genocide as an almost natural event will continue to justify it in the sense of convincing people that nothing can be done.

The Whitaker Report establishes the principle that there is an inherent justification of intervention "to prevent and punish violations of the crime by others" (6:18). Through its recommendations for the expansion of the definition of genocide under the United Nations Convention, it also expands the basis for concepts of prevention. The report recommends including political genocide, mass murder of a sexual group, genocide of one's own people, and also recommends the possible consideration of cultural genocide or ethnocide, and the consideration of ecocide—adverse impacts on the ecological environment. It also recommends the study of apartheid for its possible relevance to genocide. Since expansion of the definition in itself implies an increased pressure on peoples and governments who might otherwise automatically undertake such types of mass killing, the proposed revisions can also be considered tools of prevention.

There are other ways in which the definition of genocide is broadened. While the report emphasizes that the legal definition of genocide is subject to an examination of the *intent* to destroy a designated group, it also calls for the inclusion of "advertent omission" to qualify as genocide. Thus allowing, let alone organizing, a policy of famine or disease would qualify as genocidal killing.

The report also seeks to place responsibility on individuals for their actions in mass killings even if they are following orders given by their superiors. "The Special Rapporteur recommends that explicit wording should be added to the Convention . . . that 'in judging culpability, a plea of superior orders is not an excusing defence,' " and calls on national codes for "armed forces, prison staffs, police officers, doctors and others, to advise and warn them that it is not only their right to disobey orders violating human rights, such as to carry out genocide and torture, but their legal duty so to disobey" (26:53).

Enforcement takes an important place in the recommendations. Whereas the convention now provides for trial of a person committting genocide in the territory in which the act was committed, or by an international penal court that has not yet been established, the report calls for universal jurisdiction, the competence of the courts of all countries, and extradition. It also calls for serious early warning and fact-finding systems, impartial publicity as a deterrent, and the development of strong international public pressure against crimes against humanity.

Other Proposals towards Prevention

Albeit slowly, over recent years we begin to hear one proposal and then another towards preventing or containing genocide.

Two attorneys, Luis Kutner, Chairman of the World Habeas Corpus organization, and Ernest Katin (1984), have proposed the development of a World Genocidal Tribunal that would be authorized to bring before it individuals as well as governments which have committed genocide. The Tribunal would also be empowered to undertake investigative actions when reports of genocide come in. Similarly, the Baha'i International Community have proposed (Knight, 1982; Whitaker, 1985) a Committee on Genocide that would hold "watching briefs" on genocide. The committee would concern itself with questions of *fact* rather than questions of law. It would be responsible for investigating allegations of genocide. As in the Kutner proposal, the committee would be empowered to summon state parties charged with genocide. "Such a committee would remove the subject of genocide as far as possible from the political arena; attract a high caliber of 'independent expert' membership; speed the international response to genocidal situations and provide the high-profile, international focus for genocide that is currently lacking" (43–44:85).

An example of a major initiative to translate a past genocide not only into a basis for powerful new awareness on the part of the world community but into an impetus to undertake dramatic new steps to prevent future genocide is the development of the Cambodia Documentation Commission under the direction of David Hawk, a former director of the U.S. branch of Amnesty. Hawk has been an intrepid researcher of the genocidal murder of Cambodians by Pol Pot's regime (*see* Chapter 7 in this book). He has painstakingly accumulated records of mass graves and executions, brought out records of the execution schedules and of a torture manual in the infamous Tuol Sleng prison in Phnom Penh. He has created a powerful photographic exhibition that has been viewed in Washington, DC (where its display was also earmarked to support the campaign to bring about ratification of the U.N. Genocide Convention by the United States Senate), and has toured the United States and other countries.

The Cambodia Documentation Commission has set for itself a goal of bringing legal action under the Genocide Convention—the first time this will have been undertaken—against the Cambodian government, whose representation in the U.N. is by the same governing group of Pol Pot that was responsible for the mass murders. Ironically, Cambodia had ratified the Genocide Convention and action can be brought, under Article IX, before the International Court of Justice.

Other initiatives to prevent genocide have been designed to influence a broad international public opinion. An important effort which intends to combine a mass-movement constituency with knowledgeable political influences on governments in the face of impending genocide is the newly founded International Alert organization. In his book, Kuper called for "an international grass-roots organization, with even more massive and influential support than the anti-nuclear movement" (p. 19), International Alert has been established with its headquarters in London and initial branch in Los Angeles. The Secretary General of the new organization is Martin Ennals, former Secretary General of Amnesty International. As an example of the alerting of world public opinion and government leaders, International Alert took as two of its first projects action to restrain mass killings in Sri Lanka and Uganda.

In connection with the development of a Genocide Early Warning System (*see* Chapter 1), Charny (1982b) also proposes convening experts in communication, including advertising professionals and mass media professionals, to look at more effective ways of disseminating information about atrocities, massacres and genocide. There are a number of serious problems connected with effective delivery of information about such dread events to viewers, listeners and readers. Many people naturally experience a rapid cutoff of their ability to apprehend news of atrocities because such information threatens their security deeply. In a paper to an Amnesty International Conference on Extra-Legal Executions, Charny (1982a) proposed creating carefully balanced announcements of news of atrocities together with messages of respect for life by respected world leaders and celebrities, also with reassuring news of rescue efforts and humanitarian aid, as examples of possible ways to counter the problem of transmitting dread news.

A proposal combining elements of the Genocide Early Warning System and International Alert was advanced by Gerald Knight of the Baha'i International Community. In an address in London in 1982, he called for a "Genocide Bureau." "It would be the body which first came to mind . . . whenever questions of genocide arose . . . the Genocide Bureau would inform itself on possible genocide trouble spots around the world" (Knight, 1982, pp. 8, 9). In a subsequent submission to the U.N. (for the Whitaker Report), the proposal was renamed a "Genocide Committee." It would be empowered to indict a State against which charges of genocide were raised, and to make confidential inquiries into such situations.

A specific example of a grass-roots public opinion campaign to advance commitment against genocide has been the successful mobilization of a public in the U.S.A. to call for ratification of the Genocide Convention by the Senate, accompanied by lobbying of members of the Senate. On 19 February 1985, by a vote of 83 to 11, the Senate consented to ratification of the Convention, thereby ending a thirty-seven-year deadlock since President Harry Truman first submitted the treaty for ratification in 1949.

An interesting symbolic effort at countering genocide is the series of Peoples' Tribunals that have been conducted over recent years. In 1966–67, the First Russell Tribunal investigated charges of genocide against the United States Forces for its role in Vietnam. The Second Russell Tribunal in 1973–75 dealt with violations of human rights in Latin America and found Brazil, Chile, Uruguay, Bolivia, Guatemala, Haiti, Paraguay and the Dominican Republic guilty of systematic violations of human rights, while Brazil was found guilty of genocide. The Third Russell Tribunal in 1978–79 dealt with violations of human rights in West Germany. The fourth Russell Tribunal investigated complaints of violations of human rights, mostly of Indians in the Americas. The Russell Tribunal was succeeded the following year by the Permanent Tribunal of the Peoples, which found San Salvador guilty of genocide for political mass murders. In 1981 and 1982, the Peoples' Tribunal held sessions on Afghanistan and found the Soviet government guilty of aggression. In 1981, the Indonesian government was found guilty of genocide in East Timor. In January 1983, the Guatemalan government was cited for genocide against its Indian population. In 1984, the Tribunal ruled that genocide had been committed by the Turks in their extermination of the Armenians in 1915–17.

The overall record of these tribunals is a mixed one. Some critics feel there has been too much looseness in the definition of charges, which detracts from the credibility of the indictments. In addition, the entire structure is such that one feels that the verdict is in before the case begins, and this makes the tribunals showcases for the foregone conclusions of liberals rather than genuine judicial or scholarly investigations. The lack of a political base for the tribunals also renders them impotent from the outset and invites a certain degree of mockery.

Legal Initiatives—Punishment

It is doubtful whether punishment of the crime is an effective deterrent. But, to date, there have been only a few isolated prosecutions in national courts for genocides committed after the framing of the Convention. In Cambodia, the government succeeding Pol Pot tried him and his deputy *in absentia* for genocide; a trial of Macias in Equatorial Guinea in 1979 found him guilty of genocide; in 1973 the government announced a trial for genocide in Bangladesh but then did not pursue it. However, the International Commission of Jurists thought that in the Macias case no genocide was committed since there was no intentional destruction of a national ethnic or religious group.

The recommendations of the Whitaker Report for the extension of legal tools to prosecute those who commit genocide virtually anywhere in the world, and to expand the definition of genocide, in effect would justify the various trials. However, it is clear that numerous problems relating to the constitutions and powers of states which would have to pass enabling legislation remain unsolved, and it is also not clear that there is sufficient international will to create a genuinely strong legal machinery to punish genocide. At best, one can foresee at this point a period of some additional national prosecutions of some individual leaders who have committed genocide. The long-range goal to develop world legal machinery against genocide remains one of the most important tasks.

Obstacles to International Action against Genocide

Without doubt, one of the greatest obstacles to progress is the fact that, with few exceptions, leaders and governments employ self-interest cruelly and unashamedly. At this point in the United Nations system, cynicism and political self-interest certainly are more the rule than positions of principle. When the question of Chinese genocide in Tibet came before the U.N., the East European socialist states, with the exception of Yugoslavia, acted as a solid bloc in defense of China. Their argument was that Tibet was an integral part of China and therefore involved an aspect of its domestic affairs, which precluded outside interference. As noted earlier, the United States remains a supporter of Pol Pot as the vested leader of the Cambodian people so as to undermine the standing of the Vietnam-supported government of Cambodia. This leaves the Soviet Union, Vietnam, and Cuba trying to unseat the Pol Pot representation. At the same time, they support Indonesia with its history of genocide in East Timor, and other "people's governments" such as Czechoslovakia, Hungary, and Romania have abstained from motions critical of Indonesia. Prior to the time that Vietnam fought against Pol Pot, the same Soviet Union was supporting the "Agrarian People's Government" of Pol Pot despite the reports of massive genocidal killing, while the United States was bringing to bear impassioned spokesmanship for human life and liberty against him. In short, corruption and demagoguery reign, and in the international forum of the United Nations we are presented with a scandalous picture of our human "civilization."

Another powerfully distressing statement of mankind's complicity in mass murders of peoples is the overwhelming indifference of governments to information about the plight of people who are being exterminated, the readiness to carry on relations as usual with the offending regime, complicity in concealing the record of the murders until it becomes too late, and often half-hearted efforts to provide relief and safety even to refugees who manage to escape. In the case of the Holocaust, for example, the record of two great democratic nations, the U.S.A. and Canada (Morse, 1968; Abella and Troper, 1982), was to bar the entry of many Jewish refugees who had managed to escape and others who might have been able to flee if the doors had been opened.

Another side of the coin of cynicism is the use of international forums for the expression of animosity and prejudice towards a specific people such as Israel. In 1982, Christian Falanges entered the Palestinian camps of Sabra and Shatilla and massacred several hundreds. An Israeli commission of inquiry concluded that there was no doubt of Israeli responsibility given Israel's military control of the area and given the history of massacres between Christians and Muslims in the past which should have alerted the Israelis to the likelihood of massacre. The United Nations in turn called for a resolution condemning the massacres as an act of genocide—a resolution that has not been applied to any of the huge genocides that have taken place in which hundreds of thousands have died. Moreover, in attributing responsibility to the Israeli government, the resolution completely omitted mention of the fact that the massacres were in fact carried out by Christian militia, the impression thus being given that the Israelis themselves were the killers. In fact, a specific suggestion in the Sub-Commission on Human Rights that reference be made to the actual killing role of the Falange militia had been rejected.

Denial of Genocide

Curiously, the cynicism seen in political circles, where there are immediate payoffs in power and position, is also carried over to extensive efforts to deny the historical record of events long past. The story of Turkish government opposition to the participation of Armenians in the International Conference on the Holocaust and Genocide in 1982 was reported in the last chapter. Many efforts at revision of the history of the Armenian genocide have been made by the Turkish government (*see* the discussions of this revisionism by Housepian-Dobkin, 1984, and Hovannisian, 1984). Similarly, there is a massive campaign in country after country to promote the claim that there never was a Holocaust (Butz, 1983). In both cases, academics and academic institutions participate in these unabashed lies about major events in history.

The Roles of Professionals

If professionals by definition are supposed to deliver services to human beings in order to make their lives safer, healthier and more satisfying, and professionalism means an ethic of responsibility, the record nonetheless shows that too many professionals aid, abet and themselves play key roles in mass destruction of human lives.

In the Holocaust, the first mass extermination program was authored and executed by physicians (Amir, 1977; Chorover, 1979). Later, in the accursed concentration camps, any number of physicians served in making "selections," or participated in heinous experiments on inmates (Lifton 1982, 1986). Lawyers, of course, participated in the processes required to define, authorize, and legitimate the persecutions, expropriations, and executions of the victims. Scientists contributed directly to the "Final Solution" and the problem of how to dispose of millions of bodies, and they made shameless use of inmates for anatomical, pharmacological, environmental, occupational, and other "research." Clergymen of many faiths, and various church leaders such as the Pope, played safe and did not challenge the killing regime. Altogether, the message for civilization is that to date no profession or groups of professionals can be counted on to stand resolutely for human life. One would hope that some day professional organizations, in all fields, will be mobilized as major agencies of international public opinion to counter human rights abuses and genocide.

Summing up the Prospects for Prevention

Two types of genocide ought to be thought of separately when we attempt to summarize the prospects for prevention of future genocide. The first is specific genocide of a particular target people in a limited geographical area. The second is the "multiple genocide" and "ecocide" and "omnicide" that are the expected results of nuclear, chemical, and other "future-weapons" warfare.

Tragically, both types can be expected to take place in our time. However, it seems possible to say that there is a clear enough conceptual base available to identify and intervene in the first type of genocide. Kuper (1981) notes that two groups "that are continually at risk" are indigenous groups and hostage groups, and he is encouraged that there are developments in the United Nations machinery, such as the U.N. Working Group on Indigenous Populations, which seek increasing international awareness to begin to lay down "an infra-structure for implementation of international obligations" (p. 212). An important report on human rights and massive exoduses presented by Prince Sadruddin Aga Khan recommended combination of an early warning system with the establishment of a supranational agency concerning potential mass exodus situations. Ultimately, a combination of international government machinery, such as the proposal for a U.N. High Commissioner for Human Rights [which Kuper (1985, p. 214) hailed "as the most promising proposal theoretically"], expansion of the definition and jurisdiction of genocide as recommended in the Whitaker Report, and a variety of nongovernmental systems and organizations such as International Alert and the International Commission of Jurists, and the various proposals for a World Human Rights and Genocide Early Warning Center, World Genocide Tribunal, and Committee on Genocide could provide the world with meaningful machinery against genocide. Thus today one can at least dream of and envisage the possibility of reducing genocide against a specific target people, although it has to be clear that even this is a *dream* that is far from reality, for as yet mankind and its governing structures have not really shown a will to stop mass killing.

On the other hand, the threat of even greater mass extermination by modern nuclear and other devastating weapons, especially in the context of "wars" that are justified by a language of national defense, seems very great and far beyond the reach of the conceptualizations we have begun to develop for genocide as persecutory campaigns against a specific, generally helpless target people. In modern nuclear wars, many different peoples are likely to die *en masse*, and it hardly seems to matter whether those who may survive will agree retrospectively that the participating powers were legitimately at war or engaged in genocide.

Ultimately, committed opposition to genocide also takes caring people squarely up to disturbing frontiers of unresolved philosophical issues such as the hazard of overpopulation in the ecology of Earth, the ultimate place of our planet and our species in the larger destinies of nature, and the extent to which our species can presume to intervene in the unknown grand scheme of the universe—and presumably universes.

Nonetheless, for many of us, the concept that lives of human beings are inviolate and sacred is a basic tenet without which we find our lives incomprehensible and not worth while, and it is from this conviction that people of goodwill commit themselves to efforts to prevent all forms of genocide. Moreover, genocide is usually preceded by many violations of human rights, and it is at this preliminary stage that prevention is more feasible and meaningful. Today we know enough to identify most societies at risk for genocide. It remains to be determined if we can develop sufficient human will to act to prevent these terrible occurrences of mass death.

This chapter and Chapter 1 were both prepared with the assistance of Professor Leo Kuper, which is acknowledged with warm appreciation.

Bibliography

References cited in the text of this chapter which were included in the annotated bibliography of Chapter 1 are not repeated in full here.

Abella, Irving, and Troper, Harold (1982). *None is Too Many: Canada and the Jews of Europe, 1933–1948*. Toronto: Lester & Orpen Dennys. 368 pp.
   This is the Canadian version of government indifference, cynicism and blatant anti-Semitism during World War II (*see* Morse, 1968, and Wyman, 1984, for the terrible U.S. story). Some Canadian government officials did everything in their power to bar the admission of Jews from Europe during the height of their suffering. The machinery of bureaucratic power and politics is seen relentlessly at work to serve a whole bevy of officials who wanted no more Jews in Canada, whether from indifference and aloofness, or dislike of Jews, or more open anti-Semitism.

Amir, Amnon (1977). Euthanasia in Nazi Germany. PhD dissertation, the State University of New York at Albany.
   A landmark study that deserves fuller publication but is available to serious scholars in its present form. Presents step by step the administrative and legal processes that authorized and implemented the mass murders of the mentally ill and defective. The narrative also succeeds in bringing alive the stories of several of the key leaders in this program, some of whom moved on to play roles as death camp commanders or medical specialists later in the "Final Solution."

Amnesty International (1983). *Political Killings by Governments*. London: Amnesty International.
   This is the final report of the Amnesty Conference on Extra-Legal Executions, which took place in April 1982 in Amsterdam. Although Amnesty maintains its historic and helpful focus on individual cases of "prisoners of conscience," it is also concerned with broader patterns and programs which are the contexts that legitimate and implement torture and death. The report calls for improved early warnings and world responses to government policies of murder as a political weapon.

Beres, Louis René (1984). Reason and *realpolitik*: international law and the prevention of genocide. In Charny (1984), pp. 306–324.
   There are now explicit and codified rules of international law against genocide. Prosecution of genocide in domestic courts is justified, and intervention in genocidal situations by outside countries also is permissible under law. Ultimately a centralized system of world law will be needed.

Buchheit, Lee C. (1978). *Secession: The Legitimacy of Self-Determination*. New Haven, CT: Yale University Press. 260 pp.
   The author deals with the implications for the international community of appeals to the principle of self-determination by secessionist groups within independent states. When these secessionist movements erupt into open warfare, they may constitute a serious threat to international peace. Where the secessionist group is a minority and a victim of oppression, violations of human rights, or of genocide, international concern may be generated. Case studies are presented of Katanga, the Kurds, Biafra, the Somali–Kenya/Ethiopia dispute, the Nagas and Bangladesh, and some suggestions are offered for establishing the legitimacy of secessionary movements.

Butz, Arthur R. (1983). *The Hoax of the Twentieth Century: The Case against the Presumed Extermination of European Jewry*. Torrance, CA: Institute for Historical Review, 1983 (copyright 1976). New York Public Library entry: Richmond, Surrey: Historical Review Press, 1975. 315 pp.
   A definitive best-selling "bible" of the "revisionists" who claim the Holocaust never took place, and is exploited by the Jews to gain other advantages in the world community. Butz is a tenured professor (of engineering) at a recognized American university that ignores his virulent anti-Semitic activities and his blatant distortions of history. Some have argued that our tradition of "academic freedom" should not be allowed to provide a cover for the like of Butz, who defies every standard of knowledge and truth.

Camus, Albert (1980). *Neither Victims nor Executioners*. Translated by Dwight MacDonald. New York: Continuum. First appeared serially in Fall 1946 in issues of *Combat*; published July–August 1947 in *Politics*.
   A moving statement of choice not to be a victim or an executioner that is as relevant today for all of us as when it first appeared.

Charny, Israel W. (1982a). Innovating communications initiatives for human rights. Paper presented to the Amnesty International Conference on Extra-Legal Executions, Amsterdam. Mimeographed.
   Calls for and gives examples of media techniques for publicizing human rights information which would attempt to reduce people's tendency to "tune out" information about atrocities and help mobilize a stronger public opinion for human rights.

Charny, Israel W. [in collaboration with Chanan Rapaport] (1982b). *How Can We Commit the Unthinkable?*. *See* Chapter 1.

Charny, Israel W. (Ed.) (1984). *Toward the Understanding and Prevention of Genocide.* *See* Chapter 1.

Chorover, Stephen L. (1979). *From Genesis to Genocide: The Meaning of Human Nature and the Power of Behavior Control.* Cambridge, MA: MIT Press. 256 pp.
A valuable probe of people-control and its ultimate manifestations in mass murder and genocide. Includes a detailed presentation of the Nazi "euthanasia program" for mental patients and mental defectives, which overall has received far too little attention.

Conflict Analysis Center (1985). *Genocide: Ratification of the Convention on the Prevention and Punishment of the Crime of Genocide.* Washington, DC: Conflict Analysis Center [POB 75034, Washington, DC 20013]. Pamphlet.
A well organized pamphlet presentation of the significance of the Convention. Published as a contribution to the campaign to gain U.S. Senate consent to ratification— which was achieved in February 1986.

Cristescu, Aureliu (1981). *The Right to Self-determination: Historical and Current Development on the Basis of United Nations Instruments.* E/CN.4/Sub.2/404/Rev. 1. New York: United Nations. 125 pp. *See* annotation to Gros Espiell (1980).

Dominguez, Jorge; Rodley, Nigel S.; Wood, Bryce; and Falk, Richard A. (1979). *Enhancing Global Human Rights.* New York: McGraw-Hill. 270 pp.
Richard Falk contributes the final section, "Responding to Severe Violations," which includes the crime of genocide. Following a brief survey of contemporary genocidal conflicts, he examines the inhibitions against humanitarian intervention, and the considerations bearing on the possibility of intervention. He concludes that the present obstacles to effective action in restraint of severe violations of human rights cannot be overcome without the emergence of a new system of world order.

Fawcett, James (1979). *The International Protection of Minorities.* London: Minority Rights Group. 20 pp.
This is a useful introduction to the basic principles governing the protection of minorities, the right to self-determination and freedom from discrimination. The author deals with different modes of relating minorities to the overall society, the extremes being represented by separation and integration. He includes a brief historical review of the development of international protection of minorities, with some discussion of international intervention.

Franck, Thomas M., and Rodley, Nigel S. (1973). After Bangla Desh: the law of humanitarian intervention by military force. *American Journal of International Law,* 67(1), 275–305.
The authors survey the history of humanitarian intervention, and the present state of the law regarding unilateral forceful intervention on humanitarian grounds. They conclude that the use of military force by a state or bloc of states to enforce human rights, prevent inhuman activities, or to ensure self-determination in other states, outside the framework of the United Nations, is not sanctioned in historic or contemporary practice. On the question of the successful intervention of India on behalf of East Pakistan, they present arguments against the desirability of regarding this as precedent setting.

Friedlander, Henry and Milton, Sybil (Eds.) (1979). *The Holocaust: Ideology, Bureaucracy, and Genocide. The San Jose Papers.* Millwood, NY: Kraus International Publications 1980.

An important anthology. One of the few sources that has treated systematically the roles of the professions in Nazi Germany: legal, medical, physical sciences, technology, government experts, church, and intellectuals in general.

Garfield, Eugene (1985). Remembering the Holocaust. Part 1. *Current Contents*, no. 27, 8 July, 3–4. Part 2. *Current Contents*, no. 28, 15 July, 3–9.
Thoughtful and moving reviews of the physiological and psychological effects of concentration-camp experiences on survivors; the role of medicine in Nazi Germany, especially "scientific experiments" on concentration-camp inmates; and the roles of science and scientists under the Nazis.

Gros Espiell, Hector (1980). *The Right to Self-determination: Implementation of United Nations Resolutions*. E/CN.4/Sub.2/405/Rev. 1. New York: United Nations. 86 pp.
The study by Espiell is concerned with the implementation of United Nations resolutions relating to the right of peoples under colonial and alien domination to self-determination. It is a radical, revolutionary document in relation to the right of colonized peoples to self-determination; at the same time, it is conservative in declaring that the right does not apply to peoples already organized in the form of independent states. The study by Cristescu deals more broadly with the development of the basic concepts involved in self-determination, and also combines a radical approach to self-determination with a protective stance toward the independent sovereign state. Both studies do introduce nuances to their conservatism, in cases when the state does not represent the whole people, or commits violations of human rights (*see* Kuper, *The Prevention of Genocide*, 1985, pp. 63–67).

Harff, Barbara (1984). *Genocide and Human Rights*. Denver, CO: Graduate School of International Studies, University of Denver. 132 pp.
A call for a humanistic legal framework which will define genocide and other serious human rights abuses as illegal under the law and will justify intervention on humanitarian grounds by the agencies of international government. Thoughtful and touching, but possibly not sufficiently tough and impersonal to be influential for legal scholars and professionals who are not already inclined to the protection of human life.

Harwood, Richard E. (1974). *Did Six Million Really Die?: The Truth at Last*. Richmond, Surrey: Historical Review Press. Pamphlet, 28 pp.
Another major "revisionist" publication that claims the Holocaust never took place. The argumentation, as if in the language of twentieth-century scholarship and accepted logic, is in fact a statement of the failure of our "civilization" that such garbage is published along with the real record of history.

Housepian-Dobkin, Marjorie (1984). What genocide? What holocaust? News from Turkey, 1915–23: a case study. *See* Chapter 1.

Hovannisian, Richard G. (1984). Genocide and denial: the Armenian case. *See* Chapter 1.

Hunt, Chester L. (1984). A critical evaluation of the resistance of German Protestantism to the Holocaust. In Charny (1984), pp. 241–254.
Most members of the Protestant church were undisturbed by Nazi anti-Semitism. Even men like Barth and Niemöller minimized its extent. When the Protestant churches were directly affected, some churchmen responded in a heroic fashion. "An earlier recognition that Jews and Gentiles were integral parts of the same body might have avoided the occasion for largely ineffective heroism."

International Alert (1986). *Emergency Sri Lanka*. Pamphlet.
This is part of a campaign against mass killing, designed to promote ethnic concilia-
tion. It reviews the issues in conflict, their historical background, the incidence of
communal violence and emphasizes the need for a devolution of power.

Internet on the Holocaust and Genocide (January–February 1985). Special issue. *See*
Chapter 1.

Journal of Historical Review. Institute of Historical Research, Torrance, California.
In name and external format, seemingly a scholarly journal. In content, a sloppy,
malevolent collection of "revisionist" anti-Semitic tripe. One could also look at the
likes of this journal as a sad, symbolic reminder of the corruptions of the scholarly
process and professionals in the Holocaust, and—one fears—in the preparations of
future nuclear genocide by thousands of scholars and professionals who staff the
nuclear and other futuristic arms industries of many countries.

Khan, Prince Sadruddin Aga (1981). *Study on Human Rights and Massive Exoduses*.
United Nations, E/CN.4/1503.
Massive exoduses of refugees are often associated with genocidal attacks on target
populations, and constitute an early warning signal. The analysis of the conditions
under which these exoduses occur, and the case studies in the original uncensored
edition, are therefore especially relevant for the prevention of genocide. So too, the
recommendations for the establishment of an early warning system and the appointment of a Special Representative for Humanitarian Questions provide a model for
preventive action against genocide.

Knight, Gerald (1982). A Genocide Bureau. *See* Chapter 1.

Kordov, Moshe (1959). *Kefar Kassim's Trial*. Tel Aviv: Narkis. (In Hebrew)
During Israel's "Operation Sinai" a curfew order was issued covering Arab villages.
In one zone the area commander ordered that violators of the curfew be shot. Most
local officers interpreted this order judiciously, and when the curfew went into effect
in the early evening simply helped residents returning late to their homes to hurry to
obey the curfew. However, in one village, Kefar Kassim, the local commander gave
orders to implement the command literally, with the terrible result that forty-nine
people were killed and thirteen wounded. This book is the dramatic report of the trial
of the officers and soldiers who executed the massacre, their conviction and
sentencing. The justices concluded adamantly, "Every officer and soldier must be
cognizant of the fact that his weapons are intended for military action against the
enemy and not for murder of a noncombatant civilian population. The eight accused
have blackened the 'purity of arms' of the Israel Defence Forces" (p. 255).

Kuper, Leo (1981). *Genocide: Its Political Use in the Twentieth Century*. *See* Chapter 1.

Kuper, Leo (1985). *The Prevention of Genocide*. *See* Chapter 1.

Kutner, Luis (1970). World Habeas Corpus: ombudsman for mankind. *University of
Miami Law Review*, 24 (Winter), 352–387.
The right to habeas corpus, under law, should not be denied any person on this
planet, regardless of the laws of the state in which one lives. A well-reasoned, practical plea for institutionalization of a World Habeas Corpus, written by a senior legal
professional who cares.

Kutner, Luis and Katin, Ernest (1984). World Genocide Tribunal: a proposal for planetary preventive measures supplementing a genocide early warning system. In Charny (1984), pp. 330–346.

A hopeful proposal for the establishment of a World Genocide Tribunal to try perpetrators of genocide directly, also with authority to conduct investigative functions, assess responsibility, and take preventive measures in conjunction with a proposed Genocide Early Warning System. The Tribunal would focus public attention on possible acts of genocide and would be authorized to issue writs of prohibition to order that actions conducive to genocide be stopped.

Lifton, Robert Jay (1982). Medicalized killing in Auschwitz. *See* Chapter 10.

Lifton, Robert Jay (1986). *The Nazi Doctors: Medical Killing and the Psychology of Genocide. See* Chapter 10.

Lifton, Robert Jay, and Falk, Richard (1982). *Indefensible Weapons: the Political and Psychological Case against Nuclearism.* New York: Basic Books. 301 pp.

The collaborative work of two outstanding professionals, a psychiatrist and a political scientist, who present a well-reasoned as well as impassioned case against "nuclear thinking" and nuclear policy.

Lillich, Richard B. (Ed.) (1973). *Humanitarian Intervention and the United Nations.* 240 pp.

This reports the proceedings of a conference by leading international lawyers, presenting a variety of views on the controversy concerning the right to forcible humanitarian intervention. In the first of the two postscripts on the conference, Ian Brownlee concludes that a rule allowing humanitarian intervention, as opposed to a discretion in the United Nations to act through the appropriate organs, is a general license to vigilantes and opportunists to resort to hegemonial intervention. Tom Farer sums up the consensus at the conference as follows: "The salient fact is that almost every member of a group representing a considerable portion of the U.S. foreign policy spectrum *agreed* on the desirability of humanitarian intervention to prevent large-scale abuse, on the appropriateness of exhausting multilateral remedies whenever time allowed, on the need to calculate the damage to the target society as well as to the imminent victims, and on the inadmissibility of interventions designed to safeguard commercial property or ideologically congenial regimes. What divided us, then was a narrow point of strategy. On the main substantive issues we were close to being united."

Morse, Arthur (1968). *While Six Million Died. See* Chapter 1.

Palley, Claire (1978). *Constitutional Law and Minorities.* London: Minority Rights Group.

An indispensable guide to the wide range of policies available in response to claims for self-determination. Palley's discussion is particularly valuable for the detailed specification of legal constitutional arrangements to promote assimilation or to balance the sharing of common institutions with a measure of institutional "separateness."

Penkower, Monty N. (1984). From Holocaust to genocides. In Charny (1984), pp. 129–136.

The West could have checked the tempo of the "Final Solution." "An obtuse world persists in disregarding the warning signals that came from the smokestacks of the crematoria; power-politics-as-usual tolerates genocides and mass murders.''

Ramcharan, B.G. (Ed.) (1985). *The Right to Life in International Law*. Dordrecht: Martinus Nijhoff.
Of general relevance for the prevention of genocide, with a few specific references, including an article by Kuper entitled "Illusion and Reality." This contrasts the commitment of the United Nations on its founding to the eradication of the twin scourges of war and genocide with its performance.

Rassinier, Paul (1978). *Debunking the Genocide Myth: A Study of the Nazi Concentration Camps and the Alleged Extermination of European Jewry*. Introduction by Pierre Hofstetter, translated from the French by Adam Robbins. Los Angeles: Noontide Press. 441 pp.
The flagship of the French "revisionists" translated into English. "Proves" that the population of European Jewry was not noticeably less after World War II; that Jews spread the lies of the Holocaust in order to gain advantages for their worldwide efforts at power. Disgusting, dangerous, and a sobering reminder that books, like people, can serve the demonic.

Ruhashyankiko, Nicodeme (1978). Report to the U.N. Sub-Commission on Prevention of Discrimination and Protection of Minorities. *Study of the Question of the Prevention and Punishment of the Crime of Genocide*. E/CN.4/Sub. 2/416, 4 July 1978. 186 pp.
A major study by the U.N. of its Convention on Genocide; the first such study since the original adoption of the Convention on Genocide in 1948. Proposed significant improvements in the Convention such as universal jurisdiction for prosecution of those who commit genocide. However, the report became most widely known not for its significant contributions to the understanding of genocide and its possible prevention, but as a focus of cynical politicization in the U.N. After unceasing political efforts and threats, the Turks succeeded in having the report revised so as not to acknowledge the Armenian genocide, action that Leo Kuper referred to as casting the Armenian genocide "down the memory hole." *See* the entry for the succeeding report in 1985 by Whitaker in the previous chapter.

Russell Tribunals.
The Russell Tribunals were instituted by Bertrand Russell in Stockholm in 1966 and in Roskilde, Denmark, in 1967. Their purpose is to create a transnational context, with a juridicial quality, to evaluate serious abuses of international law. The tribunals are public events conducted in the manner of court proceedings and conclude with a formal judgment. The citations below refer to the Second Tribunal, which dealt with violations of human rights in Latin America; the Third Tribunal in re West Germany; the Fourth on the rights of Indians in the Americas. The Permanent Peoples' Tribunal was initiated in 1979. It has rendered two advisory opinions in Western Sahara and has held nine sessions: Argentina, Philippines, El Salvador, Afghanistan I and II, East Timor, Zaire, and Guatemala, and the genocide of the Armenians. This latter instance of genocide is the subject of the last citation below, *A Crime of Silence*.

Russell Tribunal (1975). Second International Tribunal. *Found Guilty*. The Verdict of the Russell Tribunal Section in Brussels. Spokesman Pamphlet 51. Nottingham: Bertrand Russell Peace Foundation.
Third International Tribunal (1975). *Berufsverbote Condemned*. Nottingham: Bertrand Russell Peace Foundation.
Fourth International Tribunal (1980). *The Rights of the Indians of the Americas*. Amsterdam: Workgroup Indian Project.

Permanent Peoples' Tribunal (1985). *A Crime of Silence: The Armenian Genocide.* London: Zed Press.

Sachs, Shimon (1985). *Action T4: Mass Murder of Handicapped in Nazi Germany.* Tel Aviv: Papyrus. 151 pp. (In Hebrew)
A well-written, responsible summary of the infamous Nazi program of euthanasia for the mentally ill and defective. This was the first program of mass exterminations implemented by the Nazis. Its "success"—the breakdown of the moral barrier that it represented and the administrative, logistical and operational experiences gained from this program—paved the way for the "Final Solution" in the early 1940s.

Snyder, Richard C.; Hermann, Charles F.; and Lasswell, Harold D. (1976). A global monitoring system: appraising the effects of government on human dignity. *International Studies Quarterly*, 20(2), 221–260.
A pioneering proposal that received considerable intellectual interest but no operational development for a worldwide monitoring system of nations based on their value positions with regard to hostility towards others, perception of threat from others, valuing of humanity and life, and so on—to provide an index of government impact on what the authors sum up as "human dignity."

Vanderhaar, Gerard A. (1984). Genocidal mentality: nuclear weapons on civilian populations. In Charny (1984), pp. 175–182.
There are striking similarities between the mentality of those who executed the Holocaust—"the single greatest evil in the history of the human race"—and those who will be ready to execute a nuclear holocaust. Two key elements are dehumanization of the victims and desensitization of self. Organized public opposition may forestall nuclear disaster: even the Nazis were responsive to public protests.

Wertham, Frederic (1966). *A Sign for Cain: An Exploration of Human Violence.* New York: Macmillan. 391 pp.
A landmark book in its time by a psychiatrist well known for his war on pornography and crime and one that is still valuable reading today. Sums up the evidence of man's passion and proclivity for genocide, including cases that tend to miss the attention even of liberals, such as the genocide of the Hereros in Africa by the German government early in the century. Wertham was one of the first and few mental health practitioners to put his finger on the roles of mental health leaders, including distinguished professors of psychiatry, in designing and legitimating the Nazi policy of mass extermination of patients for eugenic reasons.

Whitaker, Ben (1985). Revised and Updated Report on the Question of the Prevention and Punishment of the Crime of Genocide. *See* Chapter 1.

Wiesel, Elie (1979). *Report to the President: President's Commission on the Holocaust.* Washington, DC: U.S. Government Printing Office. Pamphlet.
An eloquent presentation that laid the basis for the creation of U.S. Holocaust Commission by President Jimmy Carter, which Elie Wiesel has headed from the outset. A plea for remembrance of the Holocaust but also for knowledge, awareness and alertness to new possibilities of genocide, to any people.

Wiseberg, Laurie and Scoble, Harry (1982). An International Strategy for NGOs Pertaining to Extra-Legal Executions. Paper presented to the Amnesty International Conference on Extra-Legal Executions, Amsterdam. Mimeographed.
A proposal for monitoring, reporting on and influencing world governments to think

twice and hopefully to be pushed to refrain from numerous extra-legal executions (including "disappearances" of thousands of people who are never heard from again, and executions on the basis of flimsily contrived pseudo-judicial processes).

Wyman, David S. (1984). *The Abandonment of the Jews: America and the Holocaust, 1941–1945*. New York: Pantheon Books. 450 pp.

Continues the thesis of Arthur Morse (1968), backed by supplemental research and the increasing perspective of additional years. The Nazis were correctly perceived by the U.S.A. as threatening not only unacceptable territorial and political domination, but as promoting blatant evil and insufferable torture of subject peoples. Nonetheless, the powerful American government refused knowingly to intervene actively and directly on behalf of the hapless Jews who were being led daily in their thousands to their deaths, and even refused for the most part to allow immigration of escaping Jews into the U.S.A. beyond the normal quotas.

3

The History and Sociology of Genocidal Killings

Frank Chalk and Kurt Jonassohn

This chapter will deal with an ancient phenomenon that was given a new name in 1944 by Lemkin. We propose to discuss definitions and typologies of genocidal killing and to follow this discussion with an analysis of a number of cases to illustrate and apply our conceptual framework. The deliberate killing of members of a group with the intention of destroying it has occurred too frequently throughout history and in too many parts of the world to make an exhaustive listing possible or desirable.

(In the Bibliography, all references to conceptual matters, such as the book by Lemkin referred to above, will be found under "Conceptual References." All references to cases will be found under their specific case names, with the exception of four sets of cases that are grouped under general headings: "Antiquity," "Colonialism . . .," "The Holocaust," and "The U.S.S.R.")

Terminology

The term "genocide," although coined in 1944, acquired its most widely accepted meaning as a result of the many political compromises that had to be agreed to in order that the United Nations could pass the Convention on the Prevention and Punishment of the Crime of Genocide in 1948 (Kuper, 1981). The Convention has been widely accepted and incorporated into much of the relevant literature and into the legal codes of many signatory countries. At the same time, this definition of genocide has been seriously questioned because it protects only groups that are specifically covered by it and also because it is unsatisfactory for purposes of research and comparative analysis (Drost, 1959). Definitions and typologies are essential tools for scholars who want to group together phenomena that are in some relevant respect comparable, who want to explore the situations and conditions under which they occur, and who want to generalize about the processes leading up to them and the consequences that result from them.

We will continue to reserve the term "genocide" for the killing of national, ethnic, racial and religious groups covered by the U.N. definition. However, to achieve a broader, more realistic definition which also lends itself to more rigorous conceptual comparisons of types of genocidal killings, we use the following definition in this chapter:

Genocidal killings are a form of one-sided mass killing in which a state or other authority intends to destroy a group, as that group and membership in it are defined by the perpetrators.

Because this definition leaves open the nature of the victim group, it allows the inclusion of groups that were excluded from the U.N. Convention. Further, it allows the inclusion of groups that had not previously been considered under the U.N. Convention as potential victim groups (such as the retarded, the mentally ill, and homosexuals, as in Nazi Germany, or city dwellers in Pol Pot's Cambodia) and groups that have no existence outside a perpetrator's imagination (such as demonic witches in western Europe and "wreckers" and "enemies of the people" in Stalin's Russia), but whose fate was no less tragic for that. The killing of combatant groups in warfare is excluded, but the one-sided killing of noncombatant groups is, of course, covered by our definition. The deliberate destruction of the culture of a group is covered by the term *ethnocide*. There are cases, such as some aboriginal tribes in the Americas and in Oceania, where groups have been deliberately destroyed as a result of colonial expansion without the state having intended to destroy them. These we shall refer to as *genocidal massacres*.

Our analysis of cases of genocidal killings will be presented in terms of the following typology:

Type I: Genocidal killings that are committed in the building and maintaining of empires. The following three motives underlie the perpetrators' actions, one of them usually being dominant: (a) to eliminate a real or potential threat; (b) to terrorize a real or potential enemy; or (c) to acquire and keep economic wealth.

Type II: Genocidal killings that are committed in the building and maintaining of nation states. The following three motives underlie the perpetrators' actions, one of them usually being dominant: (a) to eliminate a real or potential threat; (b) to terrorize a real or potential enemy; or (c) to implement a belief, theory, or ideology by destroying either a real group, or a pseudo-group (see discussion below).

Type I and Type 11 genocidal killings, apart from distinguishing between perpetrators (empires v. nation states), also represent a crucial distinction between types of victims and types of consequences for the perpetrator state. The victim groups in Type I are always groups outside the perpetrator's state, while the victim groups in Type II are usually within the perpetrator's state (Nazi Germany being a notable exception in that it victimized groups in its occupied territories as well). The consequences of genocidal killings of Type I were that the perpetrator realized significant material benefits from his actions, while the consequences of Type II were that the implementation of the perpetrator's belief system was only achieved at the cost to the perpetrator of enormous direct and indirect losses in human capital, losses that had grave short and long-term results for the state.

History

The first genocidal killing is lost in antiquity. It seems improbable that any occurred when people were still nomads, if only because there were so few of them and they were very thinly scattered over large territories. After the invention of agriculture, serious warfare occurred when nomads raided settled communities to benefit from their harvest. But these raids did not usually lead to any large-scale killing because it was in the nomads' interest to be able to repeat their raids. The settled people may have had better motives, but usually lacked the means to destroy the nomads.

When agricultural methods improved, especially with the invention of irrigation, and produced surpluses large enough to support city states, wars over scarce resources became more frequent. Given the methods of the day, they were rarely conclusive. The defeated party would withdraw to lick its wounds, to rebuild its resources, and to seek revenge in renewed warfare. Finally someone decided—we do not know who—to put an end to this pattern of warfare by destroying the defeated enemy, not only their army and weapons, but also their women, their children, their old, and their sick. This was the first of many genocidal killings.

We have indirect evidence to support this assertion. Firstly, a large number of peoples in the Fertile Crescent seem to have disappeared without leaving evidence as to how they disappeared, among them being the Amorites, Aramaeans, Cimerians, Elamites, Kassites, Lulubaeans, Mittani, Hittites, Lydians, Parthians, Sumerians, and the Urartus. Some of them were sold into slavery, some of them assimilated, some of them migrated, but some of them were almost certainly destroyed by killing. Secondly, we have clear references in the Old Testament to cases where a people, including women and children, were slain, as in the case of the Amalekites. There are several descriptions of a policy of slaying all the members of a vanquished people which hardly leave the reader with the impression that this was a previously unknown phenomenon.

These cases from antiquity seem to have been committed primarily in order to eliminate a present or future threat and thus would come under our Type I(a).

At the same time, the perpetrators would produce terror among other peoples that were real or potential rivals. Since the people that are terrorized and the people that are destroyed are not the same, both motives can coexist. The Roman destruction of Carthage in 146 B.C. is probably the most famous later example of a genocidal killing to eliminate a real or potential threat, but the Romans were also interested in terrorizing their real or potential enemies. A successful destruction also means that the property and wealth of the victims is acquired by the perpetrators. Because all three motives are thus present in almost all cases, we are treating them as sub-types. In assigning concrete cases to one of the sub-types it is necessary to decide which of the three motives played a dominant role.

Although the first Type I genocidal killings were aimed at the elimination of a real or potential threat, many of the later genocidal killings had the spread of terror (Type I(b) as their major objective. There is a striking parallel between the cases of Melos (416 B.C.), Jerusalem (A.D. 73), the victims of the Mongols (thirteenth century), and of Shaka Zulu in southern Africa (1818–28). In each case, the perpetrator sought to demonstrate to other real or potential enemies that the price of resistance or rebellion was the destruction of the offending group. Europe's expansion into the Americas, Asia, and Africa produced a number of genocidal killings intended to acquire and keep economic wealth (Type I(c)), usually in the form of land. There are strong similarities between the fate of the Pequots of New England (1637), several of the Indian tribes of Virginia (seventeenth and eighteenth centuries), and the Hereros of South West Africa (1904–07). In contrast, little evidence of genocidal killings exists in the early South American mines and plantations, where Europeans needed a large labor supply.

Very extensive killings resulted from European expansion when frontier settlers embarked on campaigns to destroy the native occupants of the land. Such devastations were often opposed by governments, but their feeble efforts to protect the natives were overwhelmed by the settlers' persistent attempts to annihilate their aboriginal neighbors. These were cases of genocidal massacre. Among the victims were the Caribs, the Tasmanians, the Beothuks of Newfoundland, several Indian tribes of California, and some of the tribes of the Brazilian Amazon. However, a far larger number of Indians were the victims of disease, devastation of their environment, alcohol, and forced labor under lethal conditions.

Although Type II genocidal killings are a modern phenomenon perpetrated by nation-states, many of the methods used were developed during two transitional cases that happened long ago.

The Cathars were a heretical group in the Languedoc in the twelfth and thirteenth century who gained widespread support not only among the common people, but also among the aristocracy, especially at the court of the count of Toulouse. After vain efforts to preach to them, the pope called for a crusade that became known as the Albigensian Crusade. This transitional case connects our two types, because from the point of view of the king of France it was an opportunity to expand his realm, while from the point of view of the pope it was necessary to eliminate heretics who did not recognize his authority. This case is also important because persecution by torture, forced confessions, and guilt by association, leading to imprisonment and death, have become standard methods in many genocidal processes of the twentieth century.

An even more important transitional case is the Great Witch-Hunt of Europe because the victim groups here were an invention of the perpetrators. Its thousands of victims were burned at the stake not as witches, but for demonic witchcraft, that is to say for *conspiracy* with the Devil. Many people doubted at the time, and everybody today doubts that there ever was such a conspiracy, that a coven of witches ever met the Devil on a mountain to plot against God, or to have sexual intercourse with him. However, although neither the group nor the conspiracy it was accused of had any reality in verifiable fact, the results were real enough: the accused were burnt at the stake. This innovation in the history of genocidal killings makes it important to distinguish in Type II(c) between *real* victim groups, regardless of whether the accusations against them were true or not, and *pseudo-groups* of victims, that can be identified only after a perpetrator labels them as such.

The question arises as to why a perpetrator would invent a pseudo-group of victims when real groups are always readily at hand. Christina Larner has suggested that the victimization of a pseudo-group for a pseudo-conspiracy serves to legitimate a new regime that is trying to impose a new discipline on a recalcitrant population. A real group would not serve this purpose nearly as well because it might be able to defend itself, because it might be able to enlist the support of sympathizers, and because its victimization might thus threaten the unity of the realm. We suspect that Stalin knew exactly what he was doing when he labeled his victims "enemies of the people" and "wreckers." The research on this hypothesis remains to be done, but it is challenging in the light of the number of twentieth-century genocidal killings that have been perpetrated by new regimes against pseudo-groups that are accused of pseudo-offences.

All of the Type II genocidal killings, with the exception of some early transitional cases, occurred in the twentieth century. Since they are dealt with in several other chapters in this volume, we shall be very brief and confine ourselves to only a few typological remarks. Among the early transitional cases, in addition to the Albigensian Crusade and the Great Witch-Hunt, were the slaughter of the non-Christian inhabitants of Antioch and Jerusalem during the Crusades (in these instances one identifies a distinct authority as perpetrator in contrast to many other instances of what we call "genocidal massacres" by roaming mobs of crusaders) and the persecutions of the Marranos and Moriscos by the Inquisition in Spain. These are all transitional cases involving religious persecution and thus have important characteristics in common with Type II(c). Other cases that fit into Type II(c) are the Armenian victims of Pan-Turkic ideology, and the Jews and the Gypsies who became the victims of Nazi race theories. Victim groups who were attacked to eliminate real or perceived threats (Type II(a)) include the educated and elite groups in what became Bangladesh and among the Hutu in Burundi, the army and party elites during Stalin's purge years, and several nationality groups in the southern U.S.S.R. at the end of World War II. Finally, there are several cases where the victim groups were destroyed in order to terrorize a real or potential enemy or opposition (Type II(b)): communists in Indonesia, political opponents in Equatorial Guinea, rebellious groups in northern Ethiopia, the peasantry in the Ukraine, as well as the "wreckers" and the "enemies of the people" during Stalin's purges. Also in the twentieth century, isolated survivals of Type I(c) cases have been reported, particularly in South America, where colonial expansion in search of resources still endangers indigenous peoples, though the colonizers have by now become nation-states with large, yet unexploited, hinterlands. (For a much more detailed presentation of our analysis, the interested reader will have to await our forthcoming volume entitled *The History and Sociology of Genocidal Killings*.)

Problems of Research

Investigations into the history of genocidal killings have only just begun, and are hampered by a series of daunting problems:

1. In both contemporary and historical accounts, there has been a collective denial of events that were not a source of pride and fame, although the level of denial has fluctuated with the ethic of the day. From the rise of the nation-state until the end of World War II, the triumph of Enlightenment values in public attitudes has increased the level of such denial.
2. For the early periods of human strife, we shall have to develop an archeology of genocide if we are ever to find out what happened to peoples that have disappeared.
3. When evidence is available, it comes either from the victims or from the perpetrators; in the rare cases where it comes from both sides, the discrepancies are often dramatic.
4. In the nature of the event under study, underreporting would be expected, but overreporting has also occurred.
5. In a number of instances, perpetrators have gone to great lengths to try to alter and even obliterate the facts of the genocides they have committed.
6. Finally, modern totalitarian regimes have developed a high degree of efficiency in controlling access to information and maintaining secrecy.

What About the Future?

Contrary to the prevailing trends in academia and in social problems movements, we do not subscribe to the theory that pessimism is the only road to wisdom. We do not believe that all twentieth-century developments hasten the end of the world. At the same time, we are painfully aware of the lack of success that all of the social sciences have when they attempt to deal with the future. (In fact, the recent popularity of futurology leads us to wonder whether it does not represent a retreat from the failure to explain the past and the present.) Our judgment leads us to make the following observations:

1. The study of genocide is rarely, if ever, motivated by disinterested intellectual curiosity alone. In our case, one of our main motives is the hope and the conviction (the two are not the same thing) that an understanding of the social processes and social situations that are conducive to genocidal killings is a prerequisite for efforts at prevention. Given the above-mentioned problems of doing research in this complex area, an adequate understanding of the relevant social dynamics will not be easy to attain. Furthermore, we have barely begun to explore the means of prevention that might be successfully deployed once predictions are so reliable that they can be used as the basis for preventive action. These areas will require much greater scholarly resources than are presently being invested in them.

2. Quite independently of scholarly research, shifts have been taking place in the norms and values that deal with human life and human rights. While the rate at which these shifts are occurring is much too slow for concerned humanists, it is quite amazing if seen in historical perspective. This is not the place to examine these shifts in detail, nor their interaction with both national and international jurisprudence. However, the broad trend seems to be clear: as the twentieth century experienced growing excesses of cruelty and brutality, a snowballing revulsion resulted in war-crimes trials and charters of human rights, United Nations Declarations and Conventions, and investigations and publicity that discredited the perpetrators. While these developments did not have the same impact or proceed at the same speed in all parts of the world, their cumulative effect is likely to decrease the frequency and the scope of genocidal killings.

Whether genocidal killings will in fact diminish, only time will tell. In the meantime, there is no excuse for complacency. People of good will must always maintain their vigilance if human life and human rights are to attain and maintain their full potential. It is not clear that genocide can be prevented in the future, but the first lesson of its past is clear: genocides and genocidal killings in their different forms have occurred throughout most of history and recognition of this fact is essential if efforts at prevention are to succeed. Research on genocide must go forward, informed by the spirit of James Baldwin's maxim that: "Not everything that is faced can be changed; but nothing can be changed until it is faced."

We would like to acknowledge extremely useful comments on our work from Norman Cohn, Helen Fein, Leo Kuper, Franziska Shlosser, and Anton

Zijderveld, whose advice we have valued even when we have sometimes begged to differ.

Bibliography

Since this chapter spans almost all of history, it is possible to give only a few key references, chosen to guide the reader into a particular literature of interest. The references for the twentieth-century cases are particularly limited because these cases are being dealt with much more intensively in several other chapters in this volume.

We have also prepared an introductory bibliography consisting of over four hundred items, which may be obtained by writing to the Montreal Institute for Genocide Studies, Concordia University, 1455 De Maisonneuve Blvd. West, Montreal, Quebec, Canada H3G 1M8.

Conceptual References

Arendt, Hannah (1958). *The Origins of Totalitarianism*. New York: Harcourt Brace Jovanovich. 527 pp. [First published in 1951]
   This is one of the classic works on the rise of the nation state and its totalitarian tendencies.

Bauer, Yehuda (1984). The place of the Holocaust in contemporary history. In Frankel, Jonathan (Ed.), *Studies in Contemporary Jewry*, Vol. 1, pp. 201–224.
   An important attempt to connect definitions of genocide and the Holocaust with historical analysis of what the Holocaust was. Bauer's critique of Lemkin's work and the U.N. definition lead him to propose a continuum of mass killings of the twentieth century. He supports his concept by presenting a revised definition of genocide and offering his own definitions of autogenocide, urbicide, and Holocaust or Shoah.

Charny, Israel W. (Ed.) (1984). *Toward the Understanding and Prevention of Genocide*. Boulder, CO: Westview Press. 396 pp.
   A collection of the best papers from the 1982 International Conference on the Holocaust and Genocide. The conceptual papers by Fein and Kuper deserve particular attention. Fein applies an interesting typology based on the motives of the perpetrator to a number of fictitious scenarios inspired by cases from the past.

Chorover, Stephen (1979). *From Genesis to Genocide: The Meaning of Human Nature and the Power of Behavior Control*. Cambridge, MA: MIT Press. 237 pp.
   In Chapter 5, "Genocide: the Apotheosis of behavior control," Chorover succinctly analyzes the participation of psychiatrists, physicians, and scientists in the administrative mass killing of at least 275,000 German psychiatric patients between 1939 and 1945. These killings of patients deemed "unfit to live," carried out at State initiative, approved by State-appointed panels of psychiatrists, and conducted with devices such as carbon monoxide-fed gas chambers are not classified as genocide under the U.N. definition. When, by the end of 1941, many of the mental patients had been murdered by the killing experts, the specialists were ordered to new locations in the East, where they turned their attention to Jews, Gypsies, and others condemned to death for the sake of the master race.

Dadrian, Vahakn (1975). A typology of genocide. *International Review of Modern Sociology*, 5, 201–212.

A pioneer attempt to develop a sociological definition and a typology of genocide, encompassing cases from the Middle Ages to the 1960s. Dadrian's definition of genocide, emphasizing the degree and type of disparity between the power of the perpetrator group and the victim group, establishes the matrix for his five-category typology. This article contains an especially interesting discussion of the problem facing researchers when they apply the modern concept of genocide as a crime to pre-modern cases. The typology of genocide suffers, however, from inconsistencies between its categories and the inclusion of cases of pure ethnocide.

Drost, Pieter N. (1959). *The Crime of State*. 2 vols. Leyden: A.W. Sythoff. 583 pp.
Drost strongly criticized the omission of political and other groups from the U.N. definition of genocide and predicted that governments which undertook genocidal action would dash through this gap in the definition. He proposed the redefinition of genocide as "the deliberate destruction of physical life of individual human beings by reason of their membership of any human collectivity as such," a position that is similar to ours.

Horowitz, Irving Louis (1980). *Taking Lives: Genocide and State Power*. 3rd edn. New Brunswick, NJ: Transaction Books. 199 pp. [First edition 1976]
Explores the nexus between genocide and statecraft. Of particular interest here is his development of an eightfold typology of states based on the extent to which they tolerate or persecute diversity and deviance: from completely permissive societies at one extreme to genocidal societies at the other.

International Commission of Jurists (1973). Bangladesh. *The Review*, 11, 30–33.

International Commission of Jurists (1979). *The Trial of Macias in Equatorial Guinea*. Report by Alejandro Artucio. Geneva: ICJ. 61 pp.
Both these items have an important bearing on proposals to extend the definition of genocide. The 1973 article presents a detailed analysis of Bangladesh's International Crimes (Tribunal) Act of 1973, introduced to permit the trial of 195 Pakistani officers held as prisoners of war. In this act, the Bangladesh Parliament extended the definition found in the Genocide Convention to include "political groups."
    The report on Macias is important for its finding that although Don Francisco Macias Nguema, the former President-for-Life and dictator of Equatorial Guinea, was responsible for "numerous and horrifying murders of political prisoners," he was innocent of the charge of genocide, in part because political groups are not covered by the U.N. definition of genocide. Artucio notes that in January 1973 the ICJ recommended that "the definition of genocide should be expanded to include acts committed with the intent to destroy, in whole or in part, a political group as such as well as national, ethnic, racial and religious groups."

Kuper, Leo (1981). *Genocide: Its Political Use in the Twentieth Century*. New Haven, CT, and London: Yale University Press. 255 pp.

Kuper, Leo (1985). *The Prevention of Genocide*. New Haven, CT, and London: Yale University Press. 256 pp.
This and the above are the two most important books to date on twentieth-century genocide.
    In *Genocide*, Kuper presents a comprehensive analysis of genocidal processes and motivation. He concludes his illuminating discussion of the debates that shaped the U.N. definition of genocide by reluctantly accepting the U.N. definition in the interest of encouraging it to undertake practical steps toward preventive action. Under the

rubric of "Related Atrocities," Kuper also examines genocidal killings directed at political and economic groups in the Soviet Union, Indonesia, and Cambodia. Although these killings fall outside the U.N. definition of genocide, Kuper views them as legitimate candidates for inclusion under a revised U.N. definition.

In his latest book, *The Prevention of Genocide*, Kuper's major focus is on the need for new international pressure groups, legal institutions, and agreements to facilitate positive and timely measures against genocides before they are carried to completion. He also presents a thoughtful discussion of the major obstacles to implementation of the U.N. Convention, emphasizing the interplay of state interests and values.

Lang, Berel (1984–85). The concept of genocide. *The Philosophical Forum*, 16 (1 and 2), 1–18.
In this sensitive essay, Lang seeks to elaborate the qualities that define the essence of genocide, using the Holocaust as his model.

Lemkin, Raphael (1944). *Axis Rule in Occupied Europe*. Washington DC: Carnegie Endowment for International Peace. 674 pp.
The now classic statement by the man who coined the term "genocide" and who was instrumental in getting the U.N. to adopt a convention against it. Lemkin carefully distinguishes between mass murder, denationalization, and genocide. His primary concern emerges from this book and his later writings as the prevention of the deliberate biological destruction of "nations" or ethnic groups, which he regarded as the building blocks of world culture. Lemkin's definition of genocide, reflected in the U.N. Convention, is limited to national, racial, religious, and ethnic groups. As Yehuda Bauer (1984) has already noted, there are some interesting contradictions between Lemkin's definition and what he actually wrote about in this book.

Porter, Jack (Ed.) (1982). *Genocide and Human Rights: A Global Anthology*. Washington, DC: University Press of America. 353 pp.
A collection of papers on twentieth-century cases, with useful bibliographies. His introduction elaborates a conceptual framework that differs from our own and that we do not agree with.

Savon, Hervé (1972). *Du cannibalisme au génocide*. Paris: Hachette. 248 pp.
This is one of the early attempts to devise a typology of genocide. While Savon emphasizes that it is the intent to exterminate that distinguishes genocide from simple massacre, he also cautions that intent is more important for the moralist than for the sociologist, whose problem it is to isolate the particular set of forces that lead to genocide. We do not think that intent can be omitted, even by the sociologist.

Whitaker, Ben (1985). *Revised and Updated Report on the Question of the Prevention and Punishment of the Crime of Genocide*. United Nations Economic and Social Council, Commission on Human Rights (E/CN.4/Sub.2/1985/6, 2 July 1985). 62 pp.
Whitaker, a U.N. Special Rapporteur, warns that "In an era of ideology, people are killed for ideological reasons." He recommends expanding the definition of genocide in the U.N. Convention to protect political, economic, and sexual or social groups. If a consensus cannot be reached, he advocates making a revised definition part of an additional optional protocol.

Antiquity

The Bible (1967). "Translated out of the original tongues by the commandment of King James the first *anno* 1611." New York: AMS Press.

Bury, J.B.; Cook, S.A.; and Adcock, F.E. (Eds.) (1970). *The Cambridge Ancient History*: Vol. 3, *The Assyrian Empire*. Cambridge: Cambridge University Press.

Ceram, C.W. (1980). *Gods, Graves, and Scholars: The Story of Archeology*. Toronto: Bantam Books. 515 pp. [First edition 1949]

Macqueen, J.G. (1975). *The Hittites and Their Contemporaries in Asia Minor*. London: Thames & Hudson. 206 pp.

Saggs, H.W.F. (1969). *The Greatness That Was Babylon: A Survey of the Ancient Civilization of the Tigris-Euphrates Valley*. New York: Frederick A. Praeger. 562 pp.
All of these above books deal with the Fertile Crescent and its peoples. The multi-volume *Cambridge Ancient History* is the most comprehensive. Both the texts and the accompanying maps refer to great numbers of peoples who appear and disappear on the stage of history. Often it is not clear where they came from, and even more often it is not clear where they disappeared to. The Bible gives clearcut descriptions of policies of conquest which require total elimination of the vanquished people, and has references to many peoples who later disappear, some of whom were undoubtedly slain.

The Armenians in Turkey

Hovannisian, Richard G. (1967). *Armenia on the Road to Independence: 1918*. Berkeley: University of California Press. 384 pp.

Hovannisian, Richard G. (1971). *The Republic of Armenia*: Vol. 1, *The First Year, 1918-1919*. Berkeley: University of California Press. 547 pp.

Trumpener, Ulrich (1968). *Germany and the Ottoman Empire: 1914-1918*. Princeton, NJ: Princeton University Press. 433 pp.
Hovannisian is the most authoritative scholar on the genocide of the Armenians in 1915 and the best starting-point for the interested reader. (*See* his Chapter 5 in the present volume for details and for a discussion of revisionist history that denies that the genocide took place.) Trumpener is cited here because he is relevant to an examination of the costs that a perpetrator is prepared to incur in order to carry out an ideological genocide. The completion of the Berlin-Baghdad railroad was considered crucial to the Central Powers' war effort. The majority of the workers on the railroad were Armenians. In spite of management's pleading, they were deported and the railroad was not completed in time to be used during the war.

Bangladesh

International Commission of Jurists (1972). *The Events in East Pakistan*. Study by the secretariat. Geneva: ICJ.

Levak, Albert E. (1975). Discrimination in Pakistan: national, provincial, tribal. In Veenhoven, Willem A. (Ed.), *Case Studies on Human Rights and Fundamental Freedoms: A World Survey*, Vol. 1, pp.281-308. The Hague: Martinus Nijhoff.

Mascarenhas, Anthony (1971). *The Rape of Bangladesh*. Delhi: Vikas Publications. 168 pp.

Satyaprakesh (Compiler and Editor) (1976). *Bangla Desh: A Select Bibliography*. Gurgaon: Indian Documentation Service. 218 pp.
> Levak, Mascarenhas, and the ICJ study will introduce the reader to the human destruction that accompanied the birth of a new nation. The genocidal killings by the West Pakistan army of the Bangladeshi separatist leadership and of the educated groups in East Pakistan in order to terrorize the survivors into submission is one of the rare cases when a genocidal killing failed to achieve its objective.

Burundi

Greenland, Jeremy (1976). Ethnic discrimination in Rwanda and Burundi. In Veenhoven, Willem A. (Ed.) *Case Studies on Human Rights and Fundamental Freedoms: A World Survey*, Vol. 4, pp. 95–133. The Hague: Martinus Nijhoff.

Lemarchand, René and Martin, David (1974). *Selective Genocide in Burundi*. London: Minority Rights Group. Report No. 20.

Meisler, Stanley (1976). Holocaust in Burundi, 1972. In Veenhoven, Willem A. (Ed.), *Case Studies on Human Rights and Fundamental Freedoms: A World Survey*, Vol. 5, pp. 227–238. The Hague: Martinus Nijhoff.
> Burundi is a classic case of conflict over and control of power and privilege between two ethnic groups. As the Tutsi saw their rule of the country threatened by upwardly mobile Hutu, they destroyed their political opponents and most of the educated Hutu in the civil service and the professions. While our conceptual framework allows the perpetrator to define the group, Lemarchand, who accepts the U.N. definition, solves the definitional problem by using the term "selective genocide" for this case, which does not strictly fit the U.N. definition. For more detail refer to Chapter 8 in this volume, by Leo Kuper.

Cambodia

Etcheson, Craig (1984). *The Rise and Demise of Democratic Kampuchea*. Boulder, CO: Westview Press. 300 pp.

Kiernan, Ben (1985). *How Pol Pot Came to Power: A History of Communism in Kampuchea, 1930–1975*. London: Verso.
> These books are among the first efforts by scholars to produce monographs on the Cambodian disaster, in which as many as 2 million out of 7 million Cambodians died. This event involved the state-organized murder of political opponents, "class enemies," and even persons guilty of the crime of living in cities stocked with large quantities of Western manufactured goods. Despite the scale and the premeditation of the killing, the Khmer Rouge killings can be called a genocide under U.N. Convention only because two relatively small groups—the ethnic Cham and the Buddhist priests—were targeted for destruction.
>   Both books suffer from limitations on access to sources, but they provide valuable information about the history of the Communist movement in Cambodia and the probable nature of the lethal struggle within the Kampuchean Communist Party that led to the genocidal killings. Etcheson is more critical than Kiernan of the Khmer Rouge and the Vietnamese. He reproduces the full text of the constitution of Democratic Kampuchea, a chilling document. For a more detailed discussion, *see* Chapter 7 in this volume, by David Hawk.

Carthage, 146 B.C.

Adcock, F.E. (1946). "Delenda est Carthago." *Cambridge Historical Journal*, 8, 117–128.

Astin, Alan E. (1967). *Scipio Aemilianus*. London: Oxford University Press. 374 pp.

Astin, Alan E. (1978). *Cato the Censor*. London: Oxford University Press. 371 pp.

Harris, William V. (1979). *War and Imperialism in Republican Rome: 327–70 B.C.* Oxford: Clarendon Press. 291 pp.

Sherwin-White, A.N. (1980) Rome the aggressor? A review essay. *Journal of Roman Studies*, 70, 177–181.

Warmington, B.H. (1969). *Carthage*. 2nd edn. London: Robert Hale. 272 pp.
　Recovering, following two titanic wars with Rome, the Carthaginians rejected Rome's hysterical demand that they move inland, abandoning the North African coast and their profitable trade. When Carthage chose to fight instead, Rome wiped the city off the face of the earth in the Third Punic War. Perhaps 50,000 out of 200,000 Carthaginians survived and were sold into slavery.
　Adcock (1946) and many other modern authors dismiss economic motives and emphasize the Romans' gnawing fear about the security of their empire. Sherwin-White (1980) argues that Rome's "neurosis of fear" was rooted in real difficulties that emerged when the demands of empire began to outstrip Rome's ability to maintain a favorable balance of strength against its rivals. Both authors believe that Rome destroyed Carthage to eliminate a rival, as well as to instill terror in others. Astin (1967, 1978) makes the case that the revival of Carthage gave Rome serious grounds for its fears. Harris (1979) rejects Astin's theory and contends that Carthage was destroyed to satisfy the Roman aristocracy's hunger for power, glory and booty. This case is a prime candidate for scholars interested in developing an archeology of genocide.

The Cathars

Hamilton, Bernard (1974). *The Albigensian Crusade*. London: The Historical Association. 40 pp.

Madaule, Jacques (1967). *The Albigensian Crusade*. Translated by Barbara Wall. New York: Fordham University Press. 177 pp.

Oldenbourg, Zoé (1961). *Massacre at Montségur: A History of the Albigensian Crusade*. New York: Pantheon. 420 pp.

Strayer, Joseph R. (1971). *The Albigensian Crusades*. New York: Dial Press. 201 pp.

Wakefield, Walter L. (1974). *Heresy, Crusade and Inquisition in Southern France, 1100–1250*. London: Allen & Unwin. 288 pp.
　The heresy of the Cathars and the Albigensian Crusade in the late Middle Ages generated a huge literature and many divergent interpretations. The only aspect on which there is no controversy at all is that the crusade was successful in destroying the Cathars. For the general reader, the nontechnical account by Oldenbourg provides the easiest access to a very complex literature. The fact that this book is a bestseller in

the south of France indicates that resentment against Paris has not disappeared after hundreds of years.

Colonialism since 1492 and Its Indigenous Victims

Bridgman, Jon (1981). *The Revolt of the Hereros.* Berkeley: University of California Press. 200 pp.

Canny, Nicholas P. (1973). The ideology of English colonization: from Ireland to America. *William and Mary Quarterly*, 30(4), 575–598.

Chanaiwa, David Shingirai (1980). The Zulu revolution: state formation in a pastoralist society. *African Studies Review*, 23(3), 1–20.

Cook, Sherburne F. (1976a). *The Indian Population of New England in the Seventeenth Century.* Berkeley: University of California Press. 91 pp.

Cook, Sherburne F. (1976b). *The Conflict between the California Indians and White Civilization.* Berkeley: University of California Press. 522 pp.

Cook, Sherburne F., and Borah, Woodrow (1971, 1974). *Essays in Population History: Mexico and the Caribbean.* 2 vols. Berkeley: University of California Press. 516 pp.

Davis, Shelton (1977). *Victims of the Miracle: Development and the Indians of Brazil.* Cambridge: Cambridge University Press. 205 pp.

Drechsler, Horst (1980). *"Let Us Die Fighting": The Struggle of the Herero and the Nama against German Imperialism (1885–1915).* Translated by Bernd Zollner. London: Zed Press. [First published 1966]

Gibson, Charles (1964). *The Aztecs under Spanish Rule: A History of the Indians of the Valley of Mexico, 1519–1810.* Stanford, CA: Stanford University Press. 657 pp.

Hemming, John (1978). *Red Gold: The Conquest of the Brazilian Indians.* Cambridge, MA: Harvard University Press. 677 pp.

Münzel, Mark (1976). The Man-Hunts: Aché Indians in Paraguay. In Veenhoven, Willem A. (Ed.) *Case Studies on Human Rights and Fundamental Freedoms: A World Survey*, Vol. 4, pp. 351–403. The Hague: Martinus Nijhoff.

Nash, Gary (1972). The image of the Indian in the southern colonial mind. *William and Mary Quarterly*, 29(2), 197–230.

Omer-Cooper, J.D. (1966). *The Zulu Aftermath: A Nineteenth Century Revolution in Bantu Africa.* Evanston, IL: Northwestern University Press. 208 pp.

Pearce, Roy H. (1952). The "ruines of mankind": the Indian and the Puritan mind. *Journal of the History of Ideas*, 13, 200–217.

Robson, Lloyd (1983). *A History of Tasmania*: Vol. 1, *Van Diemen's Land from the Earliest Times to 1855.* Melbourne: Melbourne University Press. 632 pp.

Ryan, Lyndall (1981). *The Aboriginal Tasmanians.* Vancouver: University of British Columbia Press. 315 pp.

Salisbury, Neal (1982). *Manitou and Providence: Indians, Europeans, and the Making of New England, 1500-1643*. New York: Oxford University Press. 316 pp.

Sheehan, Bernard (1980). *Savagism and Civility: Indians and Englishmen in Colonial Virginia*. Cambridge: Cambridge University Press. 258 pp.

Simmons, William S. (1981). Cultural bias in the New England Puritans' perception of Indians. *William and Mary Quarterly*, 38(1), 56-72.

Upton, Leslie F.S. (1977). The extermination of the Beothuks of Newfoundland. *Canadian Historical Review*, 58, 133-153.

Walter, Eugene Victor (1969). *Terror and Resistance: A Study of Political Violence*. Oxford: Oxford University Press. 385 pp.

The term "colonialism," as used in this section, refers to three distinct sets of conditions: the founding of colonies that were incorporated into an empire; the expansion of a state by conquering neighboring territories and peoples; and a state policy of treating native inhabitants like dependent colonial subjects. Certain relevant cases—the Athenians, the Romans, the Mongols, Nazi Germany, and the Soviet Union—are treated in other parts of this chapter and elsewhere in this book, but others must be omitted for reasons of space. Cook and Borah (1971, 1974), Gibson (1964), and Hemming (1978) meticulously examine the demographic consequences of the European conquest of the New World, concluding that the decimation of the Indians was primarily the result of European and African epidemic diseases spread by the colonists' hunger for labor and the missionaries' search for converts. Canny (1973) finds that the secular ideology developed by Englishmen to justify their colonization of Ireland and their slaughter of numbers of the Irish played an important part in the Elizabethan claim to moral respectability for American colonization and massacres of native peoples. Cook (1976a) estimates the Indian population of seventeenth-century New England, nation by nation, while Pearce (1952), Salisbury (1982), and Simmons (1981) demonstrate that, in their thought, the New England Puritans equated the Indians with the devil and demonic witchcraft, a myth that provided a rationale for the destruction or enslavement of entire populations of Indians. Sheehan and Nash report that settlers in Colonial Virginia evolved an image of the natives much like that found in New England. Cook (1976b) has also examined the decimation of the California Indians in the periods of Spanish and U.S. rule. He concludes that once again alien microbes were most responsible for massive population losses among the Indians, but he also presents new evidence underlining the contribution to the destruction of the fabric of Indian societies of frequent kidnappings, rapes and killings by American settlers. Upton's account (1977) of the destruction of the Beothuks reveals a similar pattern in Newfoundland. Turning to our own time, Münzel's account (1976) implicates the government of Paraguay in genocidal killings aimed at destroying the Aché Indians.

A number of native peoples in Asia and Oceania, as well as the Americas, have been the victims of genocidal massacres. Of these, the Tasmanians are probably the best known. Robson's is a scholarly presentation (1983) of the standard history of Tasmania, including the details of the death of the last aborigine in 1876. Ryan's important work (1981) shows that the last Tasmanian did not die in 1876, but that this supposed death became a self-serving myth which legitimated the ignoring of the Tasmanians and their problems. Davis's account (1977) of the process that is destroying Indian peoples of the Amazon region in Brazil improves our understanding of the native population losses occurring in many parts of Central and South America as a consequence of modern road building, settler intrusions, and mining.

Genocidal killings are also associated with colonial expansion in Africa, where they were committed by both Africans and Europeans. Shaka ruled the Zulu kingdom from 1818 until his assassination in 1828. He conquered over three hundred chiefdoms, annihilating some and fusing the members of others into one Zulu nation. In 1826, he attacked his most determined African enemies, the Ndwandwes, a nation of some 40,000 persons, ordering his soldiers to kill every last man, woman, and child. At the victorious conclusion of this war, his soldiers executed his order. Walter (1969) presents an incisive analysis of Shaka's uses of terror. Omer-Cooper (1966) describes the role in Shaka's expansion of population pressure intensified by white settlement and gives a thorough account of his rule. Chanaiwa (1980) is primarily concerned with Shaka's contribution to state formation, but he also disputes Walter's sources, criticizes Omer-Cooper's hypothesis and presents a more favorable interpretation of Shaka than Walter.

Germany waged a colonial war against the Herero people of South West Africa (modern Namibia) from 1904 to 1907. The Germans aimed at seizing land for railroads linking German ranches with the coast. Long after the Hereros offered to give up, the German military commander refused to accept surrenders and turned the Hereros, including women and children, back into the desert to die of thirst and hunger. By 1911, roughly 64,000 of the 80,000 Herero people had perished. The history of this episode is covered in depth by Bridgman (1981) and Drechsler (1980).

Crusades

Runciman, Steven (1962). *A History of the Crusades*: Vol. 1, *The First Crusade and the Foundation of the Kingdom of Jerusalem*. Cambridge: Cambridge University Press. 3 vols.
See especially for the details of the conquests and the ensuing massacres of the population of Antioch and Jerusalem.

The Holocaust

Cohn, Norman (1981). *Warrant for Genocide: The Myth of the Jewish World Conspiracy and the Protocols of the Elders of Zion*. Chico, CA: Scholars Press. 303 pp. [First published in 1967]

Hilberg, Raul (1985). *The Destruction of the European Jews*. New York: Holmes & Meier. 3 vols. Rev. edn. 1312 pp. [First published 1961]

Kenrick, Donald, and Puxon, Gratton (1972). *The Destiny of Europe's Gypsies*. New York: Basic Books. 256 pp.
Of the huge literature on the Holocaust, we cite here only Cohn (1981), because he details the origin and spread of the most infamous anti-Semitic myth of modern times, and Hilberg (1985), because his is the classic study of the genocidal process at the centre of the Holocaust. By contrast, there is a quite limited literature on the annihilation of the Gypsies during the Holocaust. Kenrick and Puxon's is the best book-length treatment (1972). Much more material on the Holocaust will be found in Chapter 4 of this volume, by Alan Berger. The interested reader may obtain a bibliography of the Gypsies' treatment by the Nazis by writing to our colleague, G. Tyrnauer, Montreal Institute for Genocide Studies, Concordia University, 1455 De Maisonneuve Blvd. West, Montreal, Canada H3G 1M8.

Indonesia

Budiardjo, Carmel (1976). The abuse of human rights in Indonesia. In Veenhoven, Willem A. (Ed.), *Case Studies on Human Rights and Fundamental Freedoms: A World Survey*, Vol. 3, pp. 209–241. The Hague: Martinus Nijhoff.

Crouch, Harold (1978). *The Army and Politics in Indonesia*. Ithaca, NY: Cornell University Press. 377 pp.
>Chapters 4 and 5 in Crouch deal with the coup attempt of 1 October 1965 and its aftermath, and present various theories about the coup. He explores the responsibility, the extent, and the estimates of victims of the ensuing massacre. He tries to give equal weight to the various interpretations of the events of which Budiardjo gives a concise summary. A good deal more detail on this case will be found in Chapter 8 of the present volume, by Leo Kuper.

The Inquisition

Guiraud, Jean (1979). *The Medieval Inquisition*. New York: AMS Press. 208 pp.

Kamen, Henry (1976). *The Spanish Inquisition*. London: White Lion Publishers. 334 pp.

Llorente, Juan Antonio (1826). *History of the Spanish Inquisition*. New York: G.C. Morgan. 271 pp.

Roth, Cecil (1964). *The Spanish Inquisition*. New York: Norton. 316 pp. [First published 1937]
>The Inquisition, which was established to eradicate the heresies of the Cathars, operated in all Roman Catholic countries, but was particularly severe in Spain. After the expulsion of the Jews and the Muslims it persecuted converted Jews who were suspected of practicing Judaism in secret (Marranos) and converted Muslims who were suspected of practicing Islam in secret (Moriscos). The question in the context of genocide studies is whether persecutions that offer a saving way out by conversion may be called genocidal. The answer depends on whether it was possible to prove that one did not still adhere to one's prior religion in secret. Our tentative answer is that, once accused, it was probably not possible.

Japan

Adachi, Ken (1976). *The Enemy That Never Was: The History of Japanese Canadians*. Toronto: McClelland & Stewart. 456 pp.

Sansom, George B. (1978). *A History of Japan*: Vol. 3, *1615–1867*. Folkestone, Kent: Dawson. 3 vols. [First published 1958]

Storry, G. Richard (1960). *A History of Modern Japan*. Harmondsworth, Middlesex: Penguin. 304 pp.
>The penetration of Westerners into Japan in the seventeenth century is a little-known episode. Adachi (1976) provides, in his first chapter, a terse summary of the fate of the Christians. Sansom (1978) provides much more detail on the Tokugawa period, the exclusion policy, the persecutions, and the final massacre after a revolt of mostly Christian peasants. Storry (1960) deals with the same materials, but also includes

brief accounts of the two Mongol invasions, attempts which are interesting because they represent rare examples of Mongol failure.

Melos, 416 B.C.

Ducrey, Pierre (1968). Aspects juridiques de la victoire et du traitement des vaincus. In Vernant, Jean-Pierre (Ed.), *Problèmes de la guerre en Grèce ancienne*, pp. 231–243. Paris and The Hague: Mouton. 320 pp.

Littman, Robert J. (1974). *The Greek Experiment: Imperialism and Social Conflict, 800–400 B.C.* London: Thames & Hudson. 180 pp.

Meiggs, Russell (1972). *The Athenian Empire*. Oxford: Oxford University Press. 382 pp.

Thucydides. *The Peloponnesian War*. New York: Bantam Book. [This edition, translated by Benjamin Jowett, published in 1960]
    The Athenian empire depended on sea power. Lacking a large standing army, the Athenians resorted to a policy of terror. In 416 B.C., the people of the strategically situated island of Melos in the Aegean Sea, nonbelligerent allies of the Spartans, rejected Athens' demand that they support the war against Sparta. Following their victory, the Athenians killed all the Melian men, enslaving the women and children, apparently reasoning that successful rejection of their demands by so weak a foe would unleash a wave of rebellion throughout their empire.
    The Melian Dialogue in Thucydides offers the classic account of the Athenian outlook. Meiggs (1972) and Littman (1974) provide useful modern interpretations of the dynamics of Athenian expansion. *See* Ducrey (1968) for the argument that residents of besieged city-states were frequently able to wring concessions from enemy commanders, saving themselves from enslavement or massacre, and that the Peloponnesian War was an exceptionally brutal war even by the standards of the ancient Greeks.

The Mongols

Boyle, John Andrew (Ed.) (1968). *The Cambridge History of Islam*: Vol. 5, *The Saljuq and Mongol Periods*. Cambridge: Cambridge University Press. 763 pp.

Dawson, Christopher Henry (Ed.) (1955). *The Mongol Mission: Narratives and Letters of the Franciscan Missionaries in Mongolia and China in the Thirteenth and Fourteenth Centuries*. Translated by a nun of Stanbrook Abbey. New York: Sheed and Ward. 246 pp.

Saunders, J.J. (1971). *The History of the Mongol Conquests*. London: Routledge & Kegan Paul. 275 pp.

Vernadsky, George (1953). *The Mongols and Russia*. New Haven, CT: Yale University Press. 462 pp.
    The Mongols, a nomadic people in Central Asia, were united in the thirteenth century under Genghis Khan. He formed them into a superior fighting force with the best light cavalry in the world. Then he implemented his vision of conquering the world and uniting it. In order to facilitate his aim, he adopted a method of conquest by terror. He offered his potential subjects a choice of submission or total extermination, a threat that was ruthlessly carried out. The Mongols have gone down in history, as recorded by their victims, as bloodthirsty savages, but they were simply better at

using methods that were in common use in their day. There is no evidence that they invented anything new.

Dawson (1955) contains the *History of the Mongols* by John of Plano Carpini, the *Journey of William Rubruck*, several letters and papal bulls, and an important introduction by Dawson himself showing that the Central Asian nomads were not quite as barbarous as their victims believed. New evidence and excavations reveal that they had their own ancient culture which was never entirely lost. Saunders (1971) provides us with a modern and balanced treatment of the Mongol Empire and a preface that gives us his critical survey of the literature. The first two chapters in Vernadsky (1953) provide a particularly clear and readable overview of the establishment of the Mongol empire, including the Yasa (law code), their arts of war, government and administration, post roads, and the Pax Mongolica. Boyle (1968) is particularly relevant for details on Mongol destructiveness and population exterminations.

The U.S.S.R.

Antonov-Ovseyenko, Anton (1981). *The Time of Stalin: Portrait of a Tyranny*. Translated from the Russian by George Saunders with an introduction by Stephen F. Cohen. New York: Harper & Row. 374 pp.

Conquest, Robert (1968). *The Great Terror: Stalin's Purge of the Thirties*. New York: Macmillan. 633 pp.

Conquest, Robert (1970). *The Nation Killers: The Soviet Deportation of the Nationalities*. New York: Macmillan. 222 pp.

Conquest, Robert (1978). *Kolyma: The Arctic Death Camps*. New York: Viking. 254 pp.

Nekrich, Aleksandr M. (1978). *The Punished Peoples: The Deportation and Fate of Soviet Minorities at the End of the Second World War*. Translated from the Russian by George Saunders. New York: Norton. 238 pp.

The history of the U.S.S.R. under Stalin includes a number of genocidal killings; they are being dealt with by James Mace in Chapter 6 of this volume. We mention Antonov-Ovseyenko (1981) here in spite of his shortcomings because he provides the reader with quantitative data on the losses among the army and the party elites, and several other victim groups. Nekrich (1978) contains much important data on the deportation of the nationalities, supported by a useful "Note on Sources." Conquest (1970) deals with the same topic and emphasizes how news about them was suppressed so that their fate became known only many years later. He not only quotes the U.N. Convention, but also the second edition of the *Great Soviet Encyclopaedia*, which describes genocide as "an offshoot of decaying imperialism." In his 1968 book, Conquest deals with the 1930s in general, and in his 1978 book he deals with the Gulag. He shows how most prisoners in Kolyma were "enemies of the people," how the few criminals had much higher status in the camps which allowed them to act as oppressors rather than as fellow prisoners, and how few of the political prisoners had a chance to survive, although they had not officially been condemned to death.

The Great Witch-Hunt

Baschwitz, Kurt (1963). *Hexen und Hexenprozesse: Die Geschichte des Massenwahns und seiner Bekämpfung*. Munich: Rütten & Loening Verlag. 480 pp.

Cohn, Norman (1975). *Europe's Inner Demons: An Inquiry Inspired by the Great Witch-Hunt*. New York: Basic Books. 304 pp.

Larner, Christina (1981). *Enemies of God: The Witch-Hunt in Scotland*. London: Chatto & Windus. 244 pp.

Baschwitz's book (*Witches and Witch-Trials: The History of a Mass Delusion*, 1963) is available only in German and French. It is important because he shows that from the beginning of the persecutions of the witches there were voices of sanity speaking out against the trials; but they were exposing themselves to persecution unless they wrote anonymously. According to Baschwitz, such mass delusions can flourish only where there is no free speech and where the law protecting individual rights is weak. Cohn's book (1975) is the authoritative work on the processes of demonizing victims leading up to the Great Witch-Hunt. He also encouraged Christina Larner to do her research on the witch-hunt in Scotland, research that led her to formulate her hypothesis (1981) on the relationship between new regimes trying to impose a new discipline on a recalcitrant population, systems of social control, and the persecution of demonic witches as enemies of God and the godly state.

4

The Holocaust: The Ultimate and Archetypal Genocide

Alan L. Berger

The systematic destruction of European Jewry, commonly termed the Holocaust, has altered in a radical way our understanding of the human condition, the notion of divine presence, and the entire enterprise of modernity. A frightening combination of technological prowess, bureaucratic expertise, religious, quasi-religious, and anti-religious components, the Holocaust raises the most profound questions about the continuity of the present with the past and any possible human future. The Holocaust, in fact, calls into question the fundamental interpretive categories of both religious and secular worlds. The twelve-year war against Jews and Judaism, the only war that Hitler won, has continuing repercussions for both Jews and non-Jews. The deaths of 6 million Jews, including a million and a half children, throws into question the credibility of virtually all pre-Holocaust thought. For example, it is not *what* Jews did, but rather *that* they were Jews which constituted their "crime." What the Nazis themselves termed the *Endlösung* was in deed and in intent an unrelenting assault upon the elemental idea of human dignity and the sanctity of life itself.

Skills and Values

The Holocaust has come to be viewed as the paradigm of genocide, revealing that both secular and religious traditions can be harnessed in the service of mass murder. Tracking its path one is struck by the exemplary nature of the killing process. Each step along the exterminatory path was undertaken with precise calculation, bringing to bear all of the vast machinery at the disposal of a modern industrial state, disclosing for the first time that killing could be accomplished as an industrial process. The so-called bureaucratic murderer compels a rethinking of the nature and extent of the contemporary problem of evil. The temptation to do away with those whom it considers superfluous is now, as Richard Rubenstein (1975, 1983) powerfully argues, a permanent possibility for any government. The willingness of the professions either to become corrupted by, or to eagerly embrace, the killing process means that serious studies of ethics and human behavior must be undertaken anew. Death camps (the German word *Vernichtungslager* means, literally, extermination camp), gas chambers, ovens, and crematoria underscore profoundly and in a demonic manner the dichotomous relationship between skills and values in modernity. Competitive bids were entered by firms seeking to profit from manufacturing crematoria. Physicians, attorneys, and PhDs, all products of advanced German universities, were the mastercraftsmen of genocide. They became what Franklin Littell (1975) has termed "technically competent barbarians."

Apathy and Contempt

The ease with which Europe's non-Jewish citizens, both Nazi and non-Nazi, embraced their roles as killers or as indifferent bystanders, combined with the near-universal apathy toward the victims' fate displayed by the democracies, compels analysis of the relationship between Judaism and Western culture. Why has this relationship, at best ambiguous, so often led at worst to genocidal actions? What are the key tensions between Judaism and Christianity? Specifically, why was none of the murderers excommunicated? What is the role of social responsibility? It is estimated, for example, that in order to maintain the Holocaust universe—freightcars of victims leaving on time, death camps, and the myriad of details associated with industrialized murder—the participation of upwards of half a million people was necessary. The Holocaust has, in fact, become the archetype of twentieth-century evil: serving, in the words of Irving Greenberg (1977), as "model and pedagogy for future generations that genocide can be carried on with impunity—one need fear neither God nor man." The historical persistence of anti-Semitism both in its medieval (religious) and modern (racial) forms requires serious attention. Here it is instructive to recall Elie Wiesel's observation concerning anti-Semitism: "At Auschwitz the victims died, but not the disease" (remarks at a conference on anti-Semitism at New York University, 1985).

Why, on the other hand, did a precious few Christians risk their lives and those of their families to hide, shelter, rescue, or otherwise assist Jews when, in their overwhelming numbers, those who professed the Christian faith were murderers, accomplices, or onlookers? Altruistic behavior of Righteous Gentiles is now a subject of increasing importance to those seeking to reconstruct the human image after Auschwitz.

The Holocaust and its Diminishment

Study of the Holocaust compels recognition of many paradoxes. The Holocaust is seen, on the one hand, as an epochal event whose very massiveness renders inadequate the attempt to seek meaning in the meaningless suffering and deaths of millions. The historian Henry Feingold (1981) has aptly noted that Auschwitz both as a specific place and a general name for the entire killing operation has entered our vocabulary as a "measuring rod," thereby "inadvertently" indicating "that something radically different had occurred in the death camps." Yet the very fact that the Holocaust and Auschwitz have entered the public domain has inexorably led to a variety of distortions. Divorcing the event from its historical moorings has meant that its Jewish specificity has frequently been abandoned, denied, distorted, or ignored by those who, for a variety of reasons, find it convenient to employ the Holocaust as a weapon or a metaphor in order to further whatever cause, political goal, or ideological struggle is currently popular. Interest in the Holocaust is also in danger of becoming a fad which, when the cultural fashion of the moment changes, may easily be discarded. Conversely, there is a trend towards domesticating the evil of Nazism by employing symbols of the Nazi era in pop art.

Contradictory Trends: Revisionist and Memorial

Two contradictory trends have emerged in regard to the Holocaust. There is, on the one hand, the contemporary anti-Semitic denial that the Holocaust ever occurred. So-called historical revisionists who are post-Holocaust Jew-haters simply contend that the Holocaust is a fraud: a sympathy-gaining strategy devised by Zionists to foster public support of Israel. Revisionists and other pseudo-scholars deny the Jewish past in order to prevent a Jewish future. Although the threat posed by these anti-Semites is manifold, it is most clearly seen on the demographic level. Approximately three-quarters of the world's population has been born since the end of World War II. From whom, and what, will they learn of the Holocaust? Those who lie about the Holocaust must be confronted with the historical evidence.

There is also the inevitable forgetfulness which follows in the wake of any historical event. It is ironic to note that certain perpetrators of both the Armenian and the Jewish genocides felt wrongly that their guilt would be everlasting. This feeling is decidedly contradicted by the evidence. It is difficult to remember, and nearly impossible to learn from, history.

On the other hand there is an enormous outpouring of memorials of the Holocaust, on the part of Jews and non-Jews, and the historical facts of the Holocaust have been carved indelibly into the historical record of our civilization.

One especially hopeful sign emerging in the contemporary study of the Holocaust and its aftermath is the growth of the Second Generation movement. This movement is made up of children of Holocaust survivors who have accepted the legacy of their parents' wartime experiences. Second Generation groups, international in scope, meet regularly and discuss issues related to their identity as children of Holocaust survivors. These children are involved in the helping professions, such as teaching, social work, psychology, psychiatry, in numbers out of proportion to their percentage in the general population. For them, the

Holocaust assumes a highly personal dimension, serving in many instances as an impetus to seek a better, more just society.

In the Jewish community social science studies have confirmed that the Holocaust is the point of entry into Judaism for many Jews whose lives were not directly or even indirectly touched by the catastrophe.

Literature and the Holocaust

The intersection of literary and theological effort in grappling with the meaning of the Holocaust deserves attention. Novelists can raise the central post-Holocaust human and religious questions without necessarily being able to posit definitive responses. Quite the contrary. It is the task of novelists to raise these questions to the level of consciousness, thereby insuring them a place in memory. The moral, ethical, and theological complexities that emerge from the Holocaust are thus revealed as unprecedented in their intensity. It is, therefore, not surprising that Holocaust literature has profoundly influenced Jewish and Christian theological responses. But, at the same time, the entire issue of whether the Holocaust defies artistic imagination is very far from being settled. Who, for example, should write of the Holocaust? What is the nature of the complex relationship between memory and imagination?

The Term 'Holocaust'

How properly to define the Holocaust and its relationship to other examples of mass murder is an elusive and complex question. It is a novum, yet it is in history and must be comparable to other genocidal events. The claim is made that the very uniqueness of the Holocaust means that it possesses universal implications. Because it happened to a specific people in a precise manner, under definite conditions, a central post-Holocaust question is framed in Yehuda Bauer's (1978a) query: Who can tell who the "Jews" will be next time? There are, moreover, substantial problems concerning the very use of the term Holocaust, which has unfortunate sacrificial connotations. Better and more accurate words are supplied by Jewish tradition itself, which utilizes either the Hebrew *Shoah* or the Yiddish *Hurban* in referring to the disaster of European Jewry. The first, derived from the Book of Job, implies a cosmic disaster; the second word denotes the desolation associated with the destruction of the Jerusalem Temple. Both terms confer the specificity of the event, thereby minimizing the danger of domesticating the horror and the temptation to label every form of unhappiness from social injustice to murder to highway accidents as a holocaust. But the Holocaust does clearly teach lessons. How are they to be taught?

Pedagogy and the Holocaust

All of education and the pedagogical enterprise may be said to be at risk after Auschwitz. Based on a rationality that served as the foundation for a value-free, problem-solving paradigm of viewing human existence, how can pedagogy continue unchanged?

Of incalculable importance in teaching the Holocaust and its lessons are the accounts of witnesses, both those who survived and those who perished. There is as well the emerging role of dialectical thinking with its emphasis on paradox, and the associated phenomenon of an espousal of Jewish mystical concepts in the search for a hidden or more profound understanding of the Holocaust and its implications for the meaning of Jewish continuity.

Other pedagogical issues which occupy a role of central importance include defining the role of power and its relationship to morality in the post-Auschwitz world. How is Israel related to contemporary Jewish and Christian perceptions of both revelation and events in the secular sphere? What is to be done about the rising tide of totalitarian movements and groups, on both the Left and the Right? Is the rise of international terrorism somehow related to the Holocaust? Here the question centers on the relationship between the negative precedent of Nazism's massive disregard for the value of human life and subsequent life-denying actions. The nature of this type of relationship is captured in Wiesel's observation: "There could have been no Hiroshima, symbolically, without Auschwitz" (Abrahamson, 1985).

The contemporary church struggle against genocidal thinking, for its part, warns against the dangers of triumphalism and the disastrous results of refusing to allow self-definition to the other.

Rational and Irrational Components

Out of the fiery domain of the concentrationery universe there have emerged, in fact, a myriad of seemingly intractable problems. It is crucial that one distinguish between the rational and the irrational components of Holocaust history. To the extent that it is possible to do so, we can expect ever greater clarity concerning the "how" questions related to the Holocaust. Researchers are discovering more documents and conducting more interviews; scholars are devoting increased attention to the Holocaust and its continuing impact. Both Jewish and Christian thinkers are grappling with the theological dilemmas posed by the Holocaust's unprecedented assault against life itself. Early-warning systems tracking the genocidal process have been proposed.

Answers to the "why" questions are, on the other hand, likely to continue to elude us. Nazism was a combination of rational and irrational components. For example, the irrational scheme of exterminating an entire people, wherever they lived, was implemented in a thoroughly rational and bureaucratically efficient manner. Modernity itself is an uncanny concatenation of the scientific and the demonic. Philosophers must continue to probe the nature of man. It is, moreover, imperative to recognize that at its core the Holocaust remains unassimilable.

Need for New Definitions

At every turn serious students of the Holocaust are faced with the necessity of new definitions in enquiring into the meaning of post-Holocaust existence. Who, for example, is the hero and what is heroic? How is the concept of resistance to be understood in light of crematoria? What was the role of choice in the kingdom of death? The literary critic Lawrence Langer (1982) has termed the situation of Holocaust victims "choiceless choice." One survivor, for example, reports that an inmate being marched to the crematorium could walk no further. He begged the Nazi guard not to beat him so that he might march with his friends to be incinerated. What human lessons can survivors teach us in the nuclear age?

Theological and Philosophical Issues

The greatest ferment in contemporary Jewish religious thought focuses on the relationship of the Holocaust to the covenantal promise of redemption. Are old, pre-Holocaust, understandings of a covenantal deity who assures meaning in history still viable? One of the great challenges to the Jewish religious imagination is to extract meaning from within traditional sources. There is, moreover, a vigorous debate within the Jewish theological community about the role of the Holocaust in Jewish existence. Certain novelists, philosophers, and theologians have compared Auschwitz and Sinal. Others contend that there is nothing revelational about the Holocaust. The debate centers on the responsibility of both God and man.

The Holocaust has grave theological consequences for Christianity as well. There is intense self-scrutiny and debate in many Christian theological circles over the issue of whether Christianity can rid itself of the moral stain of the teaching of contempt and a theology of supersession. What will be the nature of this new Christianity which embraces, rather than rejects, its Jewish roots? This question is at the heart of serious Christian introspection after Auschwitz. Post-Holocaust interfaith dialogue must confront the changes in both Jewish and Christian thought arising out of the Holocaust.

Philosophical thought has, until recently, refrained from confronting the Holocaust. There are, however, beginning to be serious attempts made in this area. Crucial studies treat the issues of uniqueness and language. There is also an attempt to distinguish between logic and, in Emil Fackenheim's (1982) words, the logic of Nazi destruction. Philosophers are concerned with the structure of human experience after the Holocaust. But perhaps the greatest challenge to philosophers is to understand the nature of evil.

Unique and Universal

Studies of genocide that treat the Jews and other groups of victims such as the Armenians and Gypsies serve to illustrate to what degree each reveals the dialectic between unique and universal elements of their tragedies. Recognizing both uniqueness and universalism heightens human sensitivity to incipient warning signs as well as revealing the distinctiveness of each case.

Debate about the meaning of the Holocaust, for example, frequently stems from wrongly assuming that one must decide whether the event was unique or universal. Proponents on both sides marshal sophisticated historical, philosophical, and theological arguments. The difference between the two positions is, however, succinctly put in terms of numbers of victims attributed to the Holocaust: 6 million according to those who contend that the Holocaust refers to Jewish specificity, or 11 million, which is the number of victims murdered in camps. Students of the Holocaust need in fact to discern both its unique and universal aspects. The murder of the Jews, for example, underscores the dangers in permitting societal isolation, and legal inferiorization, of a group. There was as well the attribution of all that was wrong in society and the world to a single group. Jews were portrayed by Nazis as "poisoners of Aryan blood" and, therefore, Nazism viewed continued Jewish existence as inimical to the creation of a new, *Judenrein* (Jew-free) world. Killing Jews thus became a "sacred" obligation whose aim was purifying and remaking the cosmos. The uniqueness of the Jewish experience is well stated by Wiesel, who observed: "Not all victims were Jews, but all Jews were victims" (Abrahamson, 1985).

The universal aspect of the Holocaust can be seen in the coming to power of a government that was determined to commit genocide and the behavior of other governments which, for whatever reasons, refrained from actively interfering in the genocidal process. Nazism began by murdering its own, non-Jewish, citizens. The so-called euthanasia program which, in reality, was State-sponsored murder—by injection and by gassing—of mental patients and others classified as undesirables, predated the death camps. During the Holocaust ever-expanding numbers of others were murdered, including Gypsies, homosexuals, Jehovah's Witnesses, Poles, Russians, other Slavs, and some Allied airmen. The vast and indiscriminate nature of Nazism's murderous reign is a universal warning of human vulnerability to State power. Thus it is possible to assert that the Holocaust was unique in its attempt to exterminate all members of an entire people, and universal in its constantly growing definition of who was to be exterminated.

Bibliography

The following bibliography reflects interdisciplinary, interfaith, and international attempts to confront the massive rupture in civilization engendered by the Holocaust. Frequently there are overlaps in the concerns of the various disciplines. For example, theological works, by their nature, impact on post-Holocaust Jewish–Christian relations.

The historical works are also moral and philosophic enquires. The philosophical entries are concerned as well with theological and historical issues. Entries dealing with the second generation, for their part, concern a variety of disciplinary configurations. Nevertheless, the bibliography has several main foci in treating contemporary implications of the Holocaust: historical, philosophical, literary, pedagogical, theological, impact on Christian thought, Second Generation, and prevention of future genocidal activity.

Abrahamson, Irving (Ed.) (1985). *Against Silence: The Voice and Vision of Elie Wiesel.* 3 vols. New York: Holocaust Library. 1,188 pp.
    An indispensable collection of the literary, philosophical, and religious thought of one of the foremost thinkers of our time.

Alexander, Edward (1979). *The Resonance of Dust: Essays on Holocaust Literature and Jewish Fate.* Columbus, OH: Ohio State University Press. 256 pp.
    An excellent collection of essays that focus on the political and Zionist lessons of the Holocaust for writers, and readers, of such literature.

Allen, Charles R., Jr. (1985). *Nazi War Criminals in America: Facts . . . Action.* New York: Highgate House. 110 pp.
    A useful study replete with names, dates, and places. Suggestions for citizen actions to deport the murderers.

Alter, Robert (1981). Deformations of the Holocaust. *Commentary*, 71(2), 48–54.
    A distinguished literary critic and interpreter of Jewish culture warns against what he views as an excessive focus on the Holocaust.

Arendt, Hannah (1965). *Eichmann in Jerusalem: A Report on the Banality of Evil.* New York: The Viking Press. 275 pp.
    Arendt's ahistorical view that the Jewish Councils in some way cooperated with the Nazis thereby causing the deaths of Jews, and that Eichmann was just a "little man" who revealed the banal nature of evil. The book caused a furor which remains to this day.

Arendt, Hannah (1966). *The Origins of Totalitarianism.* New York: Harcourt, Brace & World. 526 pp. [First published 1951]
    Here Arendt, writing as a political philosopher grounded in the historical data, analyzes the essence of both Hitler's and Stalin's totalitarian rule. The essence of such regimes is their exercise of "total domination."

Baron, Lawrence (1981). Teaching the Holocaust to non-Jews. *Shoah*, 2(2), 14–15.
    A wise and helpful statement concerning appropriate universalizing of the Holocaust's lessons.

Baron, Lawrence (1985). *The Dynamics of Decency: Dutch Rescuers of Jews during the Holocaust.* Frank P. Piskor Faculty Lecture. St. Lawrence University. 1–18. Available by writing Office of the Dean, St. Lawrence University, Canton, NY 13617, U.S.A.
    A variety of reasons and motivations, both religious and nonreligious, entered into decisions of rescuers to rescue Jews.

Baron, Lawrence, and Midlarsky, Elizabeth (Eds.) (1986). *Altruism and Prosocial Behavior.* A special issue of *The Humboldt Journal of Social Relations*, 12(2).

A useful collection of theoretical perspectives on and case studies of altruistic behavior.

Bauer, Yehuda (1970). *From Diplomacy to Resistance: A History of Jewish Palestine 1939-1945*. New York: Atheneum. 432 pp. [First published in Hebrew in 1966]
A penetrating study of Israel's simultaneous efforts at helping European Jewry and building a state.

Bauer, Yehuda (1978a). The Holocaust and American Jewry. In Bauer, Yehuda, *The Holocaust in Historical Perspective*, pp. 7-29. Seattle: University of Washington Press.
An important contribution to issues dealing with epistemology, as well as historical, political, and psychological impediments confronting American Jewry.

Bauer, Yehuda (1978b). Against mystification: the Holocaust as a historical phenomenon. In Bauer, Yehuda, *The Holocaust in Historical Perspective*, pp. 30-41. Seattle: University of Washington Press.
Important typological discussion of the Holocaust as the ultimate genocide—which, although aimed specifically at eliminating the Jews, has universal implications.

Bauer, Yehuda (1982). *A History of the Holocaust*. New York: Franklin Watts. 398 pp.
Israel's preeminent historian of the Holocaust examines the destruction within the larger perspective of Jewish history. After a thorough analysis, he inquires whether ours will be the first generation that is able to learn from history.

Berenbaum, Michael (1979). *The Vision of the Void: Theological Reflections on the Works of Elie Wiesel*. Middletown, CT: Wesleyan University Press. 220 pp.
An exploration of Wiesel's theological position vis-à-vis views of Eliezer Berkovits, Emil Fackenheim, and Richard Rubenstein. The author argues for the presence in Wiesel's fiction of what Berenbaum terms an "additional covenant."

Berenbaum, Michael (1981). The uniqueness and universality of the Holocaust. *American Journal of Theology and Philosophy*, 2(3), 85-96.
Analysis of the positions of Elie Wiesel and Simon Wiesenthal. Suggestions are given for authentic universalizing of Holocaust.

Berger, Alan L. (1982). Academia and the Holocaust. *Judaism*, 31(2), 166-176.
A critique of the moral failure of academics, then and now, when dealing with the Holocaust.

Berger, Alan L. (1984). Reflections on teaching the Holocaust: the American setting. *Shofar*, 2, 21-26.
Argues for an intermingling of cognitive and affective learning strategies in confronting the Holocaust's challenge to the human community.

Berger, Alan L. (1985). *Crisis and Covenant: The Holocaust in American Jewish Fiction*. Albany: State University of New York Press. 226 pp.
A study which focuses on Holocaust fiction in terms of its relationship to covenantal Judaism.

Bergmann, Martin S., and Jucovy, Milton E. (Eds.) (1982). *Generations of the Holocaust*. New York: Basic Books. 338 pp.
Psychoanalytic case studies of children of survivors and of murderers. Examples are taken from America and Europe.

Berkovits, Eliezer (1973). *Faith after the Holocaust*. New York: KTAV. 180 pp.
   An Orthodox rabbinic scholar analyzes the problem of theodicy, concluding that
   Christianity and Western civilization (not God) are accountable for the Holocaust.

Berkovits, Eliezer (1979). *With God in Hell: Judaism in the Ghettos and Deathcamps*.
New York: Sanhedrin Press. 166 pp.
   An account of the behavior of pious Jews during the Holocaust.

Bettelheim, Bruno (1960). *The Informed Heart: Autonomy in a Mass Age*. Glencoe: The
Free Press. 309 pp.
   A psychologist imprisoned in Dachau and Buchenwald, and released in 1939,
   Bettelheim controversially stresses the value of personal autonomy in helping survi-
   vors survive.

Bezwinska, Jadwiga, and Czech, Danuta (Eds.) (1973). *Amidst a Nightmare of Crime*.
Poland: Publications of the State Museum at Oswiecim 207 pp.
   Four manuscripts left by Jewish *Sonderkommandos*, those whom the Nazis forced to
   unload the gas chambers and burn the corpses. Unspeakable horrors confronted by
   doomed human beings.

Blatter, Janet, and Milton, Sybil (1981). *Art of the Holocaust*. New York: The Rutledge
Press. 272 pp.
   An impressive volume that bears witness to the human creative capacity even under
   the most horrible of conditions. Includes biographies of the artists.

Blumenthal, David R. (1978–79). Scholarly approaches to the Holocaust. *Shoah*, 1,
21–27.
   A survey of socio-political and religio-moral interpretations.

Borowitz, Eugene (1980). *Contemporary Christologies: A Jewish Response*. New York:
Paulist Press. 203 pp.
   Insightful review of both European and American Christological views. The author
   concludes by observing that any meaningful Jewish–Christian dialogue must be
   based on respect for Jewish theological sensitivities after Auschwitz.

Borowski, Tadeusz (1976). *This Way for the Gas, Ladies and Gentlemen*. New York:
Penguin Books. 180 pp. [First published in Polish in 1959]
   A soul-searing collection of memoirs written by a non-Jewish survivor of Auschwitz
   who, after the war, committed suicide by gassing himself.

Borth, William F. (1983). Holocaust studies: we need to do more. *Clearing House*, 56,
345–356.
   Fewer than one percent of America's high schools teach the Holocaust.

Braham, Randolph (Ed.) (1983). *Contemporary Views on the Holocaust*. Boston,
London, The Hague: Kluwer-Nijhoff Publishers.
   Essays on post-Holocaust ethics.

Brenner, R. Reeve (1980). *The Faith and Doubt of Holocaust Survivors*. New York: The
Free Press. 266 pp.
   Empirical social science study of Holocaust survivors living in Israel. The major
   finding is that those who believed in God prior to the Holocaust continue, with few
   exceptions, to do so now. Similarly, those who had little or no belief prior to the
   conflagration by and large maintain their position in the post-Holocaust world.

Bronsen, David (1981). Child of the Holocaust. *Midstream*, 27(4), 50–56.
Sensitive psychological portrait of a young Hungarian refugees's post-Holocaust American life, which culminated in suicide. Reveals that even those who were spared direct experience of the camps were frequently irreparably damaged.

Bulka, Reuven P. (Ed.) (1981). *Holocaust Aftermath: Continuing Impact on the Generations*. A special issue of *Journal of Psychology and Judaism*, 6(1).

Butz, Arthur R. (1975). *The Hoax of the Twentieth Century*. Richmond, Surrey: Historical Review Press. 315 pp.
Notorious example of contemporary Jew-hatred which denies the Holocaust. Ludicrous and patently false "explanations" are dignified with footnotes.

Cain, Seymour (1971). The question and the answers after Auschwitz. *Judaism*, 20(3), 263–278.
Perceptive analysis of the theological views of Ignaz Maybaum, Richard Rubenstein, and Emil Fackenheim.

Cargas, Harry James (Ed.) (1976). *Harry James Cargas in Conversation with Elie Wiesel*. New York: Paulist Press. 126 pp.
Wide-ranging discussion in which Wiesel articulates the mystical and moral foundations of his Holocaust literature.

Cargas, Harry James (Ed.) (1978). *Responses to Elie Wiesel*. New York: Persea Books.
Significant essays by Jewish and Christian thinkers reflecting the impact of Wiesel's thought on the post-Holocaust moral, literary, and religious imagination.

Cargas, Harry James (1981). *When God and Man Failed: Non-Jewish Views of the Holocaust*. New York: Macmillan. 238 pp.
A collection of previously printed papers which serve as a helpful reference.

Carmon, Arye (1980). Problems in coping with the Holocaust: experiences with students in a multinational program. *Annals of the American Academy of Political and Social Science*, 450, 227–236.
Examines the question of whether pedagogy has a special task in the post-Auschwitz world. Coping with moral dilemmas in Israel, America, and West Germany.

Charny, Israel W. (1982). In collaboration with Chanan Rapaport. *How Can We Commit the Unthinkable?: Genocide, The Human Cancer*. Boulder, CO: Westview Press. 430 pp.
An important study treating the psychological aspects of genocide. Recognizing genocide as a process, Charny proposes establishing a Genocide Early Warning System that will include procedures for tracking and reporting the sequence of events.

Charny, Israel W. (Ed.) (1984). *Toward the Understanding and Prevention of Genocide: Proceedings of the International Conference on the Holocaust and Genocide*. Boulder, CO: Westview Press. 396 pp.
A significant collection of selected papers dealing with various aspects of genocide: scenarios, case studies, dynamics, arts, religion and education, and intervention and prevention. An invaluable resource for both scholars and lay people.

Cohen, Arthur A. (1981). *The Tremendum: A Theological Interpretation of the Holocaust*. New York: Crossroad. 110 pp.

Cohen argues that the Holocaust is a caesura in Jewish and human history; a *tremendum* that must be subscended. His reconstructive efforts utilize concepts from the Lurianic Kabbalah (sixteenth-century Jewish mysticism) and the Gospel of John.

Dawidowicz, Lucy (1966). Belsen remembered. *Commentary*, 41(3), 82–85.
Leading historian's tribute to Joseph Rosensaft, founder of the Bergen–Belsen Survivors group, and a plea for special prayer or liturgical poetry to help American Jewry remember the Holocaust. Two decades later these prayers and poetry do exist.

Dawidowicz, Lucy S. (1975). *The War against the Jews 1939–1945*. New York: Holt, Rinehart & Winston. 460 pp.
A classic work dealing primarily with Eastern European Jewry. Arguing that the Holocaust was a "new phenomenon in human history," Dawidowicz writes both a history and an inquiry into moral and philosophical matters. The book confronts three vital questions. How was it possible for a modern state systematically to murder an entire people because they were Jews? How did a whole people allow itself to be destroyed? Why did the world permit the destruction?

Dawidowicz, Lucy S. (1980). Lies about the Holocaust. *Commentary*, 70 (6), 31–37.
The author raises moral and historical questions concerning the activities of the so-called revisionists who deny the Holocaust.

De Celles, Charles (1982). The importance of dialoguing on the Holocaust. *American Benedictine Review*, 33(1), 75–101.
An elucidation of the political, religious, and social lessons of the Holocaust, and how they might serve to stimulate interfaith efforts.

Des Pres, Terrence (1976). *The Survivor: An Anatomy of Life in the Death Camps*. New York: Oxford University Press. 218 pp.
A landmark study of those enmeshed in Nazi and Soviet camps. The book argues for the existence of a biological/ethical imperative to survive.

Dimsdale, Joel E. (Ed.) (1980). *Survivors, Victims, and Perpetrators: Essays on the Nazi Holocaust*. Washington, Hemisphere. 474 pp.
Historical and psychosocial interpretations of the Holocaust's uniqueness and its continuing impact on both victims and murderers.

Dinnerstein, Leonard (1982). *America and the Survivors of the Holocaust*. New York: Columbia University Press. 409 pp.
An important and shocking political history which reveals that Jewish displaced persons suffered prolonged misery after the Holocaust. Jews continued to be forgotten and frequently fared worse than their German tormentors.

Donat, Alexander (1970). A letter to my grandson. *Midstream*, 16(6), 41–45.
A survivor tells his grandson that covenantal Judaism has perished in the Holocaust.

Donat, Alexander (1978). *The Holocaust Kingdom*. New York: Holocaust Library. 361 pp. [First published 1963]
A powerful account by a survivor who raises the compelling moral, political, and religious issues of Jewish and human existence after Auschwitz.

Eckardt, A. Roy (1971). The nemesis of Christian antisemitism. In Wood, James E., Jr.

(Ed.), *Jewish–Christian Relations in Today's World*, pp. 45–62. Waco, Texas: Baylor University Press.
An analysis of Christian anti-Semitism as a collective pathological state.

Eckardt, A. Roy (1973). *Elder and Younger Brothers: The Encounter of Jews and Christians.* New York: Schocken. 172 pp. [First published 1967]
An essay on Christian theological ethics which combats traditional elements of Christian anti-Semitism by examining their biblical roots.

Eckardt, A. Roy (1980). Contemporary Christian theology and a Protestant witness for the *shoah. Shoah*, 2(1), 10–13.
The *Shoah* transmutes the messiahship of Jesus through the obliteration of the Jews.

Eckardt, A. Roy, and Eckardt, Alice L. (1982). *Long Night's Journey into Day: Life and Faith after the Holocaust.* Detroit: Wayne State University Press. 206 pp.
A detailed study and critique of Jurgen Moltmann's post-Holocaust theology. The authors' theological reconstruction of Protestant Christianity radically questions the meaning of the Resurrection in light of the Holocaust.

Eckardt, Alice L. (1974). The Holocaust: Christian and Jewish responses. *Journal of the American Academy of Religion*, 42(3), 543–469.
Survey of theological implications on selected interfaith thinkers.

Eckardt, Alice, and Eckardt, Roy (1978). Studying the Holocaust's impact today: some dilemmas of language and method. *Judaism*, 27(2), 222–232.
A cross-cultural study of the contemporary interpretations and lessons of the Holocaust.

Eckardt, Alice, and Eckardt A. Roy (1980). The Holocaust and the enigma of uniqueness: a philosophical effort at practical clarification. *Annals of the American Academy of Political and Social Science*, 450, 165–178.
Draws a distinction between three types of uniqueness, ending with the Holocaust which is termed uniquely unique. The article links social ethics and the sociology of knowledge.

Edelman, Lily; Bernards, Solomon S.; and Klenicki, Leon (Eds.) (1979). Building a Moral Society: Aspects of Elie Wiesel's Work. A special issue of *Face to Face: An Interreligious Bulletin*, 6.
Wiesel's vision of ethical theology and the moral society is discussed by a panel of distinguished interfaith scholars.

Epstein, Helen (1979). *Children of the Holocaust: Conversations with Sons and Daughters of Survivors.* New York: G.P. Putnam's Sons. 348 pp.
The first book to bring the Second Generation phenomenon to popular attention.

Ericksen, Robert P. (1985). *Theologians under Hitler: Gerhard Kittel, Paul Althaus and Emanuel Hirsch.* New Haven: Yale University Press. 245 pp.
The political attitudes of many within the academy and the church reveal the crisis of reason in modernity.

Ezrachi, Sidra (1973). Holocaust literature in European languages. In Rabinowitz, Louis I. (Ed.), *Encyclopaedia Judaica Year Book*, pp. 106–119. Jerusalem: Keter.

An exploration of various themes that emerge in European Holocaust literature ranging from those viewing the catastrophe within the continuum of Jewish history to those adopting an apocalyptic stance.

Ezrachi, Sidra DeKoven (1980). *By Words Alone: The Holocaust in Literature*. Chicago: University of Chicago Press. 262 pp.
An intelligent typological study of European and American Holocaust literature.

Fackenheim, Emil L. (1970). *God's Presence in History: Jewish Affirmations and Philosophical Reflections*. New York: New York University Press. 104 pp.
Distinguished Holocaust thinker articulates his view of a Commanding Voice of Auschwitz and the contemporary applicability of the midrashic method for confronting the Holocaust.

Fackenheim, Emil L. (1977). Post-Holocaust anti-Jewishness, Jewish identity and the centrality of Israel. In Davis, Moshe (Ed.), *World Jewry and the State of Israel*, pp. 11–31. New York: Arno Press.
Fackenheim outlines reasons why Israel is decisive for authentic post-Holocaust Jewish identity for world Jewry.

Fackenheim, Emil L. (1978). *The Jewish Return into History: Reflections in the Age of Auschwitz and a New Jerusalem*. New York: Schocken. 296 pp.
A collection of essays treating the moral, philosophical, and theological implications of the Holocaust and the State of Israel.

Fackenheim, Emil L. (1982). *To Mend the World: Foundations of Future Jewish Thought*. New York: Schocken. 362 pp.
A major study treating crucial logical and theological issues. Distinguishes between the logic of destruction and Nazi destruction. Outlines ways in which Jewish philosophy and theology can begin to mend the rupture of the world caused by the Holocaust.

Fackenheim, Emil L. (1985). The Holocaust and philosophy. *Journal of Philosophy*, 82(10), 505–514.
The Holocaust is a *novum* in the history of evil. Philosophy tends not to treat this problem.

Fasching, Darrell J. (1984). *The Jewish People in Christian Preaching*, Vol. 10. New York: The Edwin Mellon Press. Symposium Series.
A discussion of post-Holocaust Jewish–Christian relations by Michael Cook, Eugene Fisher, Krister Stendahl, and Paul M. VanBuren.

Feig, Konnilyn (1979). *Hitler's Death Camps: The Sanity of Madness*. New York: Holmes & Meier. 547 pp.
Well documented history of the death camps and their juxtaposition of bureaucracy and murder; includes section on lessons of the Holocaust.

Fein, Helen (1979). *Accounting for Genocide: National Responses and Jewish Victimization during the Holocaust*. New York: Free Press. 468 pp.
A major work utilizing both social science concepts and literary accounts by victims. In those countries where Jews were viewed as inhabiting the same "universe of moral obligation," resistance to Nazism was greatest. The book also sheds much light on both the similarities and the differences between the genocide of the Armenians and that of the Jews.

Feingold, Henry L. (1980). *The Politics of Rescue: The Roosevelt Administration and the Holocaust, 1939–1945*. New York: Holocaust Library. 416 pp. [First published 1970]
A classic study analyzing Roosevelt's indifference. Feingold's basic truth is that "European Jewry was ground to death between the twin millstones of a murderous Nazi intent and a callous Allied indifference."

Feingold, Henry L. (1981). Determining the uniqueness of the Holocaust: the factor of historical valence. *Shoah*, 2(2), 3–11, 30.
The Holocaust is both a warning and a portent because, argues Feingold, the chimneys of the crematoria "inform mankind what the ultimate destiny of [the technological system] may be."

Feingold, Henry L. (1985). *Did American Jewry Do Enough During the Holocaust?* Twenty-third annual B.G. Rudolph Lecture in Judaic Studies. Syracuse, NY: Syracuse University. 33 pp.
A sober and intelligent inquiry into what was, and what was not, possible for American Jewry to accomplish.

Ferencz, Benjamin B. (1979). *Less than Slaves: Jewish Forced Labor and the Quest for Compensation*. Cambridge, MA: Harvard University Press. 249 pp.
Concerning the complicity of major German industrial firms and their refusal of either legal or moral responsibility.

Fine, Ellen S. (1982). *Legacy of Night: The Literary Universe of Elie Wiesel*. Albany: State University of New York Press. 200 pp.
Excellent study of the themes that dominate Wiesel's writings.

Fine, Ellen S.; Gerber, Jane; Hamaoui, Lea; and Lamont, Rosette C. (Eds.) (1980). *The Holocaust*. A special issue of *Centerpoint*, 4(13).
Excellent essays on literature, film, poetry and history of the Holocaust.

Fisher, Eugene (1977). *Faith without Prejudice: Rebuilding Christian Attitudes towards Judaism*. New York: Paulist Press. 179 pp.
Ways are suggested for implementing strategies aimed at overcoming past misconceptions. Readers are urged to recognize the pluralism of Jewish expression.

Flannery, Edward H. (1985). *The Anguish of the Jews: Twenty-Three Centuries of Antisemitism*. New York: Paulist Press. 369 pp. [First published 1965]
Classic study of forms of Christian anti-Semitism by a renowned Catholic priest. Updated with an assessment of the last twenty-five years.

Fleischner, Eva (Ed.) (1977). *Auschwitz: Beginning of a New Era?* New York: KTAV. 469 pp.
An invaluable collection of papers delivered at an international symposium on the Holocaust held at the Cathedral of St. John the Divine. An excellent starting-point for grasping how the world has been changed by the Holocaust event.

Flender, Harold (1963). *Rescue in Denmark*. New York: Simon & Schuster. 223 pp.
Account of Danish national assistance to Denmark's Jews.

Frank, Anne (1953). *The Diary of a Young Girl*. New York: Pocket Books. 258 pp. [First published in Dutch in 1947]

Poignant and bittersweet diary entries made by an adolescent girl who, after hiding in an Amsterdam attic for over two years, was murdered in Bergen–Belsen.

Frankl, Viktor E. (1963). *Man's Search for Meaning: An Introduction to Logotherapy*. New York: Pocket Books. 156 pp. [First published in German in 1947]
A psychiatrist survivor atributes his survival to religious and spiritual values which enabled him to remain mentally healthy.

Friedlander, Henry (1979). Toward a methodology of teaching about the Holocaust. *Teachers College Record*, 80(3), 519–542.
An insightful and bibliographically rich essay focusing on "why, how, and to whom the Holocaust ought to be taught."

Friedlander, Henry, and Milton, Sybil (Eds.) (1980). *The Holocaust: Ideology, Bureaucracy, and Genocide*. Millwood, New York: Kraus International Publications. 361 pp.
A very helpful collection of papers delivered at the San Jose Conference on the Holocaust. Essays range from history to literature to social sciences.

Friedlander, Saul (1976). The historical significance of the Holocaust. *The Jerusalem Quarterly*, (1), 36–59.
Examines the unique character of the Holocaust by investigating the behavior of the exterminators, the onlookers, and the victims. A crucial study linking rational elements with factors of true insanity.

Friedlander, Saul (1979). *When Memory Comes*. New York: Farrar, Straus & Giroux. 186 pp. [First published in French in 1978]
A powerfully evocative memoir recalling a Jewish orphan's Holocaust experience and later his life as an Israeli professor. An important work for post-Holocaust Jewish identity.

Friedlander, Saul (1984). *Reflections of Nazism: An Essay on Kitsch and Death*. New York: Harper & Row. 143 pp. [First published in French in 1982]
Well reasoned and illuminating discussion of contemporary exorcism of Nazi evil by its neutralization through "displacements of meaning, aesthetization, linguistic artifice, and inversion of symbols."

Friedmann, Thomas (1984). *Damaged Goods*. Sag Harbor, New York: The Permanent Press. 269 pp.
An excellent novel by a child of survivors revealing the complexities of the relationships between survivors and their children and between orthodoxy and the Holocaust.

Friedrich, Otto (1981). The kingdom of Auschwitz. *The Atlantic*, September, 30–60.
A philosophico-moral treatise concerning the discomfiting light shed on the nature of humanity by the evil of Auschwitz.

Gilbert, Martin (1986). *The Holocaust: A History of the Jews of Europe during the Second World War*. New York: Holt, Rinehart & Winston. 959 pp.
Distinguished historian combines historical research with survivor testimony to underscore the uniqueness of the war against the Jews and the determination of survivors to testify.

Gordis, Robert (1972). A cruel God or none—is there no other choice? *Judaism*, 21(3), 277–284.

Critiquing Rubenstein's death-of-God position, the author suggests that post-Holocaust Judaism may still find meaning within the roots of Jewish tradition.

Greenberg, Irving (1975a). Judaism and Christianity after the Holocaust. *Journal of Ecumenical Studies*, 12(4), 521–551.
A detailed exposition of dialectical faith; one which lives in the tension between hope and despair.

Greenberg, Irving (1975b). Lessons to be learned from the Holocaust. Unpublished paper presented at the International Conference on the Church Struggle and the Holocaust, Hamburg.
Important discussion of the post-Holocaust relationship of power to morality, and the overwhelming need for recreating human existence as divine image.

Greenberg, Irving (1977a). Cloud of smoke, pillar of fire: Judaism, Christianity, and modernity after the Holocaust. In Fleischner, Eva (Ed.), *Auschwitz: Beginning of a New Era?*, pp. 7–55. New York: KTAV.
Seminal article that outlines a neo-Orthodox theological position: the concept of moment-faith; utilization of three models of arguing with, while remaining in the tradition: Job, Isaiah's Suffering Servant, and the writings of Elie Wiesel; and an articulation of the collapse of the sacred–secular distinction.

Greenberg, Irving (1977b). The interaction of Israel and the diaspora after the Holocaust. In Davis, Moshe (Ed.), *World Jewry and the State of Israel*, pp. 259–282. New York: Arno Press.
The author sketches what he terms a post-modernist outline of Jewish culture whose linchpin is the State of Israel.

Greenberg, Irving (1979). Judaism and history: historical events and religious change. *Shefa*, 2(1), 19–37.
A neo-Orthodox interpretation of the relationship between history and revelation.

Greenberg, Irving (1981). *The Third Great Cycle in Jewish History*. New York. National Jewish Resource Center. 44 pp.
Following the examples of the biblical and rabbinic eras, the Holocaust era compels an examination of the divine–human relationship.

Greenberg, Irving (1983). *Are We Focusing on the Holocaust Too Much?* New York: National Jewish Resource Center.
On the transformative nature of the Holocaust which compels the retaining of tension between Nazi nihilism and Jewish life-affirmation.

Grynberg, Henryk (1982). Appropriating the Holocaust. *Commentary*, 74(5), 54–57.
The author argues that the Holocaust was exclusively designed to end the Jewish presence on earth, and warns against a false universalizing.

Gundersheimer, Werner L. (1983). Genocide and utopia. *Jerusalem Quarterly*, 26, 22–33.
Useful survey of the historical antecedents of modern genocide followed by analysis of several intellectual contexts in which genocide is viewed as civilizational progress. Articulates conditions for the success of genocide.

Hallie, Philip (1979). *Lest Innocent Blood Be Shed*. New York: Harper & Row. 303 pp.

Stirring testament to the courage of the people of the village of Le Chambon, whose valor in saving Jews remains a beacon in the darkness.

Hart, Kitty (1982). *Return to Auschwitz: The Remarkable Story of a Girl Who Survived the Holocaust*. New York: Atheneum. 178 pp.
An important account of a survivor's postwar return to Auschwitz with her son. Raises issues of Jewish identity and continuity.

Hauerwas, Stanley (1981). Jews and Christians among the nations: the social significance of the Holocaust. *Cross Currents*, 31(1), 15–34.
An essay recognizing the Holocaust as decisive for anyone wishing to think ethically as a Christian. Calls on the Christian community to eschew false universalism when remembering the Holocaust.

Hausner, Gideon (1968). *Justice in Jerusalem*. New York: Schocken. 528 pp. [First published 1966]
Chief prosecutor's account of the trial of Adolf Eichmann. Noting the trial's educational role, Hausner affirms personal responsibility as a universal rule of law.

Heer, Frederick (1971). The Catholic Church and the Jews today. *Midstream*, 22(5), 20–31.
A distinguished Catholic scholar calls for a revision of the Roman Church's triumphalistic approach to Judaism. The light of the ovens of Auschwitz should compel the church to rediscover its Jewish origins.

Herman, Simon (1970). *Israelis and Jews: The Continuity of an Identity*. New York: Random House. 331 pp.
A social science study in which the Holocaust emerges as a major ingredient in Jewish identity.

Hilberg, Raul (1985). *The Destruction of the European Jews*. New York: Holmes & Meier. 3 vols. 1123 pp. [First published 1961]
The standard reference for those interested in the mechanisms of the Holocaust's destruction. Hilberg's comprehensive study reveals the massiveness of societal participation in the Holocaust.

Hirsch, David H., and Pfefferkorn, Eli (Eds.) (1986). *Holocaust Literature*. A special issue of *Modern Language Studies*, 16(1).
Holocaust literature is analyzed from both a theoretical and case study perspective. International in scope.

Horowitz, Irving Louis (1976). *Genocide: State Power and Mass Murder*. New Brunswick, NJ: Transaction Books. 80 pp.
A comparative study of the relationship between types of genocide and socio-political organization.

Horowitz, Irving Louis (1981). Many genocides, one Holocaust?: the limits of the rights of States and the obligations of individuals. *Modern Judaism*, 1(1), 74–89.
A social science critique of Emil Fackenheim's position. Underscores both the differences and commonalities between sociological and theological approaches to genocide.

Idinopulos, Thomas A., and Ward, Roy Bowell (1977). Is Christology inherently anti-

Semitic?: a critical review of Rosemary Ruether's *Faith and Fratricide*. *Journal of the American Academy of Religion*, 45(2), 193–214.
  Challenges Ruether's theological explanation of Christian anti-Judaism, and argues that the phenomenon arose from historical and political contexts.

Insdorf, Annette (1983). *Indelible Shadows: Film and the Holocaust*. New York: Vintage Books. 234 pp.
  Exploration of the degree to which Holocaust films confront or retreat from moral issues. The moral dimension is juxtaposed with questions of artistic integrity.

Kakutani, Michiko (1981). Wiesel: no answers, only questions. *New York Times*, 7 April.
  In this interview Wiesel castigates contemporary trivialization of the Holocaust by those who fail to see it as a watershed for civilization.

Katz, Fred E. (1982). A sociological perspective to the Holocaust. *Modern Judaism*, 2(3), 273–296.
  Theoretical discussion of the Holocaust as routinization of monstrous behavior. The theory is applied to the specific example of Rudolf Hoess, commandant of Auschwitz.

Katz, Jacob (1975). Was the Holocaust predictable? *Commentary*, 59(5), 41–48.
  Distinguished social historian traces the history of modern anti-Judaism while contending that the Holocaust was not predictable. He wonders, however, if Judaism is moving in the direction of rehabilitation or Holocaust.

Katz, Steven T. (1975–76). Jewish faith after the Holocaust: four approaches. In Omer-Man, Jonathan; Rabinowitz, Louis I; and Wigoder, Geoffrey (Eds.) *Encyclopaedia Judaica Year Book*, pp. 92–105. Jerusalem: Keter.
  Explanation and critique of the theological positions of Richard Rubenstein, Emil Fackenheim, Ignaz Maybaum, and Eliezer Berkovits.

Katz, Steven T. (1981). The "unique" intentionality of the Holocaust. *Modern Judaism*, 1(2), 161–183.
  Uniqueness of the Holocaust is to be found in Nazism's *genocidal intent* against the Jewish people. That intent was metaphysical: to rule over a world which had been recreated as *Judenrein* (free of Jews).

Katz, Steven T. (1983). *Post-Holocaust Dialogues: Critical Studies in Modern Jewish Thought*. New York: New York University Press. 327 pp.
  Series of essays on selected Jewish theologians revealing the range of post-Holocaust reflection operative in Judaism.

Keneally, Thomas (1982). *Schindler's List*. New York: Simon & Schuster. 400 pp. [Published in the U.K. as *Schindler's Ark*. Sevenoaks, Kent; Hodder & Stoughton.]
  The remarkable true tale of Oskar Schindler, a German Catholic industrialist, whose courage saved thousands of Jewish lives.

Knopp, Josephine Z. (1975). *The Trial of Judaism in Contemporary Jewish Writing*. Urbana: University of Illinois Press. 164 pp.
  A study which concludes that Judaism is reaffirmed, even after catastrophes, through the evolution or rediscovery of a moral code—*mentshlekhkayt*—which is central to the Judaic tradition.

Knopp, Josephine Z. (Ed.) (1979a). *The International Conference on Lessons of the Holocaust*. Philadelphia: National Institute on the Holocaust.
A helpful collection of pedagogical and historical reflections.

Knopp, Josephine Z. (Ed.) (1979b). *International Theological Symposium on the Holocaust*. Philadelphia: National Institute on the Holocaust.
Christian theologians discuss the impact of the Holocaust on Christianity.

Korczak, Janusz (1978). *Ghetto Diary*. New York: Holocaust Library. 192 pp.
A compelling look at the thoughts of one of the moral giants of the twentieth century.

Korman, Gerd (1972). The Holocaust in American historical writing. *Societas*, 2(3), 251–270.
History of the evolution of the word "Holocaust" to describe what befell European Jewry.

Kraus, Ota, and Kulka, Erich (1966). *The Death Factory: Document on Auschwitz*. London and New York: Pergamon Press. 284 pp. [First published in Czech in 1946]
A chilling account by two survivors; includes testimony from the 1964 Auschwitz trials.

Kraut, Benny (1982). Faith and the Holocaust. *Judaism*, 31(2), 185–201. Insightful discussion of Berkovits's *With God in Hell* and Brenner's *The Faith and Doubt of Holocaust Survivors*.

Kren, George M., and Rappoport, Leon (1980). *The Holocaust and the Crisis of Human Behavior*. New York: Holmes & Meier. 176 pp.
Study of the Holocaust from a psychosocial perspective which argues for the event's singular nature.

Kuper, Leo (1981). *Genocide: Its Political Use in the Twentieth Century*. New Haven, CT: Yale University Press. 255 pp.
A comparative study of the genocidal process which rightly laments politicization of the genocide issue.

Kuper, Leo (1985). *The Prevention of Genocide*. New Haven, CT: Yale University Press. 282 pp.
Discussion of the continuing risks of omnicide owing to inability of the United Nations to implement existing structures. Includes proposals for an early warning system that combines normative regulation and surveillance institutions.

Lang, Berel (Ed.) (1984–85a). *Philosophy and the Holocaust*. A special double issue of *The Philosophical Forum*, 16(1&2).
Essays by American and Israeli scholars treating philosophico-moral problems engendered by the Holocaust.

Lang, Berel (1984–85b). The concept of genocide. *The Philosophical Forum*, 16(1&2), 1–18.
Any claim for the distinctiveness of genocidal action must be measured by the destruction of the Jews.

Langer, Lawrence L. (1975). *The Holocaust and the Literary Imagination*. New Haven: Yale University Press. 300 pp.

A ground-breaking work whose purpose was to inquire about the relationship between normality and horror in the literary works of survivors.

Langer, Lawrence L. (1982). *Versions of Survival: The Holocaust and the Human Spirit*. Albany: State University of New York Press. 267 pp.
An important literary study of survival that demonstrates the uniqueness of the Holocaust by distinguishing between fate, which implies choice, and doom, which is the death of choice.

Lanzmann, Claude (1985). *Shoah: An Oral History of the Holocaust*. New York: Pantheon. 200 pp.
The script of the widely acclaimed film, which consists of interviews with victims, murderers, and bystanders. Scholarly testimony by Raul Hilberg and Jan Karski is included.

Laqueur, Walter (1980). *The Terrible Secret: Suppression of the Truth about Hitler's "Final Solution"*. Boston and Toronto: Little, Brown. 262 pp.
Eminent historian suggests that the failure of the Allies to act was a demonstration that democratic societies "are incapable of understanding political regimes of a different character."

Levi, Primo (1961). *Survival in Auschwitz*. New York: Collier Books. 157 pp. [First published in Italian in 1958]
A profound account by an assimilated Italian chemist of his death-camp experiences. Levi probes deeply into questions about faith, the essence of man, and the moral life.

Lipstadt, Deborah E. (1979). We are not Job's children. *Shoah*, 1(4), 12–16.
Explores the tension between seeking Holocaust answers and the realization that we may only be able to ask the right questions.

Lipstadt, Deborah E. (1981). Invoking the Holocaust. *Judaism*, 30 (3), 335–343.
A warning against contemporary exploitation of the Holocaust in the educational, communal, religious, and political arenas.

Lipstadt, Deborah E. (1985). *Beyond Belief: The American Press and the Coming of the Holocaust, 1933–1945*. New York: The Free Press. 370 pp.
A study of the woeful inadequacy on the part of the majority of the American press to report the extermination of European Jewry accurately. Especially censured is *The New York Times* because it set the standard for many lesser papers.

Littell, Franklin H. (1969). *Wild Tongues: A Handbook of Social Pathology*. New York: Macmillan. 173 pp.
A model study in early warning systems for the emergence of totalitarian movements. Littell develops a fifteen-point grid for tracking the development of such groups.

Littell, Franklin H. (1971). *Kirchenkampf* and Holocaust: the German Church struggle and Nazi anti-Semitism in retrospect. In Wood, James E., Jr. (Ed.), *Jewish–Christian Relations in Today's World*, pp. 45–62. Waco, Texas: Baylor University Press.
On the dangers involved when Christianity is removed from its Semitic base and deteriorates into a culture religion.

Littell, Franklin H. (1973). Christendom, Holocaust and Israel. *Journal of Ecumenical Studies*, 10(3), 483–497.

Leading Protestant theologian argues that Christian teaching of the theology of supersession has blinded Christianity to the reality that "the Holocaust and the restoration of Israel are basic events in Christian history of the same order as the Exodus, Sinai, and the fall of Rome."

Littell, Franklin H. (1975). *The Crucifixion of the Jews*. New York: Harper & Row. 153 pp.

A pioneering study on the damage done by Christianity's teaching of contempt for Judaism. Littell offers a statement of conscience for Christians and suggests a Christian *Yom HaShoah* liturgy.

Littell, Franklin H., and Locke, Hubert G. (Eds.) (1974). *The German Church Struggle and the Holocaust*. Detroit: Wayne State University Press. 328 pp.

An important collection of articles from the first Scholars' Conference on the Church Struggle and the Holocaust.

McGarry, Michael B. (1977). *Christology After Auschwitz*. New York: Paulist Press. 119 pp.

Useful survey by a Catholic priest of church statements and theological revisions made since Vatican II.

Magurshak, Dan (1980). The "incomprehensibility" of the Holocaust: tightening up some loose usage. *Judaism*, 29(2), 233–242.

Study that distinguishes types of incomprehensibility and concludes that the Holocaust is, in principle, comprehensible except in theological terms of asking why it happened.

Mesher, David R. (1982). Reading the Holocaust. *Judaism*, 31(2), 177–184.

Analysis of four books of Holocaust literary criticism highlighting the distinction between Holocaust literature and other forms of literary expression.

Milgram, Stanley (1974). *Obedience to Authority: An Experimental View*. New York: Harper & Row. 224 pp.

A classic that looks penetratingly at the conflict between conscience and authority.

Morley, John F. (1980). *Vatican Diplomacy and the Jews during the Holocaust 1939–1943*. New York: KTAV. 327 pp.

A Catholic scholar documents the fact that the pope's timid diplomatic efforts failed Jews and Catholics during Hitler's murderous reign.

Morse, Arthur D. (1968). *While Six Million Died: A Chronicle of American Apathy*. New York: Random House. 420 pp.

One of the early studies indicting the political and moral failure of American policy toward the Jews during the Holocaust.

Moskovitz, Sarah (1983). *Love despite Hate: Child Survivors of the Holocaust and Their Adult Lives*. New York: Schocken. 245 pp.

A bittersweet analysis of child survivors initially cared for in England, and their postwar existence in America and Israel.

Nomberg-Przytyk, Sara (1985). *Auschwitz: True Tales from a Grotesque Land*. Chapel Hill: University of North Carolina Press. 185 pp. [Translated from Polish]

An absorbing and incredible collection that reveals the depravity of Nazism and the varied Jewish responses.

Oliner, Samuel P. (1984). The unsung heroes in Nazi occupied Europe: the antidote for evil. *Nationalities Papers*, 12(1), 129–136.
On the importance of teaching about rescuers and altruists as moral role models to emulate.

Oshry, Ephraim (1983). *Responsa from the Holocaust*. New York: Judaica Press. 228 pp. [First published in Hebrew in 1977]
Shows how Jews utilized normative Jewish teachings in attempting to respond to Nazi evil.

Ozick, Cynthia (1976–77). A liberal's Auschwitz. *The Pushcart Prize: Best of the Small Presses*, Yonkers, pp. 149–153. New York: Pushcart Book Press.
A critique of the novel *Sophie's Choice*, underscoring the dangers of antihistorical methods in dealing with the Holocaust.

Pawlikowski, John T. (1980a). The Holocaust and Catholic theology: some reflections. *Shoah*, 2(1), 6–9.
Post-Holocaust christological claims must be freed from inherent injustices.

Pawlikowski, John T. (1980b). *What Are They Saying about Christian–Jewish Relations?* New York: Paulist Press. 165 pp.
A helpful primer on this vital post-Holocaust topic.

Pawlikowski, John T. (1987). *The Challenge of the Holocaust for Christian Theology*. New York: Anti-Defamation League of B'nai B'rith. 45 pp. [First published 1982]
A leading Catholic theologian articulates the demands on Catholic theology that will cause it to cease practices and teachings which carry genocidal weight.

Peck, Abraham J. (Ed.) (1982). *Jews and Christians after the Holocaust*. Philadelphia: Fortress Press. 111 pp.
An important group of theological essays by Catholic, Jewish, and Protestant scholars treating the Holocaust's impact on their traditions.

Penkower, Monty N. (1983). *The Jews Were Expendable: Free World Diplomacy and the Holocaust*. Urbana: University of Illinois Press. 429 pp.
A well documented study detailing international indifference to the plight of the Jews.

Porter, Jack Nusan (1983). *Confronting History and the Holocaust: Collected Essays 1972–1982*. Lanham, MD: University Press of America. 148 pp.
Several important essays treating the sociological and religious implications for children of Holocaust survivors.

Prince, Robert M. (1985). *The Legacy of the Holocaust: Psychohistorical Themes in the Second Generation*. Ann Arbor MI: UMI Research Press. 223 pp.
Discussion that combines psychoanalytic and moral issues in the lives of the second generation.

Quaytman, Wilfred (Ed.) (1980). *Holocaust Survivors: Psychological and Social Sequelae*. A special issue of *Journal of Contemporary Psychotherapy*, 2(1).
Several articles combining theoretical issues and case studies.

Rabinowitz, Dorothy (1976). *New Lives: Survivors of the Holocaust Living in America*. New York: Alfred A. Knopf. 242 pp.
  A helpful study disclosing the resilience and moral tenacity of Holocaust survivors determined to seek meaning without illusions.

Reichek, Morton A. (1976). Elie Wiesel: out of the night. *Present Tense*, 3(3), 41–47.
  Wiesel articulates his view that the Holocaust is a mystical subject and that it is being cheapened by contemporaries.

Ringelblum, Emmanuel (1975). *Notes from the Warsaw Ghetto: The Journal of Emmanuel Ringelblum*. New York: Schocken. 369 pp. [First translated and published in 1958]
  A professional historian who perished in Auschwitz wrote his observations on the structure, organization, religious life, and Jewish response of the doomed ghetto. An invaluable testament.

Rittner, Carol (1983). The message of the Holocaust. *Shofar*, 2(1), 17–21.
  The moral obligations of, and the pitfalls involved in, Holocaust pedagogy.

Robinson, Jacob (1965). *And the Crooked Shall Be Made Straight: The Eichmann Trial, the Jewish Catastrophe, and Hannah Arendt's Narrative*. New York: Macmillan. 406 pp.
  A well reasoned and meticulously researched refutation of Arendt's banality-of-evil thesis.

Rosenbaum, Irving J. (1976). *The Holocaust and Halakha*. New York: KTAV. 177 pp.
  A scholarly study of the ultimate test of traditional guidelines in light of unprecedented evil.

Rosenberg, Alan (1981). Philosophy and the Holocaust: suggestion for a systematic approach to the genocidal universe. *European Judaism*, 14(2), 31–38.
  The philosophical significance of the Holocaust is that it threatens our self-understanding as human beings.

Rosenberg, Alan (1983). The philosophical implications of the Holocaust. In Braham, Randolph L. (Ed.), *Perspectives on the Holocaust*, pp. 1–18. Boston, London and The Hague: Kluwer-Nijhoff Publishers.
  Concerning the usefulness of philosophy in uncovering the Holocaust's transformational nature in order to probe longstanding moral and ethical values by which culture is defined.

Rosenberg, Alan, and Bardosh, Alexander (1981). The Holocaust and historical crisis: a review essay. *Modern Judaism*, 1(4), 337–346.
  Insightful analysis of the Kren and Rappoport study (1980) as an important first step toward a psychosocial understanding of the Holocaust's uniqueness.

Rosenfeld, Alvin H. (1980). *A Double Dying: Reflections on Holocaust Literature*. Bloomington: Indiana University Press. 210 pp.
  A sensitive study that outlines the distinctiveness of Holocaust literature as this literature attempts to "express a new order of consciousness."

Rosenfeld, Alvin H. (1979). The Holocaust according to William Styron. *Midstream*, 25(10), 43–49.

A critique of *Sophie's Choice* that underscores the pitfalls and distortions of an antihistorical approach to the Holocaust and its implications.

Rosenfeld, Alvin H. (1985). *Imagining Hitler*. Bloomington: Indiana University Press. 121 pp.
Discussion of the contemporary fascination with, and distortion of, Hitler and the evil of Nazism.

Rosenfeld, Alvin H., and Greenberg, Irving (Eds.) (1978). *Confronting the Holocaust: The Impact of Elie Wiesel*. Bloomington: Indiana University Press. 239 pp.
Interfaith and international literary and theological reflections on the significance of Wiesel's work.

Rosenfeld, Harvey (1982). *Raoul Wallenberg: Angel of Rescue: Heroism and Torment in the Gulag*. Buffalo, NY: Prometheus Books. 261 pp.
Well written comprehensive study of Wallenberg's heroic actions and mysterious fate.

Rosensaft, Menachem Z. (Ed.) (1965). *Bergen-Belsen Youth Magazine*. New York: World Federation of the Bergen-Belsen Survivors.
Those born in Bergen-Belsen shortly after the war reflect on the meaning of the Holocaust to Judaism through short stories, poetry, and essays.

Rosensaft, Menachem Z. (1981). Reflections of a child of Holocaust survivors. *Midstream*, 27(9), 31-33.
On the historical distinctiveness of the Second Generation and determination to fight racial, ethnic, and religious hatred.

Rosensaft, Menachem Z. (1985). We are our brothers' keepers. *Keeping Posted*, (5)13.
Articulates the moral role of children of Holocaust survivors.

Ross, Robert W. (1980). *So It Was True: The American Protestant Press and the Nazi Persecution of the Jews*. Minneapolis: University of Minnesota Press. 374 pp.
The author contends that the Protestant religious press provided all the details about the Holocaust, but nothing was done to protest.

Roth, John K. (1979). *A Consuming Fire: Encounters with Wiesel and the Holocaust*. Atlanta: John Knox Press. 191 pp.
Theological and moral issues arising out of Wiesel's work as novelist and witness. Implications are drawn for American life.

Roth, John K. (1981a). A theodicy of protest. In Davis, Stephen T. (Ed.), *Encountering Evil*, pp. 9-22, 30-37. Atlanta: John Knox Press.
Advocates a post-Holocaust theodicy which, while recognizing the dreadfulness of the human condition, refuses to yield to the despair generated by this recognition.

Roth, John K. (Ed.) (1981b). *American Theology after Auschwitz*. A special issue of *American Journal of Theology and Philosophy*, 2(3).
Two Jewish and two Christian scholars discuss the American impact of the Holocaust on their traditions.

Rubenstein, Richard L. (1966). *After Auschwitz: Radical Theology and Contemporary Judaism*. Indianapolis: Bobbs-Merrill. 287 pp.

A series of penetrating essays in which the author first articulates his death-of-God position, which radically challenges the idea of covenantal Judaism.

Rubenstein, Richard (1968). Homeland and Holocaust: issues in the Jewish religious situation. In Cutler, Donald R. (Ed.), *The Religious Situation: 1968*, pp. 39–111.
Programmatic essay in which Rubenstein asserts the failure of traditional covenant Judaism to deal with either the Holocaust or the State of Israel. He posits a neopagan espousal of nature rather than a covenantal sanctification of history. The language of power is to replace that of theological election.

Rubenstein, Richard L. (1975). *The Cunning of History: The Holocaust and the American Future*. New York: Harper & Row. 113 pp.
A provocative essay contending that ours is a "functionally godless" age whose major task is to prevent Metropolis from becoming Necropolis. The theological significance of genocide is that the Holocaust was the inevitable outcome of Western civilization.

Rubenstein, Richard L. (1983). *The Age of Triage: Fear and Hope in an Overcrowded World*. Boston: Beacon Press. 301 pp.
An exploration of the socioeconomic and cultural forces in modernity that produce unemployment, which leads to genocidal remedies. Rubenstein calls for a new (Eastern) religious leader, untainted by Western rationalism, in order to save the world from cataclysm.

Ruether, Rosemary Radford (1974). *Faith and Fratricide: Theological Roots of Anti-Semitism*. New York: Seabury Press. 294 pp.
Ruether argues that anti-Semitism is the "left hand" of Christology and offers suggestion for theological reform in Catholicism. The book caused a storm in Catholic circles and stimulated much response.

Schatzker, Chaim (1980). The teaching of the Holocaust: dilemmas and considerations. *Annals of the American Academy of Political and Social Science*, 450, 218–226.
An illuminating discussion by an Israeli scholar of Jewish and universal elements in the Holocaust's lessons.

Schwarzschild, Steven S.; Fackenheim, Emil L.; Steiner, George; Popkin, Richard; and Wiesel, Elie (1967). Jewish values in the post-Holocaust future: a symposium. *Judaism*, 16(3), 266–299.
A valuable discussion focusing on theological issues and the relationship of Jews everywhere to the Holocaust.

Sereny, Gitta (1983). *Into That Darkness: An Examination of Conscience*. New York: Vintage. 380 pp.
Based on interviews with Franz Stangl, commandant of the notorious death camp Treblinka. Stangl is morally blind to the immense crimes he committed.

Sherwin, Byron L. (1969). Elie Wiesel and Jewish theology. *Judaism*, 18(1), 39–52.
Kabbalistic teachings on evil as found in Wiesel's Holocaust stories.

Sherwin, Byron L. (1972). Elie Wiesel on madness. *Journal of the Central Conference of American Rabbis*, 19, 24–32.
Wiesel's use of moral madness, as for example caring in spite of an indifferent and hostile world.

Sherwin, Byron L. (1979a). Jewish and Christian theology encounters the Holocaust. In Sherwin, Byron L. and Ament, Susan G. (Eds.), *Encountering the Holocaust: An Interdisciplinary Survey*, pp. 407–442. Chicago: Impact Press.
Survey and critique of representative theologians.

Sherwin, Byron L. (1979b). Philosophical reactions to and moral implications of the Holocaust. In Sherwin, Byron L. and Ament, Susan G. (Eds.), *Encountering the Holocaust: An Interdisciplinary Survey*, pp. 443–472. Chicago: Impact Press.
Brief analysis of Karl Jaspers' reaction to German guilt, followed by helpful classroom models for confronting the Holocaust's moral dilemmas.

Shur, Irene G., and Littell, Franklin H. (Eds.) (1980). *Reflections on the Holocaust: Historical, Philosophical, and Educational Dimensions*. A special issue of *Annals of the American Academy of Political and Social Science*, 450.
Valuable essays on antecedents, Holocaust, meanings, and teaching the lessons.

Sichrovsky, Peter (1986). *Strangers in Their Own Land*. New York: Basic Books. 165 pp. [First published in German in 1985.]
Disturbing interviews with children of Holocaust survivors living in Austria and Germany.

Smith, Lacey Baldwin (Ed.) (1977). *Dimensions of the Holocaust*. New York: Anti-Defamation League of B'nai B'rith. Pamphlet, 63 pp.
Lectures by Elie Wiesel, Lucy Dawidowicz, Dorothy Rabinowitz, and Robert McAfee Brown in reaction to revisionist lies about the Holocaust.

Steiner, George (1971). *In Bluebeard's Castle: Some Notes towards the Redefinition of Culture*. New Haven: Yale University Press. 141 pp.
Distinction between instinctual and religious life seen in Judaism's "blackmail of transcendence" vis-à-vis Western civilization.

Steinitz, Lucy Y., and Szonyi, David M. (Eds.) (1979). *Living after the Holocaust: Reflections by Children of Survivors Living in America*. New York: Bloch Publishing. 175 pp.
Reminiscences, conversation, poetry, and philosophical, psychological, and theological works.

Suhl, Yuri (Ed.) (1975). *They Fought Back: The Story of Jewish Resistance in Nazi Europe*. New York: Schocken. 327 pp. [First published in 1967]
Examples of resistance, correcting the mistaken view that Jews went passively to their deaths.

Syrkin, Marie (1976). *Blessed is the Match: The Story of Jewish Resistance*. Philadelphia: The Jewish Publication Society of America. 366 pp. [First published 1947]
Important study of the variety of Jewish resistance in Europe and Palestine.

Syrkin, Marie (1985). The teaching of the Holocaust. *Midstream*, 31(2), 47–49.
Assessment of the damage done by those who, following the lead of Hannah Arendt, began "ferreting out wrongs committed by Jews" during the Holocaust.

Tal, Uriel (1979a). Excursus on the term *shoah*. *Shoah*, 1(4), 10–11.
Hermeneutical value of the term *shoah*.

Tal, Uriel (1979b). On the study of the Holocaust and genocide. In Rothkirchen, Livia (Ed.), *Yad Vashem Studies*, 13, 7–52. Jerusalem: Yad Vashem Martyrs' and Heroes' Remembrance Authority.
Invaluable study of the Holocaust's metahistorical uniqueness.

Talmon, Jacob L. (1965). Uniqueness and universality of Jewish history: a mid-century revaluation. In Talmon, Jacob L., *The Unique and the Universal*, pp. 64–90. New York: George Braziller.
An exquisite piece of historiography which argues that the Holocaust was a focal point in twentieth-century history.

Talmon, Jacob L. (1974). European history as the seedbed of the Holocaust. In Arad, Yitzhak (Ed.) *Holocaust and Rebirth: A Symposium*, pp. 11–75. Jerusalem: R.H. Hacohen Press.
The Holocaust viewed as confrontation between morality and paganism. The author wonders whether Auschwitz was a warning, or a portent of the future.

Tec, Nechama (1983). Righteous Christians in Poland. *International Social Science Review*, 58(1), 12–19.
Distinguishes normative from autonomous altruism. The latter is practiced even though opposed by the environment.

Tec, Nechama (1984). *Dry Tears: The Story of a Lost Childhood*. New York: Oxford University Press. 242 pp. [First published 1982]
Compelling account of eleven-year-old Jewish girl and her family hidden by Polish Christians during the Holocaust.

Theological implications of the State of Israel (1974). In Rabinowitz, Louis I. (Ed.), *Encyclopaedia Judaica Year Book*, pp. 148–173. Jerusalem: Keter.
Analyses by major Jewish, Protestant, and Catholic scholars.

Trepp, Leo (1986). Toward a *s'lihah* on the Holocaust. *Judaism*, 35(3), 344–350.
Profoundly moving statement by a survivor who calls for days of Holocaust commemoration to be on Tisha b'Av and Yom Kippur, thereby linking the fallen with normative Jewish tradition.

Trunk, Isaiah (1972). *Judenrat: The Jewish Councils in Eastern Europe under Nazi Occupation*. New York: Macmillan. 664 pp.
The heartbreaking situation of Jewish leadership and the terrifying decisions imposed upon them.

Trunk, Isaiah (1982). *Jewish Responses to Nazi Persecution*. New York: Stein & Day. 371 pp. [First published 1979]
Eyewitness accounts of Jewish reactions to Nazi horrors. Essential reading for those who think Jews did not resist, or who think of resistance only in physical terms.

Weinberg, Werner (1984). Survivor of the first degree. *The Christian Century*, 10 October, 922–926.
Account of the stages through which survivors pass, and the continuing trauma of the Holocaust in their lives.

Wells, Leon W. (1977). *The Death Brigade*. New York: Holocaust Library. 307 pp. [First published 1963]

A philosophically minded and sensitive account by a survivor who wonders if the world cares.

Wiesel, Elie (1969). *Night*. New York: Avon. 127 pp. [First published in French in 1958]
A classic in Holocaust memoir literature. All subsequent themes of Wiesel's fiction are present here.

Wiesel, Elie (1974). *The Oath*. New York: Avon Books. 286 pp.
The preeminent Holocaust witness turns his attention to Jewish–Christian relations.

Wiesel, Elie (1979). *A Jew Today*. New York: Vintage. 247 pp. [First published in French in 1978]
Character portraits and essays that illuminate the complexities of post-Auschwitz Jewish life.

Wiesel, Elie (1982). *Legends of Our Time*. New York: Schocken. 197 pp. [First published 1968]
Essays and tales illuminating both the moral indifference of the world, and the theological dilemmas of Judaism.

Wiesel, Elie (1983). Does the Holocaust defeat the artist? *The New York Times*, 17 April.
Wiesel argues that the Holocaust's universality resides in its Jewish uniqueness. While the cataclysm defies artistic representation, its survivors are committed both to life and truth.

Wiesel, Elie (1985). *The Fifth Son*. New York: Summit. 220 pp. [First published in French in 1984]
A symbolic tale of the Holocaust's continuing impact on children of survivors.

Wiesenthal, Simon (1976). *The Sunflower*. New York: Schocken. 216 pp. [First published in German in 1969]
A profound and autobiographical moral tale about the dimensions of forgiveness. Interfaith symposiasts offer their comments in the book's second section.

Williamson, Clark M. (1982). *Has God Rejected His People?* Nashville: Abingdon. 190 pp.
Analysis of the ideology of Christian anti-Judaism and proposals for overcoming this phenomenon.

Willis, Robert E. (1975). Christian theology after Auschwitz. *Journal of Ecumenical Studies*, 12(4), 493–519.
Traditional Christian theology is unable to confront either the Holocaust or Israel.

Willis, Robert E. (1985). The burden of Auschwitz: rethinking morality. *Soundings*, 68(2), 273–293.
Moral life is grounded in a tradition's narrative power. Christian self-understanding requires grappling with the Holocaust as part of its own narrative.

Wurzburger, Walter S. (1980). The Holocaust—meaning or impact? *Shoah*, 2(1), 14–16.
Orthodox view of the relationship between history and revelation.

Wyman, David S. (1978). Why Auschwitz was never bombed. *Commentary*, 65(5), 37–46.

Demonstrates the inconsistent American position of aiding other groups while refusing aid for the Jews despite knowledge of the death camps.

Wyman, David S. (1984). *The Abandonment of the Jews: America and the Holocaust 1941–1945*. New York: Pantheon. 444 pp.
A thoroughly documented investigation of the political, religious, and cultural dimensions of American apathy.

Wyschogrod, Michael (1971). Faith and the Holocaust. *Judaism*, 20(3), 286–294.
Review essay criticizing Emil Fackenheim's contention that there is a Commanding Voice of Auschwitz.

Wyschogrod, Michael (1977). Auschwitz: beginning of a new era? Reflections on the Holocaust. *Tradition*, 17(1), 63–78.
An Orthodox response to Irving Greenberg's theory of post-Holocaust moment faith.

Yerushalmi, Yosef Hayim (1982). *Zakhor: Jewish History and Jewish Memory*. Seattle: University of Washington Press. 144 pp.
The image of the Holocaust is being shaped more by novelists than by historians.

Zerner, Ruth (1979). Holocaust: a past that is also present. *Journal of Ecumenical Studies*, 16(3), 518–524.
A lucid exploration of why the Holocaust is becoming a focal point in American culture.

5

The Armenian Genocide

Richard G. Hovannisian

Seven decades after the Armenian genocide, there is no complete or annotated bibliography on the subject. Thousands of newspaper accounts and journal articles were written about the massacres at the time and many memoirs and secondary works appeared subsequently. But as international interest in the Armenian Question waned, so too did scholarly and public attention. Moreover, for the survivor generation, there never seemed to be a need to document and create bibliographies of a calamity so immense and fathomless that it was inconceivable the world could ever doubt or forget what had occurred. Yet within the lifetime of those survivors, forces of denial have emerged which seek ways to obscure and rationalize the elimination of the Armenian population of the Ottoman Empire.

The preparation of bibliographic aids therefore has both scholarly and humanistic aspects. On the scholarly level, it should facilitate the study, analysis, and comparison of the phenomenon of genocide. On the humanistic level, it may help in the work of preventing and punishing the crime of genocide and providing psychological relief to the victims and their progeny in the face of an organized campaign of denial. It was for these purposes that I prepared what may be the first bibliography on the subject, *The Armenian Holocaust: A Bibliography Relating to the Deportations, Massacres, and Dispersion of the Armenian Population of the Ottoman Empire, 1915–1923* (Cambridge, MA: Armenian Heritage Press, 1980), which lists several archival holdings and a few hundred books on the subject. It does not, however, include the many articles in periodicals or the works and studies in Armenian and other non-Western languages. In the bibliography in this chapter, a number of the most significant or representative books and articles will be annotated.

The general public and even many historians today know very little about the

Armenian genocide perpetrated during World War I. Mass killings during wartime did not, of course, begin with the decimation of the Armenians. Civilian populations have fallen victim to the brutality of invading armies, bombing raids, poisonous contamination, and other forms of indiscriminate killing. In the Armenian case, however, the government of the Ottoman Empire, dominated by the so-called Committee of Union and Progress or Young Turk party, abandoned the obligation to defend its citizenry and instead turned against a segment of its own population. In international law there were certain accepted laws and customs of war which were aimed in some measure at protecting civilian populations, but these did not cover domestic situations or a government's treatment of a constituent ethnic group among its own people. Nonetheless, at the time of the Armenian deportations and massacres in 1915, many governments and statesmen called the atrocities crimes against humanity. Several of the principal organizers were subsequently tried as war criminals, albeit the vast majority of the implicated were never called to account and the victims were in no way compensated or rehabilitated.

Scholars have begun to categorize types, circumstances, and motivations of genocide. Applied to the Armenian case, these include the existence of a plural society with significant racial, religious, and cultural differences and tensions; the process of creating a nation state or new regional order during which the perpetrators eliminate groups that pose real, potential, or perceived threats; the espousal and propagation of an ideology or belief system emphasizing the nobility and righteousness of one group as opposed to the alien and exploitative nature of the other; the mobilization of state power and the military establishment for action against the victim group; and seizure and retention of the economic wealth of the dispossessed victims. Government and party merged in the Ottoman Empire as the Young Turk dictatorship created the "Special Organization" to supervise the elimination of the Armenians, form butcher battalions, and remove weakhearted and recalcitrant officials. Moreover, even in a country as little developed as Turkey, the use of technological advances such as the telegraph allowed for unprecedented coordination in the genocidal process.

Descriptions of the Armenian deportations and massacres were broadcast the world over by newspapers, journals, and eyewitnesses. Except for the Young Turk dictators, no government denied or doubted what was occurring. In the United States charity drives began for the remnants of the "starving Armenians," and in Europe the Allied Powers gave public notice that they would hold personally responsible all members of the Turkish government and others who had planned or participated in the massacres. Between 1915 and 1918, hundreds of declarations, promises, and pledges were made by world leaders regarding the emancipation, restitution, and rehabilitation of the Armenian survivors. Yet within a few years those same governments and statesmen turned away from the Armenian Question without having fulfilled their pledges. And after a few more years the Armenian calamity had virtually become the "forgotten genocide." In view of this outcome, a brief sketch of the events leading to and following the Armenian genocide may be instructive.

History of the Genocide

Most of the territories that had once formed the ancient and medieval Armenian kingdoms were incorporated into the Ottoman Empire in the sixteenth century. The Armenians were included in a multinational and multireligious realm, but as a Christian minority they had to endure official discrimination and second-class citizenship, including special taxes, inadmissibility of legal testimony, and the prohibition on bearing arms. Down through the centuries, many Armenians converted to Islam to be relieved of these disabilities and periods of persecution. There were, of course, prosperous Armenian merchants, traders, artisans, and professionals in Constantinople (Istanbul), the Ottoman capital, and other parts of the empire, as the minority populations played prominent roles in international commerce, in the highly skilled professions, and as interpreters and intermediaries. Still, most Armenians remained rooted in their historic territories, becoming for the most part tenant farmers or sharecroppers under a dominant Turkic feudal military elite.

Despite their second-class status, most Armenians lived in relative peace so long as the Ottoman Empire was strong and expanding. But as the empire's administrative, fiscal, and military structure crumbled under the weight of internal corruption and external challenges in the eighteenth and nineteenth centuries, oppression and intolerance increased. The breakdown of order was accelerated by Ottoman inability to modernize and compete with the West. The legal and practical superiority of one element over all others continued, and the lavish and uncontrolled spending of the Ottoman court led to ever more oppressive taxation and exploitation.

The decay of the Ottoman Empire was paralleled by cultural and political revival among many of the subject peoples. The national liberation struggles, supported at times by one or another European power, resulted in Turkey's loss of most of the Balkan provinces in the nineteenth century and aggravated the Eastern Question: that is, what was to happen to the enervated empire and its constituent peoples. The British, concerned that the dissolution of the Ottoman Empire would hurt their economic interests and undermine their mastery of the seas, tried to preserve it as a weak buffer state and lucrative marketplace but realized that it would not be possible to do so without effective administrative reforms and the elimination of the worst abuses of government. A growing circle of Ottoman liberals also came to believe that the empire's survival depended on reform. These men became the movers behind several significant reform measures promulgated between 1839 and 1876. Yet time and again the advocates of reform became disillusioned in the face of the entrenched vested interests that stubbornly resisted change.

Of the various subject peoples, the Armenians perhaps sought the least.

Unlike the Balkan Christians or the Arabs, they were dispersed throughout the empire and no longer constituted a majority in much of their historic home-lands. Hence, Armenian leaders did not think in terms of independence. Expressing loyalty to the sultan and disavowing any separatist aspirations, they petitioned for the protection of their people and property from corrupt officials and marauding bands. The Armenians had passed through a long period of cultural revival. Thousands of youngsters enrolled in elementary and secondary schools and hundreds of students traveled to Europe for higher education. Many returned home imbued with contemporary social and political philosophies to engage in teaching, journalism, and literary criticism. As it happened, however, this Armenian self-discovery was paralleled by heightened administrative corruption, economic exploitation, and physical insecurity. It was this dual development, the conscious demand for security of life and property on the one hand and the growing insecurity of both life and property on the other, that gave rise to the Armenian Question as a part of the larger Eastern Question.

In 1876, Sultan Abdul-Hamid II (1876–1909), reacting to widespread unrest in the Balkans and attempted European intercession, promulgated a liberal constitution drafted by sincere advocates of reform. Had the sultan been as sincere in implementing the constitution, he could have removed the major grievances of the subject peoples. But having warded off European inter-ference, Abdul-Hamid soon suspended the constitution. The tribulations of the Armenians, instead of abating, multiplied. Robbery, murder, and kidnapping became commonplace in a land where even the traditional feudal protective system had broken down. During the Russo-Turkish war of 1877–78, much of the Armenian plateau was occupied by the Russian armies. The resulting peace treaty, aside from granting independence or autonomy to several Balkan states, stipulated that the Russian armies would continue to occupy the Armenian provinces until the Ottoman government implemented reforms to guarantee the safety and security of the Armenian population.

Great Britain regarded the treaty as a serious threat to the balance of power and forced Russia to back down. Consequently, as a result of the Congress of Berlin in mid-1878, the Russian armies were required to withdraw immediately on the pledge of Sultan Abdul-Hamid that he would undertake reforms and report to the European powers collectively about the progress made. The depar-ture of the Russian armies removed the pressure for reforms. Yet, despite the setback, Armenian leaders had not lost hope, declaring that they still had faith in the Ottoman government and its introduction of the necessary improve-ments. The Armenian patriarch swore fidelity to the sultan and emphasized that efforts to overcome Armenian misfortunes would be made within the estab-lished legal framework of the Ottoman homeland. At a time when most Balkan peoples had won independence or autonomy, the Armenians still shunned talk of separatism.

The Congress of Berlin elevated the Armenian Question to the table of international diplomacy, but the Armenians gained no advantage from that status. On the contrary, tribesmen, organized and armed by Abdul-Hamid's men, spread havoc over the Armenian provinces. Neither the petitions of the patriarch nor the detailed reports of European consuls helped to alleviate the situation. For two years the European powers reminded the sultan of his treaty obligations, but then became too involved in colonial expansion elsewhere to concern themselves with the Armenians and thus quietly shelved the Armenian Question.

Feeling abandoned and betrayed, some Armenians began to preach resistance. Local self-defense groups gradually gave way to broadly based clandestine political societies. Still, few members were prepared to expound national independence as a goal. Rather, the Armenian revolutionaries sought cultural freedom and regional autonomy, equality before the law, freedom of speech, press, and assembly, unhindered economic opportunity, and the right to serve in the armed forces. Thus, while the Armenian religious leaders in Constantinople continued supplications, the exponents of the new mentality called for resistance. Under such influence the rugged villagers of the Sassun district refused to pay an extortionary protection tax to Kurdish chieftains. In 1894, when the Kurds were unable to subdue their former clients, they appealed to Ottoman officials, accusing Sassun of sedition. Regular Turkish regiments joined the irregular cavalry and ultimately massacred several thousand Armenians without regard to age or sex.

The Sassun crisis revived the European call for Armenian reforms. In May 1895, a joint British, French, and Russian plan was submitted, which with many amendments and modifications was finally accepted by Sultan Abdul-Hamid in October. As before, however, European intercession unsustained by force only compounded Armenian troubles. Even as Abdul-Hamid gave notice of his assent to the revised reform plan, Armenians at Trebizond on the Black Sea were being massacred. In the following months, systematic pogroms swept over every district inhabited by Armenians. The slaughter of up to 200,000 people, the exile of thousands of other Armenians, the forced conversion of scores of villages, and the looting and burning of hundreds of settlements became Abdul-Hamid's actual response to European meddling. His use of violent methods was a desperate attempt to maintain the status quo in the face of external and internal challenges. In this regard, the major difference between Abdul-Hamid and his Young Turk successors was that he unleashed massacres in an effort to maintain a state structure in which the Armenians would be kept submissive, unable to resist tyrannical rule, whereas the Young Turks were to employ the same tactic on a grander scale to bring about fundamental and far-reaching changes in the status quo and create an entirely new frame of reference that did not include the Armenians at all.

Disillusion weighed heavily upon the Armenians after the calamities of 1894–96, yet some comfort was found in the fact that various non-Armenian elements were also trying to organize against the sultan's tyranny. Several of those opposition groups merged into the Committee of Union and Progress, popularly referred to as the Young Turks. In 1908 a military coup led by the Young Turks forced Abdul-Hamid to restore the constitution he had prorogued more than three decades earlier. The Armenians hailed the victory of the army and its Young Turk commanders amid manifestations of Christian and Muslim Ottoman brotherhood.

One of the most unanticipated and for the Armenians most tragic developments in modern history was the process from 1908 to 1914 in which the seemingly liberal, egalitarian Young Turks became transformed into xenophobic nationalists bent on creating a new order and eliminating the Armenian Question by eliminating the Armenian people. European exploitation of Turkish weaknesses after the 1908 revolution and the Turkish loss of more territory in the Balkans contributed to this process. In 1909 some 20,000 Armenians were massacred in Cilicia. The Young Turks blamed Abdul-Hamid and deposed him, but there were strong indications that adherents of the Young Turks had themselves participated in the carnage. The crisis prompted the Young Turks to declare a state of siege and suspend constitutional rights for several years.

It was during this period that the concepts of "Turkism" and exclusive nationalism attracted several prominent Young Turks, who began to envisage a new, homogeneous Turkish state in place of the enervated and exploited multinational Ottoman Empire. In another coup in 1913 the ultranationalist faction of the Young Turk party seized control, and thereafter, until the end of World War I in 1918, the government was dominated by a triumvirate composed of Minister of War Enver, Minister of Internal Affairs Talaat, and Minister of the Navy Djemal. With the ideology of Turkism expounded by writers such as Zia Gökalp, the Young Turk extremists began to contemplate ways to abandon multinational "Ottomanism" for exclusivist "Turkism" and so transform the Ottoman Empire into a homogeneous Turkic domain.

The outbreak of World War I in the summer of 1914 deeply alarmed Armenian leaders. If the Ottoman Empire entered the conflict on the side of Germany, the Armenian plateau would become the inevitable theater of another Russo-Turkish war. In view of the fact that the Armenian homelands lay on both sides of the frontier, the Armenians would suffer severely no matter who might eventually win the war. For these reasons, Armenian spokesmen implored the Young Turk leaders to maintain neutrality and spare the empire from disaster. Despite these appeals, the Germanophile Young Turk faction, led by Enver and Talaat, sealed a secret alliance with Berlin in August and looked to the creation of a new Turkish realm extending into Transcaucasia and Central Asia. Turkey's surprise attack on Russia in October voided the possibility of solving the Armenian Question through administrative reform. Rather, Turkism was to supplant Ottomanism and give purpose and justification to unlimited violence for the greater good of producing a homogeneous state and society. In *Accounting for Genocide*, Helen Fein (1979, pp. 29–30) has concluded: "The victims of twentieth-century premeditated genocide—the Jews, the Gypsies, the Armenians—were murdered in order to fulfill the state's design for a new order . . . War was used in both cases . . . to transform the nation to correspond to the ruling elite's formula by eliminating the groups conceived of as alien, enemies by definition." Any vacillation that may still have lingered following the Ottoman Empire's entry into the war was apparently cast aside after the tragic Caucasus campaign, in which Enver Pasha sacrificed an entire army to his militarily unsound obsession to capture Transcaucasia in the dead of winter, and after an Allied expedition had landed at Gallipoli in an abortive attempt to capture Constantinople and knock Turkey out of the war. The military setback and external threat gave the Young Turk extremists the excuse to scapegoat the Armenians and accuse them of treachery.

On the night of 23/24 April 1915, Armenian political, religious, educational, and intellectual leaders in Constantinople were arrested, deported into Anatolia, and put to death. Then in May, after mass deportations had already begun, Minister of Internal Affairs Talaat Pasha, claiming that the Armenians were untrustworthy, could offer aid and comfort to the enemy, and were in a state of imminent rebellion, ordered *ex post facto* their deportation from the war zones to relocation centers—actually the barren deserts of Syria and Mesopotamia. The Armenians were driven out, not only from areas near war zones but from the length and breadth of the empire, except Constantinople and Smyrna, where numerous foreign diplomats and merchants were located. Often Armenian Catholics and Protestants were exempted from the deportation decrees, only to follow once the majority belonging to the Armenian Apostolic Church had been dispatched.

Secrecy, surprise, and deception were all a part of the process. The whole of Asia Minor was put in motion. Armenians serving in the Ottoman armies had already been segregated into unarmed labor battalions and were now taken out in batches and murdered. Of the remaining population, the adult and teenage males were, as a pattern, swiftly separated from the deportation caravans and killed outright under the direction of Young Turk agents, the gendarmerie, and bandit and nomadic groups prepared for the operation. The greatest torment was reserved for the women and children, who were driven for months over mountains and deserts, often dehumanized by being stripped naked and repeatedly preyed upon and abused. Intentionally deprived of food and water, they fell by the thousands and the hundreds of thousands along the routes to the desert. In this manner an entire nation was swept away, and the Armenian people was effectively eliminated from its homeland of several millenia. Of the refugee survivors scattered throughout the Arab provinces and Transcaucasia, thousands more were to die of starvation, epidemic, and exposure, and even the memory of the nation was intended for obliteration, as churches and cultural monuments were desecrated and small children, snatched from their parents, were renamed and farmed out to be raised as Turks.

Interpreting the Genocide and Its Sequelae

Although the decimation of the Armenian people and the destruction of millions of persons in central and eastern Europe during the Nazi regime a quarter of a century later each had particular and unique features, historians and sociologists who have pioneered the field of victimology have drawn some striking parallels. The similarities include the perpetration of genocide under the cover of a major international conflict, thus minimizing the possibility of external intervention; conception of the plan by a monolithic and xenophobic clique; espousal of an ideology giving purpose and justification to racism, exclusivism, and intolerance toward elements resisting or deemed unworthy of assimilation; imposition of strict party discipline and secrecy during the period of preparation; formation of extralegal special armed forces to ensure the rigorous execution of the operation; provocation of public hostility toward the victim group and ascribing to it the very excesses to which it would be subjected; certainty of the vulnerability of the targeted group (demonstrated in the Armenian case by the previous massacres of 1894–96 and 1909); exploitation of advances in mechanization and communication to achieve unprecedented means for control, coordination, and thoroughness; and the use of sanctions such as promotions and the incentive to loot or, conversely, the dismissal and punishment of reluctant officials and the intimidation of persons who might consider harboring members of the victim group.

In laboring over a definition of genocide, the United Nations ultimately adopted a compromise version and listed five categories, any one of which would constitute the crime of genocide. That article reads: "In the present Convention, genocide means any of the following acts committed with intent to destroy, in whole or in part, a national, ethnical, racial or religious group, as such: (a) killing members of the group; (b) causing serious bodily or mental harm to members of the group; (c) deliberately inflicting on the group conditions of life calculated to bring about its physical destruction in whole or in part; (d) imposing measures intended to prevent births within the group; and (e) forcibly transferring children of the group to another group." It is noteworthy that the actions taken against Armenians and the subsequent victims of the Holocaust qualified as genocide under each and every category.

The Turkish wartime denials and rationalizations were roundly refuted by statesmen and humanitarians. Not Armenian treachery, wrote Johannes Lepsius (*see* the various publications by Lepsius in the bibliography), but the exclusivist nationalism of the Young Turks lay at the root of the tragedy. The elimination of the Armenians would do away with European intervention in the name of this Christian minority and would remove the major racial barrier between the Ottoman Turks and the Turkic peoples of the Caucasus and Transcaspia, the envisaged new pan-Turkish realm. United States ambassador Henry Morgenthau (1918, p. 322) summarized the reports of numerous American diplomatic and missionary personnel: "I am confident that the whole history of the human race contains no such horrible episode as this. The great massacres and persecutions of the past seem almost insignificant when compared to the sufferings of the Armenian race in 1915.'' Even Turkey's allies, Germany and Austria–Hungary, stopped making excuses and in their internal correspondence acknowledged that the Armenians were being subjected to a policy of ''race extermination.''

The defeat of the Ottoman Empire and its allies at the end of 1918 raised the possibility of enacting the numerous pledges concerning the punishment of the perpetrators and the rehabilitation of the Armenian survivors. After the Young Turk dictators had fled the country, the new Turkish prime minister admitted that they had committed such misdeeds ''as to make the conscience of mankind shudder forever.'' Returning from an inspection tour of the former Armenian population centers in 1919, the U.S. general James G. Harbord (1920, p. 7) reported on the organized nature of the massacres and concluded: ''Mutilation, violation, torture and death have left their haunting memories in a hundred beautiful Armenian valleys, and the traveler in that region is seldom free from the evidence of this most colossal crime of all the ages.'' The Paris Peace Conference declared that the lands of Armenia would never be returned to Turkish rule, and a Turkish military court martial tried and sentenced to death *in absentia* Enver, Talaat, Djemal, and Dr. Nazim, a notorious organizer of the genocide. No attempt was made to carry out the sentence, however, and thousands of other culprits were neither tried nor even removed from office. Within a few months the judicial proceedings were suspended and even accused and imprisoned war criminals were freed and sent home.

The release of the perpetrators of genocide signaled a major shift in the political winds. The former Allied Powers, having become bitter rivals over the spoils of war, failed to act in unison in the imposition of peace or in dealing with the stiff resistance of a Turkish nationalist movement headed by Mustafa Kemal Pasha. They concurred that the Armenians should be freed and rehabilitated but took no effective measures to achieve that objective. They hoped that the United States would extend a protectorate over the devastated Armenian regions, but the United States was recoiling from its involvement in the world war and turning its back on the League of Nations. Unable to quell the Turkish nationalist movement, which rejected the award of any territory for an Armenian state or even unrestricted repatriation of the Armenian refugees, the Allied Powers in 1923 made their peace with Mustafa Kemal. They acknowledged that the new Turkey would incorporate all the Ottoman territories in which the Armenians had lived. No provision was made for the rehabilitation, restitution, or compensation of the Armenian survivors. Western abandonment of the Armenians was so complete that the revised peace treaties included no mention whatsoever of ''Armenians'' or ''Armenia.'' It was as if the Armenians had never existed there. The Republic of Turkey became the beneficiary of the Young Turk policies aimed at creating a homogeneous nation-state at the expense of the minority populations.

The Armenian survivors were condemned to a life of exile and dispersion, being subjected to inevitable acculturation and assimilation on five continents and facing an increasingly indifferent world. With the consolidation of totalitarian regimes in Europe during the 1920s and 1930s, memory of the Armenian cataclysm gradually faded, and in the aftermath of the horrors and havoc of World War II it virtually became the "forgotten genocide." Turkish policy during these years was to downplay and prevent discussion of the Armenian tragedy and to focus upon the secularization and modernization of the Turkish republic. This policy was based on the belief that the Armenian survivors or their children would assimilate wherever they had taken refuge and that the Armenian Question would thus disappear permanently from international forums. All attempts by the scattered Armenian communities to bring their case before world opinion were quietly and successfully countered through diplomatic channels. Illustrative of this success was an affair relating to plans by MGM Studios to film a motion picture based on Franz Werfel's (1983) *The Forty Days of Musa Dagh*, a saga of some 4,000 Armenian villagers near the Mediterranean Sea who in 1915 resisted the deportation decrees and endured great hardship with legendary courage until they were miraculously rescued by Allied naval vessels. News that a script for the film was being prepared elicited formal protests from the Turkish government, intercession by the Department of State, and pressure on MGM and the Motion Picture Producers and Distributors of America. These channels were ultimately sufficient to force MGM to shelve the project, and all subsequent efforts to revive it were met by a repetition of protest, intercession, pressure, and cancellation.

The "Forgotten Genocide" Becomes the "Controversial Genocide"

The helpless silence of the dispersed Armenian communities was broken briefly on the fiftieth anniversary of the genocide in 1965, when Armenians the world over descended into the streets to call attention to their trauma. A new and angry generation demanded an end to world indifference and an acknowledgment by the Turkish government of the wrongs of its Ottoman and Young Turk predecessors in the manner that the German government accepted and made recompense for the crimes of the Nazi regime. Subsequently, a few Armenians even resorted to acts of violence to pressure the Turkish government and the international community. Coverage of Armenian demonstrations and violence now often also included background material on the Armenian massacres and deportations.

The Armenians, lacking a sovereign nation-state to sponsor their cause or the political, economic, and military means to influence the course of international relations, did nonetheless create a major annoyance for the Turkish government. Both Turkish civilian and military governments have reacted sharply to the Armenian challenge through the use of diplomatic channels and a well-financed campaign of denial and refutation. The Turkish information agencies and historical societies were mobilized to plan the strategy to discredit the revived charge of genocide. The resulting initial brochures and booklets published in the 1960s were clumsy and crude, but by the 1970s and especially 1980s, scholars and publicists who were native speakers of English, French, German, and other languages were enlisted, together with foreign public relations firms, to produce much more plausible propaganda that appealed to a sense of fair play and a willingness to hear the "other side" of a misunderstood issue. These recent materials take a relativist approach showing that all humanity suffers during wartime and that, while Armenian losses are undeniable, they were not inordinate when compared with the suffering of the Turkish and other elements. Concurrently, deniers of the Holocaust point out that far more Germans than Jews perished in World War II.

Some of the accomplices in this campaign play the "numbers game," minimizing the number of Armenians living in the Ottoman Empire in 1915 in order to minimize the number that could have perished. Others emphasize the decrease in Turkish and other Muslim population in Anatolia during the war years to show that Armenians, like everyone else, died mainly from famine and disease and not from a premeditated plan of annihilation. They try to cloud the issue further by pointing to "intercommunal" warfare between Armenians and Muslims and equating this to the intercommunal strife in Lebanon without noting that in 1915 the Ottoman government and army stood on one side and a defenseless Armenian subject population composed, after the first few weeks, overwhelmingly of women and children was on the other. The scattered Armenian attempts at self-defense are cited as proof of treachery and insurrection. Following this logic, the rising of the Warsaw ghetto may be taken as evidence of Jewish treachery and reason for the harsh Nazi reprisals. The same writers ignore cause and effect relationships. They not only deny the genocidal intent of the Turkish government, but they draw attention to the excesses of Armenian bands in 1918 in territories occupied by the Russian armies in order to show that there was mutual suffering and that the Armenians were as guilty as the Turks and therefore have no call for redress. They do not take into account either the scope or the cause of the Armenian excesses and pay no heed to the fact that nearly all implicated Armenians were either uprooted survivors or family members of the victims of the genocide that had begun three years earlier in 1915.

The renewal of discussion about the Armenian experience in World War I has turned the "forgotten genocide" into the "controversial genocide." The controversy is manifested in newspaper articles, editorials, and letters, brochures and booklets, radio and television programs, public and scholarly forums, and classroom instructional materials. The tendency of some academics to support the Turkish state-sponsored version of what occurred to the Armenians is a matter of concern. Clearly, scholars are not free of their own political predilections. In a world beset by power blocs and cold wars, some use defense considerations to downplay, rationalize, or deny what happened. As early as 1951, a Princeton professor, Thomas (Thomas and Frye, 1951, p. 61) while admitting that the Turks had overreacted to the perceived Armenian threat, concluded: "Had Turkification and Moslemization not been accelerated there [in Anatolia] by the use of force, there certainly would not today exist a Turkish Republic, a Republic owing its strength and stability in no small measure to the homogeneity of its population, a state which is now a valued associate of the United States." The implications of this approach and the warrant for violence implicit in it require no commentary.

The process of rationalization and denial has made great strides since the 1950s. Several American and Turkish historians now claim that the Armenians were removed only from zones of war in 1915 and not the whole of Anatolia, that the government did everything in its power to safeguard the deportees during their "transportation," that orders were issued to provide adequate food, water, and medications *en route* to the "relocation centers," that the goods and properties of the deportees were inventoried so that they could be returned to their owners once the war was over, and that special accounts were opened so that anyone using those properties in the interim could pay rent for the benefit of their owners. They attempt to discredit the hundreds of eyewitness accounts by Western observers as being prejudiced in favor of the Armenian Christians and even to explain away the incriminating evidence in the archives of Germany and Austria–Hungary, both of them wartime allies of the Ottoman Empire. Slight technical irregularities in any report or document are held forth as evidence of fraudulence and deception. An explanation for everything allows for a denial of everything. In a society overwhelmed with information, especially conflicting information, it becomes increasingly difficult to distinguish truth from disinformation.

On the official level, perceptions of state interests have prompted several governments that condemned the genocide in no uncertain terms in 1915 and whose archives abound with documents attesting to the process of "race extermination" to collaborate in efforts to suppress discussion of or cast doubts on the actuality of an Armenian genocide. From 1985 to 1987, for example, the United States Department of Defense, Department of State, and White House all actively lobbied against passage of Congressional resolutions intended to set aside a day of commemoration of man's inhumanity to man with special reference to the Armenian genocide. The protests of the Turkish government and threats regarding American–Turkish relations, American military bases in Turkey, and the entire NATO connection were enough to enlist the most powerful agencies of the United States into the campaign of denial. Those agencies alluded to the "ambiguous" nature of what had occurred in 1915 and warned of the sensitivities of the allied Turkish government as well as the aid and comfort that terrorists would receive from passage of a commemorative resolution. Both Turkish and American officials pointed to Soviet-sponsored attempts to undermine Turkey and the NATO alliance and implied that the passage of a commemorative resolution would constitute a victory for the strategists of destabilization.

Pressure by the forces of denial has not been limited to Congress. Thousands of schools, libraries, and teachers have received copies of the denial literature, and almost every plan to include discussion of the Armenian experience in teaching units on human rights and genocide has been met with protests and counter-literature. Many curriculum writers and teachers, trying to avoid controversy, back away from the subject. The decision of the United States Holocaust Council to include exhibits and learning materials on the Armenian genocide in the Holocaust museum being constructed in Washington, DC has also evoked an intense campaign to excise the Armenian segment. Once again, high-ranking U.S. officials and even Jewish leaders in Turkey have been pressed into service. Dissociation of the two genocides is fundamental in the strategy of the deniers as they repeatedly contrast the truth and horror of the Holocaust with the hoax of an alleged Armenian genocide. One can only conjecture what might happen if the German government predicated American–German relations and military alliances on whether or not the Holocaust was acknowledged by the U.S. government and included in the activities of museums, schools, and other institutions.

The powerful campaign first to make the Armenian genocide controversial and then to make it forgotten again and forever has not been limited to the United States and Europe. Tracts are put out in Arabic and Persian, and the government of Israel, in particular, has been targeted for direct pressure. In 1982, for example, Turkey first used diplomatic channels and then serious threats to have the Israeli government preclude discussion of the Armenian genocide at the International Conference on the Holocaust and Genocide. Professor Israel Charny and his associates of the organizing committee were thrust into chaos by the covert and overt threats to the wellbeing of the Jewish community in Turkey and elsewhere. In his careful accounting of the episode, Charny (in Charny and Davidson, 1983) lays bare the moral dilemmas that came into play in the ultimate decision to proceed with the conference even though sponsorship by the government and state-sponsored institutions was withdrawn. Many scholars in attendance vocalized their sense of outrage that Israel and the Jewish people should be placed in the position of being pressured to deny the genocide of another people, especially when much was known and criticized about the silence of the world during the Holocaust. It was nonetheless a reality that Israeli officials, who are in a unique position to understand the unacceptability of silence regarding the crime of genocide, were unable to rebuff external coercion and blackmail.

This discussion raises questions about how a people lacking a sovereign nation state and government can place their case before national and international bodies that operate within the framework of nation states. How is it possible to seek legal recourse, to penetrate the mutual protective systems of nation states, to have truth prevail over perceived national interests, and to liberate history from politics? How can vulnerable and dependent governments withstand blackmail involving individual and collective rights? Are effective measures for the prevention and punishment of genocide really possible in a world dominated by so-called national interests? Perhaps hope is offered by the example of the Israeli organizers of the international conference, who opted for truth and morality at great personal sacrifice and who had confidence in the strength of individuals and their collective reservoir of goodwill and influence.

The literature pertaining to the Armenian genocide is extensive. Examination of the indexes of major newspapers and journals shows that hundreds of articles on the subject appeared between 1915 and 1922. Other contemporary publications include collections of documents, accounts and memoirs of foreign diplomats and eyewitnesses, and appeals and tracts by Armenophiles in the West. There are also accounts of Armenian survivors, and a variety of secondary studies. All of these are included in the bibliography that follows as well as selected references from the literature of denial.

References

Fein, Helen (1979). *Accounting for Genocide*. New York: Free Press.

Harbord, Major-General James G. (1920). In U.S. Congress, Senate, 66th Cong., 2nd session, Senate Document no. 266. *Conditions in the Near East: Report of the American Military Mission to Armenia*. Washington, DC: Government Printing Office.

Thomas, Lewis V. and Frye, Richard N. (1951). *The United States and Turkey and Iran*. Cambridge, MA: Harvard University Press.

Bibliography

Collections of Documents

Anassian, H.S. (1983). *The Armenian Question and the Genocide of the Armenians in Turkey: A Brief Bibliography of Russian Materials*. Los Angeles: American Armenian International College. 177 pp.

This bibliography includes 662 titles in the Russian language relating to the fate of the Armenians in the Ottoman Empire. The materials deal not only with the genocide but also with the Armenian problem before and during World War I. Newspaper and journal articles, books, and translations into Russian are listed. The Russian text in the bibliography is followed by the English translation, with corresponding entry numbers.

Andonian, Aram (Ed.) (1920). *Documents officiels concernant les massacres arméniens*. Paris: H. Turabian. 168 pp. Published in English as *The Memoirs of Naim Bey*. London: Hodder & Stoughton, 1920, 83 pp.

Most caravans of Armenian deportees were directed toward Aleppo, whence they were dispatched to the desert. A minor official in the office dealing with the deportations was Naim Bey, who after the war sold copies of documents incriminating Minister of Interior Talaat Pasha and other Young Turk leaders and showing the organized and premeditated nature of the Armenian genocide. The authenticity of these documents has recently been challenged by Turkish writers. *See*, for example, Orel (1985–86). However, their charges have been refuted by Dadrian (1986).

Armenian National Committee (1983). *The Armenian Genocide as Reported in the Australian Press*. Sydney: Armenian National Committee. 119 pp.
The volume includes photoreproductions of newspaper articles reporting the Armenian genocide in the Australian publications *The Age*, *The Daily Telegraph*, *The Sydney Morning Herald*, and *The World's News*, for the period 1915–17.

Beylerian, Arthur (1983). *Les grandes puissances: L'Empire ottoman et les Arméniens dans les archives françaises (1914–1918)*. Paris: Sorbonne. 792 pp.
The 757 documents from the French archives cover the period from the autumn of 1914 to the spring of 1919 and include reports and memoranda relating to the Armenian Question, Armenian refugees, and the French-sponsored Légion d'Orient. Several of the documents relate directly to the deportations and massacres, but most pertain to their consequences and the future of the Ottoman Empire and of the Armenian people. The editor introduces the collection with a fifty-page discussion of the Armenian Question and the bearing of the documents upon that issue.

Dadrian, Vahakn (1986). The Naim–Andonian documents on the World War I destruction of the Ottoman Armenians: the anatomy of genocide. *International Journal of Middle East Studies*, 18(3), 311–360.
An important publication reasserting the authenticity of the documents. *See* the annotation of Andonian (1920).

Great Britain. Parliament (1916). *The Treatment of the Armenians in the Ottoman Empire: Documents Presented to Viscount Grey of Fallodon, Secretary of State for Foreign Affairs*. Preface by Viscount Bryce. London: Sir Joseph Causton & Sons. 684 pp. Also in French and Armenian.
This Blue Book, compiled by Arnold Toynbee, includes 149 documents, many of them eyewitness accounts by American, British, and German diplomatic and missionary personnel. The documents are organized to reflect the general situation in the Ottoman Empire and then to show what was happening to the Armenians province by province. Devastation, dehumanization, torture, death, and cries for help are detailed in the volume, which concludes with Arnold Toynbee's "A summary of Armenian history up to and including the year 1915." The identity of some informants and place names was not published in the original for reasons of security, but the key was preserved in the Foreign Office and has been included in a republication of the volume (Beirut: Doniguian & Sons, 1972).

Hovannisian, Richard G. (1980). *The Armenian Holocaust: A Bibliography Relating to the Deportations, Massacres, and Dispersion of the Armenian People, 1915–1923*. Cambridge, MA: Armenian Heritage Press. 43 pp.
The bibliography lists the files relating to the Armenian deportations and massacres in Armenian, Austrian, British, French, German, and U.S. archives. The second part of the bibliography lists more than 400 published memoirs, accounts, collections of documents, and studies on the subject.

Institut für Armenische Fragen (1987). *The Armenian Genocide*, Vol. 1. Munich: Institut für Armenische Fragen. 655 pp.
Documents and excerpts relating to the Armenian Question since 1878.

Kloian, Richard D. (Ed.) (1985). *The Armenian Genocide: News Accounts from the American Press, 1915–1922*. 3rd edn. Berkeley, CA: AAC Books. 388 pp.

Consists of photoreproductions of newspaper and journal articles describing the persecutions and massacres of the Armenians. The reproductions, taken from *The New York Times*, *Literary Digest*, *Missionary Review*, *The Outlook*, *Current History*, *The Survey*, *The Independent*, *The Atlantic Monthly*, and *The New Republic*, show that the American public was well informed about the genocide and that there was no question at the time that an organized scheme of annihilation was being enacted. The volume ends with an index of relevant articles appearing in the *Readers' Guide to Periodical Literature* from 1890 to 1931.

Lepsius, Johannes (Ed.) (1919). *Deutschland und Armenien, 1914–1918: Sammlung diplomatischer Aktenstücke*. Potsdam: Tempelverlag. 541 pp.

Lepsius was an influential German religious leader who, despite official censorship on matters relating to the Armenian genocide, brought the plight of the Armenian people to the attention of the German people. After World War I, he published documents on the subject, taken from the German archives and other official sources. The 444 documents in this volume do not tell everything about the role of the German government, but they leave no doubt about what was happening to the Armenian population in the Ottoman Empire and about the full knowledge of these events by the German authorities. The fact that the German and Ottoman empires were allied makes these documents all the more interesting and revealing. The introduction by Lepsius describes the deportation process, the involvement and motives of Talaat Pasha and other Young Turk leaders, and the attitude of German officials.

Orel, Sinasi (Winter, 1985–86). The facts behind the telegrams attributed to Talat Pasha by the Armenians. *Turkish Review Quarterly Digest*, pp. 83–102.

Questions the authenticity of the Andonian documents. *See* the annotation to Andonian (1920).

Eyewitness and Contemporary Accounts

Elliott, Mabel Evelyn (1924). *Beginning Again at Ararat*. New York: Fleming H. Revell. 341 pp.

In 1919 the American Near East Relief intensified efforts to assist homeless refugees and survivors. Dr. Mabel Elliott of the American Women's Hospitals first served at Marash, where she witnessed renewed massacres in 1920, then transferred to Ismid, near Constantinople, before moving on to Soviet Armenia to work at Alexandropol, known as "orphan city." Hers is the story of an American medical and missionary official striving to keep the survivors alive. Chapters 5–9 entail her eyewitness account of the Turkish attack upon the Armenians of Marash in 1920.

Gibbons, Herbert Adams (1916). *The Blackest Page in Modern History: Events in Armenia in 1915: The Facts and the Responsibilities*. New York and London: G.P. Putnam's Sons. 71 pp. Reissued, New York: Tankian Publishing Corp., 1975. Also French, Russian, and Armenian editions.

This is an example of contemporary Western responses to the Armenian genocide, drawing attention to the horrors and denouncing the Turkish perpetrators and their German allies.

Glockler, Henry W. (1969). *Interned in Turkey, 1914–1918*. Beirut: Sevan. 154 pp.

Born of British parents in Beirut and living there at the outbreak of World War I, the author was deported to the interior of Turkey for the duration of the war. Chapters

3–5 describe the siege, defense, and destruction of the Armenian quarter of Urfa. Glockler discusses the attitudes of German missionaries and military personnel and of Americans remaining at their posts in the interior.

Kerr, Stanley F. (1973). *The Lions of Marash: Personal Experiences with American Near East Relief, 1919–1922.* Albany: State University of New York Press. 318 pp.

Following World War I, many Americans volunteered for service with the Near East Relief. Stanley Kerr was assigned to Marash, a mountainous city on the periphery of the historic region of Cilicia. There, while working with the Armenian survivors returning to the city, he witnessed a new inferno when in February 1920 the French army of occupation secretly withdrew from the district and the panic-stricken Armenians tried to flee during a raging blizzard. As the city burned, the Armenians turned into frozen mounds in the snow. This was the beginning of the final phase of the expulsion of the Armenians from Turkey.

Lepsius, Johannes (1916). *Bericht über die Lage des armenischen Volkes in der Türkei.* Potsdam: Tempelverlag. 303 pp.

Lepsius, Johannes (1918). *Le rapport secret du Dr. Johannès Lepsius, président de la Deutsche Orient mission et de la Société germano-arménienne, sur les massacres d'Arménie.* Paris: Payot. 332 pp.

Lepsius, Johannes (1930). *Der Todesgang des armenischen Volkes: Bericht über das Schicksal des armenischen Volkes in der Türkei während des Weltkrieges.* 4th printing. Potsdam: Missionshandlung. 314 pp.

These are important sources based on first-hand reports and primary documentation relating to the destruction of the Armenian people. Lepsius gives many details of the tragedy and raises the questions of cause and responsibility, the role of the German press, and the possibility of alleviation. His works include statistical tables on the Armenian population of the Ottoman Empire and the numbers of deportees, refugees, and women and children confined to Muslim households.

Mandelstam, André (1926). *La Société des Nations et les puissances devant le problème arménien.* Paris: A. Pedone. 355 pp.

This study focuses on the Armenian Question in international law, on humanitarian intervention on behalf of oppressed peoples, and specifically on the role of the Allied Powers and League of Nations in the future and fate of the Armenians. Mandelstam analyzes international agreements on the subject, the ultimate abandonment of the Armenians by the Allied Powers in 1923, and the failure of the League of Nations to uphold human and national rights.

Morgenthau, Henry (1918). *Ambassador Morgenthau's Story.* Garden City, NY: Doubleday, Page. 407 pp.

The author was U.S. Ambassador to Turkey from 1913 to 1916. He was well acquainted with the Young Turk leaders and tried to dissuade them from their anti-Armenian policies. He informed the Department of State of what was happening to the Armenians but received only limited support from his government. His account is a first-hand narrative of what was transpiring in the Ottoman capital during the deportations and massacres, the admissions and denials of Turkish officials, and the degree of German complicity. Chapters 22–27 deal specifically with the Armenian genocide, or as Morgenthau labels it, "the murder of a nation." After seven decades this remains one of the most important sources regarding the attitudes of Minister of War Enver, Minister of the Interior Talaat, and other Young Turk organizers of the genocide.

Nansen, Fridtjof (1928). *Armenia and the Near East*. New York: Duffield. 323 pp. First published in Norwegian as *Gjennem Armenia*. Also Armenian, British, French, and German versions.

> Nansen, who was the League of Nations' High Commissioner for Refugees, describes efforts to resettle thousands of Armenian refugees in Soviet Armenia in the 1920s. He reports on his investigation in Armenia and the Caucasus, on plans for refugee resettlement, and on the circumstances that brought about the massacres and dispersal of the Armenians of the Ottoman Empire.

Niepage, Martin (1917). *The Horrors of Aleppo, Seen by a German Eye-Witness*. London: T. Fisher Unwin. 24 pp. Also New York: George H. Doran, 1918. 26 pp. Reprinted by New Age Publishers, 1975.

Niepage, Martin (1919). *Eindrucke eines deutschen Oberlehrers aus der Türkei*. Potsdam: Tempelverlag. 14 pp.

> This and the above are accounts of a German headmaster, testifying to the Turkish policy of annihilation and the agonies of the Armenians.

Nogales, Rafael de (1926). *Four Years beneath the Crescent*. New York and London: Charles Scribner's Sons. 416 pp. First published in Spanish. Also German and Turkish editions.

> Venezuelan by birth and soldier of fortune by profession, de Nogales served in the Ottoman army during World War I as inspector-general of the Turkish army on the eastern front. The first nine chapters describe the military campaigns on that front, the Turkish siege of Van, and the Armenian massacres. The author admits, despite his personal dislike for Armenians and many of their traits, that an organized scheme of massacre was implemented. He absolves the regular army of guilt. The account is of particular interest because of the author's position in the Turkish forces besieging the Armenians of Van.

Toynbee, Arnold (1915). *Armenian Atrocities: The Murder of a Nation*. London: Hodder & Stoughton, 1915. 117 pp. New York: George H. Doran. 117 pp. Also French and Dutch editions. Reissued, New York: Armenian Apostolic Church of America, 1975. 126 pp.

Toynbee, Arnold (1917a). *The Murderous Tyranny of the Turks*. London: Hodder & Stoughton. 35 pp. New York: George H. Doran. 26 pp. Reissued, New York: Tankian Publishing Corp., 1975. 48 pp.

Toynbee, Arnold (1917b). *Turkey: A Past and a Future*. London: Hodder & Stoughton. New York: George H. Doran. 85 pp.

> These works by historian Toynbee are typical of the pamphlets, articles, and sermons decrying the persecution of the Armenians, denouncing the policies of the Young Turks and the Turkish government, and calling for an end to Turkish dominion over other peoples. Toynbee backed away into a relativist position during the Greco-Turkish war of 1921–22, showing that atrocities were being committed on both sides, but returned in his memoirs, *Acquaintances*, 1967, and *Experiences*, 1969 (both published by Oxford University Press), to characterize in no uncertain terms as genocide the Turkish policies against the Armenians.

Ussher, Clarence D., and Knapp, Grace H. (1917). *An American Physician in Turkey: A Narrative of Adventures in Peace and in War*. Boston and New York: Houghton Mifflin. 339 pp.

Dr. Ussher served at Harput and Van in the Armenian provinces of the Ottoman Empire from 1898 to 1915. Present and active during the Turkish siege and Armenian defense of Van, he gives a first-hand account of the resistance and final Armenian exodus. He refutes Turkish claims that the Armenians were organizing a rebellion and shows that Djevdet Bey, the governor and Enver Pasha's brother-in-law, deliberately engaged in provocative actions in order to find an excuse to victimize the Armenians.

Wegner, Armin T. (1919). *Offener Brief an den Präsidenten der Vereinigten Staaten von Nord-Amerika, Herrn Woodrow Wilson, über die Austreibung des armenischen Volkes in die Wüste*. Berlin: O. Fleck. Also in English translation.

A German medical officer in Turkey during the war, Wegner witnessed and photographed scenes of the Armenian annihilation. Assisting the Armenian deportees in whatever way he could, Wegner after the war called upon President Wilson and the United States to extend their protection over the Armenians. This and other pieces are included in his *Die Verbrechen der Stunde—die Verbrechen der Ewigkeit* (Hamburg: Buntbuch, 1982), published posthumously by his widow, Irene Kowaliska-Wegner.

Voices of the Survivors

Armaghanian, Arsha Louise (1977). *Arsha's World and Yours*. New York: Vantage Press. 96 pp.

One of the more than fifty survivor accounts in English.

Bedoukian, Kerop (1978). *The Urchin: An Armenian's Escape*. London: John Murray. 186 pp. Also published as *Some of Us Survived*. New York: Farrar, Straus & Giroux, 1979. 241 pp.

Through the lively, inquisitive eyes of an Armenian child, a story of deportation and death unfolds. It is a saga of women and children struggling to survive from day to day with feats of great courage and ingenuity. The poignant narrative leads from Sivas (Sebastea) to the desert and bewildering loss, miraculous rescue, orphanage life, and passage to Canada. It is an effectively told story that brings genocide down to a personal level.

Caraman, Elisabeth (1939). *Daughter of the Euphrates*. New York: Harper. 277 pp. Reprinted, Paramus, New Jersey: Armenian Missionary Association, 1979.

Hartunian, Abraham H. (1968). *Neither to Laugh nor to Weep; A Memoir of the Armenian Genocide*. Boston: Beacon Press. 206 pp. Reprinted by the Armenian Missionary Association, 1976, and Armenian Heritage Press, 1987.

The author was a Protestant minister who witnessed the Armenian pogroms of 1895–96 and 1909 and who then himself suffered the harrowing experiences of the deportations and massacres of 1915. Armenian Protestants at first believed that they would be spared, only to be driven out and massacred shortly after the others had been herded away. The moving account takes place in the regions of Diarbekir, Aintab, and Marash. The minister faced numerous moral dilemmas and tests of faith. In 1919, he returned to Marash with other survivors, but the Armenians were beset by new tribulations, now by the adherents of the Turkish Nationalist cause. Abandoned by the French garrison in 1920, they were victimized yet another time. Hartunian's memoir includes the activities of American missionaries and teachers during and after the genocide.

Keyan, Haykas (1978). *No Choice but One*. New York: Armen House. 318 pp.

Kherdian, David (1979). *The Road from Home: The Story of an Armenian Girl*. New York: Greenwillow Books. 238 pp.

This is the story of the author's mother, whose idyllic childhood in a prosperous Armenian family was shattered by deportations and massacres. The story is told through the eyes of a young Armenian girl who witnessed unspeakable horrors yet somehow never lost hope. She left her shattered world behind as she went to the United States as a picture bride.

Shipley, Alice M. (1983). *We Walked, Then Ran*. Phoenix, AZ: A.M. Shipley. 290 pp.

Taft, Elise Hagopian (1981). *Rebirth*. Plandome, New York: New Age Publishers. 142 pp.

Elise was born in Bandirma in western Asia Minor, far removed from zones of war or land that could ever be reconstituted as an Armenian state, yet she too was caught up in the genocide that swept away countless thousands of young children in 1915. The saga leads from the destruction of a secure and happy home life to the routes of deportation and death for all her loved ones, rescue and orphanage life for her, the burning of Smyrna, flight to Athens, and eventually "rebirth" in Syracuse, New York.

Zaroukian, Antranik (1985). *Men without Childhood*. New York: Ashot Press. 162 pp.

Translated stories about the orphan generation of survivors.

Secondary Works

Arlen, Michael J. (1975). *Passage to Ararat*. New York: Farrar, Straus & Giroux. 293 pp. Paper edition, Ballantine Books, 1976.

This is the saga of an acculturated half-Armenian on a real and symbolic passage back to Ararat in search of his roots. First published in serial form in the *New Yorker*, it is an effective personal narrative that brings to life issues strongly felt by many Armenians but little known to the public at large.

Armenian Review (1984). *Genocide: Crime against Humanity*. Special issue of the *Armenian Review*, 37(1). 202 pp.

Contributors to this special issue include I. Louis Horowitz, James Reid, Armen Hairapetian, and Armen K. Hovannisian. Horowitz considers claims on "the exclusivity of collective death" and includes a critique of the propositions of Emil L. Fackenheim's "What the Holocaust was not." Reid analyzes the way in which the Armenian massacres are portrayed in Turkish historiography. Hairapetian and Hovannisian examine the records pertaining to the Armenian genocide in the United States National Archives.

Bardakjian, Kevork B. (1985). *Hitler and the Armenian Genocide*. Cambridge, MA: Zoryan Institute. 81 pp.

The Armenian genocide and Jewish Holocaust are symbolically linked by Adolf Hitler's rhetorical question, "Who, after all, speaks today of the annihilation of the Armenians?" Recently, revisionist writers have tried to disprove the authenticity of such a statement. Bardakjian examines the issue, presenting the published variants of the speech made in 1939, and shows that Hitler not only understood the lesson to be learned from world nonintervention during the course of the Armenian genocide but that he also made other statements bearing on the subject.

Carzou, Jean-Marie (1975). *Un génocide exemplaire: Arménie, 1915*. Paris: Flammarion. 252 pp.
A history of the Armenian Question and the process of genocide is followed by translations of excerpts from the Turkish military court martial proceedings against the Young Turk perpetrators at the end of World War I.

Charny, Israel W. (Ed.) (1984). *Towards the Understanding and Prevention of Genocide*. Boulder, CO, and London: Westview Press. 396 pp.

Charny, Israel W., and Davidson, Shamai (Eds.) (1983). *The Book of the International Conference on the Holocaust and Genocide*: Book 1, *The Conference Program and Crisis*. Tel Aviv: Institute of the International Conference on the Holocaust and Genocide. 348 pp.
This volume contains the abstracts of the papers given during the international conference at Tel Aviv, 20–24 June 1982. The second section, written by Israel Charny, is entitled "The Conference Crisis: The Turks, Armenians and the Jews." In this discussion (pp. 269–315), Charny discloses efforts of the Turkish government to prevent mention of the Armenian genocide, the responses of the Israeli government and conference organizers, and the serious implications of this episode. It is, in fact, a day-by-day and blow-by-blow exposé, with no party spared the potentially embarrassing revelations. Serious questions are raised about moral dilemmas in dealing with cases of international blackmail. Selected conference papers are included in the companion volume by Charny (1984).

Commission of the Churches on International Affairs (1984). *Armenia: The Continuing Tragedy*. Geneva: World Council of Churches. 55 pp.
This informational booklet on the genocide and its effects includes issues relating to the Armenian diaspora, Armenian claims and grievances, the Armenian church, and ecumenical responsibility. Intended for mass distribution, the publication provides a brief introduction to the Armenian tragedy.

Dadrian, Vahakn N. (1971). Factors of anger and aggression in genocide. *Journal of Human Relations*, 19(3), 394–417.

Dadrian, Vahakn N. (1972). The methodological components in the study of genocide. In [no editor] *Recent Studies in Modern Armenian History*, pp. 83–103. Cambridge, MA: Armenian Heritage Press.

Dadrian, Vahakn N. (1975). The common features of the Armenian and Jewish cases of genocide: a comparative victimological perspective. In Drapkin, Israel, and Viano, Emilio (Eds.), *Victimology*, Vol. 4, pp. 99–120. Lexington, MA: D.C. Heath.

Dadrian, Vahakn N. (1976). An attempt at defining victimology. In Viano, Emilio (Ed.) *Victims and Society*, pp. 40–42. Washington, DC: Visage Press.

Dadrian, Vahakn N. (1976a). Some determinants of genocidal violence in intergroup conflicts—with particular reference to the Armenian and Jewish cases. *Sociologus*, 12(2), 129–149.

Dadrian, Vahakn N. (1976b). A theoretical model of genocide with particular reference to the Armenian case. *Sociologia Internationalis*, 14(1/2), 99–126. Reprinted in *Armenian Review*, 1978, 31(2), 115–136.

Dadrian, Vahakn N. (1984). The structural functional components of genocide: a victimological approach to the Armenian case. In Drapkin, Israel, and Viano, Emilio (Eds.), *Victimology*, pp. 123–135. Lexington, MA: D.C. Heath.

Dadrian, Vahakn N. (1986). The role of Turkish physicians in the World War I genocide of Ottoman Armenians. *Holocaust and Genocide Studies*, 1(2), 169–192.

  Dadrian has pioneered the study of the Armenian genocide from a sociological perspective. His studies consider the framework within which the genocide occurred and examine factors common to the genocide and the Holocaust. Dadrian addresses both the specific and the universal aspects of the subject. *See also* Dadrian's 1986 study of Naim–Andonian documents, listed above.

Grabill, Joseph L. (1971). *Protestant Diplomacy and the Near East: Missionary Influence on American Policy, 1810–1927*. Minneapolis: University of Minnesota Press. 395 pp.

  Grabill traces American Protestant influence in the making and conduct of American foreign policy in the Near East. During the genocide, missionaries played a major role in relief efforts but were also instrumental in forestalling an American declaration of war against Turkey. Ultimately they made their peace with the new Turkey of Mustafa Kemal and abandoned "clamorous Armenianism." The study is based on the records of the American Board of Commissioners for Foreign Missions and other missionary archives.

Housepian, Marjorie (1972). *Smyrna 1922: The Destruction of a City*. London: Faber & Faber. 275 pp.

  At the culmination of the war between the Greeks and Nationalist Turks, the victorious army of Mustafa Kemal entered Smyrna. The Christian quarters then went up in flames and the hapless population was literally driven into the sea, where Allied naval vessels bore cold witness to one of the closing episodes of the genocide. Most of the Armenians of Smyrna and Constantinople had been spared during the deportations and massacres in 1915 but now had the water hoses of American naval vessels turned upon them as they swam toward the ships and tried to climb to safety. The book was published in the United States as *The Smyrna Affair* (New York: Harcourt Brace Jovanovich, 1966), but the British edition has fewer printing errors and is more precise in its system of notation.

Hovannisian, Richard G. (1967). *Armenia on the Road to Independence*. Berkeley and Los Angeles: University of California Press (4th printing, 1982). 364 pp.

  This study places the Armenian Question in local, regional, and international perspectives and focuses on the events that led to the elimination of most of the Armenian population in the Ottoman Empire and the creation of a small Armenian republic on territory formerly within the Russian Empire. Chapters 3 and 4 deal with World War I and the Armenian genocide, and Chapters 7–9 detail the uncharted road to Armenian independence. The volume is a forerunner to the projected three-volume history of the Republic of Armenia (Vol. 1, 1971; Vol. 2, 1982).

Hovannisian, Richard G. (Ed.) (1986). *The Armenian Genocide in Perspective*. New Brunswick, NJ: Transaction Press—Rutgers University. 215 pp.

  The volume represents a multidisciplinary approach to examining the genocide. The eleven articles encompass the fields of ethics, history, literature, political science, psychiatry, and sociology. Seven of the articles were presented at the International Conference on the Holocaust and Genocide in Tel Aviv in 1982. In a thought-provoking introduction, Terrence Des Pres issues a call and challenge to scholars in the face of all the forces that find it expedient to forget, ignore, or deny what has occurred. Robert Melson and R. Hrair Dekmejian consider the ideological components of the genocide; Leo Hamalian and Vahé Oshagan discuss the literary impact; Vigen Guroian and Donald and Lorna Miller raise theological and moral issues; Levon Boyajian and Haigaz Grigorian take a preliminary look at psychosocial effects; and Marjorie Housepian, Richard Hovannisian, and Leo Kuper place the genocide in historical and historiographical contexts.

Lang, David Marshall, and Walker, Christopher J. (1981). *The Armenians*. London: Minority Rights Group, Report no. 32 (revised). 24 pp. and appendix.

The report of the Minority Rights Group sketches the history of the Armenian people, their status under Ottoman dominion, the era of pogroms, the "false dawn" of the Young Turk revolution, the genocide and its aftermath, and the Armenian dispersal and current problems. It is a concise and useful overview, with maps and a brief bibliography and film guide.

Miller, Donald E., and Miller, Lorna T. (1982). Armenian survivors: a typological analysis of victim response. *Oral History Review*, 10, 47–72.

The authors are pioneers in scholarly application of oral histories of Armenian survivors. Their study divides the responses of the survivors into various categories, but these are not firm, for sometimes lurking just under the surface of responses classified as resignation and reconciliation are sentiments of rage and revenge.

Permanent Peoples' Tribunal (1985). *A Crime of Silence: The Armenian Genocide*. Preface by Pierre Vidal-Naquet. London: Zed Press. 245 pp. French edition, *Le crime de silence*. Paris: Flammarion, 1984. 380 pp.

The Permanent Peoples' Tribunal, which has evolved from the tribunal established by Bertrand Russell, considered the case of the Armenian genocide during a sitting at the Sorbonne in Paris, 13–16 April 1984. The evidence submitted included the testimony of experts on Armenian history, on British and German sources relating to the genocide, and on international law, as well as of Armenian survivors now living in France and the United States. A statement was also accepted from the late Yilmaz Güney, a noted filmmaker of Kurdish origin. The Turkish position, as stated in a publication of the Turkish Foreign Policy Institute, was read into the record. The Tribunal's verdict confirmed that the Armenians had been the victims of genocide, that the crime was not subject to any statute of limitations, and that the United Nations and its member states should recognize "the reality of the genocide" and take measures to mitigate its effects. The entire proceedings of the session and the Tribunal's verdict are published in this volume.

Sachar, Howard M. (1969). *The Emergence of the Middle East: 1914–1924*. New York: Alfred A. Knopf. 518 pp.

Sachar's history covers the final years of the Ottoman Empire and the impact of that decade on Arabs, Jews, Turks, and Armenians. Chapter 4 describes the Armenian genocide and Chapter 11 examines United States postwar policy regarding the Armenians and a solution to the Armenian Question. The fate of the Armenian people is placed in the larger context of Near Eastern, European, and American history.

Strom, Margot Stern, and Parsons, William S. (1982). *Facing History and Ourselves: Holocaust and Human Behavior*. Watertown, MA: Intentional Educations. 400 pp.

This text and resource book raises issues such as prejudice and discrimination, conditioning and obedience, choice and judgment. The authors develop a methodology for facing the Holocaust and other genocides. Chapter 11 (pp. 317–382) deals specifically with the Armenian genocide and includes selected readings and points for discussion and individual and collective development. Students are encouraged to confront themselves as a way of dealing with the kinds of human behavior that can nurture intolerance and even genocidal acts.

Ternon, Yves (1977). *Les Arméniens: histoire d'un génocide*. Paris: Editions du Seuil. 318 pp.
    This is one of several books on the Armenian genocide, written or edited by Ternon. He uses many published documents and secondary sources to show how the Armenians were the victims of geopolitics and international cynicism. He assesses the ideology and policies of the Young Turks, their perversion of State power, and their process of genocide, province by province.

Trumpener, Ulrich (1968). *Germany and the Ottoman Empire, 1914–1918*. Princeton, NJ: Princeton University Press. 433 pp.
    Many contemporary sources implicated the Germans in the Armenian genocide. The fact that a German regime itself perpetrated genocide only a quarter of a century later makes the issue all the more relevant. Trumpener's study, based largely on archival materials, shows that Germany did not in fact plan or participate in the annihilation of the Armenians but, on the other hand, did not intercede in a forceful manner to prevent or put an end to the massacres. Germany alone, as the senior ally and financial mainstay of the Young Turk government, could have intervened effectively. Rather, a policy of expediency was adopted. Chapters 6 and 7 point up the tension between the two allied Central Powers over the Armenian issue and rivalry for control of Transcaucasia.

Walker, Christopher J. (1980). *Armenia: Survival of a Nation*. New York: St. Martin's Press. 446 pp.
    Walker traces the development of the Armenian Question and particularly the role and responsibility of Great Britain, whose policies are sharply criticized. The section dealing with the genocide is entitled "The Death of Turkish Armenia" and includes descriptions of the destruction of the Ottoman Armenian population district by district. The volume includes a chapter on Armenian efforts to create an independent republic and a useful biographical glossary.

Werfel, Franz (1983). *The Forty Days of Musa Dagh*. New York: Carroll & Grat [Copyright 1933 Paul Zsolnay Verlag AG; 1934, 1962 Viking].
    A factually based novel about Armenian villagers who fight courageously against Turkish extermination. An effort "to snatch from the Hades of all that was, this incomprehensible destiny of the Armenian nation."

Zarevand (1971). *United and Independent Turania: Aims and Designs of the Turks*. Translated by V.N. Dadrian. Leiden: E.J. Brill. 174 pp.
    The Armenian genocide is viewed within the context of pan-Turanism. The political and ideological aspects of genocide are stressed. The original work was published in Boston in 1926.

Rationalization, Revision, and Denial

Assembly of Turkish American Associations (1986). *Armenian Allegations: Myth and Reality: A Handbook of Facts and Documents*. Washington, DC: ATAA. 139 pp.

Ataov, Türkäyya (1984). *A Brief Glance at the "Armenian Question."* Ankara: Ankara University.

A typical example of recent Turkish revisionist and denial literature, often first published in Turkish for domestic distribution and then translated into various Western languages. These booklets try to show that "Armenia" was never more than a geographic expression, having little or no political connotation, that the Armenians were always a minority in the land called Armenia, that they had lived in peace and harmony in the Ottoman Empire until they were subverted by Russia and their own revolutionaries, that they took arms against the state in World War I, that certain preventive measures were taken but there was no plan to annihilate the Armenians, that various documents and circumstantial evidence used against Turkish officials were either forgeries or untrue, that the release by the Allies of many captured Turkish leaders after the war is proof of their innocence, that no more than 100,000 to 200,000 Armenians perished during the war years, a figure not disproportionate to the number of Turks and other Muslims who died, that attempts to revive the "Armenian Question" today are directly related to the schemes of international terrorists to destabilize Turkey and undermine NATO, and that the time has come for the truth to be known and for unfavorable stereotypes of Turkey and the Turks to be done away with. *See also* Karal (1975), Özkaya (1971), Şimsir (1984).

Djemal Pasha (1922). *Memories of a Turkish Statesman, 1913-1919.* London: Hutchinson. 302 pp. Also in Arabic, Armenian, French, German, Russian, and Turkish.

Djemal and Talaat (*see* Talaat Pasha, 1921) were members of the Young Turk triumvirate that controlled the Ottoman Empire during World War I. Both were condemned to death *in absentia* by a Turkish court martial in 1919, and both were hunted down and killed by Armenians. Before their deaths, each denied any participation in measures to eliminate the Armenians. Talaat confessed that certain elements composed of common criminals and zealous patriots committed excesses and that the government did not intercede forcefully but that these "excesses" were no different from what was happening in other countries. Djemal insisted that the decision to deport the Armenians had been made without his participation and that in fact he managed to save as many as 150,000 widows and orphans, an indirect confirmation that the male population had already been annihilated by the time the caravans reached Aleppo, where Djemal was commanding an Ottoman army.

Emin, Ahmed (1930). *Turkey in the World War.* New Haven, CT: Yale University Press. 310 pp.

Of the postwar Turkish writers, American-educated journalist Ahmed Emin (Yalman) was the most candid in admitting that genocidal acts had occurred. Without discarding the standard rationalizations about the Armenian threat to state security, he wrote that certain influential Young Turks wanted to use the deportations as a means of achieving "the extermination of the Armenian minority in Turkey with the idea of bringing about racial homogeneity in Asia Minor." Chapter 18 is entitled "The Armenians and the War."

Gürün, Kâmuran (1985). *The Armenian File: The Myth of Innocence Exposed.* London: Weidenfeld & Nicolson; Nicosia: K. Rustem. 323 pp. Also in Turkish and in French.

Published and distributed by reputable publishing houses in France, Great Britain, and the United States, this volume is the culmination of many years of trial and error by Turkish revisionist writers. Adopting Western styles of organization and notation, Gürün has brought together all the Turkish arguments that (a) belittle or discount any significant Armenian national history, (b) minimize the number of Armenians living in the Ottoman Empire, (c) claim that the Armenians became rebels, revolutionaries, and terrorists, (d) assert that the Armenians were disloyal during World War I and had to be "transferred" from the war zones, and (e) show that the Armenians became the victims of European imperialism and their own self-deception.

Karal, Enver Ziya (1975). *Armenian Question (1878–1923)*. Ankara: Gunduz. 26 pp.

National Congress of Turkey (1919). *The Turco-Armenian Question: The Turkish Point of View*. Constantinople: Société Anonyme de Papeterie et d'Imprimerie. 157 pp.
This is an example of postwar efforts by Turkish leaders to avoid a harsh peace treaty by persuading the Allies that the former Young Turk government had been an aberration of the normal tolerant behavior of Ottoman rulers and that the Turkish people should not be held responsible or made to pay for the criminal actions of a dictatorial clique. It admits that some Young Turk leaders carried out a policy of extermination against the Armenians, but also alleges that the Armenians had engaged in subversive activities, that their relocation from the war zones was justified, that they, too, had committed excesses against innocent Muslims, and that their claims to territorial autonomy were baseless.

Özkaya, Inayetullah Cemal (1971). *Le peuple arménien et les tentatives de rendre en servitude le peuple turc*. Istanbul: Institute for the Study of Turkey. 336 pp.

Shaw, Stanford J., and Shaw, Ezel Kural (1977). *History of the Ottoman Empire and Modern Turkey*. Vol. 2. Cambridge: Cambridge University Press. 518 pp.
The Shaws have created the archetype of revisionist and denial history relating to the Armenian genocide. In a few pages (200–205, 314–317), the authors work to reverse a century of historiography on the Armenian Question, portraying the Armenians as not victims but victimizers, the privileged rather than the oppressed. Their treatment of the Armenian massacres of 1894–1896 and of 1915 not only disguises the truth but transcends all previous levels of revisionism. They claim that after great patience, the Turkish government in 1915 found it necessary to "transport" Armenians living near the war zones to relocation centers (never identified as deserts), that everything possible was done to provide the affected population with food and supplies, and that trust funds were even established in the names of the deportees so that anyone using their properties in their absence would pay rent, which would be given to the deportees, along with the return of their properties, once the crisis had passed. The fact that such absurdities have been published by Cambridge University Press may be indicative of how far revisionist and denial literature has advanced. For a critique of Shaw's historical methodology, *see* Vryonis (1983).

Şimsir, Bilâl N. (1984). *The Deportees of Malta and the Armenian Question*. Ankara: Foreign Policy Institute.

Sonyel, Salahi, P. (1978). *Displacement of the Armenians: Documents*. Ankara: Turkish Historical Society. 13 pp. (text also in French and Turkish).
The author's introduction summarizes the arguments in revisionist literature:
"In the country which was in a struggle for life and death, some of our Armenian citizens, forgetting their citizenship, attempted to rise as a result of external agitations as well as the instigation and provocation of certain fanatical circles and planned to continue their actions during the war in spite of all the warnings".
"In the face of those facts, the Ottoman Empire planned to displace some of the Armenian citizens temporarily to other parts of the country, taking the most humane

measures, in order to ensure, at the rear front, the security of the Ottoman armies, fighting at various fronts, following the example of other countries which did the same in different periods of history. Although this is a historical fact, there are some people who claim that this event is a genocide and these are malicious persons who want to threaten world peace and especially to incite a conflict in the Middle East.''

Talaat Pasha (1921). Posthumous memoirs of Talaat Pasha. *Current History*, 15 (Nov.), 287–295.

Turkey, Foreign Policy Institute (1982). *The Armenian Issue in Nine Questions and Answers*. Ankara. 39 pp.

Turkey, Government of (1916). *Aspirations et agissements révolutionnaires des comités arméniens avant et après la proclamation de la constitution ottomane*. Constantinople. 416 pp.

Turkey, Government of (1916). *Vérité sur le mouvement révolutionnaire arménien et les mesures gouvernementales*. Constantinople. 15 pp.
These Turkish wartime publications were issued in response to the worldwide condemnation of the Armenian massacres. They were intended to demonstrate Armenian disloyalty and sedition and thereby to justify what were then claimed to be limited preventive measures. Repudiated at the time by the Allied powers, these arguments are being reiterated by contemporary Turkish officials and revisionist historians.

Turkey, Prime Ministry (1982). *Documents*. Ankara: Directorate General of Press and Information. 289 pp.

Turkey, Prime Ministry (1983). *Documents on Ottoman Armenians*. Ankara: Directorate General of Press and Information. 187 pp.
These two companion volumes include 142 documents from the period 1914–18. Most of the documents relate to Turkish–Armenian hostilities on the Caucasus front in 1918. By showing that the Russian Armenians were fighting against the Turks and were oppressing Muslims on their side of the line in 1918 (while at the same time leaving out documents and descriptions of the massacres of Armenians in the Ottoman Empire in 1915–16), the compilers of these documents create an anachronism in an attempt to deflect the charges against the Turkish government and to demonstrate that Armenian losses were linked with military action and insurrection. The documents that do relate to 1915 are largely military communiqués in which those Armenians who tried to resist deportation are referred to as ''rebels,'' ''bandits,'' or ''gangs.'' Even these carefully selected documents, however, include evidence of the wholesale removal of the Armenian population, contrary to recent claims that only the war zones were affected.
Many internal contradictions exist in these documents, as they do in Sonyel's pamphlet (1978), listed above.

Vryonis, Speros, Jr. (1983). Stanford J. Shaw, *History of the Ottoman Empire and Modern Turkey*: Volume 1 . . . A Critical Analysis, *Balkan Studies*, 24(1), 126 pp. Offprint published as a separate volume by the Institute for Balkan Studies, Thessalonika.

6

Genocide in the U.S.S.R.

James E. Mace

The question of genocide in the U.S.S.R. is inevitably connected with the policies of social engineering carried out under the leadership of Joseph Stalin from the late 1920s until his death in 1953. The main transformations of this period include the forced collectivization of agriculture on the basis of the liquidation of the kulaks as a class, rapid industrialization made possible by the lowering of real labor costs through the drastic reduction in the living standards of free workers and the extensive use of forced labor, the absolute stand- ardization of all spheres of intellectual activity and their strict subordination to state priorities, and the integration of a large and varied collection of national and religious groups into a Russocentric political structure. Moreover, a massive blood purge of real and imagined "enemies of the people" took place.

These transformations were accomplished only at the cost of millions of lives. For purposes of comparison, the 20 million Soviet deaths attributed to World War II and often cited as evidence of the tremendous sacrifice of the "Soviet peoples" in that war may well be exceeded by the number of lives claimed by the Soviet government itself in peacetime under Stalin.

There is no scholarly consensus on the total number of "unnatural deaths," that is, the number of individuals whose premature demise is attributable to state policies, under Stalin. Serious demographic estimates range from 9.1 million in 1926–39 (Maksudov, 1977) to over 28.6 million and perhaps as many as 32.4 million in 1929–49 (Rosenfielde, 1983). Part of the controversy hinges upon the reliability of the 1939 Soviet census, which is actually a summary of a census conducted less than two years after officials in charge of the 1937 census had been executed for their alleged participation in a plot to discredit Stalinist policies by deliberately undercounting the population. The fact that top census officials were shot for not finding enough people in 1937 and that the 1939 census has never been published in full would tend to indicate that the 1939 count, accepted as accurate by Maksudov, inflates the Soviet population to some extent. Even Rosenfielde's most outspoken critic (Wheatcroft, 1984) concedes that the 1939 census probably overcounted the Soviet population to some degree.

The mass murder of millions, however, does not necessarily indicate that genocide took place. Murder is a crime against individuals, even if it is indiscriminate and the number of its victims runs into the tens of millions. Genocide, by contrast, is a crime against humanity as such because it is an attempt to destroy an irreplaceable component of humanity, whether that component is racial, ethnic, national, or religious, and killing members of that group is only one of a number of actions defined as genocidal by international convention. An act or policy may be considered genocidal only if it directed against specific target groups with intent to destroy them, wholly or in part, as such.

The most obvious case of genocide in the U.S.S.R. is the deportation of whole nations during and immediately after World War II. Germans, Crimean Tatars, Kalmyks, Chechens, Ingushes, Meskhetians, Karachai, Balkarians, and Greeks were deported *in toto* because they were held to be collectively guilty (including infants and persons who served in the Red Army) of collaboration with the enemy in the World War II (Conquest, 1970; Nekrich, 1978). Mortality rates approaching 50 percent and the absence of any national cultural institutions in places of exile indicate that the deportations were carried out in a manner calculated to destroy the victimized groups as such. Indeed, such a policy of compulsory resettlement involving massive loss of life invites comparison with the massacre of Armenians in the Ottoman Empire.

These so-called "punished peoples" were not unique, since smaller and lesser-known groups were deported *en masse* and at times *in toto* as early as the first half of the 1930s, usually from border areas (Mironenko, 1958; Ammende, 1984). During the Great Purge of the late 1930s, smaller urban minorities were also arrested as groups and sent for forced labor (Weissberg, 1951).

The famine of 1932–33 poses particular problems from the standpoint of internationally accepted definitions of genocide, since its focus was geographic, rather than discriminatory against specific groups within a given area, and it was clearly not an attempt to destroy all members of a given group. Rather, as this writer has argued, its national and ethnic target (i.e. genocidal nature) must be inferred from the clarity with which it was geographically focused against areas containing target populations and from the particularly harsh policies of the Soviet authorities in the national sphere as applied to the main victimized group, the Ukrainians (Mace, 1984b, c).

With the famine and other policies that have been argued to have been genocidal, the issue of intent is particularly difficult because the Soviet state, including Stalin, decreed a massive denial of everyday reality from the very pinnacle of authority to the lowest level of execution and victimization. When a

Ukrainian official at the height of the famine confronted Stalin with the situation, the latter accused him of spinning fictions. And, as survivors often state, starving villagers themselves were accused of engaging in counterrevolutionary propaganda if they mentioned that they or their neighbors were hungry (*Black Deeds*, 1953–55). As for Stalin himself, he not only denied reality and insisted upon such denial from subordinates, he seemed to be so obsessed with avoiding responsibility for actions that he often avoided giving direct orders, confining himself to saying thus and so was a problem, then punishing the subordinate if his wishes were not carried out or shifting blame on to the subordinate if the given action proved counterproductive (Souvarine, 1981). In such circumstances, subordinates might well be unaware as to the rationale for a given action or the official reason might not be the real one. We have little choice, in such a situation, but to attempt to extrapolate intent from circumstantial evidence.

Another thorny problem connected with the famine of 1933 is whether the other main target group, aside from the Ukrainians, was a victim of genocide. Unlike the Ukrainians, who received certain limited cultural and political concessions until the 1930s, the Cossacks received no official recognition by Soviet authorities after the abolition of their autonomous Soviet republics in the early 1920s. Indeed, even the very name "Cossack" was banned by a decree of 1923 (Glaskow, 1958). In the early 1930s entire settlements were often deported, and the area was targetted for famine in 1932–33. Clearly, there was an attempt to destroy the group as such. But the problem arises in connection with whether they were an ethnic group, and thus protected by the genocide convention, or a social group, and therefore not falling within the definition of genocide. In some ways a military caste and in other ways possessing a sense of cultural unity and a national ideology, the Cossacks seem to have been at least a protonational group, analogous perhaps to the Vlachs of the premodern Balkans in that they were defined in both ethnic and social terms.

Religious groups such as the Buddhists, the Ukrainian Autocephalous Orthodox, Ukrainian (Uniat) Catholic, and Belorussian Autocephalous Orthodox were also destroyed, or attempts were made to destroy them, as such. In these cases, destruction was accomplished or attempted not so much through mass murder—except of clergy and recalcitrants among the faithful—as through forced liquidation, closing of religious establishments, and the destruction of institutional frameworks. These religions were without exception connected with nationality (Buddhism with the Kalmyks mainly) and discriminatory religious policy was certainly a function of nationality policy. In the sense that the genocide convention lists inflicting mental or bodily harm upon members of a group with intent to destroy it as a genocidal act, these groups may be considered to have been victims of genocide, if only because the suppression of a religion cannot avoid inflicting severe mental harm upon those who have faith in that religion.

A variety of other groups have claimed to have been victims of genocide in the

U.S.S.R. because certain segments of their societies and aspects of their culture have been destroyed. Even members of the dominant nation and faith, the Russians (Dudin and Miller, 1958) and the Russian Orthodox (Teodorovich, 1958c), have made such claims. Some claims of partial destruction which involved exceptionally large-scale and brutal executions, arrests, and deportations, principally in areas annexed by the U.S.S.R. in 1939–44, may well have had genocidal aspects, but a definitive answer will have to await further refinement of the concept of genocide. The Katyn massacre of a large part of the Polish officer corps in 1940 (*Crime of Katyn*, 1965; Jagodziński, 1982) was indeed probably genocidal in that it represented a first step in an effort to extirpate any trace of Polish nationality (and Poles) from areas annexed by Stalin during his short-lived alliance with Hitler in 1939.

The problem of Soviet Jewry has been arbitrarily excluded from this analysis both because of its unique complexity and because the large volume of literature on the subject would necessitate a separate article. However, circumstantial evidence—particularly the alleged Doctor's Plot of 1952 and the campaign against "rootless cosmopolitans" (i.e. Jews) in Stalin's later years—points toward a massive assault against Soviet Jews which could well have led to genocide had Stalin lived but a few years longer.

The principal problem in defining genocide in the U.S.S.R. stems from the fact that Soviet ideological imperatives deal with class, and national and religious identities are strictly subordinated to the needs, real or perceived, of the State. In the Stalin period, the Soviet State did not hesitate to attempt the complete destruction of such identities and those who bore them, if they were perceived to be hindrances to the State's complete integration and subordination of all forces in society to Stalin's goals. Genocide took place as a mechanism of removing obstacles. And though the mass bloodletting stopped with Stalin's death, the machinery that made it possible remains in place and essentially unaltered.

Any views expressed in this chapter are solely those of the author, and do not necessarily represent either the views of the Ukraine Famine Commission or those of any of its members.

Bibliography

Abbe, James E. (1934). *I Photograph Russia*. New York: McBride. 324 pp.
   Freelance photographer in the U.S.S.R. during the Ukrainian famine relates difficulty in photographing even the most common scenes of everyday life and especially of the famine itself.

Agursky, Mikhail (1980). *Ideologiia natsional-bol'shevizma* (Ideology of National Bolshevism). Paris: YMCA. 321 pp.
   How Soviet Marxism assumed an *étatist* Russian national content.

Alexeyeva, Ludmilla (1985). *Soviet Dissent: Contemporary Movements for National,*

Religious and Human Rights. Middletown, CT: Wesleyan University Press. 521 pp. [Translated from Russian]
  Useful source on the subsequent fate of groups victimized under Stalin.

Ammende, Ewald (1984). *Human Life in Russia*. Cleveland: Zubal. 319 pp. [First published in England in 1936 and in Vienna in German in 1935]
  Important work by the head of Interconfessional Relief Committee, appointed by Cardinal Innitzer of Vienna in 1933. Primarily about the Ukrainian famine, it also contains information not otherwise available on the 1930s deportations of Poles, Finns, and others from border areas, foreshadowing the more massive deportations of the 1940s.

Anders, Władisław (1949). *Katyn*. Paris: Editions France-Empire. 349 pp. [subsequently published in various languages]
  Massacre of Polish officer corps by the Soviets in 1940 following partition of the Polish Republic between Hitler and Stalin.

Arbakov, Dorzha (1958). The Kalmyks. In *Genocide in the U.S.S.R.*, pp. 30–35.
  Deported in their entirety with high mortality, remnants of the Kalmyk nation were later rehabilitated and allowed to return.

Avtorkhanov, A. (1952). *Narodoubiistvo v S.S.S.R.: ubiistvo chechenskogo naroda* (Genocide in the U.S.S.R.: the murder of the Chechen people). Munich: Svobodnyi Kavkaz. 69 pp.
  Background and accomplishment of the Soviet deportation of the entire Chechen–Ingush nation.

Avtorkhanov, A. (1960). Forty years of Sovietization of Chechen–Ingushia. *Caucasian Review*, 10.
  Summarizes 1952 Russian-language account.

Balinov, Shamba (1958). The Kalmyk Buddhists. In *Genocide in the U.S.S.R.*, pp. 193–196.
  Complete destruction of Buddhist monkhood and of organized Buddhism by the Soviet state.

Bira, Mirza (1958). The Azerbaidzhanis. In *Genocide in the U.S.S.R.*, pp. 63–76.
  Partial destruction.

The Black Deeds of the Kremlin: A White Book (1953; 1955). Toronto: DOBRUS and SUZERO. 2 vols.
  The most extensive collection of eye-witness and other materials on the Ukrainian famine and related events, published by U.S. and Canadian organizations of famine survivors.

Bociurkiw, Bohdan (1984). *Ukrainian Churches under Soviet Rule: Two Case Studies*. Cambridge, MA: Ukrainian Studies Fund. 74 pp.
  Reprints two articles by the leading authority on the forced liquidation of the Ukrainian Autocephalous Orthodox and Uniate Catholic Churches, attempts to destroy religious groups as such.

Bolubash, Anna (1978–79). The Great Ukrainian Famine as an instrument of Russian nationalities policy. *Ukrainian Review*, 26(4), 11–23; 27(1), 31–59.
  Perceptive treatment of basic issue.

Carynnyk, Marco (1983). The famine *The Times* couldn't find. *Commentary*, 76 (November), 32–40.
Based largely on Crowl's monograph, treats Walter Duranty's role in concealing the Ukrainian famine.

Chamberlin, William Henry (1934). *Russia's Iron Age*. Boston: Little, Brown. 400 pp.
By a *Christian Science Monitor* correspondent in Moscow who reported frankly about the famine. *See also* his series of articles in *The Monitor*, 28 May–18 June 1934.

Chamberlin, William Henry (1935). Soviet taboos. *Foreign Affairs*, 140, 432–435.
Reporting the famine was taboo to the Western press.

Chub, Dmytro (pseudonym of D. Nytczenko) (1984). *Vidlunnia velykoho holodu v spohadakh ochevidtsiv i v ukrains'kii literaturi* (Echo of the Great Famine in eyewitness memoirs and Ukrainian literature). Toronto: Kiev Printers. 16 pp.
Useful survey of literature on Ukrainian famine.

Comité Central des Organisations Ukrainiennes en France (1983). *1933–1983: 50ème anniversaire de la famine—génocide en Ukraine*. Paris: CCOUF (mimeographed). 2 vols.
Volume 1 reprints French press coverage of the famine in the 1930s and selected documents. Volume 2 contains press coverage of fifty years afterwards.

Committee on Agriculture, Nutrition and Forestry. U.S. Senate (1984). *Collectivization and Its Impact on the Ukrainian Population and on Soviet Agriculture: Hearing*. Washington, DC: GPO. 124 pp.
Concerning the 15 November 1983 Senate committee hearing on the Ukrainian famine.

Conquest, Robert (1968). *The Great Terror: Stalin's Purge of the Thirties*. New York: Collier. 844 pp.
Definitive treatment on a subject which, while not in itself genocidal, is essential background for issues of group victimization.

Conquest, Robert (1970). *The Nation Killers: The Soviet Deportation of Nationalities*. New York: Macmillan. 222 pp. [First published in 1960 as *Soviet Deportations of Nationalities*]
Along with Nekrich (1978), the definitive treatment of the deportation in the 1940s of Soviet Germans, Kalmyks, Crimean Tatars, Karachai, Chechens, Ingushi, Balkarians, Meskhetians, and Soviet Greeks, all on charges of collaboration with the Germans in World War II. Mortality rates of nearly 50 percent invite comparison with the Armenian genocide in the Ottoman Empire.

Conquest, Robert (1986). *The Harvest of Sorrow: Soviet Collectivization of Agriculture and the Terror Famine*. London: Hutchinson. 384 pp.
The most extensive scholarly account of the Soviet man-made famine of 1932–33 and its background.

Conquest, Robert; Dalrymple, Dana; Mace, James; and Novak, Michael (1984). *The Man-Made Famine in Ukraine*. Washington, DC: American Enterprise Institute. 39 pp. (AEI Studies No. 404.)
Round-table discussion among scholars of the subject.

The Crime of Katyn: Facts and Documents (1965). London: Polish Cultural Foundation. 303 pp.
Documents on the Soviet massacre of the Polish officer corps.

The Crime of Moscow in Vynnytsia (1952). Edinburgh: Scottish League for European Freedom. 32 pp.
Mass graves in Ukraine uncovered during World War II.

Crossman, Richard (Ed.) (1950). *The God That Failed*. New York: Harper & Row. 248 pp. (published in many editions).
Koestler's essay contains an interesting eyewitness account of the Ukrainian famine.

Crowl, James William (1982). *Angels in Stalin's Paradise: Western Reporters in Soviet Russia, 1917 to 1937, A Case Study of Louis Fischer and Walter Duranty*. Washington, DC: University Press of America. 224 pp.
Best study to date on the role of Western reporters in aiding Soviet official denials of famine in 1932–33.

Czapski, Jozef (1946). *The Mystery of Katyn*. Bombay: Indo-Polish Library. 59 pp.
Soviet massacre of the Polish officer corps in the Katyn Forest in 1940.

Dalrymple, Dana (1964). The Soviet famine of 1932–34. *Soviet Studies*, 15(3), 250–284.
First scholarly study of the Ukrainian famine by a Western sovietologist.

Dalrymple, Dana (1965). The Soviet famine of 1932–34: some further references. *Soviet Studies*, 16(4), 471–474.
Cites testimony of psychologist William Horsley Gannt, told by Soviet public health officials that famine mortality might have reached 15 million in 1932–33.

Death at Katyn (1944). New York: National Committee of Americans of Polish Descent. 48 pp.
Early account of the Soviet massacre of Polish officers.

Deker, Nikolai K. (1958). The meaning of genocide. In *Genocide in the U.S.S.R.*, pp. 1–2.
Early attempt to apply genocide convention to Stalin's policies.

Djabagui, Vassan-Ghiray (1955). Soviet nationality policy and genocide. *Caucasian Review*, 1, 71–80.
Stalin's deportation of whole nationalities involved the death of almost half their population in some instances, and was genocidal.

Dolot, Miron (pseudonym) (1984). *Who Killed Them and Why?* Cambridge, MA: Ukrainian Studies Fund. 34 pp.
Famine survivor tries to analyze the Ukrainian famine.

Dolot, Miron (1985). *Execution by Hunger: The Hidden Holocaust*. New York: Norton. 231 pp.
The extensive individual eye-witness account of the Ukrainian famine.

Dór, Remy (1976). Orature du nord-est Afghan. *Turkica*, 8(1), 87–116.
Text of "Balchibek" (Song of Abdul Satar), a Kirgiz epic of Bolshevik oppression, brought to Afghanistan by refugees *c.* 1935.

Dudin, Leo, and Miller, Michael (1958). The Russians. In *Genocide in the U.S.S.R.*, pp. 111–126.
Claims partial destruction.

Duranty, Walter (1935). *I Write As I Please*. New York: Simon & Schuster, 347 pp.
Best-seller by a *New York Times* correspondent who helped suppress the news of famine.

Duranty, Walter (1944). *U.S.S.R.: The Story of Soviet Russia*. Philadelphia: J.B. Lippincott.
Belatedly admits the extent of the 1933 famine after years of denial.

Dushnyk, Walter (1983). *50 Years Ago: The Famine Holocaust in Ukraine*. New York: World Congress of Free Ukrainians. 56 pp.
Commemorative pamphlet citing scholarly literature.

Dyadkin, Iosif (1983). *Unnatural Deaths in the U.S.S.R., 1928–1954*. New Brunswick, NJ, and London: Transaction Books, 63 pp. [Translation]
Dissident Russian demographic study concludes that Stalin killed around 20 million Soviet citizens.

Echanges: Revue Franco-Ukrainienne (1983), 54–55. Paris: l'Association Franco-Ukrainienne.
Special issue of eight articles on the Ukrainian famine of 1933.

Fainsod, Merle (1958). *Smolensk under Soviet Rule*. New York: Vintage Russian Library. 485 pp.
Classic study based on captured Soviet archive taken from Germans. Cites reports on local response to Ukrainian refugees from the famine in 1933 (p. 267) and an order to resettle several Jewish families to Jewish collective farms in the Ukrainian steppe, which had been depopulated by the 1932–33 famine (p. 444).

La famine en U.R.S.S. (1933). *Cilac*, 15 August, 141–152.
French rightists criticize Edouard Herriot for refusing to see famine on his visit to Ukraine.

First Victims of Communism: A White Book on Religious Persecution in Ukraine (1953). Rome. 115 pp.
Official church report on the Soviet attempt to destroy the Ukrainian Catholic (Uniate) Church by forced liquidation.

Fitzgibbon, Louis (1971). *Katyn: A Crime Without Parallel*. London: Tom Stacey Ltd. 285 pp.
Soviet execution of thousands of Polish officers.

Fitzgibbon, Louis (1972). *The Katyn Cover-Up*. London: Tom Stacey Ltd. 185 pp.
Documents on the Katyn massacre.

Fitzgibbon, Louis (1977). *Katyn Massacre*. London: Corgi, 252 pp.

Gaev, Arkady (1958). Genocide, the Inevitable Concomitant of Soviet Communism. In *Genocide in the U.S.S.R.*, pp. 16–19.

Galay, Nikolay (1958). Political Groups. In *Genocide in the U.S.S.R.*, pp. 217–228.

Ganzha, I.F.; Slin'ko, I.I.; and Shostak, P.V. (1963). Ukrainskoe selo na puti k sotsializmu (Ukrainian village on the path to socialism). In Danilov, V. (Ed.), *Ocherki istorii kollektivizatsii sel'skogo khoziaistva v soiuznykh respublikakh* (Sketches on the history of the collectivization of agriculture in the Union republics), pp. 151–223. Moscow: Gospolitizdat.
 Still the best Soviet account of collectivization in Ukraine, containing some rather startling admissions about the famine.

Genocide in the U.S.S.R.: Studies in Group Destruction (1958). Munich: Institute for the Study of the U.S.S.R. 280 pp.
 Still the classic collection on the issue. Individual chapters are listed in this bibliography under their authors' names.

Glaskow, W.G. (1958). The Cossacks as a group. In *Genocide in the U.S.S.R.*, pp. 242–252.
 Glaskow, Ataman-President of the Supreme Representation of Cossacks in Exile, considers the Cossacks to be a nation. If indeed they are, they clearly were victims of genocide.

Glowinskyi, Eugen A. (1958a). The Western-Ukrainian Greek Catholic (Uniat) Church. In *Genocide in the U.S.S.R.*, pp. 177–180.
 Destruction of a religious group through forced liquidation.

Glowinskyi, Eugen A. (1958b). The Western Ukrainians. In *Genocide in the U.S.S.R.*, pp. 147–154.
 Mass arrests and deportations after the Hitler–Stalin Pact and from 1944 on.

Goldelman, Solomon (1958). The Jews. In *Genocide in the U.S.S.R.*, pp. 94–110.
 Partial destruction.

The Great Famine in Ukraine: The Unknown Holocaust (1983). Jersey City, NJ: Svoboda Press. 88 pp.
 Contents: Omeljan Pritsak, Foreword; James Mace, "The man-made famine of 1932–33;" Myron Kuropas, "America's 'red decade' and the great famine cover-up;" Marco Carynnyk, "Malcolm Muggeridge on Stalin's famine;" "Eyewitness recollections;" "Dissidents on the famine."

Grigorenko, Petro (1982). *Memoirs.* New York: Norton. 462 pp.
 Former Soviet general turned dissident and now in the West writes about the Ukrainian famine in Chapter 4.

Grudzinska-Gross, Irena, and Gross, Jan Tomasz (Eds.) (1981). *War through Children's Eyes: The Soviet Occupation of Poland and the Deportations, 1939–1941.* Stanford: Hoover Institution Press. 260 pp.
 Stalin's initial collaboration with Hitler in World War II gave the U.S.S.R. the ethnically Lithuanian Vilnius region (shortly thereafter transferred to Lithuania), western Ukraine, and western Belorussia. From these areas an estimated 900,000 Poles, Ukrainians, Belorussians, Jews, and others were deported to Russia. Thousands of surviving Poles, including children, were released to Iran after Hitler turned on his erstwhile ally and Poles in the U.S.S.R. were allowed to form an army. This important source is compiled from accounts by Polish children in Iran during the war.

Haliy, M., and Novits'kyi, B. (1934). *Het' masku! Natsional'na polityka na Rad. Ukraini v svitli dokumentakh* (Away with the mask! Nationality policy in Sov. Ukraine in light of the documents). Prague and L'viv: Všetečka. 128 pp.
   Valuable source on the famine and suppression of Ukrainian national self-assertion *c*. 1933, using extensive quotations from the Soviet press.

Haliy, Mykola (1958). The 25th anniversary of the great famine in Ukraine. *Ukrainian Quarterly*, 16(3), 204–214.
   Contains useful Soviet material.

Harvard University Refugee Interview Project.
   Unpublished transcripts of interviews with displaced persons, housed in the Harvard Russian Research Center and containing material on virtually all aspects of Soviet policy under Stalin. File 12 is most useful on the Ukrainian famine.

Holubnychy, Vsevolod (1979). The causes of the famine of 1932–33. *Meta*, 2(2), 22–24. [Translated from 1958 Ukrainian version]
   Marxist analysis, concentrating on economic factors leading the Soviet authorities to seize the 1932 harvest in Ukraine.

Hryshko, Wasyl (1983). *The Ukrainian Holocaust of 1933*. Toronto: Bahrany Foundation. 165 pp. [Translated from Ukrainian]
   The author, a famine survivor, bases his study primarily on Soviet materials. While anti-Soviet, his perspective is that of left-wing socialism, reflecting the views of the Ukrainian Revolutionary–Democratic Party, of which he has long been a leading member.

The hunger revolt in northern Caucasia (1933). *Literary Digest*, 28 January, 12.
   Virtually the only published account of the revolt of the Ukrainian-speaking Kuban Cossacks against State grain seizures in 1932–33.

Imniashvili, Nikolaus (1958). The Georgians. In *Genocide in the U.S.S.R.*, pp. 89–93.
   Partial destruction.

Ingilo, Ralph, and Uratadze, George (1958). The Georgian Autocephalic Orthodox Church. In *Genocide in the U.S.S.R.*, pp. 165–171.
   Partial destruction.

Istoriia kolektyvizatsii sil'skoho hospodarstva v Ukrains'kii R.S.R., 1917–1937 rr.: Zbirnyk dokumentiv i materialiv u tr'okh tomakh (History of the Collectivization of Agriculture in the Ukrainian S.S.R., 1917–1937: A Collection of Documents in Three Volumes) (1962–1971). Kiev: Akademiia Nauk U.R.S.R. 3 vols.
   Standard Soviet Ukrainian collection of documents on the collectivization of agriculture. An essential, if tendentious, source for the study of the Ukrainian famine.

Jagodziński, Zdisław (1982). *The Katyn Bibliography*. London: Polish Combatants Association. 48 pp.
   Lists 496 items in various languages on the Katyn Forest massacre of thousands of Polish officers by the Soviets in 1940.

Kabysh, Simon (1958). The Belorussians. In *Genocide in the U.S.S.R.*, pp. 77–88.
   Partial destruction of a national group.

Kaelas, Aleksander (1950). *Human Rights and Genocide in the Baltic States.* Stockholm: Estonian Information Centre. 57 pp.
Partial destruction through arrests, deportations, executions, etc.

Kalynyk, O. (1955). *Communism: The Enemy of Mankind.* London: Ukrainian Youth Association. 144 pp. [Translated from Ukrainian]
Contains authentic archival documents from the Krynychiansk *raion* relating to the Ukrainian famine. The original documents may be consulted with the permission of the Shevchenko Scientific Society in New York. A microfilm of the documents is on permanent loan to Columbia University as "Ukrainian Famine of 1933."

Kantemir, Ali (1958). The Moslems. In *Genocide in the U.S.S.R.*, pp. 197–202.
Partial destruction, obviously unsuccessful given current growth.

Karatnycky, Nadya (Ed.) (1985). *Holod na Ukraini, 1932–1933* (Famine in Ukraine, 1932–1933). Munich: Suchasnist'. 143 pp.
Selected articles on the Ukrainian famine.

Karcha, Ramazan (1956). Genocide in the North Caucasus. *Caucasian Review*, 2, 74–84.
Deportations of the Karachai, Balkars, Chechen–Ingush, etc. in their entirety, and mortality of nearly 50 percent.

Karcha, Ramazan (1957). The restoration of the liquidated republics and the rehabilitation of the deported peoples. *Caucasian Review*, 5, 41–46.
The 1957 rehabilitation with right to return affected the surviving Chechen–Ingush, Karachai, Balkars, and Kalmyks, but not the Meskhetians, Crimean Tatars, and Germans.

Karcha, Ramazan (1958). The peoples of the north Caucasus. In *Genocide in the U.S.S.R.*, pp. 36–48.
Updated version of Karcha (1956).

Khrushchev, Nikita (1970). *Khrushchev Remembers.* Boston: Little, Brown. 639 pp.
Khrushchev's frank testimony on the Ukrainian famine is on pp. 73–74.

Kirimal, Edige (1958). The Crimean Turks. In *Genocide in the U.S.S.R.*, pp. 20–29.
Deportation of the entire nation.

Koestler, Arthur (1945). *The Yogi and the Commissioner and Other Essays.* New York: Macmillan. 247 pp.
Eyewitness account of the Ukrainian famine on pp. 136–138.

Kopelev, Lev (1980). *The Education of a True Believer.* New York: Harper & Row. 328 pp.
Sent to the Ukrainian countryside in 1933 to help collect grain, the author gives a valuable analysis of how he and his companions were able to dehumanize the victims of the famine so as to be able to carry out grain seizures from a dying populace.

Kostiuk, Hryhory (1960). *Stalinist Rule in the Ukraine, 1929–1939: A Study in the Decade of Mass Terror.* London: Atlantic Books. 162 pp.
Still the best study of the political context in which the famine of 1933 took place.

Kravchenko, Victor (1946). *I Chose Freedom: The Personal and Political Life of a Soviet Official.* New York: Scribner's. 496 pp.

One of the best memoirs ever written about Stalin's U.S.S.R., used extensively for Hannah Arendt's *Origins of Totalitarianism*. Chapters 8 and 9 deal with the collectivization of agriculture and famine, which the author witnessed at close hand in Ukraine.

Kravchenko, Victor (1950). *I Chose Justice*. New York: Scribner's. 493 pp.
When a pro-Soviet French publication called Kravchenko a liar, he sued and won. This book, based on trial testimony, includes several eyewitness accounts of the Ukrainian famine of 1933.

Krawchenko, Bohdan (1982). The Great Famine of 1932–33 in the Soviet Ukraine. *One World*, 20(1), 17–23.
Concise survey from special genocide issue of the journal of the Social Studies Council of the Alberta (Canada) Teachers' Association.

Krawchenko, Bohdan (1984). The man-made famine of 1932–33 in Soviet Ukraine. *Conflict Quarterly*, 4(2), 29–39.
By one of the leading Canadian–Ukrainian social scientists.

Krawchuk, Andrii (1983). Protesting against the famine: the statement of the Ukrainian Catholic bishops in 1933. *Journal of Ukrainian Studies*, 8(2) (Winter), 59–62.
Text translated from Ukrainian with introductory comments.

Kvitovs'kyi-Kvitka, Denys (1968). *Represii v Ukraini v svitli mizhnarodnoi konventsii pro zlochyn genotsydu* (Repression in Ukraine in light of the International Convention on the Crime of Genocide). Toronto: New Pathway. 31 pp.
Ukrainian famine and related repressions as genocide.

Lang, Harry (1935). Series of articles in *New York Evening Journal*, 15–23 April.
Editor of New York *Jewish Daily Foreword* went to Ukraine and wrote about famine upon return. Translated from *Der Forvaerts*.

Lebed, Andrei (1958a). Destruction of national groups through compulsory migration and resettlement. In *Genocide in the U.S.S.R.*, pp. 6–8.
Stalin's mass deportations of whole nations as genocide.

Lebed, Andrei (1958b). Genocide as a means of creating a unified socialist nation. In *Genocide in the U.S.S.R.*, pp. 3–5.
Soviet nationalities policy and genocide.

Letgers, Lyman H. (1984). The Soviet Gulag: is it Genocidal? In Charny, Israel W. (Ed.), *Toward the Understanding and Prevention of Genocide: Proceedings of the International Conference on the Holocaust and Genocide*, pp. 60–66. Boulder, CO, and London: Westview Press.
Discusses difficulties in classifying Soviet mass murder as genocide and concludes that the failure so to classify some part of it would lead to the weakening of genocide as a juridical concept.

Lewin, Moshe (1974). 'Taking grain': Soviet policies of agricultural procurement before the war. In *Essays in Honour of E.H. Carr*, pp. 281–323. n.p.: Archon.
Procurement policies created the Ukrainian famine, but on the subject of the famine itself the author merely reiterates Dalrymple.

Liubchenko, Arkadii (1943). Ioho taiemnytsia (His secret). *Novi dni*, 2(5), 4–5.
A close friend recalls the last days of Mykola Khvyl'ovyi, the leading Ukrainian Soviet writer who committed suicide to protest the famine of 1933.

Liubchenko, Arkadii (1948). Mykola Khvyl'ovyi i holod na Ukraini (Mykola Khvyl'ovyi and the famine in Ukraine). *Shliakh molodi*, 2(4–5), 3–7.
Later, expanded version of the above, evidently unfinished.

Liutarevych, Pavlo (1955). Tsyfry i fakty pro holod v Ukraini (Figures and facts on the famine in Ukraine). *Ukrains'kyi Zbirnyk*, 2, 80–98.
Based on archival documents from the Chornukhy district, Poltava *oblast*.

Lorimer, Frank (1946). *The Population of the Soviet Union: History and Prospects.* Geneva: League of Nations. 289 pp.
Classic study of Soviet demographic trends, which underestimates mortality because of its conservative estimate of deaths at the top and bottom of the age structure, groups which would have been most vulnerable to famine.

Lykho, P.S. (pseudonym) (1958). Soviet rule at close quarters: the work of the party in a typical *raion* in the Ukraine, 1921–41. *Ukrainian Review*, 6, 126–169. [Translated from *Ukrains'kyi Zbirnyk* (1957), 8, 99–172]
A rare cache of Soviet archival documents which the Soviets left behind in 1941 from the Chornukhy district, Poltava *oblast*.

Lyons, Eugene (1937). *Assignment in Utopia.* New York: Harcourt Brace. 658 pp.
The author was Moscow correspondent for the Associated Press during the Ukrainian famine.

Mace, James E. (1983a). *Communism and the Dilemmas of National Liberation: National Communism in Soviet Ukraine, 1918–1933.* Cambridge, MA: Harvard Series in Ukrainian Studies. 334 pp.
Political background of the famine of 1933 and brief treatment of it in connection with the suppression of Ukrainian national self-assertion in 1933.

Mace, James E. (1983b). The Ukrainian Komitety Nezamozhnykh Selyan and the structure of Soviet rule in the Ukrainian countryside, 1920–1933. *Soviet Studies*, 25(4), 487–503.
On the role of the KNS as the regime's principal support organization in the Ukrainian countryside before and during the famine of 1933.

Mace, James E. (1984a). A case of genocide. *Quadrant*, April, 55–58.
Excerpt from Congressional testimony on the Ukrainian famine.

Mace, James E. (1984b). Famine and nationalism in Soviet Ukraine. *Problems of Communism*, 33(3), 37–50.
Attempts to place the 1933 famine within the context of Soviet nationalities policy. *See also* discussion of the article between the author and S.G. Wheatcroft in *POC*, 34(2), 132–138.

Mace, James E. (1984c). The man-made famine of 1933 in the Soviet Ukraine: what happened and why? In Charny, Israel W. (Ed.), *Toward the Understanding and Prevention of Genocide: Proceedings of the International Conference on the Holocaust and Genocide*, pp. 67–83. Boulder, CO, and London: Westview Press.

Brief introduction to the Ukrainian famine as a function of Soviet nationality policy, an attempt to destroy a nation as such by bringing about the death of roughly 20 percent of its number, destroying its elites, and sanitizing its national culture.

Mackiewicz, Josef (1951). *The Katyn Wood Murders*. London: Hollis & Carter. 252 pp.
Katyn Forest massacre of Polish officers by the Soviets in 1940.

Makohon, Pavlo (1983). *Witness: Memoirs of the Famine of 1933 in Ukraine*. Toronto: Anabasis. 89 pp. [Translated from Ukrainian]
Eyewitness account by villager from the Dnipropetrovsk region.

Maksudov, Sergei (pseudonym) (1977). Perties subies par la population de l'U.R.S.S., 1918-1958. *Cahiers du Monde Russe et Soviétique*, 18(3), 223-266.
Rigorous attempt to determine how many people Stalin killed.

Maksudov, Sergei (1983). The geography of the Soviet famine of 1933. *Journal of Ukrainian Studies*, 8(2), 52-58. [Translated from Russian]
Demographic evidence of the famine's geography.

Malyi, V. (1952). *Selo Druha Korul'ka* (Village of Druha Korul'ka). Munich: Logos. 23 pp.
Eyewitness account of the Ukrainian famine of 1932-33.

Markus, Vasyl (1975). Religion and nationality: the Uniates of the Ukraine. In Bociurkiw, Bohdan, and Strong, John (Eds.), *Religion and Atheism in the U.S.S.R. and Eastern Europe*, pp. 101-122. London: Macmillan.
Banned by the Soviet government, the Uniate (Ukrainian Catholic) Church is both a religious group and an underpinning of national existence in Western Ukraine.

Martin, Jean, and Briquet, Pierre-E. (1934). *L'U.R.S.S. à Genève*. Geneva: Journal de Genève. 117 pp.
Compilation of press reports surrounding Soviet entry into the League of Nations, including much material on the Ukrainian famine.

Martyrolohiia ukrains'kykh tserkov (Martyrology of Ukrainian Churches) (1985-   ). Baltimore: Smoloskyp. 3 vols.
Two volumes are out:
Vol. 1: *Ukrains'ka pravoslavna tserkva* (The Ukrainian Orthodox Church). Baltimore and Toronto: Smoloskyp, 1987. 1,029 pp.
Vol. 2: *Ukrains'ka katolyts'ka tserkva* (The Ukrainian Catholic Church). Baltimore and Toronto: Smoloskyp, 1985. 839 pp.
These first two volumes document attempts to destroy the Ukrainian Autocephalous Orthodox and Uniate Catholic churches as such. A forthcoming third volume will cover the persecution of Protestant groups in Ukraine.

Massacre at Vinnitsia (1953). New York: Ukrainian Congress Committee of America. 16 pp.
Mass graves in Ukraine uncovered during German occupation.

Minority Rights Group (1980). *The Crimean Tatars, Volga Germans and Meskhetians: Soviet Treatment of Some National Minorities*. London: Minority Rights Group. (MRG Report No. 6.)
Concerns the three national groups that were deported *in toto* by Stalin and have never been allowed to return to their homelands.

Minority Rights Group (1981). *The Ukrainians and the Georgians*. London: Minority Rights Group. (MRG Report No. 50.)
Historical survey of Soviet treatment of two nations.

Minority Rights Group (1984). *Religious Minorities in the Soviet Union*. London: Minority Rights Group. (MRG Report No. 1.)
The sections on Ukrainian Catholics and Kalmyk Buddhists fit most fully the convention's definition of genocide.

Mironenko, Yuri (1958). Other national groups. In *Genocide in the U.S.S.R.*, pp. 55–57.
Deportations *in toto* of Soviet Greeks, Bulgars, Estonians outside Estonia, Izhors, and Vlepsy.

Mlynovets'kyi, R. (1958). *Holod na Ukraini v svitli uriadovykh danykh* (Famine in Ukraine in light of government data). Detroit. 60 pp.
Famine of 1933 as reflected in official data.

Motyl, Alexander J. (1983). The Great Ukrainian Famine. *American Spectator*, 16(8), 24–26.
Survey of recent work by R. Conquest and J. Mace.

Muggeridge, Malcolm (1933). The Soviets' war on the peasants. *Fortnightly Review*, 39, 558–564.
By a British reporter on the famine of 1933. Best of the Western observers.

Muggeridge, Malcolm (1934). *Winter in Moscow*. Boston: Little, Brown. 247 pp.
Muggeridge, Moscow correspondent of the *Manchester Guardian*, slipped his official shadowers, went to Ukraine at the height of famine, writes about it, and takes colleagues to task for failing to do likewise.

Muggeridge, Malcolm (1973). *Chronicles of Wasted Time*: Vol. 1 *The Green Stick*. New York: Morrow. 284 pp.
The section on the famine is a sort of key to his earlier, 1934 account.

Muggeridge, Malcolm (1983). "Hunger" is the word I heard most. *New Perspectives*, 19 February.
Interviewed by Marco Carynnyk about the Ukrainian famine in 1933.

Nekrich, Aleksandr (1978). *The Punished Peoples: The Deportation and Tragic Fate of Soviet Minorities at the End of the Second World War*. New York: Norton. 238 pp.
A basic work on Stalin's deportation of whole nations.

Oleskiw, Stephen (1983). *The Agony of a Nation: The Great Man-Made Famine in Ukraine, 1932–33*. London: National Committee to Commemorate the Fiftieth Anniversary of the Artificial Famine in Ukraine. 72 pp.
Commemorative pamphlet with foreword by Malcolm Muggeridge.

Orlov, Alexander (1953). *The Secret History of Stalin's Crimes*. New York: Random House. 366 pp.
Best memoir by a secret-police defector.

Pidhainy, Alexandra (1968). The Great Famine in the Ukraine, 1932–33: a bibliography. *New Review*, 8(3), 123–135.
Bibliography of sources in various languages.

Pidhainy, Alexandra (1973). The Great Famine in the Ukraine, 1932–1933: a bibliography. *New Review*, 13(4), 32–68.
More extensive than the 1968 version, but it deletes some items. For this reason, both versions should be consulted.

Pidhainy, Semen (1947). *Ukrainska intellihentsiia na Solovkakh* (The Ukrainian intelligentsia on the Solovki Islands). n.p.: Prometei. 93 pp.
Excellent source on the fate of prominent Ukrainian intellectuals arrested at the time of the famine, by a survivor who met them in the Solovki Islands camps.

Plyushch, Leonid (1977). *History's Carnival: A Dissident's Autobiography*. New York: Harcourt Brace Jovanovich. 429 pp.
Memoir of a former dissident whose manuscript on the famine was seized by the KGB. Some information about the study is herein.

Plyushch, Vasyl (1973). *Genocide of the Ukrainian people: the artificial famine in the Years 1932–33*. Munich: Institut für Bildungspolitik. 29 pp.
Not a rigorous study.

Poppe, Nicholas N. (1958). The Buddhists. In *Genocide in the U.S.S.R.* pp. 181–192.
Complete destruction of religious group.

Postanova TsK VKP(b) z 24 sichnia 1933 ta zavdannia bil'shovikiv Ukrainy (The 24 January 1933 decision of the All-Union Communist Party Central Committee and the task of Ukraine's Bolsheviks) (1933). *Bil'shovyk Ukrainy*, (3), 3–20.
Text and official commentary of the decision by which the Soviet central authorities at the height of the Ukrainian famine found the Ukrainian Communist authorities "criminally negligent" for their failure to meet grain quotas and took direct control of the Ukrainian republic apparatus. The single most important document for fixing responsibility for the Ukrainian famine.

Postyshev, P.P., and Kossior, S.V. (1933). *Soviet Ukraine Today*. New York: International Publishers. 116 pp. [Translated from Ukrainian]
Slightly sanitized versions of statements by the two top Communist officials in Ukraine immediately after the famine, outlining the "successes" attained in agriculture and nationality policy in 1933.

Potychnyj, Peter (1977). The struggle of the Crimean Tatars. In Kaminetsky, Ihor (Ed.), *Nationalism and Human Rights*, pp. 228–243. Littleton, CO: Association for the Study of Nationalities.
Exiled *in toto* by Stalin, the Crimean Tatars are still denied the right to return to the Crimea.

Pravoberezhnyi, F. (pseudonym of Pigido, Fedir) (1951). *8,000,000: 1933-i rik na Ukraini* (8,000,000: 1933 in Ukraine). Winnipeg: Kul'tura i Osvita. 83 pp.
Memoir and brief exposition of the famine of 1932–33.

Radziejowski, Janusz (1980). Collectivization in Ukraine in light of Soviet historiography. *Journal of Ukrainian Studies*, 9, 3–17.

Surveys post-Stalinist Soviet scholarship relating to the forced collectivization of agriculture and famine of 1932–33 in Ukraine. Extremely useful survey by Poland's leading specialist on interbellum Ukrainian communism.

Rosenfielde, Steven (1983). Excess mortality in the Soviet Union: a reconsideration of the demographic consequences of forced industrialization, 1929–1949. *Soviet Studies*, 35(3), 385–409.
   Argues that collectivization, famine, forced labor, and terror claimed the lives of 21.4–24.4 million adults and 7.2–8.0 million children in the period, thus exceeding the 20 million Soviet deaths attributed to World War II.

Rudnyts'ka, Milena (1958). Borot'ba za pravdu pro velykyi holod (Struggle for truth about the Great Famine). *Svoboda*, (134–152).
   Former deputy in the Polish Sejm on the West Ukrainian response to the man-made famine of 1932–33 in Soviet Ukraine.

Schmitz, Gerald (1982). *The Famine in the Ukraine, 1932–33: A Canadian Retrospective after Fifty Years*. Ottawa: Library of Parliament. 47 pp.
   Surveys English-language materials, emphasizing Canadian responses.

Select Committee on Communist Aggression, U.S. House of Representatives (1954). *Investigation of Communist Takeover and Occupation of Non-Russian Nations of the U.S.S.R.* Washington, DC: Government Printing Office. 370 pp.
   Testimony includes accounts of the Ukrainian famine along with deportations and executions in the Baltic states. Committee reports Nos. 4 and 14 contain further information.

Semenko, Iurii (Ed.) (1963). *Holod 1933 roku v Ukraini* (The famine of 1933 in Ukraine). Munich: Ukrains'kyi Selianyn. 79 pp.
   Important Ukrainian-language collection of eyewitness accounts of the Ukrainian famine of 1932–33.

Serbyn, Roman (1968). British public opinion and the famine in Ukraine. *New Review*, 8(3), 89–101.
   British responses to the famine of 1932–33.

Shimotomai, Nobuo (1983). A note on the Kuban Affair (1932–33): the crisis of kolkhoz agriculture in the north Caucasus. *Acta Slavica Iaponica*, 1, 39–56.
   One of the very few works on the famine of 1932–33 in the north Caucasus, with particular reference to the largely Ukrainian Kuban.

Siryk, Hryst'ko (1982–83). *Pid sontsem obezdolennykh* (Under the Sun of the Dispossessed). Toronto: Author. 3 vols.
   Memoir of collectivization and the man-made famine of 1932–33 in Ukraine. Volume 3 deals with the author's experiences as one of the great number of homeless orphans (*bezprizornie/bezprytul'ni*) who wandered the Soviet Union in the 1930s.

Slyn'ko, I.I (1961). *Sotsialistychna perebudova i technichna rekonstruktsiia sil's'koho hospodarstva Ukrainy (1927–1932 rr.)* (Socialist Transformation and Technical Reconstruction of Ukraine's Agriculture, 1927–1932). Kiev: Akademiia Nauk U.R.S.R. 326 pp.
   The section on grain procurement campaigns (pp. 281–303) is very useful on the extractive policies that brought about the famine.

Sodnom, Kol'dong (1984). *Sud'ba donskikh kalmykov, ikh very i dukhovenstva* (Fate of the Don Kalmyks, Their Faith and Clergy). U.S.A.: Author. 196 pp.
Documents the deportation of the Kalmykhs and the destruction of organized Buddhism in the Don region.

Solovey, Dmytro (Ed.) (1953). *The Golgotha of Ukraine: Eyewitness Accounts of the Famine in Ukraine Instigated and Fostered by the Kremlin in an Attempt to Quell Ukrainian Resistance to Soviet Russian National Enslavement of the Ukrainian People.* New York: Ukrainian Congress Committee of America. 44 pp.
Eyewitness accounts, taken from the longer Ukrainian version.

Solovey, Dmytro (1955). Ukrains'ka selo v rokakh 1931–33 (Ukrainian village in 1931–33. *Ukrains'kyi Zbirnyk*, 2, 64–79.
Study of the Ukrainian famine by one of the best émigré scholars of his generation.

Solovey, Dmytro (1963). On the thirtieth anniversary of the great man-made famine in Ukraine. *Ukrainian Quarterly*, 19(3–4).
Contains useful references to official Soviet materials.

Souvarine, Boris (1939). *Stalin: A Critical Survey of Bolshevism.* New York: Longman & Green. 690 pp.
First and in some ways still the best book on Stalin. The final chapter contains useful and long-neglected sources.

Souvarine, Boris (1981). Last conversation with Isaac Babel. *Dissent*, 28(3), 319–330.
Posthumously published, this sheds much light on Stalin's style of rule which allowed him to avoid responsibility and always retain the ability to shift blame on to subordinates.

Sova, H. (1948). *Holod na Ukraini 1933 roku* (Famine in Ukraine in 1933). Munich: Author. 14 pp.
Pamphlet by Ukrainian economist on the 1933 famine.

Stadnyuk, Ivan (1963). *People Are not Angels.* London: Monography. 238 pp.
Soviet historical novel that is quite frank about the famine, within the obvious limits.

Stepovyi, Iurko (1955). *Smikh kriz' sl'ozy: Povisti* (Laughter through Tears: Stories). Chicago: Filiia DOBRUSu. 68 pp.
Important source by a former Soviet journalist who took part in creating a Potemkin village for Edouard Herriot's visit to Ukraine at the height of the 1933 famine.

Supreme Lithuanian Committee of Liberation (1951). *Appeals to the United Nations on Genocide.* N.p.: Lithuanian Foreign Service. 80 pp.
Texts of appeals by the Lithuanian government in exile and of joint appeals of the three Baltic governments in exile, with three appendices consisting of statements by individuals who escaped Soviet persecution.

Suslyk, L.P. (1951). *Sumni spohady: 1933 rik na Poltavshchyni* (Sad memories: 1933 in the Poltava region). N.p.: Author. 29 pp.
Eyewitness account of the Ukrainian famine of 1932–33.

Svabe, Areds (1952). *Genocide in the Baltic States.* Stockholm: Latvian National Fund in the Scandinavian Countries. 50 pp.
Partial destruction through executions, arrests, and mass deportations.

Swianiewicz, Stanisław (1976) *W cieniu Katynia* (In the shadow of Katyn). Paris: Instytut Literacki. 359 pp.
   Concerning the Katyn massacre of the Polish officer corps in 1940.

Tachmurat, Murat and Berdimurat, Aman (1958). The Turkistanis. In *Genocide in the U.S.S.R.*, pp. 127–137.
   Claims partial destruction of Uzbeks, Kazakhs, Kirgiz and Tadzhiks, who were collectively known as Turkmen or Turkistanis before Soviet rule.

Teodorovich, Nadezhda (1958a). The Belorussian Autocephalic Orthodox Church. In *Genocide in the U.S.S.R.*, pp. 160–164.
   Complete destruction of a religious group by the Soviet State.

Teodorovich, Nadezhda (1958b). The Roman Catholics. In *Genocide in the U.S.S.R.*, pp. 211–216.
   Claims partial destruction.

Teodorovich, Nadezhda (1958c). The Russian Orthodox. In *Genocide in the U.S.S.R.*, pp. 203–210.
   Claims partial destruction. In reality, the Russian Orthodox Church was given the spoils from religious groups that really were destroyed, more than making up for what it lost in various antireligious campaigns.

Tillett, Lowell (1969). *The Great Friendship: Soviet Historians on the Non-Russian Nationalities*. Chapel Hill, NC: University of North Carolina Press. 468 pp.
   How history in the U.S.S.R. is used as a tool of national integration by creating and reinforcing the myth that the histories of non-Russian national groups culminate in their inclusion into the Russian Empire and Soviet Union.

Timoshenko, V.P. (1956). Soviet agricultural policy and the nationalities problem in the U.S.S.R. In *Report on the Soviet Union in 1956: A Symposium*, pp. 31–56. New York: Institute for the Study of the U.S.S.R.
   Crucial in assessing issues of genocide and group victimization in the U.S.S.R.: how social policies vary in application and impact relative to different national groups.

Torossian, Sarkis V. (1958a). The Armenians. In *Genocide in the U.S.S.R.*, pp. 58–62.
   Claims partial destruction.

Torossian, Sarkis V. (1958b). The Armenian Gregorian Church. In *Genocide in the U.S.S.R.*, pp. 155–159.
   Claims partial destruction.

Ukraina hyne z holodu: vidozva Ukrains'koho Zhinochnoho Soiuzu v Prazi do ukrains'koho hromadianstva vsikh krain svitu (1933) (Ukraine is dying of hunger: appeal of the Ukrainian Women's Union in Prague to Ukrainians of the world). Prague.
   Appeal to Ukrainian communities during the Great Famine of 1933.

Ukrainian Congress Committee of America (1973). *Soviet Russian Genocide in Ukraine—40th Anniversary of the Man-Made Famine: Memorandum to the Honorable Dr. Kurt Waldheim, Secretary General of the United Nations*. New York: UCCA. 8 pp.
   Memorandum on the 1933 famine and continued russification in Ukraine.

The Ukrainian holocaust: Alberta's survivors mark the Soviet destruction of 7 million people (1983). *Alberta Report*, 31 October, 28–33.
   Focuses on Canadian research and Alberta survivor Prof. Yar Slavutych.

Ulam, Adam B. (1973). *Stalin: The Man and His Era*. New York: Viking. 760 pp.
Standard biography.

U.S.S.R. Special Commission (1944). *Statement of Special Commission for the Estab-
lishment and Investigation of the Circumstances of the Shooting of Polish Officer
Prisoners of War, in the Katyn Forest by the German-Fascist Invaders*. Moscow: Foreign
Languages Publishing House. 39 pp.
Soviet denial of the Katyn massacre of Polish officer corps.

Vardys, Stanley (1971). The case of the Crimean Tatars. *Russian Review*, 30(2), 101–110.
The Crimean Tatars were deported *in toto* by Stalin and are still denied the right to
return.

Verbyts'kyi, M. (Ed.) (1952). *Naibil'shyi zlochyn Kremlia* (The Kremlin's Biggest
Crime). London: DOBRUS u Britanii. 94 pp.
Important collection of eyewitness accounts of the Ukrainian famine of 1933.

Voinov, Nicholas (pseudonym) (1955). *The Waif*. New York: Pantheon. 292 pp.
Memoir by one of the *bezprizornie*, the homeless children who wandered the
U.S.S.R. in the 1930s.

Vvedensky, George (1958). The Volga Germans and other German groups. In *Genocide
in the U.S.S.R.*, pp. 49–54.
The Volga Germans were exiled *in toto* with near 50 percent mortality and never
allowed to return.

Weissberg, Alexander (1951). *The Accused*. New York: Simon & Schuster. 518 pp.
Held for three years without trial in the Kharkiv GPU prison, the author observed
various population categories arrested during the Great Purge in the former Ukrainian
capital. Small minorities such as the Armenians in the city were arrested *in toto*.

Wells, Carveth (1933). *Kapoot: The Narrative of a Journey from Leningrad to Mount
Ararat in Search of Noah's Ark*. New York: McBride. 264 pp.
The author describes the Ukrainian famine.

Wheatcroft, S.G. (1982). Famine and factors affecting mortality in the U.S.S.R.: the
demographic crises of 1914–1922 and 1930–1933. *CREES Discussion Papers: Soviet
Industrialization Series*, 20. Birmingham, UK: University of Birmingham Centre for
Russian and East European Studies. 30 pp. and supplementary appendices.
Argues that the number of Stalin's victims is exaggerated, published in a format
where it is to be used only with the author's permission. Attacks Maksudov's higher
calculations and believes that even Soviet mortality estimates are "uninspired" and
exaggerated.

Wheatcroft, S.G. (1984). A note on Steven Rosenfielde's calculations of excess mortality
in the U.S.S.R., 1929–1949. *Soviet Studies*, 36(2), 277–281.
Attacks Rosenfielde (1983). The Wheatcroft–Rosenfielde controversy illustrates the
difficulties in quantifying the number of unnatural deaths in the Soviet Union under
Stalin.

Wittlin, Tadeusz (1965). *Time Stopped at 6:30. The Untold Story of the Katyn Massacre*.
Indianapolis: Bobbs-Merrill. 317 pp.
Stalin's massacre of the Polish officer corps.

Wójcicki, Bolesław, *Prawda o Katyniu* (The truth about Katyn). Warsaw: Czytelnik. 188 pp.
    Polish Communist version of the Katyn Massacre, supporting the Soviet denial.

Woropay, Olexa (1983). *The Ninth Circle: In Commemoration of the Victims of the Famine of 1933*. Cambridge, MA: Ukrainian Studies Fund. 62 pp.
    An agronomist in the Vinnytsia *oblast* during the famine of 1933, the author divides the narrative into what he personally saw and what he was able to collect from other eyewitnesses.

Yaremovich, Anthony (1978). Collectivization through famine. *Ukrainian Quarterly* 34(4), 349–362.
    Commemorative article on the Ukrainian famine.

Yurchenko, Alexander V. (1958a). Genocide through destruction of national culture and sense of nationality. In *Genocide in the U.S.S.R.*, pp. 8–15.
    On Soviet attempts to destroy self-assertive national groups by creating cultural conditions making it impossible to maintain their national distinctiveness.

Yurchenko, Alexander V. (1958b). The Ukrainian Autocephalous Orthodox Church. In *Genocide in the U.S.S.R.*, pp. 172–176.
    Complete destruction of a religious group through forced liquidation.

Yurchenko, Alexander V. (1958c). The Ukrainians. In *Genocide in the U.S.S.R.*, pp. 138–146.
    Ignores the famine, probably because of Russian émigré domination of the conference, but still claims partial destruction.

Zerkov, Mikhail (1958). Social groups. In *Genocide in the U.S.S.R.*, pp. 229–241.
    Destruction of social groups in the U.S.S.R., particularly the so-called kulaks and private traders.

7

The Cambodian Genocide

David Hawk

In 1950 Cambodia acceded to the Convention on the Prevention and Punishment of the Crime of Genocide. Democratic Kampuchea, as the Khmer Rouge renamed Cambodia, continues to be an officially recognized state, party to the Genocide Convention and bound by its standards and obligations.

As defined by the Genocide Convention, genocide is the intentional destruction in whole or in part of a national, ethnic, racial or religious group by means such as killings, serious bodily or mental harm, the conditions of life to which a group is subjected, the prevention of births within the group, or forcibly transferring children of one group to another group.

All told, it is reliably estimated that 1 to 2 million of Cambodia's 6 to 7 million people died in three and one half years from executions or from what the Genocide Convention terms the "conditions of life" to which they were subjected. This constitutes the partial destruction of the Cambodian national group itself.

In Cambodia groups of persons deemed by the Khmer Rouge leadership to have no place in the revolutionary social order were legally prohibited, sociologically dissolved, and, as necessary, physically liquidated. Groups were banned, or not recognized to exist in the Constitution of Democratic Kampuchea. The Khmer Rouge term for sociological dissolution was *khchatkhchay os roling*, which is translated "scatter them out of sight" or "scatter them to the last one." Of course in real life, entire groups of people cannot be simply legislated or defined out of existence and legal prohibition and sociological dissolution were accompanied by substantial physical liquidation.

Leadership elements of groups to be eradicated were executed, as were portions of the group that resisted dissolution. Many more died because of the extremely cruel conditions of life to which they were deliberately subjected:

combinations of induced starvation (food rations were withheld by the State and private food gathering was prohibited and often severely punished as "theft"); and untreated disease stemming from the dissolution of the preexisting medical system and the execution of many identifiable trained medical personnel because of their educational level or training abroad.

Groups singled out for eradication by the leadership of the ruling Communist Party of Kampuchea (the formal name for the Khmer Rouge) included Cambodia's preeminent religious group, the Buddhist monkhood, Cambodia's ethnic minorities, and the large portion of the Cambodian "national group" deemed to be tainted by "feudal," "bourgeois" or "foreign" influences.

The Complete Destruction of a Religious Group

The Khmer Rouge had an extraordinary animus toward all religions—which they considered to be uniformly "reactionary." This hatred fell most heavily on Buddhism, prior to 1975 Cambodia's state religion, and the Therevada Buddhist monkhood, a mendicant, celibate, contemplative and teaching religious order. Outside of the cities, from which the inhabitants had been evacuated, Buddhist temples, formerly the center of Cambodian village life, were destroyed or converted to secular use (warehouses, animal stables, prison-execution centers, etc.). Statues of Buddha, Buddhist literature and other religious relics and artifacts were desecrated or destroyed. Pali, the language of Khmer Buddhism, was prohibited, as were prayer, meditation and all other forms of worship.

The Khmer Rouge denounced the monks as "leeches and bloodsuckers" and within days of taking power the Buddhist monkhood was ordered to disband or disrobe—the Buddhist equivalent of disbarment or disordination in that in Therevada Buddhism, without his saffron robe the monk cannot be a monk. The leadership of the clergy, the most venerated monks and those who refused to disrobe were executed. All others, including the elderly, were ordered to perform manual labor (which was prohibited to the monkhood). The complete elimination of the Cambodian Buddhist monkhood (*Sangha*) was everywhere fully carried out as the Khmer Rouge consolidated their control over the provinces.

Prior to 1975 there were approximately sixty thousand monks. After 1979 fewer than three thousand had survived and returned to the site of their former temples. Many had been executed or died of forced labor and starvation. Others had been forced to marry (and hence to become ineligible for the clergy) or otherwise choose not to reveal their former identity and to remain in secular life. Most of the monks had disappeared and their fate cannot be traced.

The Substantial Destruction of an Ethnic Group

The Khmer Rouge similarly proclaimed ethnic minorities no longer to exist, and all indices of ethnicity such as language, dress, custom, festivals and ethnic holidays were prohibited. These prohibitions were extended to all minorities including ethnic Chinese, Vietnamese and Thai residing in Cambodia. Khmer Rouge publications proclaimed Cambodia to now be 99 per cent Khmer.

The deliberate and forceful eradication of ethnic groups fell most heavily on the "Cham," the remnants of the Kingdom of Champa on the central coastline of what is now Vietnam, who had migrated into Cambodia after the seventeenth century and settled largely as fishermen along Cambodia's rivers and the Tonle Sap lake. The Cham were Islamic in religion and lived apart from the Khmer in their own villages or neighborhoods. The Cham had their own language, hairstyle, costume, holiday and dietary and burial customs.

Cham villages were broken up and the Cham dispersed among the larger Khmer population. Many Cham religious and community leaders ("Haikim" and "Haji") were executed, and Cham were forced to eat pork—prohibited to Muslims—as evidence of "Khmerization." Some Cham villages resisted the suppression of their religious practice and their residential dispersion, but resistance led the Khmer Rouge to massacre entire villages. Perhaps as many as one-half of the Cham people did not survive Khmer Rouge rule. Some survivors remain in Cambodia, while many other Cham sought refugee status in Malaysia. A small number now reside in the U.S.A.

The Partial Destruction of the National Group

The Khmer Rouge also believed that, along with religious and ethnic groups, a substantial portion of the Cambodian "national group" itself was irremediably tainted by feudal, bourgeois, or foreign attitudes or associations. Using the language of "purification," the Khmer Rouge sought to identify and eliminate the tainted portions of the Cambodian people. Purging the population of bourgeois traits and associations is what the well known, shocking and precipitate evacuation of the cities and towns was intended to bring about. The former urbanities were explicitly defined to be without "rights." Many were literally worked to death, while others died from the rigors of extended migrations or forced marches under tropical conditions. The State controlled agricultural production and consumption, and food was restricted or withheld from the overworked population.

A shifting series of subgroups were successively targeted for liquidation as the revolution progressed from one state to the next. Close examination of the major massacres indicates that executions were, in these instances, directed not only at real, potential or presumed "political" enemies, but extended to the general population deemed tainted merely by virtue of having resided in areas formerly under the jurisdiction of "tainted" political groups.

There existed a nationwide system of prison–interrogation–execution centers of all levels of Khmer Rouge administration to identify those to be eliminated (who were routinely and systematically tortured into confessing to be "enemies" of the revolution). This nationwide system of execution centers culminated in the infamous "S21" facility, an extermination center where nearly twenty thousand were executed and from where there were only seven known survivors—prisoners whose skills were judged useful to the Khmer Rouge prison authorities.

As indicated earlier, it is reliably estimated that 1 to 2 million of Cambodia's 6 to 7 million people died. A slaughter of this magnitude constitutes the partial destruction of the Cambodian national group itself.

Accountability and Response

Even though it is widely known that gross and terrible human rights violations occurred in Cambodia (Democratic Kampuchea) under Khmer Rouge rule, the international community has never considered or condemned the Khmer Rouge genocide. While the U.N.'s official human rights experts specifically recognized the Cambodian situation to be the worst to have occurred since Nazism, the United Nations Commission on Human Rights pointedly avoided considering the reports of those experts. While the U.N. General Assembly frequently passes resolutions reconfirming the principles of the Genocide Convention and pledging cooperation among member states to oppose genocide, the General Assembly has never condemned the Cambodian genocide.

Those most responsible for the Cambodian genocide—the 1975-79 members of the Standing Committee of the Central Committee of the Communist Party of Kampuchea, the Khmer Rouge military commanders whose troops committed so much of the killing, those officials who oversaw, directed, and ran the nation-wide network of torture chambers, prison-execution centers and extermination facilities, etc.—continue to remain active in Cambodian and international political life. Based in enclaves along the Thai–Cambodia border, they conduct guerrilla war seeking to return to power in Phnom Penh. Neither the state of Democratic Kampuchea nor those individuals bearing responsibility for the genocide have been held accountable for their crimes under international law.

Introduction to the Literature and Definitions

There is a substantial and growing body of literature on the human, social, and cultural destruction that occurred in Cambodia (Democratic Kampuchea) under Khmer Rouge rule. Most of this literature has been written by journalists or Cambodia specialists with a background in political science or history. Very little of the present Cambodia literature deals with the concept of genocide as defined by law, or as defined by scholars who have reformulated the concept of genocide so as to compensate for some of the perceived inadequacies of the Convention on the Prevention and Punishment of the Crime of Genocide.

However there is, in the literature discussed below, ample primary and secondary discussion of the component parts of genocide as defined by the

Genocide Convention: the destruction in whole or in part of racial, religious, ethnic, or national groups, by such means as killings, mental or physical harm, the separation of children from parents, and deaths resulting from deliberately imposed conditions of life imposed on the group.

There has been some confusion over the application of the term "genocide" to the Cambodia under Khmer Rouge rule. The Khmer Rouge or Pol Pot massacres have been widely termed genocide in the commonplace use of the word as State-sponsored mass murder. But because the most widely known aspect of Khmer Rouge policy was the ceaseless physical liquidation of real, suspected, and imagined political opponents of the regime, there has been question about the application of the term "genocide" to the Cambodian massacres because the Genocide Convention excludes "political groups" from its coverage. The fact that under Khmer Rouge rule there was also substantial destruction of religious and ethnic groups is less widely known or sometimes subordinated to the general suffering of the population as a whole.

There has also been some confusion caused by the use of the term "autogenocide" to describe the Cambodian massacres. But "autogenocide" does not differ from what the Genocide Convention defines as the "partial" destruction of the "national" group. There is nothing in either the language of the Convention or the legislative history of the Convention to warrant the conclusion that government directed mass murder must be conducted against the "national group" of another state to fit the legal definition of genocide.

Apart from the literature described below, there will be additional, forthcoming studies that analyze the Cambodian "genocide" according the precise categories and terms of the Genocide Convention. A preliminary study that follows the terms and provisions of the Genocide Convention was completed by Hawk (1986). A version of this analysis is also available in the oral and prepared statement of David Hawk to hearings on "political killings by governments" before the Subcommittee on Human Rights and International Organizations of the Committee on Foreign Affairs of the United States House of Representatives (1983). Appended in the record of the same hearings are two studies prepared at the Yale Law School. On the Genocide Convention and Khmer Rouge policy by Walter Siegel, and on the construction of an interstate submission to the International Court of Justice by Eric Biel.

The Cambodia Documentation Commission

The Cambodian Documentation Commission is a group of Cambodian refugees, Cambodia scholars, human rights specialists, and legal scholars who since 1982 have been working to: "document the immense human, social and cultural destruction in Cambodia under Khmer Rouge rule; analyze those events according to the norms and standards of international human rights; seek the review and redress available under international human rights law; and make recommendations to better enable the international community to prevent, retard, and oppose future outbreaks of mass murder by government.''

Documentation

Since 1982 hundreds of hours of taped oral histories and systematic interviews have been conducted with select categories of Cambodian survivors residing inside Cambodia, in the refugee camps in Thailand, and among Khmer now residing in the United States and Canada.

Hundreds of photographs have been taken of the execution centers, mass graves, and the destroyed Buddhist temples and statuary—the remaining physical evidence of the Khmer Rouge attempt completely to destroy Cambodian Buddhism. Fifty of these photographs were displayed in an exhibit—*Cambodia Witness*, sponsored by Amnesty International, U.S.A.—that first appeared in the Rotunda of the Russell Senate Office Building in 1983 and which continues to circulate to museums, art galleries and public spaces in the United States and Europe.

Thousands of pages of Khmer Rouge extermination facility archives have been obtained. These archives include: (a) arrest forms on individual prisoners; (b) day-by-day arrest logs denominated by name, alias, sex, function or position; (c) mug-shot arrest photographs taken by Khmer Rouge officials of prisoners to be executed; (d) daily charts on the prison population denominated by place of arrest and occupational unit or function; (e) handwritten ''confessions'' of prisoners to be executed; (f) typed summaries of prisoners' ''confessions''; (g) signed notes reporting on the torture of prisoners; (h) photographs of tortured and executed prisoners; (i) reports on the medicine administered to prisoners wounded or ill from torture; (j) signed execution orders; and (k) signed daily execution logs denominated by name, alias, age, sex, position and date of arrest. The Documentation Commission has obtained photographs and biographies of the extermination facility employees, and correspondence between extermination camp officials and the leadership of the Communist Party of Kampuchea indicating that these facilities were known to and directed by the highest government officials of Democratic Kampuchea.

The Commission has also obtained an extraordinary forty-two-page ''Interrogator's Manual'' providing extensive and detailed instructions on the Khmer Rouge philosophy and practice of torture, and other archival material from smaller, local-level prison–execution facilities.

Cambodian refugees and Cambodia scholars in Europe, Asia, and North America have been translating these archives into English.

Research and Analysis

Cambodia scholars and specialists in Europe, Asia, and the United States have worked with these other data to prepare scholarly analyses of important aspects of the Khmer Rouge genocide. The first such study, by Australian scholar Ben

Kiernan (1986), detailing the largest single massacre or related series of massacres, was published by the Center for the Study of Human Rights at Columbia University. Additional studies will be forthcoming on the virtually complete destruction of the Buddhist monkhood, Cambodia's preeminent religious group; the substantial destruction of the Cham, an ethnic minority group; and a statistical survey of causes and instances of mortality under Khmer Rouge rule.

Legal research applying the terms and provisions of the Genocide treaty to Cambodia was undertaken at the Lowenstein Human Rights Law Project at Yale Law School, the Clinical Law Program at Harvard Law School, the Holocaust and Human Rights Research Project at the Boston College Law School, and the Rutgers and University of Minnesota Law Schools. This research has been analyzed and written up by leading legal scholars and practicing attorneys in international human rights law. Utilizing the factual and legal research, a 200-page draft model dispute to the World Court under the provisions of Article IX of the Genocide Convention was prepared by Hurst Hannum, Director of the Procedural Aspects of International Law Institute, and David Hawk, Director of the Documentation Commission.

References

Biel, Eric (1983). Issues relating to the construction of an interstate subcommission to the International Court of Justice under Article IX of the Genocide Convention. Appendix to the Hearings before the Subcommittee on Human Rights and International Organization, Committee of Foreign Affairs. First Session, Ninety-eighth Congress, 16, 17 November. Political killings by governments of their citizens.

Hawk, David (1983). Statement before U.S. House of Representatives, *ibid*.

Hawk, David (1986). International human rights law and Democratic Kampuchea. *International Journal of Politics*, 16(3), Fall.

Siegel, Walter (1983). The Genocide Convention and Khmer Rouge policy. Appendix to the Hearings of U.S. House of Representatives, *ibid*.

Bibliography

Pre-1980 Accounts

Books and monographs

The following are accounts written prior to the 1979 Vietnamese invasion of Cambodia which pushed the Khmer Rouge from the capital of Phnom Penh to the Thai–Cambodia border.

Barron, John, and Paul, Anthony (1977). *Murder in a Gentle Land.* New York: Reader's Digest Press. 209 pp.
    Murder in a Gentle Land was the first book-length account of the Khmer Rouge atrocities to appear in English. It is based on the accounts of the earliest refugees who fled to Thailand from Cambodia's northwest provinces of Battambang and Siem Reap. The first sentence of the preface noted that the events recounted in this book

reflect a horror so alien and difficult to comprehend that it tends to be incredible.

Written by nonspecialists, the book has been criticized for relatively less important errors. For example, Khieu Samphan is less important and powerful as a Khmer Rouge leader than he is portrayed herein, and Cambodia was never a particularly "gentle land." The extreme violations and events portrayed in this book pertain particularly to the provinces of Battambang and Siem Reap, where the situation was particularly bad at the outset of Khmer Rouge rule.

Ponchaud, François (1978). *Cambodia: Year Zero*. New York: Holt, Rinehart & Winston. 193 pp.

Originally published in French in 1977 by Editions René Julliard, this influential account was also based on extensive interviews with Cambodian refugees fleeing from Battambang and Siem Reap, along with the official Khmer Rouge propaganda from Democratic Kampuchea radio broadcasts from Phnom Penh. Ponchaud is a Khmer-speaking French priest who had lived in Cambodia for a decade before being one of the last foreigners expelled to Thailand from the French Embassy in Phnom Penh, a scene portrayed in the motion picture *The Killing Fields*. His command of the Khmer language and knowledge of Cambodian culture enable Ponchaud expertly to provide the background and context of the Khmer Rouge revolution.

Both this volume and Barron and Paul (1977) have stood the test of time and are still well worth reading as basic accounts of the Khmer Rouge program of state-sponsored mass murder.

Quinn, Kenneth (1976). Political change in wartime: the Khmer Krahom revolution southern Cambodia, 1970–1974. *U.S. Naval War College Review*, Spring.

This account by a American Foreign Service Office is of considerable historical significance. Quinn interviewed Cambodian refugees who fled into South Vietnam in 1973–74 from areas under Khmer Rouge control in southeastern Cambodia. ("Krahom" is the Khmer-language term for "red," or in French "rouge.")

This article, an edited version of a lengthy report to the U.S. Department of State, analyzes the extreme and brutal social revolution which the Khmer Rouge began in 1973 in areas under their control—policies extended after 1975 to the entire country and population. From these earliest refugee accounts of Khmer Rouge brutality Quinn was able to distill almost the full set of Khmer Rouge policies: forced labor, forced population movements, the collectivization and State organization of agricultural production, the extreme hostility to religion and ethnic minorities, and the murderous revolution within the revolution. That is, factions of the Khmer Rouge loyal to Pol Pot began killing off their Sihanoukist and Vietnamese allies in the 1970–75 civil war against the U.S.-backed Lon Nol regime so that when the Khmer Rouge side won the civil war the Pol Pot faction would come out in complete control. Quinn's analysis, which was publicly available to Cambodia specialists, provides the policy program or plan that makes sense of the earliest refugee horror stories.

United Nations Documentation

It took three years to have the terrible Khmer Rouge human rights violations put on to the agenda of the United Nations. However, in 1987 five governments and two nongovernmental organizations submitted a considerable body of documentation to the United Nations Commission on Human Rights. This material includes numerous citations from refugee testimony and also includes part of the testimony presented at a set of public hearings conducted in Oslo, Norway. These submissions to the Commission on Human Rights are obtainable through their U.N. Documentation classifications as follows:

Government of Australia, U.N. Doc. E/CN.4/Sub.2/Add.8, 20 September 1978.

Government of Canada, U.N. Doc. E/CN.4/Sub.2/Add.1, 14 August 1978, and E/CN.4/Sub.2/Add.7, 8 September 1978.

Government of Great Britain, U.N. Doc. E/CN.4/Sub.2/Add.3, 17 August 1978.

Government of Norway, U.N. Doc. E/CN.4/Sub.2/Add.2, 18 August 1978.

Government of the United States, U.N. Doc. E/CN.4/Sub.2/Add.4, 14 August 1978.

Amnesty International, U.N. Doc. E/CN.4/Sub.2/Add.5, 15 August 1978.

International Commission of Jurists, U.N. Doc. E/CN.4/Sub2/Add.6, 16 August 1978.

U.N. Doc. E/CN.4/Sub.2/Add.9, 20 September 1987.
   Democratic Kampuchea's response to U.N. inquiry in a telegram dated 16 September 1978 from the Minister for Foreign Affairs of Democratic Kampuchea addressed to the Sub-Commission on Prevention of Discrimination and Protection of Minorities was to denounce this "impudent, criminal imperialist maneuver," which the Democratic Kampuchea's Foreign Ministry vowed "to make mincemeat of"—a successful boast inasmuch as the U.N. Human Rights Commission never recognized or condemned the extreme Khmer Rouge violations.

U.N. Doc. E/CN.4/1335/1979 (Boudhiba).
   The U.N. Commission on Human Rights has a subsidiary body of experts, the Sub-Commission on the Prevention of Discrimination and the Protection of Minorities, whose members are often appointed by the Commission on Human Rights to analyze materials on human rights violations provided to the Commission by U.N. member states and nongovernmental organizations in consultative status with the Economic and Social Council of the United Nations. The submissions cited above were examined by Mr. Boudhiba, a Tunisian jurist who was the Chairman of the Sub-Commission. The Boudhiba Report, entitled "Analysis prepared on behalf of the Sub-Commission by its Chairman of materials submitted to it and the Commission on Human Rights under decision 9 (XXXIV) of the Commission on Human Rights," analyzed the violations contained in the submission according to the articles of the Universal Declaration of Human Rights. One of the most thorough reports on a situation of human rights violations to have been prepared by a U.N.-appointed expert, the Boudhiba Report provides the context of a consistent pattern of gross violations of human rights in which the specific acts of genocide were committed. The report concluded that the situation in Kampuchea was the worst to have occurred since Nazism and constituted nothing less than "auto-genocide." Regrettably, the Commission on Human Rights pointedly declined to consider the report it had commissioned by the Chairman of the Sub-Commission.

U.N. Doc. E/CN.4/Sub.2/1985/6 (Whitaker)
   Subsequently, a 1986 report, "Revised and Updated Report on the Question of the Prevention and Punishment of the Crime of Genocide" prepared by Special Rapporteur Ben Whitaker, a British member of the Sub-Commission, also noted that specific acts of genocide were committed in Kampuchea and that "at least two million people were killed by Pol Pot's Khmer Rouge government of Democratic Kampuchea out of a total population of seven million." Unfortunately, this report was not forwarded by the Sub-Commission to the Commission for its consideration.

Initially the official response by the Khmer Rouge was to blame deaths occurring in Cambodia on the United States (*see* the U.N. document E/CN.4/Sub.2/Add.9, cited above). After 1979 the Khmer Rouge blamed Vietnam for the deaths of 2½ million Cambodians (*see* Note 6/page 97 Chapter IV. "Human Rights," *Multilateral Treaties for which the Secretary-General Acts as Depositary* [ST/LEG/SER.D/13] for Democratic Kampuchea's 9 November 1981 objection as a U.N.-recognized state, party to the Genocide Convention, to the U.N. Secretary-General with regard to the accession by Vietnam to the Convention on the Prevention and Punishment of the Crime of Genocide).

Post-1980 Accounts

The following are accounts written after Cambodia had been reopened to foreign journalists and researchers.

Survivor Literature

There is a small but growing number of survivor accounts of the Cambodian genocide, first in French, more recently in English. These invaluable resources recount the sufferings, observations and reflections of Cambodians as they experience personal and national loss.

May, Someth (1986). *Cambodian Witness*. New York: Random House; London: Faber & Faber.
> By a student and journalist in Phnom Penh before 1975, this excellent account portrays May's experiences and the deaths of his father, two of his sisters, three of his brothers, and his brother-in-law.

Ngor, Haing, with Warner, Roger (forthcoming). *Cambodian Odyssey*. New York: Macmillan; London: Chatto & Windus.
> Dr. Haing Ngor is the Academy Award-winning actor who played the part of Dith Pran in the motion picture *The Killing Fields*. A medical doctor in pre-revolutionary Cambodia, Haing Ngor is a survivor of the Korh Kra Lar prison–execution center in Battambang province where he was repeatedly and horribly tortured.

Phandara, Y. (1982). *Retour à Phnom Penh: le Cambodge du génocide à la colonisation*. Paris: Editions A.M. Metailie.
> Phandara was a sympathizer of the Cambodian revolution living in France who did not believe the early refugee accounts and voluntarily returned to Cambodia after 1975 to help rebuild the country after the Khmer Rouge victory in the 1970–75 civil war. He was immediately imprisoned by the Khmer Rouge in a "reeducation camp" set up at Boeung Trabeck in Phnom Penh for returning Khmer intellectuals and diplomats.

Picq, Laurence (1984). *Au dela du ciel: cinq ans chez les Khmer Rouges*. Paris: Editions Bernard Barrault.
> Picq was the French wife of a Khmer Rouge official who was allowed to remain with her husband in Phnom Penh working as a translator in Democratic Kampuchea's Ministry of Foreign Affairs, one of the most privileged of positions during Khmer Rouge rule. Her account contradicts assertions by Khmer Rouge Foreign Ministry officials that they were unaware of what was happening during Khmer Rouge rule.

Schanberg, Sydney (1985). *The Death and Life of Dith Pran*. London: Penguin.

An expanded version of the *New York Times Sunday Magazine* story that formed the basis of the motion picture *The Killing Fields*.

Stuart-Fox, Martin and Ung, Bunheang (1985). *The Murderous Revolution: Life and Death in Pol Pot's Kampuchea*. Chippendale, Australia: Apcol Press.
   This interesting and useful account has three aspects: Bunheang Ung's story as recounted to Martin Stuart-Fox; sixty drawings by Bunheang Ung, a former art student in Phnom Penh, of life under the Khmer Rouge; and Martin Stuart-Fox's balanced and concise analysis of Democratic Kampuchea's policy and practice. Bunheang Ung was evacuated from Phnom Penh to a village in the Cambodian "Eastern Zone" that borders on Vietnam. His story is well expanded on by Martin Stuart-Fox's background chapters, which set Ung's personal situation into the overall developments during Khmer Rouge rule.

Syzmusiak, Molyda (1986). *The Stones Cry Out: A Cambodian Childhood*. New York: Hill & Wang. [Originally published in French as *Les pierres crieont*, Editions La Découvert, Paris, 1984]
   Syzmusiak is the name of the family who adopted Molyda in France, Molyda being the young daughter of a minor member of the Sisowath branch of the Cambodian royal family. This is the sad story of Khmer Rouge rule as seen from the eyes of a small child. Most of her family, whose identity was successfully disguised to avoid execution, died from starvation, exhaustion, and disease.

Yathay, Pin (1979). *L'utopie mertrière: un rescapé du génocide cambodgien temoigné*. Paris: Robert Laffont.
   Pin Yathay is a former irrigation engineer whose family died of illness.

Secondary Accounts

Ablin, David and Hood, Marlowe (Eds.) (forthcoming). *The Cambodian Agony*. Armonk, NY: M.E. Sharpe.
   The Cambodian Agony is a collection of papers delivered at a 1982 conference dealing with several aspects of the Cambodian situation as of the early 1980s. Several chapters are of immediate relevance. These include "Revolution and reformation of Cambodian village culture," by anthropologist May Ebihara; "Patterns of Cambodian politics," by Serge Thion, a French Cambodia specialist who traces political continuities among successive Cambodian regimes; "Revolution in full spate: Communist party policy in Democratic Kampuchea," by David Chandler, and "International human rights norms and Democratic Kampuchea" by David Hawk.

Barnett, Anthony; Boua, Chanthou; and Kiernan, Ben (1980). The bureaucracy of death. *New Statesman*, 2 May, 669–676.
   This magazine story is, together with Hawk (1986), the best account of the S.21 (Tuol Sleng) extermination facility in Phnom Penh, where the Khmer Rouge left behind approximately 100,000 pages of self-incriminating archives including signed execution orders, signed torture accounts, etc.

Becker, Elizabeth (1986). *When the War Was Over: The Voices of Cambodia's Revolution and Its People*. New York: Simon & Schuster.
   This is by far the best account yet available of Cambodia under Khmer Rouge rule. It also provides an extensive account of the civil war period (1970–75) that led to Pol Pot's victory, events covered by Ms. Becker as a reporter for the *Washington Post*. It deals with the social, political, and economic aspects of Khmer Rouge policy. It also

covers the abolition of religion and the persecution of ethnic minority groups, and the search for and elimination of perceived enemies of the revolution, including the purges within the Khmer Rouge itself. The book uses cases of Cambodian survivors and the extermination camp "confessions" of several Cambodians who did not survive to illustrate her well told story.

Ms. Becker was one of the very few Western journalists to be allowed into Cambodia during the reign of Pol Pot and she visited Phnom Penh just weeks before the Vietnamese invasion. She also returned to Cambodia after the overthrow of Pol Pot.

Boua, Chanthou; Chandler, David; and Kiernan, Ben (Eds.) (forthcoming). *Pol Pot Plans the Future*. New Haven, CT: Yale University, Southeast Asia Studies Program Monograph Series.

This volume contains eight Khmer Rouge (Communist Party of Kampuchea) documents. Several of these translated manuscripts are the "plans" for the "building of socialism;" that is, the radical transformation of Cambodian society after 1975 (what the Khmer Rouge termed the "super great leap forward").

Two of the shorter documents are particularly relevant: "Summary of the Results of the 1976 Study Session" and "Abbreviated Lessons on the History of the Kampuchean Revolutionary Movement Led by the Communist Party of Kampuchea." These Khmer Rouge attempts at self-understanding and explanation speak of the complete "scattering," that is, the sociological dissolution of unwanted elements of the population, the need to deal with the "hated remnants of the former [that is, scattered] classes," eliminating "family-ism" and "property-ism," and the need to relentlessly uncover and eliminate enemies of the revolution and resolve the "life and death contradictions," that is, perceived social tensions deemed so severe that they can only be dealt with through armed force. These documents indicate that the Communist Party of Kampuchea recognized that part of the population was going hungry. Yet the Party resolved not to allow private food gathering or consumption lest it lead to a restoration of privatism and the return of capitalism.

Another important document in this collection is the translated "confession" of Hu Nim, a popular Phnom Penh radical in the 1960s and 1970s, who was tortured (and later executed) as part of Khmer Rouge's Stalinist purge of the Communist Party of Kampuchea and the elimination of potential rivals to Pol Pot's dictatorial control.

Chandler, David, and Kiernan, Ben (Eds.) (1983). *Revolution and Its Aftermath in Kampuchea: Eight Essays*. New Haven, CT: Yale University, Southeast Asia Studies Program Monograph Series.

Some of the essays in this book have found fuller expression elsewhere. Most useful are Serge Thion's "Chronology of Cambodian communism," a translation by David Chandler from Thion's *Khmer Rouge: matériaux pour l'histoire du communisme au Cambodge* (Paris: A. Michel, 1981), the essays by William Shawcross, "Cambodia: some reflections on a disaster," which examines the perception and reporting on Cambodia in the West, and Anthony Barnett's "Democratic Kampuchea: a highly centralized dictatorship".

In this last work, Barnett challenges the theory or "model" of the Khmer Rouge revolution which holds that the Khmer Rouge were without central authority or State power (in which case the execution, starvation and forced labor were not consequences or responsibilities of deliberate decisions by the political leadership) or that executions and deaths resulting from the imposed conditions of life were unintended consequences of Khmer Rouge policy. Barnett argues that "terror" was the form of Khmer Rouge rule and that the Democratic Kampuchea leadership cannot escape responsibility for the killings and deaths by starvation, exhaustion, and disease.

Etcheson, Craig (1984). *The Rise and Demise of Democratic Kampuchea*. Boulder, CO: Westview Press; London: Frances Pinter.

The Rise and Demise of Democratic Kampuchea is a useful, if highly schematized, account by an international-affairs specialist. Based on other secondary sources, this volume reviews the then available Cambodia literature and many of the controversies over the rise and fall of Pol Pot's Khmer Rouge. It has a good bibliography and chronology.

Etcheson examines phases of the development of communism in Cambodia and attempts to delineate the factions within the Khmer Rouge that led to the murderous feuds and purges. He covers the role of Buddhism in prewar Cambodia and its elimination by the Khmer Rouge. Unfortunately, his understanding of genocide is uninformed by any of the serious literature on the subject. While positing that the Khmer Rouge revolution resulted in the deaths of one-third to one-half of the Cambodian people, he defines genocide in such a way as to be able to deny that it occurred in Cambodia. Even more oddly, Etcheson lauds the "denial" literature (*see below*) for exposing the "flimsy and contradictory" nature of the early refugee accounts.

Hawk, David (1986). Tuol Sleng Extermination Center. *Index on Censorship*, 15(1), January, 25–31.

See the annotation to Barnett *et al.* (1980).

Jackson, Karl (Ed.) (forthcoming). *Rendezvous with Death: Democratic Kampuchea 1975–1978*. Princeton, NJ: Princeton University Press.

This volume contains a collection of thoughtful and stimulating essays by several American specialists and by François Ponchaud, whose landmark volume *Cambodia Year Zero* is noted above. Tim Carney provides a brief chapter, "Unexpected victory," outlining how the Khmer Rouge came to power and a detailed description of the party, government and state, "The organization of power in Democratic Kampuchea." This latter chapter updates Carney's 1976 analysis of the same subject. Karl Jackson surveys the sources of the mentality of the Khmer Rouge leadership, "The ideology of Democratic Kampuchea: motivations for total revolution." Charles Twining analyzes the Cambodian economy under Khmer Rouge rule.

Kenneth Quinn, whose landmark 1976 study outlining the harsh imposition of Khmer Rouge social policy within those areas under their control after 1973 is discussed above, analyzes the pattern and scope of violence in Democratic Kampuchea in terms of (a) breaking the social, political, economic and cultural infrastructure of the old society; (b) forcing the entire society into new socioeconomic cultural patterns; (c) using purge and execution to prevent "revisionism" or "coups from within"; and (d) preemptively defending against external enemies and their perceived internal allies.

Another chapter by Kenneth Quinn analyzes the Chinese cultural revolution as a source of inspiration for Khmer Rouge terror, while Father Ponchaud provides an invaluable and suggestive essay on what was uniquely Cambodian in the Khmer Rouge ideology and program. This is a necessary perspective to add to the more readily available view of what was adopted from French, Vietnamese, and Chinese sources of influence.

This volume also contains a lengthy appendix of Khmer Rouge documents including Pol Pot's monumental speech of 27 September 1977, translated articles from the Khmer Rouge periodical, *Revolutionary Flags*, and a translated document, "The last plan," from the archives of the central interrogation and extermination facility in Phnom Penh.

Katuichi, Honda (1981). *Journey to Cambodia*. Tokyo: International Edition Meiwa to Podo Kaihan.

This is an English translation of a series of newspaper stories that first appeared in a leading Japanese paper, *Asahi Shimbun*. Reporter Honda Katuichi went into Cambodia and interviewed several hundred family members or village leaders about the numbers and causes of deaths among their families or villages. He then reconstructed the family trees of these 216 families, which show a mortality rate of 44 percent.

Kiernan, Ben (1986). *Cambodia: The Eastern Zone Massacres*. New York: Center for the Study of Human Rights, Columbia University.

This 100-page "Report on Social Conditions and Human Rights Violations in the Eastern Zone of Democratic Kampuchea under the Rule of Pol Pot's (Khmer Rouge) Communist Party of Kampuchea" details the largest single massacre or related series of massacres, which occurred in mid to late 1978 in those Cambodian provinces bordering on Vietnam. Based on eighty-seven interviews with present or former Eastern Zone residents, this report is of particular interest because much of the refugee testimony depicts conditions in the northwest areas of Cambodia closest to the Thai border. This account also details the deterioration of conditions as the central authorities of Democratic Kampuchea consolidated their control over these provinces.

Kiernan, Ben, and Boua, Chanthou (Eds.) (1982). *Peasants and Politics in Kampuchea 1942–1981*. London: Zed Press; Armonk, NY: M.E. Sharpe.

This anthology contains a number of chapters by Ben Kiernan that are more fully developed in other works. It also contains earlier writings on Cambodia by Hou Youn and Hu Nim, two Khmer Rouge leaders purged and executed by Pol Pot and translations of refugee testimony on "life under the Khmer Rouge."

Kinzie, J. David; Fredrickson, R.H.; Rath, Ben; Fleck, Jenelle; and Karls, William (1984). Posttraumatic stress disorder among survivors of Cambodian concentration camps. *American Journal of Psychiatry*, 141(5), 645–650.

Kinzie, J. David; Sack, William; Angell, Richard; Manson, Spero; and Rath, Ben (1987). The psychiatric effects of massive trauma on Cambodian children. *Journal of the American Academy of Child Psychiatry*, 25(3), 370–376.

This is beginning of a growing body of literature on the enduring mental harm to Cambodians stemming from Khmer Rouge rule. These and other forthcoming studies are the most clinically detailed interviews conducted with Cambodian survivors by trained psychiatrists and mental health workers. The impact on the reader is devastating as these surveys measure the extreme damage done to the lives of individual victims and survivors.

Vickery, Michael (1984). *Cambodia 1975–1982*. Boston: South End Press.

Michael Vickery is an American scholar of medieval Cambodia, working in Australia. *Cambodia* is an idiosyncratic book, combining valuable insight and thorough research and analysis with ideological polemic. Of great value is his description of a Cambodian backwoods or "outer" society with little or no connection to towns or urban life, beyond the few paved roads, removed from the main rice-growing areas—one of the sectors of Cambodian society from which the Khmer Rouge drew much of their hardcore recruits. Vickery also provides a most useful analysis of social conditions by the district, regional and zonal administrative divisions of Khmer Rouge rule. This allows the complexity of the reality of the Khmer Rouge policy and practice to emerge more clearly.

Unfortunately, the analysis is marred by Vickery's polemic against those who criticized the Khmer Rouge "too soon," "for the wrong reasons" or "by the wrong people"—those, in effect, who did not originally support the Cambodian revolution. The book is further marred by his castigations against the early refugees whose depictions of life under the Khmer Rouge were not, on the whole, incorrect. Vickery also devotes a chapter to blaming Pol Pot's destructive policies on "peasant populism". This is suggestive in that the Khmer Rouge did have the some of the same flavor as millenarial medieval European peasant revolts against the towns. But this insight is then, in effect, extended to deny the Marxist ideological inspiration of the educated, urbanized Khmer Rouge leadership.

Literature of Denial

The genocide in Cambodia, like other genocides, has its deniers, minimizers and obfuscators. Curiously, perhaps coincidentally, there is a connection and overlap between the deniers of the Holocaust and obfuscators of the Cambodian genocide. The primary inspiration of early obfuscation regarding the Cambodia genocide came from radical critics of the U.S.A.'s Vietnam policy who were unwilling or unable to consider that the romanticized Third World opponents and victims of U.S. policy were themselves conducting mass murder.

Chomsky, Noam, and Herman, Edward (1979). *After the Cataclysm: Postwar Indochina and the Reconstruction of Imperial Ideology* (*The Political Economy of Human Rights*, Vol. 2). Boston: South End Press. 392 pp.

When early Cambodian refugees escaped to Thailand and provided accounts that disputed the notion that Khmer Rouge rule would lead to economic development and social justice, the line of argument was developed first, that the refugee accounts were unreliable and, second, that the press and publications that reported those stories were propaganda tools to justify U.S. policy retroactively, or deflect attention from human rights violations in countries allied with the United States.

This obfuscation of Khmer Rouge atrocities takes the form of a critique of Western press coverage of the early refugee accounts of Communist atrocities and "the alleged genocide in Cambodia." It is particularly directed against two books cited above, Barron and Paul (1977) and Ponchaud (1978), and "establishment" newspapers such as *The New York Times* and *The Washington Post*. Ostensibly an investigation of the "refraction of [the facts about Cambodia] through the prism of Western ideology," this volume attacks the methodology and good faith of those who gathered and published evidence of the Khmer Rouge human rights violations.

As is the case with other instances of genocide, there were minor inaccuracies in the refugee testimony, and some of the accounts of life and death under Khmer Rouge rule were utilized for partisan political purposes. On the other hand, the early refugee accounts were overwhelmingly corroborated by the much more voluminous first-person testimony available after 1979. After Cambodia was reopened to journalists and scholars and the secret extermination facilities uncovered, it became apparent that there were aspects of Khmer Rouge rule that were even worse than the early refugee accounts had indicated.

Hildebrand, George, and Porter, Gareth (1976). *Cambodia: Starvation and Revolution*. New York: Monthly Review Press. 124 pp.

This "favorable picture of [the Khmer Rouge] program and policies" (*The Nation*) seeks to defend the urban evacuations of April 1975 as rational and humanitarian policies against press reports and government condemnations of cruelty. According to Hildebrand and Porter, the criticism by U.S. officials and the Western press of the forced evacuations—"an atrocity of major proportion" (Henry Kissinger), "beyond the bounds of moral decency" (Assistant U.S. Secretary of State Philip Habib), "a new brand of cruelty" (*Wall Street Journal*), "a monstrosity of epic proportions" (*Washington Star*), and "the greatest atrocity since the Nazis herded Jews into the gas chambers" (syndicated columnist Jack Anderson)—were designed to shift the burden of guilt from the U.S.A. to the Khmer Rouge.

The second part of *Cambodia: Starvation and Revolution* is an attempt based on the theoretical and academic writings of Khmer Rouge leaders and post-1975 Democratic Kampuchea official pronouncements to defend Khmer Rouge agricultural policies, which were taken at face value and accepted as "the first steps toward agricultural development in centuries," "releasing the creative energies of the people at the same time as allocating resources nationally," leading to the "overall development of the economy and the community in which [the peasants] lived."

Related Books

The Vietnamese invasion of Cambodia in 1979 expelled Pol Pot's Khmer Rouge from Phnom Penh and pushed its members to the Thai–Cambodia border from where they fight a guerrilla war seeking to return to power. Several important books cover the causes and ongoing consequences of Khmer Rouge rule. Those consequences include large-scale refugee flows, famine and an international political and military conflict in and over Cambodia.

Amnesty International (1987). *Kampuchea: Contemporary Political Imprisonment and Torture*, London.
> Report on human rights violations against Cambodians inside Cambodia, inside Thailand, and along the Thai–Cambodian border after 1979.

Chanda, Nayan (1986). *Brother Enemy: A History of Indochina since the Fall of Saigon*. New York: Harcourt Brace Jovanovich.
> By a veteran diplomatic correspondent for the *Far Eastern Economic Review*, this is the definitive historical account of how Vietnam, Cambodia and China, all communist countries, fell out of alliance and into war after the defeat of the Americans in Indochina. It covers Khmer Rouge foreign policy and its relationship to Khmer Rouge domestic repression, as well as the slide into hostilities between Cambodia and Vietnam, and China and Vietnam. Its immediate relevance is that it was the Vietnamese invasion that drove Pol Pot's Khmer Rouge from Phnom Penh to the Thai–Cambodia border. Yet it is Cambodia's neighbors' fear about Vietnam's long-term intentions toward Cambodia that has led to the internationally supported revival of the Khmer Rouge in order to fight Vietnam's occupation.

Chandler, David (1983). *A History of Cambodia*. Boulder, CO: Westview Press. 237 pp.
> This highly readable one-volume history covers two thousand years of Cambodian history from its origin as an "Indianized" kingdom up to Cambodia's independence from France. This volume provides the historical setting from which the Khmer Rouge attempted their disastrous "super great leap forward" to modernity. Chandler is also working on a follow-up volume which will cover history from independence to the fall of Democratic Kampuchea.

Charney, Joel and Spragens, John, Jr. (1984). *Obstacles to Recovery in Vietnam and Kampuchea*. Boston: Oxfam America.
> Chapter 3 covers the problems of famine relief and rehabilitation work in the interior of a country shattered by over a decade of war, genocide and famine.

Evans, Grant, and Rowley, Kelvin (1984). *Red Brotherhood at War*. London: Verso.
   Red Brotherhood covers the same territory as did Chanda but more thematically and
   without Chanda's unparalleled access to policy makers on all sides.

Finnish Inquiry Commission on Kampuchea (1982). *Kampuchea in the Seventies*.
Helsinki. Also published as: Kiljunen, Kimmo (Ed.) (1984). *Kampuchea: Decade of the
Genocide*. London: Zed Press.
   This 100-page overview briefly covers the 1970–75 civil war, the Khmer Rouge
   period, the Vietnamese-installed People's Republic of Kampuchea, the famine relief
   and refugee aid program, and the international political conflict.

Greve, Hannah Sophie (forthcoming). *Kampuchean Refugees: Between the Tiger and
the Crocodile*. New York: Oxford University Press.
   A massive, definitive account of the problems of the Cambodian survivors who
   sought refuge in Thailand after 1979.

Kiernan, Ben (1985). *How Pol Pot Came to Power*. London: Verso. 430 pp.
   This invaluable history of the Communist party of Kampuchea situates the Khmer
   Rouge in Cambodian politics from the early emergence of modern Cambodian
   nationalism after World War I to the end of the 1970–75 civil war that brought Pol
   Pot to power. The book discusses in great depth the various political tendencies and
   personalities within the Khmer Rouge. Most germane here is the wealth of information on the careers and political developments of those personalities whose rule would
   be so brutal. Its focus is more closely on how Pol Pot gained predominance within the
   Communist party of Kampuchea and somewhat less on why Marxist–Leninist
   nationalism prevailed over royal, liberal, and reactionary nationalism in Cambodian
   politics.
   A follow-up volume on the 1975–79 period is expected, based on Kiernan's extensive research inside Cambodia after 1980.

Lawyers Committee for Human Rights (1985). *Kampuchea: After the Worst*.
New York.

Lawyers Committee for Human Rights (1987). *Seeking Shelter: Cambodians in
Thailand*. New York.
   Reports on human rights violations against Cambodians inside Cambodia, inside
   Thailand, and along the Thai–Cambodian border after 1979.

Mason, Linda and Brown, Roger (1983). *Rice, Rivalry and Politics: Managing
Cambodian Relief*. Notre Dame, IN: University of Notre Dame Press.
   Covers the famine relief program along the Thai–Cambodia border where the Khmer
   Rouge co-mingled with scores of thousands of Cambodians who had fled the Khmer
   Rouge.

Shawcross, William (1984). *Quality of Mercy: Cambodia, Holocaust and Modern Conscience*. New York: Simon & Schuster.
   This book covers the international response to the Cambodia crisis after 1979; the
   refugee program in Thailand, the famine relief program inside Cambodia and along
   the Thai–Cambodian border, as well as reflections on Cambodia's tragedy after the
   end of the destruction directed and supported by the United States which Shawcross
   had documented in his best-selling book *Sideshow: Nixon, Kissinger and the
   Destruction of Cambodia* (New York: Simon & Schuster, 1979).

Sihanouk, Prince Norodom (1980). *War and Hope: The Case for Cambodia*. New York: Pantheon Books. [Originally published in French as *Chroniques de guerre et d'espoir*. Paris: Hachette/Stock, 1979]

Prince Sihanouk's insights and reflections on Cambodia's suffering during the Khmer Rouge years and the Vietnamese occupation.

8

Other Selected Cases of Genocide and Genocidal Massacres: Types of Genocide

Leo Kuper

Genocide is a subject that covers a vast field, and, given limitations of space, many genocides have to be excluded from consideration in this chapter. Instead, I present selected cases to exemplify different manifestations of genocide.

There is as yet no satisfactory classification of genocides. Most classifications deal with what may be described as "domestic" genocides, that is to say, genocides arising on the basis of internal divisions within a society, as distinct from those committed against enemies in the course of international war, though it should be noted that under contemporary conditions there is almost invariably some international involvement in the domestic genocides.

Toynbee (1969, pp. 241–242) viewed the twentieth century as initiating a new process in genocide, characterized by the deliberate fiat of the holders of despotic power, employing all the resources of modern technology and organization to render the massacres systematic and complete. Arlen (1975, pp. 243–244) similarly emphasizes centralized control availing itself of modern technological and organizational resources. Fein (1979, p. 8) differentiates primitive genocides, directly related to the social organization of the society, and the modern premeditated genocides that are mediated by a political formula or myth.

Dadrian (1974–75, pp. 100–102) draws on a number of dimensions, primarily objectives, as a basis for a more comprehensive typology with the following categories: (a) Cultural; (b) Violent–Latent (that is, genocide as a by-product of other operations); (c) Retributive, either punitive or admonitory; (d) Utilitarian; and (e) Optimal (massive, relatively indiscriminate, sustained and aiming at total obliteration—a category that includes the modern premeditated genocide).

Kuper (1984, pp. 5–9) adopts the definition of genocide in the Genocide Convention, distinguishes the genocides of international war from the "domestic" genocides, and uses as a basis for his classification of the domestic genocides the various categories of victimized groups in their societal context. This pragmatic classification is used here. It yields the following categories: Genocides of Indigenous Groups; Genocides of Hostage Groups; Genocides in Struggles for Power or for Self-Determination; and Genocides in the Course of War.

If it is accepted that the domestic genocides are phenomena of plural societies (that is to say, societies characterized by pervasive cleavages and issues of conflict between racial, ethnic, or religious groups), then a more theoretically oriented and systematic classification of domestic genocides could be developed by relating the genocides to a typology of plural societies.

Genocides of Indigenous Groups

Colonization has been a major source of genocide against indigenous groups. Sartre (1968), in his indictment of the U.S.A. on a charge of genocide in Vietnam, tended to equate colonization with genocide. He argued that the colonial troops maintained their authority by perpetual massacre aimed at the destruction "of part of an ethnic, national, or religious group," and were thus genocidal in character. However, he introduced the qualification that the extent of physical destruction was restrained by the colonizer's dependence on the labor of the colonized.

In fact, much colonization proceeded without genocidal conflict. Maunier's (1949) distinction between colonies of exploitation and colonies of settlement is relevant, with colonies of settlement more threatening to the survival of indigenous groups. But the effects of colonial settlement were quite variable, dependent on a variety of factors, such as the number of settlers, the forms of the colonizing economy and competition for productive resources, policies of the colonizing power, and attitudes to intermarriage or concubinage.

Among the many indigenous groups annihilated in the course of colonization were the Tasmanians, the Hereros in South West Africa, the Aztecs and Incas in the Americas, and the Tainos, Gibonese, and Arawak Indians in the Caribbean. It should be noted that some of the annihilations of indigenous peoples arose not so much by deliberate act, but in the course of what may be described as a genocidal process: massacres, appropriation of land, introduction of diseases, and arduous conditions of labor. Though most of the world is now decolonized, at any rate in the formal sense of recognition as sovereign independent states, there are still episodes of colonizing genocides, as notably in the Indonesian colonization of East Timor, and the Chinese colonization of Tibet. (The Chinese, however, contend that Tibet was traditionally an integral part of China.)

Most of the postcolonial successor states are plural societies, and many have indigenous groups occupying a marginal position in the society. Small indigenous groups, usually hunters and gatherers, inhabiting, or moving over, areas with potential productive resources, are perpetually at risk of genocidal massacre. These are the so-called victims of progress, victims, that is to say, of predatory economic development. Large indigenous groups of settled agriculturalists may also be exposed to genocidal massacre as they resist continued exploitation, domination and spoliation. The processes involved in these massacres are not very different from the genocides of colonization.

Genocides of Hostage Groups

These groups, cast in the role of hostages to the fortunes of the host society, of scapegoats, are also perpetually at risk. Attacks on them are difficult to predict since they may be quite unrelated to the events that precipitate them: a catastrophe such as the Black Death in Europe in the Middle Ages, or periods of religious effervescence, as for example the Crusades or the celebration of Easter, or conflicts that do not directly involve the hostage groups. Generally speaking, hostage groups are small and vulnerable, of different religion and ethnic background from the majority in the society, and with a section engaged in trade, industry, or finance. Attacks on them may take the form of summary expulsion, as for example the expulsion of Indians from Uganda in 1972. These expulsions can have genocidal consequences if the outside world is unwilling to receive the victims. Jews in Europe were the archetypal hostage groups (*see* Chapter 4 on the Holocaust, and also the bibliographic references in the present chapter to the Baha'is). The present persecution in Iran of the Baha'is is essentially religiously motivated, but they are also cast in the role of scapegoats.

Genocides in Struggles for Power or against Discrimination or for Self-Determination

Most domestic genocides and mass killings arise in the course of struggles for power by racial, ethnic or religious groups, or struggles for greater autonomy or for secession, or simply for more equal participation and freedom from discrimination, or for change in the conditions of political incorporation. Somewhat related are the genocides that arise in the course of the consolidation of despotic power. The U.N. Genocide Convention excludes from the definition of genocide the destruction of political groups. The line, however, is not easily drawn between the political on the one hand and the ethnic, racial or religious on the other. How is one to describe the massacres of Hutu in Burundi, when the ethnic divisions themselves were politicized, and ethnic relations polarized in the struggle for political power? In any event, in the consolidation of despotic power, there have often been annihilations of racial, ethnic, and religious groups, which fall within the U.N. definition of genocide. (*See* the entries below under Fegley, 1981, and under International Commission of Jurists, 1979, for

Equatorial Guinea, and under International Commission of Jurists, 1974 and 1977, Kyemba and Martin for Uganda. *See also* entries in Chapter 7 on Cambodia, relating to the annihilation of the Muslim Cham and the attempt to eliminate Buddhism in the country.)

Genocides in the Course of War

This chapter deals essentially with the domestic genocides, but brief references must be made to the genocides in the course of war. These arise at different levels. They may be part of the actual military operations. In ancient times, it was common enough practice to destroy besieged cities and to slaughter their inhabitants, or their male defenders, while taking the women and children into slavery. In a later period, the names of Genghis Khan and of Timor Lenk became synonyms for genocides in the course of war. The large-scale massacres of Poles by Germans in World War II belong in this category, and I would include also in this category the atomic bombing of Hiroshima and Nagasaki by the U.S.A., although such a categorization is controversial. The present stockpiling of atomic weapons by the superpowers threatens genocide as an almost inevitable consequence of their use in warfare, since they are weapons of overwhelmingly destructive power, and weapons moreover of indiscriminate effect, obliterating the distinction between military and civilians. At a different level, warfare facilitates the commission of genocides not directly related to the military campaigns, as in the Turkish genocide of Armenians in World War I, and the German genocide of Jews and Gypsies in World War II.

There is an extensive literature dealing with genocides in the course of war, some of which is referred to in other sections. Here I include only a few bibliographic citations relating to charges of genocide against the two superpowers whose present policies threaten human survival.

References

Arlen, Michael J. (1975). *Passage to Ararat*. New York: Farrar, Straus & Giroux. 293 pp.

Dadrian, Vahakn (1974–1975). The structural functional components of genocide. In Drapkin, Israel, and Viano, Emilio (Eds.), *Victimology,* Vol. 4, pp. 123–135. Lexington, MA: Lexington Books.

Fein, Helen (1979). *Accounting for Genocide: National Responses and Jewish Victimization during the Holocaust*. New York: The Free Press. 468 pp.

Kuper, Leo (1982). *International Action against Genocide*. London: Minority Rights Group. 17 pp.

Porter, Jack Nusan (Ed.) (1982). *Genocide and Human Rights: A Global Anthology*. Washington, DC: University Press of America. 353 pp.

Sartre, Jean-Paul (1968). On genocide. *Ramparts*, February, 37–42.

Toynbee, Arnold (1969). *Experiences*. London: Oxford University Press. 417 pp.

Bibliography

Genocides of Indigenous Groups: Genocides of Colonization

Maunier, René (1949). *The Sociology of Colonies*. London: Routledge. 2 vols. 767 pp.
This pioneering study provides general background on colonization, with analysis also of genocidal conflict. Book 4 deals with "Results of race contact," Chapter IX being devoted to "Opposition." Elimination is described as one of the possible results of opposition in race contact. It may come about by destruction in war, or as a side effect of conquest. Or it may take the form of spontaneous depopulation, as a result of such physical causes as alcoholism, and such spiritual causes as give rise to a loss of the will to survive. (The English anthropologist, G. Pitt-Rivers, was influential in propagating the theory of the failure in the will to survive as a potential result of the clash of cultures.)

German Genocide of the Hereros

Bley, Helmut (1971). *South West Africa under German Rule 1894–1914*. London: Heinemann Educational Books. Biblio. 303 pp.
Part III, Chapter 1 deals with the policy of extermination pursued by the German military command in suppression of the Herero revolt of 1904.

Bridgman, J.M. (1981). *The Revolt of the Hereros*. Berkeley and Los Angeles: University of California Press. Bibliographic essay. 184 pp.
Chapters 3–5 describe the Herero revolt and the annihilation of the Hereros in the German reprisals. Strong evidence is presented of the intention of the German High Command in South West Africa to destroy the Hereros utterly.

Drechsler, Horst (1980). *"Let Us Die Fighting": The Struggle of the Herero and the Nama against German Imperialism*. Translated by Bernd Zollner. London: Zed Press. Biblio. 278 pp.
The study is distinctive for its extensive use of primary materials, notably German archival materials, its careful documentation of German exterminatory policies against the Herero and sections of the Nama, and its systematic development of a Marxist interpretation of German colonial policy. The early chapters deal with German penetration of South West Africa, the expropriation of land, and the internal conflict between the Herero and Nama peoples. These are followed by accounts of the Herero and Nama uprisings, and the exterminatory reprisals by the German High Command, completing the expropriation of land and the subjugation of the survivors. An epilogue introduces the contemporary struggle by the Namibian peoples for the liberation of their country from South African domination.

First, Ruth (1975). *South West Africa*. Gloucester, MA: Peter Smith. Biblio. 269 pp.
Pages 78–81 deal with the annihilation of the Hereros. There is a reference to the British government's atrocity blue book of 1918 (officially declared destroyed), which cites the German general's extermination order, and reports the killing of prisoners, wounded and unwounded, women, girls, and little boys. "German General Staff records and commentaries are more nebulous and claim that a counterinstruction to the extermination order was issued by Berlin" (p. 80).

Goldblatt, I. (1971). *History of South West Africa from the Beginning of the Nineteenth Century*. Cape Town: Juta. 273 pp.
An account of the Herero War will be found in Chapter 24.

Conquest of the Aztecs and Incas

Hemming, John (1970). *The Conquest of the Incas*. London: Macmillan. Biblio. 641 pp.
  The chapter entitled "Oppression" in this detailed account of the conquest of the
  Incas describes the many factors that contributed to the depopulation of the Incas:
  disease, profound cultural shock and chaotic administration, the effects of civil wars
  (their own and those of the Spanish invaders), the despoliation, the imposition of
  conditions of work inimical to survival, and the neglect of the irrigation system.

Innes, Hammond (1963). *The Conquistadors*. London: Collins. 336 pp.
  Chapter 7 deals with the defeat and conquest of the Aztecs by Cortes, Chapter 11 with
  Pizarro's conquest of the Incas. Both contain accounts of genocidal massacres.

Prescott, William H. (1887). *Conquest of Mexico*. London: Richard Bentley. Vol. 1, 442
pp., vol. 2, 439 pp., vol. 3, 455 pp.
  This is the classic account of the Spanish conquest of Mexico, with an extensive
  description of Aztec civilization, now extinct. In Vol. 2, Book 4, Chapter 8, Prescott
  describes a great massacre of unarmed Aztecs.

Ribeiro, Darcy (1971). *The Americas and Civilization*. London: Allen & Unwin. Biblio.
492 pp.
  The author comments briefly on Aztec civilization, political constitution, social
  structure and religious beliefs and organization. He quotes from Spengler that "All
  this was not broken down in some desperate way, but washed out by a handful of
  bandits in a few years, and so entirely that the relics of the population retained not
  even a memory of it all." Contributory causes cited are religious beliefs, ethnic
  tensions in the Aztec confederation, virulent epidemics, and a hierarchical system of
  social organization in which the ruling strata could readily be replaced by the Spanish
  conquistadors (pp. 106–113). According to an estimate cited by Ribeiro, the population of the Inca Empire declined by a ratio of 20–25:1 in 1650. "The principal factor
  in this depopulation was the destruction of the system of irrigation agriculture and
  the simultaneous constriction of the population to serve the economic objectives of
  the colonizer" (p. 143, and more generally, pp. 99–100 and 137–143).

Demographic Tragedy in Brazil

Hemming, John (1978). *Red Gold: The Conquest of the Brazilian Indians*. Cambridge,
MA: Harvard University Press. Biblio. 677 pp.
  Hemming estimates that the population of Brazil in 1500 was 2,431,000, and that
  there were, at the time of writing, about 100,000 surviving Indians in Brazil. He
  comments that "the debate about the original native population of Brazil will continue. But there can be no question that an appalling demographic tragedy of great
  magnitude has occurred" (p. 492). Of the causes of this "demographic tragedy,"
  Hemming writes: "The colonial conquest of Brazil was often brutal. But the ultimate
  objective of both colonists and missionaries was to subdue rather than to destroy the
  Indians. The colonists wanted Indian labour, and the missionaries wanted converts.
  It was disease that annihilated the Indians. Native bravery and fighting skills were
  nullified by a lack of genetically inherited defences against European and African
  diseases. Decimation by disease has condemned Brazilian Indians to near extinction.
  Instead of repossessing a decolonised country, they are now reduced to a pathetic
  minority on the fringe of a successful European society" (p. xv).

North American Colonization

Nash, Gary B. (1982). *Red, White and Black: The Peoples of Early America*. Englewood Cliffs, NJ: Prentice-Hall. Extensive bibliographic essay. 330 pp.

An indispensable work of reference on the colonization of eastern North America. The many references to genocidal policies and genocidal attacks on Indians include the destruction of the Pequots in New England, and of the Westos and Savannahs in South Carolina. The introduction of diseases, the "virgin soil" epidemics, contributed to the decimation of Indians, as did the rivalries among Indians themselves, and the enlisting of these rivalries by the settlers in pursuit of their own policies. (*See*, for example, the Iroquois war of extermination against the Hurons, pp. 90–91.) The study is particularly interesting for the comparative material on the policies of settlers of different nationalities in different social and environmental settings, the role of religious differences, and the religious and other justifications for annihilatory policies.

Australian Colonization

Jacobs, Wilbur R. (1971). The fatal confrontation: early native–white relations on the frontiers of Australia, New Guinea, and America—a comparative study. *Pacific Historical Review*, 40(3), 283–309.

This comparative study emphasizes dispossession from the land as a major factor in the destruction of indigenous societies and cultures. It attributes the more favorable situation of the peoples of Papua–New Guinea to the fact that they were not deprived of their lands by an encompassing frontier of white settlements. The situation has, of course, changed in West Irian with the proposed "transmigration" of an estimated 1 million Indonesians, and the consequent threat to the survival of the indigenous population. The article contains extensive references to the literature on the colonization of these areas, and interesting observations on the dehumanizing stereotypes of the aborigines.

Rowley, Charles Dunford (1970). *Aboriginal Policy and Practice*. Canberra: Australian National University Press. 3 vols. Biblios. 430 pp., 472 pp., 379 pp.

Vol. 1, Part II deals with the destruction of aboriginal society in the frontier clashes and in their aftermath, resulting in a decline in the aboriginal population from about 200,000–300,000 to 62,000 at the time of the 1921 census.

Travers, Robert (1968). *The Tasmanians: The Story of a Doomed Race*. Melbourne: Cassell, Australia. Biblio. 244 pp.

This account of the total extinction of the Tasmanians deals briefly with what is known of traditional Tasmanian life and describes the early contacts with Europeans, the increasing tensions and conflicts, culminating in an organized manhunt, and the banishment of the surviving Tasmanians to an inhospitable island. *See also* James Morris (1972). The final solution, Down Under. *Horizon*, 14(1), 60–71.

Caribbean

Black, Clinton V. (1965). *The Story of Jamaica from Prehistory to the Present*. London: Collins. Biblio. 256 pp.

Contains a brief reference to the extinction of the Arawak Indians under Spanish rule by massacres, harsh conditions of living, suicide, pestilence and the introduction of animals that destroyed Arawak cultivation.

The San of the Kalahari

Stephen, David (1982). *The San of the Kalahari*. London: Minority Rights Group. Biblio. 16 pp.

The report gives some background to the San, surviving mainly in Botswana, and deals with their way of life and government policies affecting them. They are extinct in South Africa, where they came under pressure from the Bantu-speaking peoples and the European settlers. (Robert Gordon is now completing a study of the Bushmen in Namibia, under the tentative title "The Bushman Myth Explored: Treating Namibia's Invisible Minority," to be published by Ravan Press, Johannesburg. In the concluding chapter he deals with policies inimical to the survival of the Bushmen in Namibia, which constitute a "slouching towards genocide." His discussion of academic justification of settler expansion is also of special interest and relevance.)

Genocides in Contemporary Colonization: East Timor

Amnesty International (1985a). *East Timor: Violations of Human Rights*. London: Amnesty International Publications. 92 pp.

This report does not charge genocide, but the volume of extrajudicial executions, disappearances and mass killings certainly provides strong corroborative evidence of the commission of the crime by the Indonesian government against the people of East Timor.

Amnesty International (1985b). *East Timor Violations of Human Rights, Extrajudicial Executions. "Disappearances," Torture and Political Imprisonment, 1975–1984*. London: Amnesty International. 92 pp.

This provides additional evidence of the violations of human rights (the atrocities) in the Indonesian colonization of East Timor.

Budiardjo, Carmel and Liong, Liem Soei (1984). *The War against East Timor*. London: Zed Press. Biblio. 248 pp.

This provides a comprehensive account of the invasion of East Timor by the Indonesian army, the military campaigns, and the massacres, murders, tortures, disappearances, and other atrocities of the conquest. Conditions in the relocation camps are described, and a detailed analysis given of the colonization in a chapter devoted to the Indonesianization of East Timor. In a well-documented study, the authors also deal with the international response to the colonization of East Timor, and the renewed struggle of its people for self-determination. An appendix of nine secret military documents provides an insight into the counterinsurgency strategy of the Indonesian army.

Retbøll, Torben (Ed.) (1980). *East Timor, Indonesia and the Western Democracies*. Biblio. 138 pp.

Retbøll, Torben (Ed.) (1984). *East Timor: The Struggle Continues*. Copenhagen: International Work Group for Indigenous Affairs. Biblio. 219 pp.

Retbøll's two volumes deal with the genocide of the people of East Timor from the time of the Indonesian invasion in 1975 to the present day. Perhaps as many as one-third of a population of 650,000 have died in the military operations, in massacres, and by disease and starvation. The edited papers cover many different aspects: traditional life, its destruction in the military campaigns, the bombardment of agricultural settlements, the corralling of inhabitants in relocation centres, torture, the operations of death squads, forced "integration," and the increasing international condonation of the Indonesian colonization of East Timor as a *fait accompli*. The work is essentially a collection of basic documents and a valuable source for reference.

TAPOL (1984). *West Papua: The Obliteration of a People*. London: TAPOL. Biblio.
122 pp.
    The present colonization of West Papua by Indonesia recalls some of the more
destructive episodes of the early periods of colonization, associated with massive
settlement by the colonizing power. These include the subsidized settlement of Indonesians in large numbers (the transmigration policy); the expropriation of land and
enforced relocation of West Papuans; cultural suppression; involvement of
transnational companies for the exploitation of rich oil and mineral resources; a
strong military presence, with mass killings of civilians in the suppression of resistance, and the customary gross violations of human rights. There is discussion also of
the role of the United Nations and of major Western powers in support of Indonesia.

Genocides in Contemporary Colonization: Tibet

International Commission of Jurists (1959). *The Question of Tibet and the Rule of Law*.
Geneva. 208 pp.
    Report of a legal inquiry committee of the International Commission of Jurists,
which found that the Chinese had killed tens of thousands of Tibetans, and that they
had killed Buddhist monks and lamas on a large scale, destroyed Buddhist
monasteries, and desecrated holy places. It concluded that the evidence pointed to a
systematic design to eradicate the separate national, cultural, and religious life of
Tibet, and that there was at least a *prima facie* case of genocide against the People's
Republic of China.

International Commission of Jurists (1960). *Tibet and the Chinese People's Republic.
Report by the Legal Inquiry Committee on Tibet*. Geneva. 345 pp.
    In this second report, the legal inquiry committee concluded that acts of genocide had
been committed in Tibet in an attempt to destroy Tibetans as a *religious group*, but
that there was not sufficient proof of the destruction of Tibetans as a race, nation, or
ethnical group to sustain a charge of genocide in international law.

Mullin, Chris, and Wangyal, Phuntsog (1981). *The Tibetans: Two Perspectives on
Tibetan-Chinese Relations*. London: Minority Rights Group. Biblio. 27 pp.
    Mullin gives a different view of the constitutional status of Tibet from that of the
International Commission of Jurists, but agrees that for thirty-eight years prior to the
invasion, Tibet was for all practical purposes independent. He perceives Tibetan
Buddhism as having deteriorated into tyrannical rule by lamas. He describes the
systematic destruction of monasteries and sacred objects during the Chinese Cultural
Revolution and the later liberalizing policies. Mullin's account of Chinese rule gives
no support for the charge of genocide advanced in Wangyal's presentation. Wangyal
describes traditional Tibetan society as a flourishing and functioning social system,
and Tibetans as a deeply religious people dedicated to Buddhism and supportive of
the existing system of values. He gives figures of massacres and executions under the
Chinese occupation, this being the basis for the charge of genocide, and he is highly
critical of the "liberalizing" policy.

Colonial and Post-colonial Victims of Progress

Arens, Richard (Ed.) (1976). *Genocide in Paraguay*. Philadelphia: Temple University
Press. Bibliographic references. 171 pp.
    Four of the articles deal directly with the annihilation of the Aché: (1) Mark Münzel,
"Manhunt," pp. 19–45; (2) Eric Wolf, "Killing the Achés," 46–57, in which he
comments generally on the destruction of hunting and gathering groups "in the
onward march of civilization," and in which he describes the National Guayaki

Colony as an extermination camp; (3) Norman Lewis, "The camp at Cecilio Baez," 58–68, of which he writes that it "seems to have been a small Belsen for Indians;" and Arens, "A lawyer's summation," 132–164, where the editor specifies the parties guilty of the genocide. (Details of the crime were contained in a complaint to the U.N. Secretary General. These details, as well as the response of the government of Paraguay, that the necessary intent was lacking, will be found in Leo Kuper (1981). *Genocide*, p. 34. New Haven, CT: Yale University Press.)

Bodley, John H. (1975). *Victims of Progress*. Menlo Park, CA, and London: Cummings. Biblio. 200 pp.

This study provides an anthropological perspective on "the worldwide regularities characterizing interaction between industrial nations and tribal cultures over the past 150 years." It is a chilling record of wholesale cultural imperialism, aggression, and exploitation that has involved every major modern national state, regardless of differences in their political, religious, or social philosophies. While blatant extermination policies have become relatively infrequent, basic native policies and the motives underlying them have remained virtually unchanged since the industrial powers began to expand more than 150 years ago (p. v).

This book is a valuable resource, with particular relevance for ethnocide, genocide and genocidal processes, the responsibility attaching to governments, multinational corporations and other agencies. On p. 39, there is a table giving figures of world tribal depopulation. The book also includes an outline for an alternative policy.

Davis, Shelton H. (1977). *Victims of the Miracle*. Cambridge: Cambridge University Press. Biblio. 205 pp.

This is a study of the impact of the Brazilian government's development program on the survival of indigenous peoples, particularly in the Amazon region. Participants in the expropriation of Indian resources are private, state, and multinational corporations. There are references to the devastating effects of diseases, the deliberate introduction in one region of smallpox, influenza, tuberculosis, and measles organisms, the attempts to exterminate the Cintas Largas tribe, and the plight of the Yanomamö tribe in an area rich in mineral resources, including uranium. In general, the study documents a genocidal developmental process. (*See also* the discussion of the reconquest of Indians in Amazonia and the rest of Brazil as a result of predatory economic development—*Survival International Review*, 4(1) (Spring 1979). Pages 18–40 deal specifically with the Yanomamö.)

Smith, Robert Jerome, and Melia, Bartomeu (June 1978). Genocide of the Aché-Guyaki? *Survival International Supplement*, 3(1), no. 21, 8–13.

An anthropological study, through genealogies, of causes of death among the Aché Indians, which established that killing of members of the group and the forcible transfer of children of the group by members of other groups have been committed with such intensity that the Aché may well soon cease to exist. The data point to frequent but unsystematic killings by Paraguayan farmers, ranchers, and laborers, rather than organized raids by army or police units. The authors believe that *de facto* genocide has occurred, for which the Paraguayan government is responsible in view of its failure to protect its citizens, but raise some questions regarding the difficulty in establishing intent. (My own view is that intent can be inputed when killings and kidnappings become an established practice.)

Hostage Groups

Threatened Genocide of Baha'is

Baha'i International Community (1981–82).

The publications of the Community in 1981, *The Baha'is in Iran* (July 1982) and *Baha'i News* (June 1982), written with restraint and careful documentation, cover the early history of the Baha'is, provide some account of their religious beliefs and the religious persecution they have suffered in the past, and particularly in the present systematic attempt by the theocratic fundamentalist regime under Khomeini to eradicate the Baha'i religion. The Community does not make a charge of genocide, but the documents and testimony clearly establish a threatened genocide, with systematic murders of religious leaders and attacks on the Baha'i Community as a whole, reminiscent of the persecution of Jews in Nazi Germany during the 1930s. At the time of writing this bibliographic note, the murders of Baha'i leaders have decreased. That the persecution of the Baha'is was religiously motivated is clear from the fact that Baha'i leaders convicted on charges of treason could have secured their release by conversion to Islam. Further information may be found in Christine Hakim (1982). *Les Baha'is ou victoire sur la violence*. Lausanne: Favre; in William Sears (1982). *A Cry from the Heart*. Oxford: George Roland; and Amnesty International, *Report 1982*, 323–329.

Cooper, Roger (1982). *The Baha'is of Iran*. London: Minority Rights Group. Biblio. 16 pp.
This report gives a somewhat different account of the early history of the Baha'is from that given in Baha'i official accounts, and provides extensive comment on the status of Baha'ism as a religion. The discussion of the persecution of the Baha'is is consistent with the documentation provided by the Baha'i International Community.

Exterminatory Anti-Semitism

Cohn, Norman (1967). *Warrant for Genocide*. New York: Harper & Row. Biblio. 303 pp.
Cohn distinguishes exterminatory anti-Semitism from the kind of anti-Semitism that is fairly closely related to the role played by Jews, or by some Jews, in the society in question and is analogous to the kind of hostility directed against Indian traders in southeastern Africa or Chinese traders in Java. The exterminatory anti-Semitism, he argues, has little to do with real conflicts of interest between living people. Its warrant for genocide derives from the belief in a Jewish world conspiratorial body, employed in medieval times by Satan for the spiritual and physical ruination of Christendom, and in modern times, banded together for the ruin and domination of the rest of mankind.

Genocides in Struggles for Power or against Discrimination or for Self-Determination

Kuper, Leo (1977). *The Pity of It All: Polarisation of Racial and Ethnic Relations*. London: Duckworth; Minneapolis: University of Minnesota Press. Biblio. 302 pp.
Conclusions in regard to the polarization of racial and ethnic relations are derived from case studies of Zanzibar, Rwanda, Burundi, and Algeria. The mass killings of Arabs in Zanzibar, of Tutsi in Rwanda, and of Hutu in Burundi are characterized as genocide, while the term "genocidal massacres" is applied to some of the mass killings in Algeria, such as the massive and indiscriminate reprisals against Algerians following the Algerian massacre of Europeans in Setif, the bombardment of Muslim villages, and the annihilation of a European mining community. A concluding chapter, "Reflections: reform or genocide," deals briefly with the relationship between plural societies and genocidal massacres.

Bangladesh

International Commission of Jurists (1971). *The Events in East Pakistan*. Study by the Secretariat. Geneva: International Commission of Jurists. Bibliographic references. 98 pp.

International Commission of Jurists (1972). Right of Self-determination in International Law. East Pakistan Staff Study. *International Commission of Jurists Review*, 8, 43–52.

Pakistan was constituted, at the time of the partition of India, from two separate areas of India, comprising peoples with very different cultures, habitat, economy and geographical orientation, but bound together by the common religion of Islam. Claims by East Pakistan (the Bengali area) for self-determination led to a conflict with West Pakistan, which sought to resolve the issue by force. The International Commission of Jurists was of the opinion that there was a *prima facie* case that in the campaign against the Bengalis, the crime of genocide was committed against the group comprising the Hindu population of East Bengal. (My own view is that the scale of the massacres, and the singling out of Bengali leaders, the elite, the educated, was such as to establish a *prima facie* case of genocide against the Bengalis as such, and not only against the Hindu population.) The ICJ studies provide, in addition to the analyses of the military campaign, background information and commentary on the issue of self-determination.

Kuper, Leo (1985). *The Prevention of Genocide*. New Haven, CT: Yale University Press. Biblio. 278 pp.

Chapters 4 and 5 deal with the genocide in Bangladesh in 1971, the failure of the United Nations to intervene, and the issues raised regarding the right to self-determination. In theory, the right is available to all peoples; in U.N. practice, it has been appreciably redefined as inapplicable to the different peoples comprising sovereign, independent states. The chapters provide bibliographical references to the genocide.

Survival International (1983). Genocide in Bangladesh. *Survival International Review*, 43, 135 pp.

An anonymous author describes the "programme of systematic extermination of indigenous nationalities of the Chittagong Hill Tracts because they are ethnically, religiously, and culturally different from the Muslim Bengalis." The area is now being colonized by Muslim Bengalis, with massacres and other killings and atrocities, burning of villages, dispossession of land holdings, herding into concentration camps, desecration of Buddhist temples, and detention, torture and murder of Buddhist monks. The article (pp. 7–25) provides a brief historical background and many references to available documentation. *See also* the account entitled "Militarisation of the Bandarban District" (pp. 26–28 in the same issue); Survival International's Urgent Action Bulletin, *Bangladesh. Chittagong Hill Tracts: More Massacres* (September 1984); and Survival International, *Bangladesh—Genocide in the Chittagong Hill Tracts—New Evidence* (May 1985).

Burundi

Lemarchand, René (1970). *Rwanda and Burundi*. New York: Praeger. Biblio. 562 pp.

This is an essential background to the genocidal conflicts in Rwanda and Burundi. It moves from the early history to the establishment of Tutsi domination over Hutu and Twa, and the later two-tier structure of domination under Belgian mandate. In Rwanda, ethnic relations rapidly polarized in the movement to independence, and in

March 1962 some murders by Tutsi bands set off massacres in which between 1,000 and 2,000 Tutsi men, women, and children were killed. After independence, and following a small but threatening invasion by Tutsi refugees, over 5,000 Tutsi were massacred in one area, and perhaps another 5,000–9,000 in other areas. In Burundi, the movement to decolonization did not result in ethnic polarization, and the indications were quite favorable for peaceful ethnic cooperation following independence. The genocide in Burundi by Tutsi against Hutu is not covered in the above book. It occurred later and it was vastly more destructive.

Lemarchand, René, and Martin, David (1974). *Selective Genocide in Burundi*. London: Minority Rights Group. Biblio. 36 pp.
This is of special interest for its account of the structural fluidity of the society, which provided many bases for cross-cutting relationships between the ethnic groups, and for its analysis of the political struggles that led to ethnic polarization, a Hutu rebellion reinforced by refugees from Zaire, and the selective genocide of Hutu by the Tutsi authorities. The term "selective genocide" refers to the fact that the educated and semieducated Hutu were special targets for annihilation. (Note: The large number of victims, between 100,000 and 200,000, indicates that the massacres extended beyond the educated and semi-educated.)

Equatorial Guinea

Fegley, Randall (1981). The U.N. Human Rights Commission: the Equatorial Guinea case. *Human Rights Quarterly*, 3(1), 34–47.
Fegley gives a brief account of the background, and some details, of the tyrannical and murderous regime of Macias. He refers to the persecution of the Bubis and Fernandinos as falling within the United Nations' definition of genocide. There is an interesting section on the involvement of outside powers in Equatorial Guinea, and their lack of concern.

International Commission of Jurists (1979). *The Trial of Macias in Equatorial Guinea*. Report by Alejandro Artucio. Geneva: International Commission of Jurists.
Following the coup in which Macias was overthrown, he was convicted of genocide and executed. In the above report, the author concluded that (1) Macias was wrongly convicted of genocide, the convention not having been signed or ratified by Equatorial Guinea, nor the crime of genocide incorporated in its laws, and (2) that though mass murder was established, the intentional destruction of national, ethnic, or religious groups in terms of the convention was not proved. (In relation to (1), note that the United Nations, in its original resolution on genocide, prior to the adoption of the convention, declared genocide to be a crime under international law, a view confirmed in an advocacy opinion by the International Court of Justice; and in relation to (2) *see* the contrary view expressed by Fegley.)

Guatemala

Nelson, Craig W., and Taylor, Kenneth I. (1983). *Witness to Genocide: The Present Situation of Indians in Guatemala*. London: Survival International. 44 pp.
An account by witnesses of murders and massacres in twenty-six separate incidents, affecting twenty-four different communities, twenty-five of the incidents being attributed to the Guatemalan armed forces. Counting only cases for which witnesses gave exact figures, some 551 people died in these incidents.

Stephen, David, and Wearne, Phillip (1984). *Central America's Indians*. London: Minority Rights Group. Biblio. 23 pp.

Part II, *Guatemala*, by Phillip Wearne, provides perspectives on Indian culture and society, on the significance of land ownership, and of the all-pervading religious values. Discrimination, expropriation of land and fragmentation of holdings, and racism have stimulated a growing political awareness and resistance to domination, exploitation and the threat to the survival of a traditional way of life. Repression, counterinsurgency strategies, massacres, disappearances, torture, scorched-earth devastation, and preventive terror have decimated the Indian population, and provide the evidence for the charges that the government is pursuing a genocidal policy against the Indians of Guatemala. (*See also* "Death and disorder in Guatemala," *Cultural Survival Quarterly*, 7(1), Spring 1982, and United Nations Document on the *Situation of Human Rights in Guatemala*, E/CN.4/1501.)

Nigeria: the Ibos

Legum, Colin (1966). The massacre of the proud Ibos. *The Observer* (London), 16 October, 12.
   This article is of interest for its discussion of the hostile dehumanizing propaganda that preceded the genocidal massacres of Easterners in northern Nigeria.

St. Jorre, John de (1972). *The Brothers' War: Biafra and Nigeria*. Boston: Houghton Mifflin. Biblio. 537 pp.
   While this study is primarily concerned with the civil war that followed the secession by the Eastern region in 1967, there is extensive analysis of ethnic relations, and many references to the massacre of Ibos in northern Nigeria in 1966. It was these massacres, which I would describe as genocidal, that led to the secession of the Eastern region. (In some respects, Ibos in Northern Nigeria constituted a hostage group, appreciably engaged in trade, and as skilled craftsmen, and with a different ethnic and religious background from the Muslim North. The massacres, however, were precipitated by ethnic conflict in the struggle for power in the federal government in Nigeria.)

Uganda

International Commission of Jurists (1974 and 1977). *Uganda and Human Rights: Reports to the United Nations*. Geneva: International Commission of Jurists.
   Between 1974 and 1977, the International Commission of Jurists submitted five complaints of human rights violations to the Secretary-General of the United Nations. These charged among other violations the arrest, detention, torture and killing of thousands of civilians, including the massacres of Acholi and Langi soldiers. [Charges of genocide by the Ugandan regime of Obote (1981–85) against the Baganda in particular are now being made. The extent of mass murder, with genocidal massacres also of other groups, appears to exceed the destruction of human life under Amin. It is too early for a full-scale study of the situation, but reference might be made, for example, to the pamphlet by Grace S. Ibingira, *Uganda's Ruin and How to End It*, March 1984, and "The fire next time," *Africa Events*, 1(7) July 1985, 14–16.]

Kyemba, Henry (1977). *State of Blood*. With a preface by Godfrey Lule. London: Transworld Publishers. 288 pp.
   Chapter 2 gives an account of the massacres perpetrated under Amin, including the massacres of soldiers recruited from the Acholi and Langi, who were supporters of the former president. *See also* the account given in David Martin (1974). *General Amin*, Chapter 8. London: Faber. (The massacres of Acholi and Langi, soldiers and villagers, would seem to fall within the U.N. definition of genocide.)

Minority Rights Group (1984). *Uganda and Sudan*. London: Minority Rights Group. 27 pp.

The report deals briefly with the historical background to the ethnic and religious conflicts in Uganda, Obote's first regime, the succeeding period of Amin's rule, and the second period of Obote's rule, following fraudulent elections. An account follows of large-scale massacres, during the second Obote regime, in the West Nile region, and there is a report also on the expulsion of the Banyarwanda. The most massive destruction of life has been inflicted on the Baganda. The two major guerrilla groups had based themselves on Baganda soil, and it was particularly in the Lowero region that the government engaged in massacres of villagers, looting, destruction of property, scorched earth, and many other atrocities, including onerous conditions in internment camps. Reference is also made to the campaign against the Karamajong.

Ukraine

The Soviet man-made famine of 1932–33 was particularly severe in the Ukraine, the Soviet Union's major grain producing area, which had been selected specially for rapid collectivization. Perhaps as many as 6 million Ukrainians died in the famine that resulted from this collectivization, brutally enforced against the resistance of the peasants, and from the seizure of their marketable grain to provide the necessary capital for industrial development. Currently it is being argued that this artificially induced famine was in fact an act of genocide, designed not only to crush peasant resistance to collectivization, but also to undermine the social basis of a Ukrainian national renaissance.

Conquest, Robert (1986). *Harvest of Sorrow: Soviet Collectivization and the Terror-Famine*. New York: Oxford University Press. Biblio. 393 pp.

The author introduces his study as follows: "Fifty years ago as I write these words, the Ukraine and the Ukrainian, Cossack and other areas to its east—a great stretch of territory with some forty million inhabitants—was like one vast Belsen. A quarter of the rural population, men, women and children, lay dead or dying, the rest in various stages of debilitation, with no strength to bury their families or neighbours. At the same time (as at Belsen), well-fed squads of police or party officials supervised the victims." The reference to Belsen is by no means extravagant.

This major study deals with the collectivization of peasant production and the concentration of peasants in collective farms under Party control; the liquidation of a class of peasants, the kulaks, in practice the most influential and resistant to the Party's plans; and the terror-famine of 1932–33 inflicted on the Ukraine and the largely Ukrainian Kuban (together with the Don and Volga areas). The estimated number of deaths is 14.5 million, made up of 11 million peasant dead in 1930–37, and 3.5 million arrested in this period and dying in camps later. Of this total, the estimated Ukrainian death roll is 5 million.

Conquest comments that "when it comes to the genocidal element, to the Ukrainian figures alone, we should remember that five million constitutes about 18.8% of the total population of the Ukraine (and about a quarter of the rural population)" (p. 304). He does not specifically charge genocide, but he clearly documents the commission of the crime: the assault by famine on the Ukrainian peasant population, with knowledge of its consequences and accompanied by a wide-ranging destruction of Ukrainian cultural and religious life and the slaughter of the Ukrainian intelligentsia—"a double blow at Ukrainian nationhood" (p. 326).

Dolot, Miron (1985). *Execution by Hunger: The Hidden Holocaust*. New York: W.W. Norton. Biblio. 231 pp.

This is an eyewitness account of the Great Famine (man-made) of 1932–33 in the

Ukraine. It is a horrendous account of unspeakable cruelty, the barbarity of bureaucratic dedication to the inhumanity of the collectivization campaign, and motivated, the author argues, by the intention to destroy Ukrainian nationalism.

Genocides in the Course of War

Soviet Russia

Conquest, Robert (1968). *The Great Terror: Stalin's Purge of the Thirties*. London: Macmillan. Biblio. 633 pp.

Conquest, Robert (1970). *The Nation Killers: The Soviet Deportation of Nationalities*. London: Macmillan. 222 pp.

Chapter 7 gives an account of the deportations from the northern Caucasus and the Crimea during World War II. The victim nations are cited as the Karachai, Balkars, Kalmyks, Chechens and Ingushi, Crimean Tatars, Volga Germans, and Meshketians (date of deportation of the latter not given). Some estimates are provided of the many who perished in the course of the deportations and resettlement. Conquest comments that they were not physically annihilated, but were destined to a more gradual oblivion. The operation falls within the United Nations definition of genocide: "(c) Deliberately inflicting on the group conditions of life calculated to bring about its physical destruction in whole or in part." For an earlier period, *see* Conquest (1968).

Nekrich, Aleksandr M. (1978). *The Punished Peoples*. Translated from the Russian by George Saunders. New York: Norton. 238 pp. Includes notes on sources.

The introductory chapters concentrate on the war years, followed in Chapter 4 by an account of the deportations and the special settlements to which the deported nations were consigned under conditions inimical to survival. Nekrich relates the deportations during the war to the deportation policies pursued more generally in Stalinist Russia (as do Solzhenitsyn and Conquest). Chapter 5 of this well researched study opens with minimal estimates of the casualties up to 1959: Chechens 22 percent, Kalmyks 14.8 percent, Ingush 9 percent, Karachai 30 percent and Balkans 26.5 percent. [Roy A. Medvedev, in Robert C. Tucker (ed.) (1977). *Stalinism: Essays in Historical Interpretation*. New York: Norton, at p. 227 gives the higher estimate that as many as 40 percent of these groups and others perished from hunger, cold, and epidemics in the uninhabited places in the east to which they were shipped by the trainload.]

Serbyn, Roman and Krawchenko, Bohdan (Eds.) (1986). *Famine in Ukraine 1932-1933*. Edmonton: Canadian Institute of Ukrainian Studies, University of Alberta.

This contributes further to the documentation of the famine as a deliberate act of genocide, directed against the resurgence of Ukrainian nationalism and culture. It includes a discussion of basic sources, outside reactions to the famine, the impact of the famine on the structure of Ukrainian society, an analysis of the famine of 1921-23 as a precursor to the later famine, and a chapter, contributed by Frank Chalk and Kurt Jonassohn, on conceptualizations of genocide and ethnocide.

Solzhenitsyn, Aleksandr I. (1974-1978). *The Gulag Archipelago*. 3 Vols. New York: Harper & Row. Vol. 1, 660 pp.; Vol. 2, 712 pp.; Vol. 3, 558 pp.

Solzhenitsyn describes different waves of slaughter in Soviet Russia during the Stalinist regime in which the victims were (a) 15 million peasants, or more, driven out into the taiga and the tundra, where they perished in the permafrost; (b) millions of communists, socialists, intelligentsia, ethnic groups; and (c) whole nations. [See Leo

Kuper's references to Solzhenitsyn in *Genocide* (New Haven, Yale University Press, 1982, pp. 140–143).] The massacres of political groups would not fall within the U.N. definition of genocide, but it is appropriately applied to the campaigns against Islam and Buddhism, and to the deportations of whole nations to the Siberian permafrost.

United States of America

Bedau, Hugo Adam (1974). Genocide in Vietnam? In Held, Virginia; Morgenbesser, Sidney; and Nagel, Thomas (Eds.). *Philosophy, Morality and International Affairs*, pp. 5–46. New York: Oxford University Press. 358 pp.

This article by Hugo Adam Bedau analyzes Sartre's argument (*see* Sartre, 1968) from a legal point of view, with an examination of possible approaches to the proof of the intent required to establish the crime of genocide. He comments further that U.S. action in Vietnam has given currency to the concept of *ecocide* as the intentional destruction of the physical environment needed to sustain human health and life in a given geographical region. Richard Falk, in his article in the same volume entitled "Ecocide, genocide and the Nuremberg tradition" (pp. 123–137), refers to "an increasing disposition by critics of American involvement to consider the indiscriminateness and magnitude of destruction on the peoples of Vietnam, Laos, and Cambodia as 'genocidal' " (pp. 123–124).

Sartre, Jean-Paul (1968). On genocide. *Ramparts*, February, 37–42.

In his indictment of the United States of America before the International War Crimes Tribunal (the Russell Tribunal on Vietnam), Sartre spoke of "villages burned, the populace subjected to massive bombing, livestock shot, vegetation destroyed by defoliants, crops ruined by toxic aerosols, and everywhere indiscriminate shooting, murder, rape, and looting. This is genocide in the strictest sense: massive extermination" (I would add to this list the establishment of free-fire zones, the search and destroy missions, the obliteration bombings, the use of high-technology weapons in counterinsurgency, and the devastation model of pacification). On the question of intent, Sartre did not assert that there was proof that the United States did in fact envision genocide. He argued simply that nothing prevented the United States from envisaging it, and that the genocidal intent was implicit in the facts.

9

Philosophy and the Contemporary Faces of Genocide: Multiple Genocide and Nuclear Destruction

William C. Gay and Ronald E. Santoni

For the first time in human history, the issue of whether or not human beings possess the capacity to destroy all life on the planet Earth is being debated. With the advent of atomic and thermonuclear weaponry, species self-destruction has become a matter of grave concern to thinkers and researchers in many fields. Graver still is the prospect that "there [may] never again be a time when self-extinction is beyond the reach of our species" (Schell, 1982).

Genocide and other forms of social madness have claimed over 100 million lives during the twentieth century (Aronson, 1983). During the last forty years a growing number of philosophers have struggled to define, understand and identify genocidal events. The splitting of the atom and the spectre of Hiroshima and Nagasaki, followed by an escalating arms race, have led to mounting philosophical concern about the meaning, roots, limits and morality of human violence, war, and more horrendous forms of human destruction. Given the awesome realities of the nuclear age, genocidal destruction seems to portend "multiple genocide" or even "omnicide." Philosophers can ignore such realities only at the risk of abandoning their vocation and their social responsibility.

Our research began with Gay's general survey of the philosophical literature on the arms race published between 1945 and 1985 (Gay, 1986). With this in hand, we chose, for the present purposes, to focus our bibliography and commentary on topics and approaches which dominate the relevant literature of the past four decades.

Social Responsibility

Throughout the nuclear age, a few philosophers have argued that the study of and a response to nuclear issues should be regarded as an appropriate, if not obligatory, professional activity; for example, Schilpp (1959), Anscombe (1961), and Shrader-Frechette (1985). Recently, Somerville (1983) and Santoni (1984) have attempted to awaken philosophers to the importance of addressing the vexing issues related to the arms race and nuclear war. Gay (1982) has argued that philosophers have a social responsibility in the nuclear age to analyze critically both public and governmental assumptions regarding nuclear war, while Govier (1983) addresses several of the areas where philosophers can apply their professional skills. Collections of essays and papers have been edited by Ginsberg (1969), Blake and Pole (1983, 1984), Gay (1984), and Fox and Groarke (1985).

Some efforts have also been made to bring together, at least in print, members of the strategic and philosophical–religious communities. These efforts reveal that most strategists are Hobbesian "realists" and most philosophers are "idealists" of one sort or another. Such efforts, however, have brought about little by way of change. Ford and Winters (1977) were among the first to bring together strategic and moral analyses, but a more recent special issue of *Ethics* on ethics and nuclear deterrence (*see* Hardin *et al.*, 1985) is likely to be influential. *See also* Cohen and Lee (1984), MacLean (1984), Paul (1985), and Sterba (1985).

Human Extinction

Throughout the nuclear arms race arguments have been offered to the effect that nuclear war could lead to human extinction. Various factors are cited, including blast effect, fallout, ozone depletion, and nuclear winter. Usually, those who make these arguments insist that nuclear war should never be waged and that nuclear weapons should be eliminated as soon as possible. The debate on this topic largely concerns the factual question of whether extinction is a likely consequence of nuclear "war," and the normative issue of whether such a horrendous consequence can or should ground a moral condemnation of nuclear war and nuclear weapons.

In 1946, Teilhard de Chardin (1964), believing our world is progressing toward increasingly integrated and higher forms, argued that we need not fear nuclear destruction. In sharp contrast, Schweitzer (1958) and Russell (1959) were among those calling for an immediate end to the nuclear arms race; they were gravely concerned about the possibility of universal nuclear destruction. Jaspers (1961), on the other side, allows conditions under which it would be moral to choose nuclear destruction. He argues that we should risk destruction in nuclear war over the alternative of our losing our "humanity" under totalitarianism.

Most of the debate on extinction has taken place in the 1980s, and it has been inspired in part by Schell's remarkable book, *The Fate of the Earth* (1982). Earlier, Somerville (1979, 1983) and Santoni (1980, 1984) warned about the peril of "omnicide"—the irreversible extinction of all sentient life—and called for a reorientation of individual and national priorities so to prevent universal nuclear destruction. They articulate some of the myths that intrude on our believing that "omnicide" is possible (*see too* Somerville, 1985, and Santoni in Gay, 1984). Schell stresses that nuclear war could lead to extinction and calls for immediate nuclear disarmament as the only moral response to what he regards as the absolute immorality of even taking the risk of human annihilation. Santoni argues, further, that because nuclear policies (of deterrence, for example), express the willingness, under certain circumstances, to incapacitate or destroy the adversary nation, they are genocidal in intention and imply "multiple genocide." Santoni appeals to such sources as the Nuremberg tradition and United Nations resolutions against genocide to condemn nuclear war planning and fighting and to demand individual and collective opposition and non violent resistance to such governmental acts.

In partial criticism, Routley (1984) argues that factually extinction is not likely and that morally the conclusions drawn are problematic. Similarly, Gay (1982, 1987b) argues that it is possible that nuclear war can have human survivors and societal recovery and that condemnation of nuclear war on the basis of worst-case scenarios is not the best ethical approach. He notes that if war at low levels is wrong, war at high levels is wrong, and he suggests that the immorality of war at even low levels provides a stronger condemnation of war than that which focuses on the prospect of omnicide. *See also* Aronson (1983), Bordo (1985), and Gallie (1983).

Domination

Much of the philosophical literature on the nuclear debate concerns issues of power and domination, as for example whether *realpolitik* is viable in the nuclear age, whether nuclear weapons render the nation state obsolete, and how an understanding of the Soviet and American systems affects the assessment of nuclear policies.

Only a few of the philosophers and theologians who address nuclear issues operate from Hobbesian assumptions. Morris (1985), for example, accepts the Hobbesian premise that once one nation attacks another, nations are in a "state of nature" (i.e. a state of war) in which principles of morality (such as noncombatant immunity) are no longer in effect. On this premise he argues that nuclear deterrence is an appropriate means of pursuing national security. Criticisms of *realpolitik* may be found in Gay (1984) and Fox and Groarke (1985). Several contributors argue that in the nuclear age Hobbesian premises hardly convey "realism:" the maximization of force (evidenced in the building of massive nuclear arsenals) and distrust (reflected in the indifference in achieving arms control treaties) leads to destruction, not security.

The thesis of global security is often debated in terms of whether it is compatible with the maintenance of the traditional concept of national sovereignty.

Schell (1982) is most widely associated with the view that elimination of nuclear weapons and maintenance of the nation-state are incompatible, although he subsequently modified his view (*see* Schell, 1984). More typically, philosophers advocate deep cuts in weapons and the pursuit of less violent and more lawful means for resolving international conflict. *See especially* Woodward (1985), Narveson (1985), and Geyer (1982).

Those who focus on the Soviet and American systems often argue that moral judgment should not be separated from an historical and political assessment of the Soviet and American systems. In their writings, the issue is often whether the Soviet Union is the "demonic enemy." Thinkers who accept some version of such contemporary Manicheism typically argue that the Soviet Union must be inhibited in its urge to dominate, even if this effort leads to nuclear war. Many of the contributors to Hardin *et al.* (1985) operate from this perspective. In sharp contrast Howard (1984), Anderson (1984), and Butler (1984) argue that the actions of both nations need to be placed in a proper historical context. They note that political domination has been characteristic of governments throughout human history and suggest that many analyses of U.S.–Soviet relations misinterpret a symptom as the cause. On these topics, Somerville (1975, 1976, 1978, 1981) has perhaps made the largest contribution. On the one hand, he questions the compatibility of U.S. nuclear policy with the principles of American democracy. On the other hand, he shows that the principles of Marxism are consistent with the aims of the peace movement in the nuclear age. *See too* Shibata (1977).

Just War

The theory of "just war" dates back to the work of St. Augustine and St. Thomas and delineates the criteria for distinguishing just from unjust war. In this regard, respect for the distinction between combatants and noncombatants made easy the transition from the critique of conventional to the critique of nuclear weapons and strategy. Before Hiroshima, Ford (in Wasserstrom, 1970) had used this distinction to argue against the shift to strategic bombing. Roszak (1963) argued early in the McNamara era that pursuit of either countervalue or counterforce nuclear policy violates just-war criteria and that since the U.S. was pursuing both (with MAD and flexible response), its nuclear policies were immoral. Although Ramsey (1968), the American Catholic Bishops (1983), and O'Brien (1983) recognize just war's presumption against the use of nuclear weapons, each permits the deployment of nuclear devices for deterrent purposes. Whether just-war theory can ever be used to sanction any nuclear options has been broadly questioned by Wells (1969, 1984). Santoni (1985), pointing to the vulnerability to accident and the technological uncontrollability of nuclear weapons, contends that nuclear weaponry demolishes the concept of a "just nuclear war" and that "nuclear pacifism" is the only morally appropriate response to the just-war themes of discrimination and restraint. Valuable surveys of the historical development and current viability of just war can be found in Churchill (1983) and Johnson (1981). *See too* Paskins and Dockrill (1979), Johnson (1984), Tucker (1985), and Walzer (1977).

Utilitarianism

Much of the work by philosophers, especially in the analytic tradition, is based on utilitarian ethics and game theory. They and their critics often begin by rehashing the debate between deontologists (e.g. moral absolutists) and consequentialists (e.g. utilitarians). Arguments continue over which approach is more applicable to nuclear issues and on what version of each approach is correct. An application of an absolutist model can be found in Kenny (1985), and a critique of the applicability of the deontic approach can be found in Shaw (1984). Strict deontologists generally find nuclear deterrence to be immoral because, should deterrence fail, it would kill innocents in acts of retaliatory horror; consequentialists, on the other hand, are more likely to condone some version of deterrence if it makes war unlikely. Among analytic philosophers, the more deontic approach is evident in Donaldson (1985). For an illustration of how one can reach negative conclusions about participation in war, whether one starts from deontological or from consequentialist premises, *see* Goodin (1985) and Stevenson (1986). *See too* Wasserstrom (1985) and Hoekema (1983).

In game theory, one sets up a model for conflict situations, assigns numerical values to alternative outcomes, and then calculates which set of moves rational players should select. This procedure can be found in Lackey (1982, 1984) and Groarke (1985). Each uses game theory to arrive at the conclusion that nuclear disarmament should be pursued. However, some philosophers who invoke game theory become advocates of nuclear deterrence. Consider Gauthier (1984), Kavka (1978), and Hardin (1983). Note too the diverse use of game theory in MacLean (1984) and Paul (1985). Rapoport (1964) and Green (1966) argued more than two decades ago that the use of game theory in planning nuclear strategy is pseudoscientific and dangerous. Among philosophers, Wolff (1970) made a similar argument in his seminal essay on the topic. *See too* Benn (1984).

Metaphysics

Those who turn to metaphysics in analyzing the nuclear age are often concerned with the conceptual choices Western people have made in their manner of relating to nature and persons—in particular the choice by Westerners to "have dominion over" or to control both. Easlea (1983) characterizes this choice in terms of the "masculine objective" of dominating nature. Some thinkers who turn to Kant have contributed essays to Ginsberg (1969). Typically, they place hope in Kant's idea of achieving peace through a federation of nations. Others, such as Butler (1984) and Parsons (1982), use Hegel to argue that peace is contingent and that the real problem lies at a level much deeper than the history of nation states. They contend that the world has not moved beyond the "master-slave dialectic," that is, the dialectic of domination. Perhaps the deepest insight into our plight has been offered by those who combine Heidegger's probing questions with Eastern alternatives. Schorstein (1962) turns to Heidegger to present the atomic bomb as one of the last and most tragic consequences of the West's loss of "nearness" to nature and persons. Weinberger (1984) uses Heidegger's comments on death and technology as a point of departure for understanding nuclear weapons. Zimmerman (1985), Heim (1984), Litke (1985), and Dombrowski (1983) either use Heidegger to thematize the West's over emphasis on control or turn to Eastern traditions for ways of relating to nature and persons that are based more on harmony than exploitation.

The feverish arms race, the possibility of human self-extinction, the horrors of nuclear reality beckon us to reexamine our self-understanding and to approach ourselves, others, and nature in a new way. In particular, Heidegger calls for a new style of thinking which is more meditative than calculative, more receptive than aggressive—one which will "let beings be." We can live in peace if we allow it. We can be open to life rather than death and create a "clearing" for Being instead of the "space" of Nothing.

Conclusions

Areas of abiding consensus appear to have developed among philosophers who address the nuclear arms race and the issues of nuclear war. Although, as a group, philosophers have been slow to incorporate these vexing issues into the mainstream of current philosophy, they often agree as to what constitute the key issues. And although they may disagree in respect to specific policies and actions, they increasingly agree that social responsibility is an essential part of their vocation as philosophers.

Consensus also appears to be emerging in regard to just-war theory. Fewer and fewer philosophers writing from the "just war" perspective find actual or possible nuclear actions and policies consistent with just war's criteria of discrimination and restraint. Only a small minority of philosophers would even attempt to offer a moral justification for the superpowers' present positions.

But there are also areas of protracted controversy. The approach of game theory remains in dispute both theoretically and practically. There is broad disagreement on whether and how to form game-theoretic models for conflict and on whether and how to assign numerical values to possible outcomes. The regularity with which diametrically opposed conclusions can be reached suggests that the prospect for eventual consensus in this area is rather bleak.

Controversy continues regarding the empirical status and normative use of the extinction thesis. Since no group, however, argues for the complete irrelevance of the extinction thesis, the prospect for consensus in this debate may be less remote.

There are areas in which philosophers are making distinctive contributions over and above the analysis and clarification of the terms of the debate. Thinkers carrying out metaphysical and psychological inquiry into the roots of destructiveness and the arms race have made noteworthy criticisms of the assumptions underlying the superpowers' strategic policies, and have suggested important alternatives to horrific military weaponry for the achievement of national or global security. By having us reexamine our self-understanding and our perception of the rest of the world, metaphysical thinkers have helped us diagnose our plight as would-be controllers (and destroyers!) of the Earth. They have also nurtured a radical rethinking of our modes of thinking and of the political arrangements of our world.

As Noam Chomsky has pointed out, no profession has a more authentic claim than philosophy to be concerned with the intellectual and moral culture of society and civilization ("Philosophers and public policy," *Ethics*, 1968, 1-9). Nor does any profession have claim to better tools for analyzing and criticizing prevailing ideology and the premises of public policy. The Socratic tradition in philosophy calls not only for the analysis and elucidation of concepts, but for a radical examination and critical scrutiny of all presupposed beliefs and established doctrines. Given contemporary beliefs about the feasibility of "nuclear deterrence," "first strike," "self-defense" or "limited nuclear war," for example, philosophers contribute distinctly to the discussion of futuristic destruction by analyzing critically the meaning, assumptions, and implications of accepted doctrines and policy alternatives—especially when these doctrines have been formulated with vested (national) interests and ideological bias, especially when their practice might spell holocaust or even extinction. By training, philosophers seem uniquely qualified to consider whether any set of values or meanings can justify resort to action that might result in the elimination of all human values and meanings. By doing this work—by making evident the implications of old value standards and foundations of meanings— philosophers are making their distinctive contribution, not simply to the creation of new meanings and values, but to the continuation of life on this planet.

As philosophers we cannot be content with analyzing and interpreting the world. We must also change it for the better, if we are to save it from grotesque destruction. That surely is our minimal social responsibility. Clearer concepts and more knowledgeable debate, more careful and sensitive reasoning, reexamined and recreated values, surely prepare us for resolute and responsible action. In that action lies our hope to prevent the unthinkable from happening.

Bibliography

American Catholic Bishops (1983). The challenge of peace: God's promise and our response. *Origins*, 12, 698-728.
  Seeing peace in the nuclear age as a moral and political imperative, this "pastoral letter" attempts to set forth Catholic teachings on war and peace. Acknowledging that the destructive potential of nuclear power threatens all the created order, the

bishops offer a "definitive and decisive" "no" to nuclear war. Although they question morality of any use of nuclear weapons, they allow deterrence as a "step on the way toward progressive disarmament."

Anderson, Lyle V. (1984). The representation and resolution of the nuclear conflict. In Gay (1984), 67–79.

Addresses how the American people and government often represent the Soviets. Shows that the question "What about the Russians?" needs to be related to historical phases of Soviet society and cannot be separated from the question "What about the Americans?"

Anscombe, G.E.M. (1961). War and murder. In *Ethics, Religion and Politics*. Oxford: Basil Blackwell. Vol. 3 of *Collected Papers of G.E.M. Anscombe*.

One of the early "classic" arguments against obliteration bombing of cities. Although critical of pacifism, repudiates the view that obliteration of innocent people can be justified by appeal to the principle of "double-effect."

Aronson, Ronald (1983). *The Dialectic of Disaster: A Preface to Hope*. London: Verso. 329 pp.

An essay on power and madness, focusing on the Holocaust, Stalin's socialism, America's Vietnam, the Zionist–Palestinian conflict, and the movement towards nuclear holocaust. Argues that each case involves a "rupturing with reality": a madness in which those holding state power, frustrated by their impotence to change reality effectively, sought to destroy it. This genocidal social dynamic of power/impotence/madness/murder has characterized our century. Still makes a passionate case for hope through reflective action.

Benn, S.I. (1984). Deterrence or appeasement: or, on trying to be rational about nuclear war. *Journal of Applied Philosophy*, 1, 5–20.

Argues that, in light of the levels of violence entailed by MAD, efforts to justify nuclear retaliation fail. Also argues that in 1939 resistance to Nazism was justified. Concludes that whereas we are justified in risking total destruction to resist evils such as Nazi genocide, we are not justified in adopting nuclear policies that include a conditional intention to perform evil on the same scale.

Blake, Nigel, and Pole, Kay (Eds.) (1983). *Dangers of Deterrence: Philosophers on Nuclear Strategy*. London: Routledge & Kegan Paul. 184 pp.

Seven essays, mostly by British philosophers, that assess nuclear deterrence. Advocates unilateralism as the best route to a politically independent Europe. Includes Gallie's critique of the apocalyptic thinking behind many unilateralist arguments. *See* Gallie (1983).

Blake, Nigel, and Pole, Kay (Eds.) (1984). *Objections to Nuclear Defense: Philosophers on Deterrence*. London: Routledge & Kegan Paul. 187 pp.

Ten essays, mostly by British philosophers, that provide moral and political objections to nuclear policies of current Western governments.

Bordo, Jonathan (1985). Nuclear weapons as a threat to the permanence of life. In Fox and Groarke (1985), 100–106.

Argues that since *any* use of nuclear weapons threatens the permanence of life, there is absolutely no justification for using them. Contends deterrence is a code word (of mystification) which the nuclear powers use to justify their use. Compare to Gauthier (1984).

Butler, Clark (1984). Peaceful coexistence as the nuclear traumatization of humanity. In Gay (1984), 81–94.
> Uses Hegel to present the notion of nuclear trauma as the result of peaceful coexistence and argues that we must either experience this destruction in fact or in imagination in order to move on to new social forms.

Churchill, Robert P. (1983). Nuclear arms as a philosophical and moral issue. *The Annals of the American Academy of Political and Social Science*, 469, 46–57.
> Assesses deterrence theory in light of the threat of nuclear annihilation. Using just-war theory, argues that threats of nuclear retaliation are immoral and that recent counterforce strategies and the Strategic Defense Initiative ("Star Wars") are also immoral since they depend on threats of nuclear retaliation.

Cohen, Avner, and Lee, Steven (Eds.) (1984). *Nuclear Weapons and the Future of Humanity*. Totowa, NJ: Rowman & Allenheld. 496 pp.
> Presents the threat of nuclear holocaust as preeminent among current apocalyptic threats. The twenty-five contributions focus largely on conceptual and moral issues. Includes several essays that address themes of apocalypse, Armageddon, final epidemic, genocide, and omnicide.

Dombrowski, Daniel (1983). Gandhi, sainthood, and nuclear weapons. *Philosophy East and West*, 33, 401–406.
> Assesses Gandhi's philosophy in light of nuclear weapons. Denies that the latter antiquate the former. Presents the options of global nonviolence or suicide of the human species.

Donaldson, Thomas (1985). Nuclear deterrence and self-defense. In Hardin *et al.* (1985), 537–548.
> Argues that a policy of nuclear deterrence is morally unacceptable because it violates certain enabling conditions for the right to self-defense. Technological recalcitrance alone of nuclear weapons inhibits the fulfillment of those enabling conditions.

Easlea, Brian (1983). *Fathering the Unthinkable*. London: Pluto Press.
> Argues that the nuclear arms race is, to a large degree, underwritten by "masculine behavior in the pursuit and application of scientific inquiry." As a masculine enterprise, modern science—in a world of highly competitive nation-states—fuels the fires of human conflict. The masculine objective of ever mounting power over nature has been the "inexorable driving force" of the arms race.

Ford, Harold P., and Winters, Francis X. (Eds.) (1977). *Ethics and Nuclear Strategy*. Maryknoll, NY: Orbis Books. 246 pp.
> Gives diverse views of strategists and ethicists on the Schlesinger doctrine of 1974, which involved a shift to greater reliance on counterforce. The editors find this doctrine to be incompatible with proper ethical principles.

Ford, John C. (1970). The morality of obliteration bombing. In Wasserstrom (1970).
> Classic critique of saturation bombing; that is, the shift from counterforce (military) to countervalue (population) targets. Written in 1945 just before Hiroshima. Stresses the immorality of intentionally killing the innocent.

Fox, Michael Allen, and Groarke, Leo (Eds.) (1985). *Nuclear War: Philosophical Perspectives*. New York: Peter Lang. 278 pp.
> Philosophers from diverse traditions provide twelve articles and fourteen

commentaries, divided into five parts on: (a) Nuclear Delusions, (b) The Individual and the State, (c) The Environment, (d) Conceptual and Psychological Dilemmas, and (e) The Pursuit of Peace. *See* Bordo (1985), Litke (1985), Narveson (1985), Shrader-Frechette (1985), Somerville (1985), Zimmerman (1985).

Gallie, W.B. (1983). Three main fallacies in discussions of nuclear weapons. In Blake and Pole (1983), 157–178.
Criticizes apocalyptic thinking (that is, the view that the human species is threatened by nuclear weapons), and suggests that such prophetic stances undercut efforts at disarmament. Notes that presenting the nuclear threat as an apocalyptic prophecy dissociates it from scientific prediction and respectability. Suggests that once an apocalyptic vision is adopted, the need to learn more about the situation ends. Concludes that apocalyptic thinking is a poor strategy because it is not an effective way to try to persuade those with power.

Gauthier, David (1984). Deterrence, maximization, and rationality. *Ethics*, 94, 474–495.
Proposes to demonstrate that deterrence can be part of a fully rational policy. On the grounds that morality follows rationality, and practical rationality focuses on the "maximization of benefit," offers an unnecessarily technical argument to show that nuclear deterrence, in spite of its horrific character, is a moral policy that aims at promoting rational interaction among nations.

Gay, William C. (1982). Myths about nuclear war: misconceptions in public beliefs and governmental plans. *Philosophy and Social Criticism*, 9, 115–144.
Argues that while less-than-all-out nuclear wars are possible and probably would have survivors, rejection of MAD and pursuit of victory are problematic.

Gay, William C. (Ed.) (1984). *Philosophy and the Debate on Nuclear Weapons Systems and Policies. Philosophy and Social Criticism*, 10 (3 & 4). 188 pp.
Fourteen articles by philosophers from continental and analytic traditions on the extinction thesis, power and domination, nuclear weapons, and the morality of deterrence and the quest for peace. All contributors are critical of current nuclear weapons systems and policies. *See* Anderson (1984), Butler (1984), Howard (1984), Routley (1984), Santoni (1984), Weinberger (1984).

Gay, William C. (1987a). The nuclear debate and American philosophers: 1945 to 1985. In Freese, Peter (Ed.). *Religion and Philosophy in the United States of America*, 303–315. Essen: Die Blau Eule.
Discusses about half of the philosophical sources on the nuclear debate. Focuses on: (a) the social responsibility of philosophers; (b) the extinction of the human species; (c) the problem of domination; (d) just-war theory and religious ethics; (e) utilitarianism and game theory; and (f) the insights of metaphysics.

Gay, William C. (1987b). Nuclear discourse and linguistic alienation. *Journal of Social Philosophy*, 18(2).
Uses F. Rossi-Landi's comparison of linguistics and economics to argue that nuclear discourse is a special sublanguage which results in linguistic alienation. Calls for abolition of nuclear discourse as a special sublanguage. Discusses the negative role of Somerville's "omnicide" and the positive role of Heidegger's "House Friend."

Geyer, Alan (1982). *The Idea of Disarmament! Rethinking the Unthinkable*. Elgin, IL: The Brethren Press. 256 pp.
A response to Herman Kahn's efforts to make nuclear war "thinkable," that is, his

views that nuclear weapons can be used and nuclear war can be won. Tries to make disarmament thinkable.

Ginsberg, Robert (Ed.) (1969). *The Critique of War: Contemporary Philosophical Explorations*. Chicago: Henry Regnery. 360 pp.
Introduction and eighteen essays, mostly by philosophers. Addresses the role of philosophers, causes of war, the war system itself, the unjustifiability of war, and the alternative to war. Several of the essays address the nuclear threat.

Goodin, Robert E. (1985). Disarming nuclear apologists. *Inquiry*, 28, 153–176.
Examines four logical uses of nuclear weapons: whether all-out or limited and whether first or second strike. Shows the immorality of each from both consequentialist and deontological perspectives.

Govier, Trudy (1983). Nuclear illusion and individual obligations. *Canadian Journal of Philosophy*, 13, 471–492.
Addresses realities and illusions concerning the nuclear arms race and calls on philosophers to address nuclear issues.

Green, Philip (1966). *Deadly Logic: The Theory of Nuclear Deterrence*. Columbus: Ohio State University Press. 361 pp.
Classic critique of systems analysis as applied to nuclear strategy. Gives special attention to Herman Kahn and to game theory. Also raises issues in ethical theory and the democratic process to criticize the propriety, as well as the adequacy, of these various academic supports for theory of deterrence.

Groarke, Leo (1985). Nuclear arms control: eluding the prisoner's dilemma. In Fox and Groarke (1985), 182–183.
Discusses the problem of the superpowers' mutual distrust in the light of the "prisoner's dilemma," a classic problem in decision theory. Argues that, in the present circumstances, there is no reason to regard the issue of disarmament as an instance of the prisoner's dilemma; that even "extreme skepticism" about Soviet intentions still entails a policy on NATO's part to pursue arms control and a massive reduction in nuclear arsenals.

Hardin, Russell (1983). Unilateral versus mutual disarmament. *Philosophy and Public Affairs*, 12, 236–254.
An extended critique of Lackey (1982).

Hardin, Russell, *et al.* (Eds.) (1985). *Symposium on Ethics and Nuclear Deterrence. Ethics*, 95. 385 pp.
Eighteen articles by philosophers and strategists. Generally speaking, the philosophers are from the "analytic" tradition and the strategists are from the "realist" tradition. Positions advocated range from a call for more counterforce and strategic defense systems to nuclear disarmament. *See* Donaldson (1985), Morris (1985), Narveson (1985), Tucker (1985). Wasserstrom (1985).

Heim, Michael (1984). Reason as response to nuclear terror. *Philosophy Today*, 28, 300–307.
A critique of Hans Ebeling, a contemporary German philosopher who turns to Kant and Heidegger for an ethical response to nuclear terror. The author largely drops Kant, keeps Heidegger, and adds the East (primarily Taoism) in the development of his critique.

Hoekema, David A. (1983). Intentions, threats, and nuclear deterrence. In Bradie, Michael; Attig, Thomas; and Rescher, Nicholas (Eds.). *The Applied Turn in Contemporary Philosophy*, pp. 111–125. Bowling Green, OH: Bowling Green State University.
Argues that although nuclear deterrence might be a "temporarily and provisionally justifiable option" for a nation in some *possible* world, it is both immoral and extremely dangerous in our *actual* post-Hiroshima, nuclear world.

Howard, Michael W. (1984). Utopianism and nuclear deterrence. In Gay (1984), 53–65.
Shows that when Catholic bishops and Walzer address the morality of deterrence, they abstract from history and that when Schell addresses the rationality of deterrence he confuses a symptom for a cause. The result is that the former end with an ambiguous ethics and the latter ends with utopian politics.

Jaspers, Karl (1961). *The Future of Mankind*. Translated by E.B. Ashton. Chicago: University of Chicago Press. 342 pp.
Originally published in German in 1958 as *Die Atombombe und die Zukunft des Menschen*. Presents the disjunction of destruction or fundamental change, but sanctions some conditions under which destruction should be chosen. Sees pure coexistence as unlikely since it would require radical isolation. Contends that there is conflict between Soviet totalitarianism and Western freedom, and rejects survival if it would result in a totalitarianism in which persons lose their "humanity."

Johnson, James Turner (1981). *Just War Tradition and the Restraint of War: A Moral and Historical Inquiry*. Princeton, NJ: Princeton University Press. 380 pp.
Sees moral life, at least in part, in terms of keeping faith with identifiable continuous values of historical communities. Attempts to identify values of just war tradition and to show how and why just war concepts have functioned in past.

Johnson, James Turner (1984). *Can Modern War Be Just?* New Haven, CT: Yale University Press. 215 pp.
Attempt by an important historian of "just war" thought to "recover" the just-war tradition for a nuclear age. Argues that permission to engage in the use of violent force goes hand in hand with the theme of restraint; that the tradition allows the justification of only "limited uses of force for limited causes." Contends that "just war" consensus implies neither militarism nor pacifism. *See* Santoni (1985) for a detailed challenge.

Kavka, Gregory S. (1978). Some paradoxes of deterrence. *The Journal of Philosophy*, 75, 285–302.
Addresses deterrence from the perspectives of the moral evaluation of actions and the moral evaluation of agents (and their states). Paradoxes arise when an effort is made to link both types of moral evaluation. Argues against the coherence of such linkage and leaves separate the two types of evaluation. Concludes that the presence of paradoxes does not undercut deterrence; rather, their presence indicates the limits of moral evaluation.

Kenny, Anthony (1985). *The Logic of Deterrence*. London: Firethorn Press. 103 pp.
Examines the logic of nuclear deterrence. Argues that although actual fighting of a nuclear war would be neither rational nor morally acceptable, it may be reasonable and right to pursue a policy of nuclear deterrence so as to prevent a nuclear war. Suggests a position of "prudent nuclear disarmament" between unilateralism and multilateralism.

Lackey, Douglas, P. (1982). Missiles and morals: a utilitarian look at nuclear deterrence. *Philosophy and Public Affairs*, 11, 189–231.

Assesses the options of superiority, equivalence, and nuclear disarmament. Counters the game-theoretic arguments in support of nuclear options. A widely reprinted article and frequently criticized by supporters of game theory. Remains one of the classic arguments that the risks of nuclear war under U.S. unilateral nuclear disarmament are less than the risks under nuclear deterrence.

Lackey, Douglas P. (1984). *Moral Principles and Nuclear Weapons*. Totowa, NJ: Rowman & Allenheld. 265 pp.

Gives an overview of moral principles and the history of nuclear weapons/strategy. Cites standards of the common good, human rights and fairness as basis for moral criticism and argues against extreme versions of pacifism and nationalism. On the basis of each of the three standards of moral criticism, concludes that nonpossession of nuclear weapons is better than either detente or victory.

Litke, Robert (1985). Consciousness, gender, and nuclear politics. In Fox and Groarke (1985), 159–172.

Points to various contrasts, such as aggressiveness and receptivity, and over emphasis on the former as basis for problems. Relates Deikman's "object" and "receptive" modes of consciousness to Gilligan's "ethics of justice" and "ethics of care," and argues for the need to balance assertiveness with receptivity at all levels of human consciousness.

MacLean, Douglas (Ed.) (1984). *The Security Gamble: Deterrence Dilemmas in the Nuclear Age*. Totowa, NJ: Rowman & Allanheld. 170 pp.

Essays by both strategists and philosophers which address the topic of deterrence, covering both the history of and options in U.S. nuclear policy and the moral justification of deterrence.

Morris, Christopher W. (1985). A contractarian defense of nuclear deterrence. In Hardin *et al.* (1985), 479–496.

A Hobbesian argument for deterrence. Concedes that counterforce is problematic, but defends countervalue. Claims nuclear retaliation (countervalue) is not immoral, because morality presupposes the condition of cooperation and an enemy attack would end cooperative relations (i.e. would return the nations to a Hobbesian amoral "state of nature"). If such a retaliation would not be morally impermissible, "threatening to retaliate with such a strike in a state of nature is morally permissible."

Narveson, Jan (1985). Getting on the road to peace: a modest proposal. In Hardin *et al.* (1985), 589–605. Also in Fox and Groarke (1985), 201–215.

Given the possibility of mutual nuclear devastation, suggests that nations renounce any military ambitions except those of defense. Proposes that each potential nuclear aggressor make clear its defensive posture by restricting itself to a force that could not plausibly be used for aggressive purposes.

O'Brien, William V. (1983). Just war in a nuclear context. *Theological Studies*, 44, 191–220.

Contends that because of the "shocking character of modern war," the just-war doctrine must be adhered to seriously. Argues that there is a strong moral presumption against the use of nuclear weapons but that nuclear war is not–like genocide–*malum in se*. Argues for a counterforce deterrence position joined to a just-war war-fighting posture. *See* Donaldson (1985) and Santoni (1984, 1985) for contrast.

Parsons, Howard L. (1982). On Hegel, Marx and nuclear war (comments on Butler). *Dialectics and Humanism*, 9, 129–137.
Notes the probability of nuclear war and the resulting genocide or biocide. Argues against the view that "the imperial lordship of the sovereign nation-state" is the central problem. Situates the problem at the level of class conflict, in particular the economic relations.

Paskins, Barrie, and Dockrill, Michael (1979). *The Ethics of War*. Minneapolis: Minnesota University Press. 332 pp.
A philosopher and a historian seek to address in detail the concrete issue of bombing cities. They consider this phenomenon as practiced by both terrorists or freedom fighters and by states, and as threatened in nuclear deterrence. They propose modified forms of the just-war tradition and pacifism and use the Nuremberg trial for criteria of when war is criminal. They claim to have established "at least a *prima facie* case" of criminality against those who have the opportunity to reflect on these issues yet have failed to raise the moral questions in the political arena.

Paul, Ellen Frankel (Ed.) (1985). *Nuclear rights/nuclear wrongs. Social Philosophy and Policy*, 3(1). 222 pp.
Eleven articles, primarily on the effectiveness and morality of various versions of deterrence. Most of the philosophers judge the versions of deterrence they analyze to be immoral, at least in part because of the catastrophic consequences, as well as risks, of nuclear war. None of the rest (broadly in political science) rejects deterrence; several focus on the Soviet threat and how to meet it.

Ramsey, Paul (1968). *The Just War: Force and Political Responsibility*. New York and London: Scribner's and University Press of America. 554 pp.
Attempts to clarify the grounds on which we "should make judgments" regarding the justice of resorting to war. Defends deterrence by arguing for the morality of "mounting a deterrent" whose effects flow from the shared fear of collateral damage from modern weapons of war.

Rapoport, Anatol (1964). *Strategy and Conscience*. New York: Harper & Row. 323 pp.
Effort by one of the developers of game theory to show the limits in the application of game theory. A passionate, yet rigorous critique of the methods of the formal nuclear strategists. Argues that, when applied to nuclear strategy, the "rational solutions" of game theory are too narrow. Presents the need to "elevate conscience" both in the game theory of strategists and the international relations of politicians.

Roszak, Theodore (1963). A just war analysis of two types of deterrence. *Ethics*, 73, 100–109.
Based on the just-war principle of noncombatant immunity. Notes that the U.S. was developing nuclear options of countervalue (with MAD) and counterforce (with flexible response). Argues that neither option meets the criteria of just-war theory and that pursuit of both is worse than pursuit of either.

Routley, Richard (1984). Metaphysical fall-out from the nuclear predicament. In Gay (1984), 19–34.
Argues that human extinction in nuclear war is not likely and, even if it were, that fact is not sufficient to show nuclear weapons to be immoral.

Russell, Bertrand (1959). *Common Sense and Nuclear Warfare*. London: Allen & Unwin. 92 pp.

Argues not only for elimination of nuclear weapons but also for an end to war, since belligerents could again make nuclear weapons. Stresses the need for reduction of East-West tension so that any arms reductions will be significant. In one of the appendices, Russell notes how the Soviet development of nuclear weapons led to the abandonment of his earlier view that the U.S. should pressure the U.S.S.R. to internationalize atomic weapons, even threatening war if necessary.

Santoni, Ronald E. (1980). Omnicide and the problem of belief. *The Churchman*, August/September, 8-9.
Discusses the myths and habits that stand in the way of our believing that nuclear omnicide is possible. Contends that not taking action against the arms race and omnicide is tantamount to casting one's lot for them.

Santoni, Ronald E. (1984a). The arms race, genocidal intent and individual responsibility. In Gay (1984), 9-18.
Draws upon the Nuremberg tradition and U.N. resolutions to characterize and criticize the arms race as genocidal in intent. On the basis of a "responsibility model" of crime suggested by Richard Falk, argues that citizens everywhere have the responsibility (i.e. obligation) to oppose and resist any government action or policy that threatens to annihilate nations or any other ethnic, political, religious or national group.

Santoni, Ronald E. (1984b). Nuclear insanity and multiple genocide. In Charny, Israel W. (Ed.) *Toward the Understanding and Prevention of Genocide*, 147-153. Boulder, CO: Westview Press.
A widely reprinted article. Contends that according both to ordinary usage and the dictionary meaning of words, the arms race is "insane" or "mad." The author offers many cases to support his contention that leaders of nations and policy makers are still proceeding according to the attitudes and rules of a pre-atomic age, and are thus involved in psychological denial of the fact that the starting of a nuclear war would likely lead to what he coins "multiple genocide."

Santoni, Ronald E. (1985). "Just war" and nuclear reality. *Philosophy Today*, 29, 175-190.
Argues that the uncontrollability and inherent indiscriminateness of nuclear weapons—their technological recalcitrance alone—preclude possibility of nuclear *jus in bello* and *jus ad bellum*. Accordingly, contends that nuclear pacifism is the only appropriate response to just-war themes of restraint and discrimination. Any attempt to justify resort to nuclear war or use of nuclear weapons is a form of "nuclear insanity."

Schell, Jonathan (1982). *The Fate of the Earth*. New York: Alfred A. Knopf. 244 pp.
One of the most important books on the nuclear predicament. Describes the overlapping ways in which the creatures of the Earth would die if the full power of our nuclear arsenals were ever unleashed. Explores the meanings of human extinction and the implications of our knowledge to bring it about. A stirring call for each of us to rearrange his or her thinking and the world's political arrangements so as to save our planet from nuclear extermination.

Schell, Jonathan (1984). *The Abolition*. New York: Alfred A. Knopf. 173 pp.
A partial rethinking of *The Fate of the Earth* (Schell, 1982). Argues against what he considers to be the reason nuclear weapons have not been eliminated: the belief (earlier shared by Schell) that world government is necessary for nuclear disarma-

ment. Suggests that nations can remain autonomous and abolish nuclear weapons. Yet a form of nuclear deterrence is advocated: nations would retain not only the knowledge but also the capacity to manufacture nuclear weapons. Since a retaliatory force could be available in about six weeks, there would be nuclear deterrence without the actual existence of nuclear weapons.

Schilpp, Paul Arthur (*c.* 1959). The abdication of philosophy. *Kant Studien*, 46, 480–495.
Notes that philosophers are ignoring the "impending doom" resulting from nuclear weapons. Argues against the style of philosophy that views "moral" and "social obligation" as meaningless and argues for what is now termed applied philosophy. Advocates that philosophers become propagandists for "saving the human race from destroying itself."

Schorstein, Joseph (1962). The metaphysics of the atom bomb. *Philosophical Journal*, 5, 1–17.
Uses Heidegger's work to suggest that the production of nuclear weapons is the final result of the "absence of nearness;" that is, what Heidegger elsewhere terms the shift from meditative to calculative thinking. Presents the destructivenesss of nuclear weapons as total negation, and relates this prospect to the concern for Being and Nothingness in metaphysics. Argues that metaphysics demands that each individual must choose "between creating and destroying, between responsibility and irresponsibility, between love and hate" and notes that affirmative choices give us hope.

Schweitzer, Albert (1958). *Peace or Atomic War?* New York: Henry Holt & Co. 47 pp.
Texts of broadcasts on "The Renunciation of Nuclear Tests," "The Danger of an Atomic War," and "Negotiations at the Highest Level." Cites scientific data on the consequences of nuclear tests and war and calls for an end to testing and for nuclear disarmament.

Shaw, William H. (1984). Nuclear deterrence and deontology. *Ethics*, 94, 248–260.
Ultimately a plea for a utilitarian approach to assessing nuclear deterrence. Argues that the deontological approach is not adequate to expose nuclear deterrence as immoral. Claims that nuclear policy is most in need of consequentialist analysis and that if utilitarians examine the facts and go beyond game theory they can make a relevant ethical contribution to the reappraisal of nuclear policy. Compare to Kenny (1985).

Shibata, Shingo (1977). The right to life vs. nuclear weapons. *Journal of Social Philosophy*, 8, 9–14.
Argues that the right to life is the most basic and that the people have a right to revolution. Argues that the right to life of smaller nations and all of humankind is threatened by U.S. nuclear policy and that the peoples of the world should defend the Declaration of Independence's right to life by eliminating all nuclear weapons.

Shrader-Frechette, Kristin. Nuclear arms and nuclear power: philosophical connections. In Fox and Groarke (1985), 85–100.
Shows the link between nuclear reactors and nuclear weapons and argues that each could lead to destruction. Points to the similarity of flaws (ethical, logical, epistemological) that appear in arguments for commercial fission technology and in arguments in support of nuclear weapons.

Somerville, John (1975). *The Peace Revolution: Ethos and Social Process.* Westport, CT: Greenwood Press. 236 pp.
Discusses the right and duty of revolution. Sees a need for a peace revolution and seeks to develop a science of peace. Addresses various nuclear issues.

Somerville, John (1976). Soviet Marxism in today's perspective. *Journal of Social Philosophy*, 7, 7–11.
Presents the prevention of nuclear war as the central problem. Suggests that action by the U.S.A. and U.S.S.R. during the Cuban missile crisis diverged from their founding theories. U.S. willingness to exterminate humanity compromised liberal capitalist theory, and Soviet adoption of nuclear pacifism compromised classical Marxist theory.

Somerville, John (1978). The contemporary significance of the American Declaration of Independence. *Philosophy and Phenomenological Research*, 38, 489–504.
Reviews the U.S. Declaration of Independence and argues that, during the Cuban missile crisis, the U.S. was prepared to exterminate the entire human race. Claims that the right to life and right of revolution cited in the Declaration of Independence provide justification for the American people to carry out a further American revolution in order to preserve and protect life.

Somerville, John (1979). Nuclear omnicide: it is now everyone's responsibility to prevent the holocaust. *The Churchman*, 113 (9, August/September).
Introduces the term "omnicide" and the founding of professional groups working for its prevention. Calls on us all to do now whatever we can to reject nuclear weapons.

Somerville, John (Ed.) (1981). *Soviet Marxism and Nuclear War: An International Debate.* Westport, CT: Greenwood Press. 166 pp.
Essays by various Marxist philosophers, including Soviets. Questions whether nuclear weapons permit justifiability of any war.

Somerville, John (1983). Nuclear omnicide: moral imperatives for human survival. *New World Review*, 20–21.
Presents the notion of "omnicide," which is defined as "the logical (and terminal) extension of the series of such nouns as suicide, homicide, genocide." Contends that the use of nuclear weapons would lead to omnicide. Argues no first use as a moral position regarding nuclear weapons. Suggests that any government which refuses to adopt such a policy abdicates the right to membership in the U.N.

Somerville, John (1985). Nuclear "war" is omnicide. In Fox and Groarke (1985), 3–9.
Presents "nuclear war" as a misnomer; it would not be war but "omnicide." Proceeds to argue against the use of nuclear weapons and uses the Declaration of Independence to argue that citizens have a right to rebel against nuclear states.

Sterba, James P. (Ed.) (1985). *The Ethics of War and Nuclear Deterrence.* Belmont, CA: Wadsworth Publishing Co. 182 pp.
Nineteen entries (articles, reprints and excerpts) on: (1) general ethical theory; (2) background information on effects of nuclear war and deterrence strategies; (3) moral assessment of nuclear war and deterrence; and (4) freeze v. military buildup.

Stevenson, Leslie (1986). Is nuclear deterrence ethical? *Philosophy*, 61, 193–214.
Argues that an absolutist ethics does not preclude deterrence strategies and a consequentialist ethics does not justify present policies of maintaining parity in a

continuing arms race. Contends that a reflective holding of either position should lead, with extreme urgency, towards moves to defuse tension, halt the arms race and reduce the world's nuclear weaponry.

Teilhard de Chardin, Pierre (1964). *The Future of Man*. Translated by Norman Denny. New York: Harper & Row. 319 pp.
Argues against the likelihood of nuclear destruction because of his belief that the world is progressing toward increasingly integrated and higher forms.

Tucker, Robert Warren (1985). Morality and deterrence. In Hardin *et al.* (1985), 461–478.
Argues that whether or not it would mean the end of humanity, the use of nuclear weaponry "invalidates" the so-called "reason for state" and is not reconcilable with any variation of the *bellum justum* doctrine. But this does not lead to rejection of deterrence altogether.

Walzer, Michael (1977). *Just and Unjust Wars*. New York: Basic Books. 361 pp.
Attempts to recapture "just war" for moral and political theory. Contends that restraint is the beginning of peace. Argues that nuclear war is morally unacceptable and that there is no case for its rehabilitation, but allows that nuclear deterrence falls, for the time being, under the "standard of necessity."

Wasserstrom, Richard A. (Ed.) (1970). *War and Morality*. Belmont, CA: Wadsworth Publishing Co., Inc. 136 pp.
Contains several classic essays relevant to the moral assessment of nuclear war. Includes William James's "The moral equivalent of war" and John C. Ford's "The morality of obliteration bombing," as well as several essays that address nuclear weapons, such as Elizabeth Anscombe's "War and murder" and Richard Wasserstrom's "On the morality of war."

Wasserstrom, Richard A. (1985). War, nuclear war, and nuclear deterrence: some conceptual and moral issues. In Hardin *et al.* (1985), 424–444.
Seeing engagement in nuclear war as the "morally worst and most despicable action conceivable," argues that the use of nuclear weapons, even for national self-defense against a murderous aggressor, would be monstrously wrong and unjustifiable. Contends that, once removed from their context of success, nuclear deterrence theories are mournfully wrong in what they propose to effect should deterrence fail.

Weinberger, David (1984). A phenomenology of nuclear weapons. In Gay (1984), 95–105.
Uses Heidegger to argue that nuclear weapons are distinctive in that they lead us to consider the possibility of collective death—termed "ontological death"—which involves the taking away of a "world" and turning into "nothing" that which we have viewed as "immortal."

Wells, Donald A. (1969). How much can "the just war" justify? *Journal of Philosophy*, 66, 819–829.
Reviews the criteria for just war and applies them to nuclear options. Suggests that while just-war theory may have had moral significance before the advent of "mega-weapons," it justifies too much when used today: a "just war" that used modern weapons would be Armageddon.

Wells, Donald A. (1984). *War Crimes and Laws of War*. Washington, DC: University Press of America. 137 pp.

Contends that there are war crimes only if there are laws of war, and crimes against the peace only if there are laws against waging war at all. Argues that so long as sovereign nations keep their "inalienable *inhuman*" right to be defender and arbiter of their ends, then no manual will ever be able to guide its readers so as to prevent war crimes and crimes against humanity.

Wolff, Robert Paul (1970). Maximization of expected utility as a criterion of rationality in military strategy and foreign policy. *Social Theory and Practice*, 1, 99–111.
Analysis and critique of the application of game theory to nuclear strategy. Shows the faulty assumptoins of those who use game theory to justify a role for nuclear weapons.

Woodward, Beverly (1985). The abolition of war. In Fox and Groarke (1985), 245–256.
Shows how pursuit of "national security" in the nuclear age increases the risks of disastrous war. Rejects the return of merely conventional war and calls for the elimination of the war system. Notes, however, that disarmament is insufficient. Addresses a comprehensive global agenda for peace and justice.

Zimmerman, Michael (1985). Anthropocentric humanism and the arms race. In Fox and Groarke (1985), 135–149.
Argues, with Heidegger, that the arms race is rooted in the superpowers' "anthropocentric humanism"—in their self-centered view of the human being and their (the superpowers') competing desires to secure and dominate the earth. Argues for a radical shift in our understanding of what it is to be "human" and for a new game for humanity—in which we bear witness to the presence of all beings.

10

Understanding the Psychology of Genocidal Destructiveness

Israel W. Charny

At this point in the history of human thought and science, we can have only a remote sense of the possibilities of translating understanding of the sources of human destructiveness into meaningful applications and tools for the *actual* prevention of genocidal killing. However, based on our faith in the process of scholarship and science, one can expect that constructive theories, observations, and experiments that will yield reliable knowledge and models of the sources of man's destructiveness in time will point the way to possible structures, interventions, and "treatments" that can be expected to reduce human violence to some extent. In this respect, the problem of genocide is no different from many other phenomena, such as plagues and climatological disasters, that today have little to no possibility of cure. We nevertheless believe that proper scientific work slowly but surely will lead us forward.

Two Total Models: Death-fulfilling Rage and the Frustration–Aggression Paradigm

Not many years ago social scientists seemed to offer nothing more than two highly simplistic, extreme, and *basically unusable* models for the explication of man's proclivity to destroy.

On the one hand, the Freudian or psychoanalytic paradigm stated that in man's true self, at the level of his basic nature in the underlying or unconscious realm of the structure of personality, there raged diabolical forces that sought to create death, essentially in fulfillment of a primordial drive towards reconciliation with or completion of the inevitable process of death that awaited each living creature.

The alternative and seemingly progressive interpretation offered by social scientists focusing on interactional processes between man and his environment, was that destructiveness is the ultimate of aggression responses that come as responses to frustration: given economic privation, sociological pressures such as discrimination, ecological limitations such as overcrowding, and psychological deprivations and aggravations such as an absence of love or a lack of support for one's dignity and self-confidence, man responds with the machinery available to him in nature: to attack and fight. This interpretation became known as the frustration–aggression hypothesis.

The former or instinctual position on the face of it implied a near-absolute hopelessness about man, that for all of our pseudo-civilization, we would never be able to restrain the destructive forces that were ultimately in the essence of our beings. The latter social interpretation, that men could live in peace given nonfrustrating conditions and structures, nonetheless also failed in the face of reality that there is no possibility whatsoever that human beings and societies can be spared all serious frustrations.

In addition, the frustration–aggression paradigm—however true as a description of frustration as a trigger of man's potential for aggression—suffered seriously from definitive proofs that even ostensibly satisfied peoples and groups were drawn by triggering mechanisms other than frustration toward terrible bestiality and murder. For example, we have learned that certain terrorist groups kill meaninglessly for pure excitement and recruit some of their most devoted members from the ranks of the rich and the spoiled. Another example directly from the area of genocide is that some of the most advanced "contributions" to mass killing have come from the intellectual aristocracy; certainly scientists have been involved, and also many other learned people such as the amazing number of physicians, educators, and lawyers who staffed the Nazi *Einsatzgruppen* that began the systematic mass killing of Jews in the early forties.

The Role of Unintentional Hence Innocent Dynamics in the Human Condition

A remarkable thesis that has entered into serious candidacy as an explicatory tool for understanding the sources of much human destruction is that there are a variety of other characteristics of human nature which *innocently* lead human beings into more and more extreme positions, without their having *intended* at all to engage in the violent behaviors that are a consequence of that position.

Moreover, once having turned to torturing and taking the lives of other human beings, the executing human beings or organizations are driven by an equally banal series of laws of human nature such as perverse, intoxicating. pleasure with their triumphant power in their status as dispensers of life and death; self-identification with their own behavior; and an inherent rigidity against being able to be self-critical and correcting of the actions with which they have become identified. Granted even the fervor and passion which many of the executioners now display as they stay committed to their evil tasks of destroying others (for example, how the guillotining French Revolution became devoted to the pageantry of its executions, and how the Nazi death machinery continued even after Hitler's fall was assured and the end of the war was in sight), the key to the continuing activity of some perpetrators still may not be a motivation and passion to destroy, but rather that they are carried along blindly by the lawfulness of chains or sequences of human behaviors that are beyond their control—incredible as it sounds.

It must be immediately added that even if true, the above thesis in no way militates against the fact that *human beings and societal organizations must be held responsible for their actions even if these are rooted in natural aspects of the human condition.* Murder of an innocent human being, cruelty, torture, slaughter, persecution, all-consuming programs of mass destruction must be defined by an intrinsic ethical imperative as evil and unlawful, so that even a person faced with structural dynamics that naturally would lead to his being a concentration camp functionary, or government policy maker for genocide, must be held responsible before a higher law of civilization.

For victim peoples, in particular, the paradigm of an essential "banality of evil," such as the classic formulation by European sociologist Hannah Arendt (1969) is insulting and infuriating, and many Jews reacted to Arendt's thesis as intolerable in its seeming implication that the victims were destroyed for no reason at all, and not because of an evil ideological mix of anti-Semitism and Nazi striving for superiority. Arendt, moreover, made reference to the compliance of the Jews as victims, and the implication that their "participation" in the chains of behaviors and events made them to some extent responsible for their destruction was the more incensing, notwithstanding the fact that the theory of Zionism and the compelling motivation for the renewal of a Jewish state in Israel in effect say the same thing, that Jews, and all peoples, must be psychologically and organizationally prepared to protect themselves against the persecutors who abound in this world.

It is certainly an important conclusion that potential victims such as a minority group must not allow themselves to be defined as intrinsically inferior to another, majority people, because under the laws of human nature this sets off chains of excesses of power and pleasures in persecution that derive from the automatic and banal laws of our human condition of becoming "drunk with power," drawn to "taking it out on the weaker person," "going all the way," and so on—even when people do not mean or intend to be evil as such.

In evaluating this hypothesis of "innocent lawfulness" in the genesis of much human destructiveness, one might also ask whether it makes sense in our theory of evolution that the human species has been assigned so many mechanisms that lead to the destruction of huge segments of our human population? Obviously, there is no answer to this question, for our species can hardly be said to have been entrusted with or to have gained the key to understanding the sources of life or the place of our species in the grand scheme of the universe, and perhaps universes. There is some sense in nature that a thinning out of the population of a species *is* part of the grand scheme, and there are some who see genocide, much like wars, as aspects of control of an exploding population and the problems of hunger that are already rampant on Earth. At the same time, it must be clear that much of the problem of starvation is a function of the inability of world society to distribute and cultivate available and potential resources.

Man as an Aberrance or Mutation

Philosopher-novelist Arthur Koestler (1967) opined that murderous *Homo sapiens* were perhaps an aberrant species, hence genocide would be natural in the ironic sense that some degree of aberrance and the unnatural are, inevitably, part of nature's grand tapestry as well. Ethologist Konrad Lorenz (1966) argued that virtually all species in the animal world restricted their killing and destroying to *extraspecific aggression* (that is, wars against other species), and almost universally refrained from *intraspecific aggression* (that is, destructive wars against their own species)—except in cases of territorial overcrowding. For Lorenz too, man as a species represents an aberrant mutation in nature.

The Natural Struggle for Survival and Dehumanization

What Lorenz did not take into account was the fact that man utilizes his powerful capacities to conceptualize and symbolize in order to achieve a redefinition of victim species as not being of one's own kind. The target people are, characteristically, the object of long-term processes of *dehumanization*, and in any case at the time when the major policy of destruction is set in motion, perceptions of the victim people generally are polarized even further to a point where the "kikes" or "gooks" or "vermin" are not human; they are sub-human, as if *not of our species*, therefore not deserving of the protections that presumably are owed to people of our own kind. Ironically, it may be that this phenomenon of dehumanization of a victim people, to the extent that they are not perceived as people, and as fathers, mothers, and children just like we are, is some measure of a saving grace for our species. For understanding how people and societies delude themselves in this way into not being aware that they are killing fellow human beings offers some explanation of man's disgusting record of murder on a basis other than an inherent availability to cruelty, sadism, or even an indifferent competitiveness that simply wipes out creatures that stand in one's way in the competition for life and its resources.

Animal-Legacy Competition for Survival

In any case, one must acknowledge that there are any number of people in our species who delight in and come to the task of destroying masses of other people with unrestrained passion. Ambitiousness, self-serving, primitive competitiveness over the resources of life, untroubled accepance of the right to execute those who stand in one's way or even arouse a sense of threat, as well as indifferent exercises of power for the intrinsic purpose of feeling powerful—all are sources, seemingly in nature, of varying measures of human destruction.

In fact, there is now considerable evidence that failure to accept to some degree the natural forces of aggression and power and self-serving in us all in itself can trigger an even greater readiness to be cruel and uncontrollably destructive. Kulscar (1978), for example, examined the arch-administrator of genocidal killing, Adolf Eichmann, and found that he was cut off from and frightened by his aggressive feelings. The murder-machinery he activated was his service to the State and a consequence of his conception that people are to be ordered and put in place like things.

The Perception of Danger

Human beings differentiate others because they are strangers, look different, speak a different language, act differently, live on the north or south of the border, engage in a different way of being in the world or style of life, pray to different gods and icons, and so on. We are afraid of differences, often blindly so, tend to hate those who are different from us, and assign them dehumanized identities. One good reason for such fear and hatred is that we know for a fact that other people are living out the aforementioned program of nature to hunt and attack other people—us. The trouble is that it is not easy to be *objective* in assessing the dangerousness of others, and people generally exaggerate considerably in their judgments that the other is out to attack them. Perhaps this is so in evolution because so much is at stake: a wrong perception means being caught unprepared. On the other hand, the very fact that one people perceives the other as intending to destroy it sets off interactions with these other people that increase the likelihood of destructive acts. Each people's perceptions feed the other, and these result in processes of escalation and self-fulfilling prophecies that move the probabilities of violence towards ever-increasing certainties. Moreover, the perceptions of danger also fuse with blind processes of dehumanization of the others. A spinning vortex of positioning oneself as superior to the stranger, and as protecting oneself from the dangers of these strangers, who in the reality of nature often *are* potentially real threats of our destruction, carries people through the ages blindly in ever-repeated historical dramas of mistrust, war and genocide.

Tragically, civilization has not yet been able to put a stop to these processes. One of the striking evidences of the twentieth century is that even a highly developed people, such as the Germans, can act bestially; and even a highly developed democratic societal structure, like the American, will engage in massive and genocidal killings, albeit the style of the killing generally tends to be more pragmatic than bestial, and based on persuasive, rational motivations of self-defense, such as the need to end a war with less loss of life to one's own people (hence the justification of the fire-bombing of Dresden and the atomic bombing of the Japanese cities).

Today, it is widely agreed that the future of life in our civilization is most at risk from the rational scientists and computer technologists who, in the sang-froid of modern electronic information-weapons systems, will someday advise of a clear and present danger from another people and call for preemptory or retaliatory nuclear strikes. "It is the sane ones, the well-adapted ones, who can without qualms aim the missiles and press the buttons that will initiate the great festival of destruction . . . The sane ones will have logical, well-adjusted reasons . . ." (Father Thomas Merton, 1967, p. 22).

The Moral Development and Potential of Man to Withstand Calls to Destructiveness

Can educated people or people with spiritual training or values withstand the pull of these many momentums towards destroying others? The evidence is increasingly clear that the great majority of people *cannot*.

Conformity–Stupidity

Blind conformity to nonsense and stupidity, if mandated by an authority, is more the case than otherwise. People follow the idiotic instructions of authorities (as in the experiments in which professors tell experimental subjects to administer potentially lethal electric shocks to other subjects who have done nothing more than give the wrong answer in a routine learning experiment). Most people are ready to abandon and blend themselves into a mass movement that is the popular form of belief in their era. Human beings can be duped easily into saying that the shorter of two lines is longer. They can be hypnotized into giving their approval to quacks and strong men with charismatic powers and go off on murderous safaris against whomever the leader designates (as in the case of the Manson group, and the bizarre story of several hundred murder–suicide deaths in Jonestown). In short, most people follow orders and adopt the prevailing norms of their immediate society, no matter how totalitarian and destructive it is.

Given these qualities, we understand more fully the considerable significance of leaders, and especially powerful leaders in a totalitarian government structure, and their use of military and police terror controls of a population. Given a charismatic leader, and dictatorial power over the people, the whim, fancy. Machiavellian policy, or psychosis of the leader will determine the fates to be assigned other vulnerable peoples. However, it is very important to realize that the powers assigned to the leader not only are inherent in the structures of government and military and secret-police powers, but derive from the complex of qualities of people and societies previously described: conformity, obedience, suggestibility, surrender of self to collective experiences, and so on. From the point of view of serious students of the evolutionary process, hopes to change the tragic predictability of future genocide must therefore lie not only with choices of the right leaders, and controls over government and military processes, and protection of human rights, but also in the possibilities of public education for the development of a new level of awareness, independence of mind, and responsibility on the part of human beings who would be able to stand up against powerful and charismatic leaders who call for destruction of others. While this kind of change seems a far-fetched hope for man as we know him today, it is not an unimaginable step in the evolution of human character and thinking.

Sociological Forerunners and Sources of Violence

Whatever the theory of the origins of destructiveness in the human soul, there are a variety of conditions under which individuals, and a variety of conditions under which groups such as nations, are more likely to be drawn towards their potential for genocidal violences. Thus, Kuper (1985) emphasizes the close relationship between "cleavage societies" and "hierarchical societies" and domestic genocide. Whenever there are conditions of "accentuated cleavage" between peoples, dominance of one people by another, a history of conflict and historical memories of same, dehumanizing and hostile perceptions, genocide becomes more probable. Such sociological, ecological and structural conditions act on a latent availability to violence within the human being. Without doubt there are a great many sociological-level determinants of violence. Thus, *war* is in itself a further source of the worst violences human beings are capable of, not only towards the opposing army, but towards victim civilian populations, and indeed it has been noted that the majority of instances of genocide take place under wartime conditions.

Education and Legitimation of Violence as Policy

When all is said and done, among the most important causes of genocide is education for violence in general, and education and legitimation of genocide specifically.

Education for violence in a society, indifference to violence, and legitimation of violence, are, each and together, sources of destructiveness as well as forces that are acting on the latent available destructiveness. Mafia families teach their children "successfully" to be criminal-killers. Nazi society socializes children and adults to celebrate humiliation, torture and murder of targeted victims. A Khomeini society trains children for martyrdom-murders by attaching explosives to them and making them living bombs. The battle of "civilization"—religious values and moral education that place human life as the supreme value—is both against the primitive side of man's nature and against the many societal institutions that adopt and promulgate genocidal violence as a legitimate, honorable, rewarding way of life.

Another source of human violence can also be identified in the repeated failure of so many people to confront morally the evils in which they have taken a part. Indeed, there is some evidence that the more a person becomes a part of a killing machinery the more "drunk" he may become, and the more he may insist on continuing far beyond what was the original definition of the program of execution. Robert Lifton (1982, 1986) reported in his study of physicians in the Nazi concentration camps that of those he interviewed, "none really confronted in a moral sense what he had done or been part of" (p. 284). The source of destructiveness that is being identified here, therefore, is the very commission of destructiveness; in itself, destroying, desensitizing, intoxicating, and legitimating more of the same. Moreover, on a group level, there are not only characteristic weaknesses in decision making at senior levels of government, but also the follies of group narcissism: pride and fear of loss of face once a group has embarked on policies of violence.

Bystanders

Another basic force that supports the possibilities of leaders and governments and societal momentums towards mass destruction is the fact that most people will *stand by* inactively in many situations where their neighbors, let alone a stranger group that has been the object of a broad propaganda of dehumanization, is subject to torture, forced migration, incarceration in concentration camps, or execution. Not only is there a crass practical decision not to endanger oneself, but a considerable body of social research of the "bystander phenomenon" has shown that even when there are no direct costs or risk, people tend to slough off responsibility for the victim to others (Sheleff, 1978).

To be a bystander is to walk past a victim who needs help as if he were not there; it is also to stand and gape and perhaps celebrate his plight; it is also to take advantage of his misfortune, such as to take his job or possessions when he loses them. In the context of governmental persecution of victims, to be a bystander is also to avoid helping the announced enemies of one's government, in all its awesome power, and likelihood of persecuting those who would help the victims. It takes a rare courage of individualism and integrity to be such a helper (Tec, 1986).

On several levels then, the mobilization of consciousness and commitment to act on behalf of life, not to be available to orders or ideologies to kill, and to be prepared to assist others in their hours of need, is a major educational and spiritual task that awaits mankind. This process can be supported under law, as for example in legislation that soldiers are forbidden to execute civilians or commit murders that are not within the purview of military operations and war, and even by laws that would require people to assist others who are injured or fleeing for their lives.

A Unified Theory of Aggression at Different Levels of Human Organization

In Charny (1982) the present author attempted to move towards a comprehensive theory of aggression that unfolds sequentially at different levels of human experience and organization. Although genocide is inherently a collective process, and the ways people behave in groups differ from their personalities as individuals, I am interested in grappling first of all with how an individual becomes able to be callously destructive of others—especially in the case of people who are not evil and violent, or identifiably criminals to begin with, but rather are "normal" people who do not intend to harm others.

Beginning with a metaphoric view of aggression as a basic power or energy process in the human personality, I postulate that this energy is inherently constructed of a dialectical integration of building or life-supporting forces and tearing down or life-destroying devices (a theory that is of course a continuation of work by many other, earlier thinkers). Destructiveness is likely, I would presuppose, when a human being fails to maintain a basic balance and integration between these two sides, in *either* direction of excess or insufficiency.

This energy is elaborated at subsequent levels of the human personality such as in connection with the defense mechanisms people employ to manage their universal experiences of anxiety. Without these defenses, no human being is capable of withstanding the terrors of life and death. These defenses may lean towards finding and giving meaning to life as an opportunity to love and help people and build a better society, or they may support destructive possibilities such as in projection, scapegoating, and dehumanization of others who are seen as inferior and lacking in order to protect one's own sense of integrity and safety from threat.

Acting on the basic energy style a person develops are the various structural and "banal" laws of dynamics of behavior, such as the tendency of people to test going "all the way" with their energy, the need for power and intoxication with power to which people succumb so easily, and tendencies to conformity and loss of identity in a collective. A great deal of even the most serious violences may not be intended, motivationally, to destroy, but represent the culmination of blind, automatic processes and chains of behavior which human beings do not know, or care to know, how to control, despite their consequences in the deaths of so many other people.

On another level, which ultimately is the crucial one, there unfold the choices of means and goals that people make. The knowledge of how to correlate the choices of means and ends with one another further defines the ways in which people use their energies for or against life. A mistaken belief that the ends justify the means leads over and over again in history to situations where in the pursuit of life, liberty, justice or religious values, human beings kill, in the name of their values and gods, anyone and everyone who seems to stand in their way. (A contrasting side of the coin is that an overemphasis on spiritual values in one's choices of means will expose caring people such as pacifists to the brutality of those who are committed to evil and are not swayed by decency and nonviolence.) Ultimately, the actual choices of goals people make are, of course, the vital central issue. Many people in our various societies are exposed to powerful institutional processes that adopt violence and genocide as their purpose. Once persons succumb to such indoctrination, it no longer matters what would have been the outcome of their own unfolding psychology of use of their aggression-energy; they are corrupted by joining the ideologies and machineries of destruction which, regrettably, abound in our world.

All of these processes take place not only in the individual as such, but in the unfolding experiences of the individual within family groups (where a great deal of emotional destruction of one another takes place); in group life where people lose themselves in the stupidity of the crowd and mass, and where never-ending prejudices and persecutions between every conceivable ethnic/racial/religious identities are formulated to satisfy needs to dehumanize others; and finally on the level of society and the decision-making of leaders, followers and bystanders in these larger collectives.

Although any current attempt at theory is inevitably going to fall short of the enormity of the task, the effort to create a unified theory of aggression at different levels of organization of behavior, ranging from the individual through the societal, is intended to open doors to new theoretical work on this most pressing psychological issue. It is the above unified theory that provides Charny (1982) with the conceptual base for the proposal of a Genocide Early Warning System, and thus provides a serious illustration of the possible application of theory in this area to the development of applied techniques for countering genocidal destructiveness.

An Emerging Consensus: Man's Fears of Death are at the Root of Much Assignment of Death to Others

Having looked at all the above organizing structures and process tendencies of man, we are still left with an important spiritual–psychological question: how is it that a human being who, in biblical metaphoric terms, is "born in the image of God"—that is, born of mother and father, undergoes a childhood with some degree of sensitivity and caring, and grows up to continue intimate relationships with a mate, children and other people—can lend himself so readily to the hell of destroying other human beings?

A new consensus of psychological thought in recent years is that the key to this readiness to destroy human life is nothing less than a bitter fear and flight from one's own mortality. Psychiatrist Robert Lifton, who has blazed a trail of exploration that began with studies of the survivors of Hiroshima (1967) and culminates most recently in the study referred to of physicians in the Nazi concentration camps, and how they were capable of killing in the name of healing, has conceptualized a series of paradigms or models through which people seek to overcome their mortality and achieve the illusion of immortality (1979).

Philosopher Ernest Becker (1973) developed the theme of the denial of death as the basis for much evil: to determine the death of another is to be like the gods, eternal, beyond vulnerability and finiteness. "If we don't have the omnipotence of gods we can at least destroy like gods" (p. 85). Charny (1982) elaborates this theme in his concept of *sacrificing*: the genocider assigns other people the fate of death he fears for himself. By sacrificing the other to that fate, the killer seeks to be spared that outcome just as in the many-centuried history of infant sacrifices. Less lethal forms of sacrificing abound in psychiatric observations of victimizing, scapegoating, and stigmatizing a weaker person in one's own family who becomes the designated carrier of mental illness, ineptitude, stupidity, and so on. Sacrificing others is an effort to escape death. A target people who have been dehumanized as not really of our species, and at the same time are perceived as overwhelmingly dangerous to the continuation of our species, is sacrificed so that we may live on.

Another Consensus: Mass Killing is Madness

Another intriguing consensus that may be beginning to emerge across a range of different disciplines is that genocide and mass killing can only be considered madness, whether on the individual level (Charny, 1986) or the societal level (Aronson, 1984; Rapoport, 1984; Santoni, 1984), and that scholars must take clear stands against destruction of life. According to ordinary usage and dictionary meanings, the nuclear arms race is indeed "insane" and "mad," argues philosopher Santoni: "Preoccupation with nuclear war, with utter destruction, is an illness, a form of extreme irrationality . . . it will eventually lead to multiple genocide or—its logical extension—*omnicide*" (p. 151).

Conclusion

It is hardly possible to say at this point that psychological theory of the sources of destructiveness has contributed meaningfully to the means of arresting future genocide. In that sense, the fledgling legal and political initiatives that are described elsewhere in this book represent much more meaningful immediate hopes for progress in our civilization of murder.

Nonetheless, there is a sense that the unfolding theoretical work on the sources of human destructiveness such as the new consensus of the bedrock significance of man's wishes to live and to defer death, and the understanding of many innocent unintentional dynamics acting on man's experience of the threat of his own inevitable death are taking us forward beyond both the sweeping nihilistic and the overly naïve, optimistic theories that dominated the psychiatric and social sciences until a few years ago. Hopefully, we shall advance further in social science's understanding of different levels of organization of the human being—individual, family, group, and society—and learn more how to identify the meaningful correspondences and transformative parallels without surrendering to a childish, literal reductionism which pretends that a dynamic force at one level of organization can explain behaviors at different levels.

In any case, the ancient philosophical and psychological fascination with the nature and sources of man's evil destructiveness will not cease to attract serious students so long as there is a human civilization.

References

Charny, Israel W. [in collaboration with Chanan Rapaport] (1982). *How Can We Commit the Unthinkable? Genocide: The Human Cancer*. New York and Boulder, CO: Westview Press. 430 pp. (*See* Chapter 1)

Koestler, Arthur (1967). *The Ghost in the Machine*. New York: Macmillan.

Merton, Thomas N. (1967). A devout meditation in memory of Adolf Eichmann. *Reflections* (Merck, Sharp & Dohme), 2 (e), 21–23.

Santoni, Ronald E. (1984). Nuclear insanity and multiple genocide. In Charny (1984), pp. 147–153. (*See* Chapter 1)

Sheleff, Leon Shaskolsky (1978). *The Bystander: Behavior, Law, Ethics*. Lexington, MA: Lexington Books (*See* Chapter 1).

Bibliography

Arendt, Hannah (1969). *Eichmann in Jerusalem. See* Chapter 1.

Aronson, Ronald (1984). Societal madness: impotence, power and genocide. In Charny (1984), pp. 137–146. (*See* Chapter 1)
    An integrated analysis of three genocides: the Holocaust, the liquidation of 20 million Soviets by Stalin, and the American war campaign in Vietnam. "Each instance comes from the depths of a society," and is an irrational or "mad" effort to rid the society of its impotence through a deranged sense of omnipotence.

Becker, Ernest (1973). *The Denial of Death*. New York: Free Press. 314 pp.
    A book that won the Pulitzer prize. Philosopher Ernest Becker sees in man's denials of his inevitable mortality, and in his unceasing efforts to create illusions of immortality and invulnerability, the seeds of evil. The desperate need to prove one will not die can lead to doing the worst to others. A book that is at once learned and sensitive.

Charny, Israel W. (1985). Sacrificing. In Charny (1982), pp. 185–211.
    A key dynamic of the genocider, that helps explain the readiness of so many people to be drawn to participating in mass murder, is the magical sense that killing others gives of one's own omnipotence and immortality. If dread of death is a powerful dynamic in human psychology, sacrificing others can be a satisfying antidote: "You die, not I!"

Charny, Israel W. (1986). Genocide and mass destruction: doing harm to others as a missing dimension in psychopathology. *Psychiatry*, 49(2), 144–157.
    A proposed revision of the standard classification of psychopathology to redefine the leaders and followers who execute genocide as abnormal. Suggests that most current

disorders can be seen as "disorders of incompetence, vulnerability, and personal weakness," and proposes adding a new dimension to classification of psychopathology: "disorders of pseudocompetence, invulnerability, and doing harm to others." "If making other people's lives miserable—persecuting, tormenting, and even killing them—cannot be linked with existing definitions of abnormality, the profession of psychology has a serious problem of credibility."

Cohn, Norman (1969). *Warrant for Genocide: The Myth of the Jewish Conspiracy and the Protocols of the Elders of Zion*. New York: Harper. 336 pp.
A classic work, by a historian, about a mythology that for centuries fed European anti-Semitism, pogroms, and ultimately the Holocaust. This is a fundamental example of the roles of projection and ideology in flaming and legitimating a genocidal process. For many years, Cohn headed an innovative Centre for the Study of Collective Psychopathology at the University of Sussex where a number of seminal studies, in various disciplines, were completed.

Cohn, Norman (1975). *Europe's Inner Demons: An Enquiry Inspired by the Great Witch-Hunt*. New York: Basic Books. 302 pp.
Cohen examines the history and mythology of witch-hunting. Beyond the fascination and significance of the subject in its own right, this is again, as in the author's *Warrant for Genocide*, an examination of the projection process, ideology and mass belief, and their roles in setting off the passions of a hunt and legitimating executions of the hunted.

Dicks, Henry V. (1972). *Licensed Mass Murder: A Socio-Psychological Study of Some SS Killers*. London: Heinemann. 283 pp.
British psychiatrist Dicks went to Europe to interview a number of Nazi war criminals serving their sentences in jail. Dicks was an outstanding Tavistock Clinic psychiatrist whose seminal work on marital problems a few years earlier is still regarded today as perhaps the most significant work in the field. He concluded, as others before him at the Nuremberg Trials, that the Nazi killers were not for the most part clinically disturbed according to the accepted mental health standards and definitions of the day.

Epstein, Lawrence (1977). The therapeutic function of hate in the countertransference. *Contemporary Psychoanalysis*, 13(4), 442–461.
One of a relatively small number of works in the field of psychotherapy that recognize and call for authentic, disciplined use of anger at patients by psychotherapists in order to achieve better treatment results. Most psychotherapists promote a counseling world of love, unconditional acceptance, and positive regard, in which patients are not judged; conventional styles of therapy confer on therapists the mantles of good, giving people, and deny their patients encounters with the anger they really do set off. *See* entry for Winnicott (1949).

Frank, Jerome D. (1967). *Sanity and Survival*. New York: Random House. 330 pp.
A sound and humane study of the processes that engender group hatred and violence, including education and public displays of indifference to human life (for example, joyous demonstrations of bayoneting techniques by the U.S. armed forces in a public setting), the psychology of misperception of others as threatening, violence and mutual escalation to violence and wars.

Frankl, Viktor E. (1970). *Man's Search for Meaning: An Introduction to Logotherapy*. New York: Simon & Schuster. 149 pp.

An all-time classic that has touched the hearts of millions of readers with its description of the greater possibilities of survival even in a concentration camp given a person's inner sense of meaning and hence a belief in the worthwhileness of life.

Fromm, Erich (1964). *The Heart of Man: Its Genius for Good and Evil*. New York: Harper & Row. 156 pp.
The same heart—the same inner nature of man—contains the potentialities for good and evil that, clearly, are expressed in diametrically opposite ways throughout human history. A modern psychological presentation of an ancient religious truth that man must choose his destiny to serve good or evil, for both are in his nature.

Fromm, Erich (1973). *The Anatomy of Human Destructiveness*. New York: Holt, Rinehart & Winston. 448 pp.
The culminating "Talmudic" work by this celebrated psychologist who in earlier works gave us powerful concepts of the misuse of people as objects (the "marketing orientation"), and how fascism thrives in man's escapes to pseudo-certainty ("escape from freedom"). Although there are too many ideas and too many words in this work, and ultimately the problem of evil continues to elude even this great thinker, the book contains many important insights. Perhaps the most troubling conclusion Fromm leaves us is that much of evil is an effort to live and to bring meaning to life.

Gilbert, G.M. (1950). *The Psychology of Dictatorship: Based on an Examination of the Leaders of Nazi Germany*. New York: Ronald. 327 pp.
Gilbert was the psychologist who examined the Nazi criminals prior to the Nuremberg Trials. He concludes that the majority were not mentally ill as such, but that overwhelming pride, ambition and narcissism, coupled with commitment to an ideology, determined their abilities to lead one of the cruelest governments in history.

Gray, J. Glenn (1967). *The Warriors: Reflections on Men in Battle*. New York: Harper & Row. 242 pp.
A classic statement of the heroic anthem that brings men happily to the grandeurs of the battlefield. The warrior discovers his error only after it is too late, when so many lay dead and so many others are shattered and broken in limb and spirit. The illusion of the heroic in destroying others dies hard.

Kelman, Herbert (1973). Violence without moral restraint. *Journal of Social Issues*, 29(4), 25–61.
Three interrelated processes are identified in the creation of *sanctioned massacres*: (1) processes of *authorization*, which define the situation as one in which standard moral principles do not apply and the individual is absolved of responsibility; (2) processes of *routinization*, which organize the action so that there is no opportunity for raising moral questions and making moral decisions; (3) processes of *dehumanization*, which deprive the victims of their human status. Kelman also mentions more briefly five targets of corrective efforts to prevent sanctioned massacres: (a) the habit of unquestioning obedience; (b) the normalization and legitimization of violence; (c) the sanctioned definition of victim categories; (d) the glorification of violence; and (e) the promulgation of transhuman ideologies which in the service of some abstract mission provide rationales for massacres.
    A thoughtful and eloquent paper that was honored with the Kurt Lewin Memorial Award by the Society for the Psychological Study of Social Issues, a division of the American Psychological Association.

Kulscar, I. Shlomo (1978). De Sade and Eichmann. In Charny, Israel W. (Ed.), *Strategies against Violence*, pp. 19–33. Boulder, CO: Westview Press.

The results of psychological and psychiatric examinations of Nazi arch criminal Adolf Eichmann. He was fearful of aggressive impulses. His overriding need was to place people as things where they belonged. In contrast, says Kulcsar, the Marquis De Sade is a symbol of the use of *fantasies* of aggression, thereby to be less prone to *actual* violences against living people.

Latane, B., and Darley, M.J. (1970). *The Unresponsive Bystander: Why Doesn't He Help?* New York: Appleton-Century-Crofts. 131 pp.
Following the New York City murder of Kitty Genovese and the failure of neighbors who heard and witnessed her efforts to flee her killer even to call the police, social scientists undertook an important series of studies of the unresponsive bystander. This book is one of the major statements of these researches. One important dynamic clarified by the author is that most people tend to assign responsibility for acting to the next person, thus allowing themselves not to have to take any responsibility or risk.

Lerner, Melvin J. (1980). *The Belief in a Just World: A Fundamental Delusion*. New York: Plenum. 209 pp.
Strangely, the continuing naïveté of belief in a just world, the source of many constructive behaviors in society, underlies a certain amount of evil. It has been observed that one reason many victims are viewed with distaste and draw further fire on them after they have already been hurt is that they "mess up" the possibilities of belief in a nice just world. Enraged by the contradiction of his belief, the frustrated believer blames the victim for bringing on himself his plight. So long as the victim "deserves" what is happening to him, the world remains a just one.

Lifton, Robert Jay (1967). *Death in Life: Survivors of Hiroshima*. New York: Random House. 576 pp.
A classic and brilliant book, which penetrates to new depths of understanding the human mind and also deserves respect for being a pioneer in its time in looking at the dread world of the survivors of the atomic bombings of Japan by the U.S.A. The concept of *psychic numbing* is introduced here to describe defenses against experiencing the unbearable horrors of the events that had taken place and scarred the survivors indelibly. In later years, this concept emerges as an important one for understanding peoples' resistance to looking at nuclear dangers of the future—an issue to which psychiatrist Lifton devotes many of his energies at the present.

Lifton, Robert Jay (1979). *The Broken Connection: On Death and the Continuity of Life*. New York: Simon & Schuster. 495 pp.
A penetrating analysis of "modes of immortality": the biological, theological, that achieved through man's work, being survived by nature itself, and a mode of "experiential transcendence" that is so intense that time and death disappear. The psychological quest for immortality determines a great range of human behaviors, and is central to the meanings people find in their lives.

Lifton, Robert Jay (1982). Medicalized killing in Auschwitz. *Psychiatry*, 45, 283–297.

Lifton, Robert Jay (1986). *The Nazi Doctors: Medical Killing and the Psychology of Genocide*. New York: Basic Books.
Another brilliant and seminal contribution by the author of "Death in Life." Probes the "medicalization of killing—the imagery of killing in the name of healing" in the Nazi camps. Based on interviews of twenty-eight former Nazi doctors and one pharmacist who, surprisingly, participated willingly. Lifton concludes: "None really

confronted in a moral sense what he had done or been part of. In many cases, the doctor interviewed would talk as if he were a third person, looking back at events as an observer.''

Proposes important concepts for our undertanding of the pyschology of genocide: ''a religion of the will''; ''the vocabulary of the genocide process''; ''the 'healing-killing' paradox''; ''the technicizing of everything''; ''doubling . . . rather than mere splitting . . . the creation of two relatively autonomous selves.''

Lorenz, Konrad (1966). *On Aggression*. New York: Harcourt, Brace & World. 306 pp.
Ethologist Lorenz achieved considerable fame for his conclusions that most species, excluding man, do not kill their own kind (''intraspecific aggression'') except under highly pressured conditions such as overcrowding, and that killing among animals is more natural in respect to members of other species (''extraspecific aggression''). Lorenz speculates that man may have suffered a mutation in the evolutionary process. Lorenz's fame was followed by some public accusations that he himself had a Nazi past, although these have no connection with his work as such.

Lorenz, Konrad (1970). On killing members of one's own species. *Bulletin of the Atomic Scientists*, October, pp. 3–5, 51–56.

Maslow, A.H. (1979). *The Journals of A.H. Maslow*. Edited by Richard J. Lowry. Vols. 1 and 2. Monterey, CA: Brooks/Cole. [Reviewed by Simpson, Elizabeth Leonie (1980). Self Report of a Complex Simplifier. *Contemporary Psychology*, 25(11), 913–914.]
This posthumous diary/autobiographical notes of the world-renowned founder of humanistic psychology is important to us because of its startling revelations of hubris, grandiosity, and intellectual statements of readiness to kill those who would stand in the way of the ''new state'' of psychological enlightenment. A reviewer of the journals wrote: ''He trusted himself more than others and holding power, he would have exercised it absolutely, abandoning Fifth Amendment protection, against such disruptive forces as civil disobedients, convicted criminals, and unemployed 'loafers' '' (p. 913). Quoting Maslow: ''As with some, nothing will work ultimately but shooting'' (Maslow, p. 631).

Milgram, Stanley (1974). *Obedience to Authority*. New York: Harper & Row.
Perhaps the most celebrated psychological experiment of our time. This is the study in which subjects were ordered to administer electric shocks to other ostensible subjects in a routine learning study whenever they gave a wrong answer. In effect, this study *proved* that most people, from all walks of life, will (a) obey authority and do what they are told; (b) administer possibly lethal punishments to others—the markings on the shock switches indicated dangerously high voltages. This study became known as the ''Eichmann Experiment.'' Many criticized Milgram for confronting the subjects with this degree of evil in themselves—as if that were more the issue than all of us facing this truth of our human nature. Any number of replications of the study have shown the same results.

Neumann, Erich (1969). *Depth Psychology and a New Ethic*. New York: Putnam's.
A thoughtful and useful probe into the nature of good and evil which examines the interrelated, dialectical nature of all human experience. To achieve an ethical position, one must also accept and take responsibility for the ''dark sides'' of one's motivations and intentions even when ''doing good.'' A straight-line pursuit of the good often ends up producing evil behaviors in the name of achieving peace, freedom, betterment of society, etc.

Rapoport, Anatol (1984). Preparation for nuclear war: the final madness. *American Journal Orthopsychiatry*, 54(4), 524–529.

"The planners of nuclear war—that is, primarily the personnel of the military establishments of both superpowers and their political entourages—satisfy two criteria for madness: they are immersed in an imaginary world of their own making, dissociated from reality, and their activities constitute a clear menace to humanity."

Schiffer, Irvine (1973). *Charisma: A Psychoanalytic Look at Mass Society*. Toronto: University of Toronto Press. 384 pp.

An intriguing, scholarly but very readable analysis of charisma—and the interaction between the Pied Pipers and the followers who march to their tune. Without doubt, this subject represents a major focus for serious students of genocide, considering how often a charismatic strong man is at the center of the events dictating the genocide of another people.

Strom, Margo Stern, and Parsons, William S. (1977). *Facing History and Ourselves: Holocaust and Human Behavior*. Brookline, MA: Facing History and Ourselves National Foundation [25 Kennard Rd., Brookline, MA 02146]. 400 pp.

An outstanding textbook for adolescents (high school and college levels) on the Holocaust, and genocide of other peoples as well. Designed to enhance active thinking and experiencing about the events themselves and about the human qualities, such as obedience and conformity, that make genocide possible. Facing History—Facing Ourselves has developed into a major educational project, providing training, teaching resources and consultations to hundreds of school systems around the United States that have adopted the program.

Tec, Nechama (1986). *When Light Pierced the Darkness: Christian Rescue of Jews in Nazi-Occupied Lands*. New York: Oxford University Press. 320 pp.

An in-depth study of Christian rescue of Jews in Poland under Nazi rule. These are people who helped not only strangers but even people they disliked, reports Tec, herself a survivor, and now an American sociologist. Individualism was the outstanding trait of altruistic helpers, she concludes.

Toch, Hans (1983). The management of hostile aggression: Seneca as applied social psychologist. *American Psychologist*, 38, 1022–1025.

This modest publication (which did not even appear as a full article but in a context similar to a letter-to-the-editor) is a gem that delights and reinspires confidence in the capacity of the human intellect to probe complex issues. Seneca was a Roman philosopher–educator–statesman who lived in the first century. He produced a three-volume treatise on ire or rage, *De Ira*, which is full of wisdom about human cruelty. Thus, "There are a sort of Men that take delight in the Spilling of Human Blood; and in the Death of those that never did them an injury . . . [men] whom we cannot so properly call *Angry*, as *Brutal*." Says Toch: "Mere forms of cruelty may remotely originate with resented injury, but can 'with frequent exercise and custom' become functionally autonomous." Seneca calls for programs of education for violence reduction and makes detailed proposals for what we would call today treatment of violence-prone individuals.

White, Ralph K. (1985). *Psychology and the Prevention of Nuclear War*. New York: New York University Press. 592 pp.

A significant anthology of possible contributions of psychology to the prevention of nuclear disaster. Includes chapters by the editor on fear and "motivated misperceptions"—concepts which he previously applied to analysis of the U.S. war in Vietnam; Jerome Frank on the role of pride in national affairs; Erich Fromm on group narcissism; Robert Lifton and Richard Falk on psychic numbing and feeling; and Irving Janis on international crisis management.

Winnicott, D.W. (1949). Hate in the countertransference. [Reprinted from *International Journal of Psychoanalysis*, 30. *Voices: The Art and Science of Psychotherapy*, 1(2), 1965, 102-109.]

An amazing paper for its time, and still ahead of many psychotherapists in looking at the naturalness of their own anger and hatred of patients, and employing them in the therapy for the patients' sake. Winnicott was a beloved and respected figure in British child psychiatry. In this paper, he proposes that many disturbed people have not learned to assimilate anger with their own sense of being lovable and loved, and therefore they remain vulnerable. He proposes that the therapist build to a point where the patient can bear to hate and as if destroy the therapist in feelings, and also receive the therapist's anger at them, in both cases surviving with a real knowledge that the anger is out of caring and part of a real relatedness. An important contribution to a psychology of healthy aggression.

Zimbardo, P.G.; Haney, C.; Banks, W.C.; and Jaffe, D. The psychology of imprisonment, privation, power and pathology. In Rosenhan, David, and London, Perry (Eds.) (1975). *Theory and Research in Abnormal Psychology*, 2nd edn., pp. 270-287. New York: Holt, Rinehart & Winston.

A classic and definitive social science experiment conducted at Stanford University. Psychology students were assigned roles as prisoners and jailers in a simulation of a prison experience. Before very long, the jailers were behaving so tyrannically to the prisoners—who in turn accepted unquestioningly the roles assigned to them—that the experiment had to be stopped.

11

The Literature, Art, and Film of the Holocaust

Samuel Totten

The creation of art, since time immemorial, has been perceived as a life-affirming act. And paradoxically, this perception has probably never been truer than when a serious writer or artist wrestles with and forges his or her art out of the terrible suffering and abject horror inherent in the subject of genocide. Such subject matter is, by its very nature, a major challenge for any writer or artist to come to grips with, for genocide is nothing less than the antithesis of the act of creation.

The very term "art" raises a host of problems when dealing with the subject of genocide. It seems as if a new, more appropriate term needs to be coined in order to do justice to the works that address such subject matter. However, since such a term is not available the following caveat is of supreme importance: the use of the term "art" in this essay in no way implies acceptance that " 'art' is a supreme good that can be made to order out of the most terrible materials" (Howe, 1980, p. 10)

Some assert that an artistic attempt at capturing the horror of genocide in art paradoxically reduces its horrific nature as well as its significance. In this regard German refugee philosopher T.W. Adorno stated: "Through aesthetic principles or stylization and even through the solemn prayer of the chorus the unimaginable ordeal still appears as if it had some ulterior purpose. It is transfigured and stripped of some of its horror and with this, injustice is already done to the victims" (Ezrachi, 1980, p. 52).

A writer or artist who sets out to create art out of a horror of such magnitude is faced with numerous dilemmas even prior to the act of creation: How does one express the ineffable? Does the creation of "art" out of such tragedies minimize or trivialize the ordeal to which the victims were subjected? Which is worse—not addressing genocide or possibly minimizing its significance and horror while attempting to probe its unfathomable dimensions?

Speaking of the Holocaust, Elie Wiesel, a survivor of Auschwitz and the writer who has been called "the messenger of the dead," has stated that "I tell of the impossibility one stumbles upon in trying to tell the tale . . . Those who never lived that time of death will never be able to grasp its magnitude or horror . . . In spite of all the movies, plays and novels about the Holocaust, it remains a mystery, the most terrifying of all times" (Wiesel, 1983, p. H 12).

Not all writers and artists, of course, wrestle with and weigh such issues prior to dealing with the subject of genocide, and this may be why a substantial number of the literary and other works of art about genocide, particularly the Holocaust and nuclear omnicide, have resulted in the trivialization of the subject matter. In this regard, certain genocidal acts have been depicted in romantic or melodramatic ways, or have been commercialized and vulgarized. On the other hand, many outstanding works have been produced. The height of artistry in many of these works is astounding.

Literature

A much greater quantity of artistic work has been created about the Holocaust than any other genocidal act in history, for a variety of reasons. Firstly, the Holocaust was "a well-calculated mass murder which took many years to plan and accomplish, and in which law-abiding German people acted in accordance with their instruction" (Zvielli, 1979, p. 13). Secondly, the crimes were committed by a highly cultured people, a fact that caused great alarm and concern among other Western nations. Then again, the use of technology horrified humanity. The perpetrators kept extensive documentation, including movies and photographs of their crimes. Many of the victims, too, including those who were destined to die in the Nazi death camps, either kept records or diaries or produced works of art that captured the horrors to which they and their people were subjected. Many of the survivors were highly literate and subsequently their experiences and those of others were related in memoirs as well as works of art. The trials of the war criminals produced voluminous and detailed records of the crimes. Finally, the brutality and the sheer number of victims contributed to its being recognized as one of the most cataclysmic events in the history of the civilized world. Perhaps the most significant reason of all is the fact that many survivors of the Holocaust believed, as Elie Wiesel does, that the Holocaust "was a satanic project, without precedent in the annals of humanity, and making it known was a duty owed to the dead" (Wiesel, 1983, p. H 12).

It should be stated at the outset that the term "literature," like that of "art," is hardly appropriate when dealing with the subject of the Holocaust. As Wiesel has noted, "there is no such thing as Holocaust literature—there cannot be. Auschwitz negates all theories and doctrines, to lock it into a philosophy is to restrict it. To substitute words, any words, for it is to distort it. A Holocaust literature? The term is a contradiction" (Wiesel, 1978, p. 234). This statement by Wiesel, like critic Irving Howe's assertion that "to relate 'art' to the Holocaust is frivolous, heartless, esthetically stupid" (Howe, 1980, p. 10), is incontestable. And yet, paradoxically, as Wiesel also points out, "the opposite of art is not ugliness but indifference" (Wiesel, 1986, p. EY 21). Thus, the point here is that the serious work about the Holocaust is ultimately combating indifference that exists in relation to the atrocities committed during the Holocaust.

Like most bodies of "literature," the quality of the novels, short stories, drama and poetry that deal with the Holocaust ranges from the mediocre to the superb. The mediocre is that which trivializes the magnitude of the Holocaust or turns it into melodrama. It is also that writing that treats the Holocaust as simply another event in history or another story to be told, without fully acknowledging its specialness. Finally, it is also that writing that uses the tragedy of the Holocaust as a background event or metaphor in order either to heighten the interest of the primary story or to draw historical or personal but flawed analogies between one event and another. The harm in using the Holocaust as such a vehicle has been addressed by Wiesel: "The massive outpouring of sensationalized books and popularized television programs and films of the Holocaust have dishonored the victims and rendered the public insensitive to the tragedy" (*Martyrdom and Resistance*, 1980, p. 8).

The styles found in literary works about the Holocaust are extremely eclectic, not surprisingly in that each and every author is dealing with the overwhelming problem of how to express the "unimaginable." Some critics assert that the documentary novel, short story or drama comes closest to truly revealing the historical accuracy of the Holocaust. Such works generally fuse journalistic conventions with fiction in order to present a heightened report of what transpired either in the ghettos or the concentration camps. Documentary works by survivors combine their personal experiences with fictional accounts, and as a result many of the works read like memoirs.

Other critics contend that the use of surrealistic images and events better serve to delineate the horror of the Holocaust because that event was nothing short of "unreal." These individuals point out that for the victims of the Holocaust the world became a nightmare in which nothing made sense, thus a literary style that uses the distortion of time, unnatural juxtapositions, and fantastic or incongruous imagery is most appropriate for trying to express such a situation.

Writers have used every available literary convention in their attempt to create works that present the "reality" of the Holocaust. In doing so, they have used rich metaphors; historical, religious, and personal allusions; myths; and intricate symbolic structures. They attempt to examine human motives, metaphysical concerns, and historical antecedents in order to come to terms with the many ramifications that the Holocaust has for humanity.

The so-called "concentrationary realists" (the short-story writer Tadeusz Borowski, a survivor of Auschwitz, is a classic example of this sort of writer), however, reject the use of aesthetic devices. Instead, they attempt to project the absolute "reality" of the hell that they, and others, experienced, by telling the "truth." They attempt to do this by using images that convey the bloody, stench-filled and brutal world of the death camps as well as by depicting actual people in actual events. And yet, as critic Irving Howe points out, "even the most vivid presentation of concrete detail and specificity, the most palpable reconstruction of Holocaust reality, is blunted by the fact there is no analogue in human experience" (Howe, 1980, p. 12).

The plots and settings of the literature are as diverse as their styles are eclectic. As in any body of literature, but possibly even more so in regard to this topic, the subject matter is dictated, to a large extent, by the individual writer's experiences and background.

In relation to the literary settings, Ezrachi (1980, p. 50) has pointed out that "In the history of Holocaust literature there are relatively few stories which are actually located in the camps; most of them either reach the periphery of the concentrationary universe—the Jewish town on the eve of deportation, the ghetto, the forests or other fugitive hideouts . . . —or relegate the camps to the contained limits of memory or imagination."

The plots deal with an incredibly diverse set of circumstances and events: the obliviousness of the European Jews to their fate during the incipient years of the Holocaust; the rising anti-Semitism in Nazi Germany; the roundups and deportations; life in the ghettos; the plight of Jews who escaped from the ghettos and death factories; the heroic efforts of some Jews to warn or to save their people from extermination; the selections and killings; the horrific "medical experiments" conducted in the concentration camps; the fight for survival in the camps; the uprisings in the ghettos and death camps; Jewish martyrdom during the Holocaust; the role of the partisans and resistance fighters to save the Jews; the role of the "righteous gentiles" in Norway and other nations who attempted to harbor and protect the Jews; the collaboration of certain nations or peoples with the Nazis' persecution and extermination of the Jews; the culpability of free nations (including the United States and Great Britain) as well as certain individuals (Pope Pius XII and American Jewry) for not doing all they could to save European Jewry; the infamous Evian Conference; God's position in relation to the Holocaust; the liberation of the concentration camps; the abysmal situation of the displaced-persons camps; Israel's relationship with survivors; the plight of survivors following the Holocaust (including their mental, spiritual and physical suffering); the survivors' role of being witnesses; the tracking down of Nazis in the postwar years; the postwar trials of those Germans guilty of crimes against humanity; the guilt of various members of German families for either their own role or the role family members had in the crimes committed against the Jews; the plight of the Gypsies during the Holocaust years, as well as many others.

Despite the breadth of topics that have covered in the literature on the Holocaust, there are still a number of areas that have not been addressed in a substantive manner. For instance, very few works deal with why and how the German people became so enamoured of Hitler that they became accomplices in such a crime against humanity. Concomitantly, there is a dearth of works on how the German people in the postwar period view their participation in such an event. Along the same lines, there is little in the way of literature as to how and why the French, Poles, and Italians capitulated to the Nazis and became accomplices in the extermination of the Jews. Neither are there many works that seek to discover what the impact of such actions has been on those nations' collective psyche. And while more and more nonfiction texts are being written about the silence of the United States during the war years vis-à-vis the Nazis' slaughter of the Jews, there has been little examination in literature of that profoundly disturbing situation. On another note, there is also a dearth of literature on the plight of the Gypsies during the Nazi reign of terror.

Films

Literally hundreds of films (archival footage produced by both the Nazis and the Allied liberators, documentaries, Hollywood-made dramas, "docudramas," feature films by Europeans, etc.) have been made about myriad aspects of the Holocaust.

Filmmakers, not surprisingly, face the same basic dilemma in their use of celluloid as writers do with words when dealing with the subject of the Holocaust: how does one depict or capture the meaning as well as the horrors of the catastrophe without undermining its terrible significance? Many fine documentary and feature filmmakers have made herculean efforts to depict at least a minute aspect of the "reality" of the Holocaust in the hope that their work would serve in some small way as a remembrance of that tragedy. Others, of course, have not made such an effort, and many have outright exploited the subject matter.

The styles of the films, among and between the various genres, are as diverse as those found in the literary works. They range from stark realism to expressionism and from black humor to surrealism. Like the writers who use surrealism to heighten the sense of disorder and madness of the Nazi era, filmmakers use a variety of stylistic devices to delineate the shocking nature of the Holocaust: "disorienting camera angles and movement, heightened lighting, distorting visual texture or color, stylized acting, contrapuntal soundtrack or music, and unconventional narrative structure" (Insdorf, 1983, p. 40).

Numerous films about the Holocaust use humor and do so for various reasons, including the depiction of the insanity of the Nazi atrocities. Some critics contend that the use of humor about such a horrific event is unconscionable, while others assert that the "serious" use of humor is a vital weapon to wake up the populace about the horrors.

The quality of the films on the Holocaust ranges from outstanding to mediocre. Among the consistently best and most significant productions are documentaries and those films that allow Holocaust survivors to tell their stories, partly because such productions pay particular attention to historical accuracy. Among the most powerful films in this category are *Camps of the Dead*, *The Eighty-First Blow*, *The Final Solution*, *Night and Fog*, *Shoah*, and *To Bear Witness*. At the other end of the scale, many Hollywood dramas and certain European feature-length productions have resulted in repugnant simplifications, distortion, and rape of the profound significance inherent in the subject matter of the Holocaust. The primary aim of the movies in this category is entertainment, and not authenticity—which is the crux of the problem. Furthermore, some of these movies use the Holocaust as a backdrop for the main story, and this use, more often than not, results in its exploitation.

Film critic Annette Insdorf (1983) perspicaciously points out that "the Holocaust is often exploited by those who simply have access to the media . . . The commercial exigencies of film make it a dubious form for communicating the truth of World War II, given box-office dependence on sex, violence, a simple plot, easy laughs, and so on" (p. xiv). Tellingly, continues Insdorf, few American feature films "have confronted the darker realities of World War II— ghettos, occupation, deportation, concentration camps, collaboration, extermination" (p. 1).

Many of the "Hollywood" productions about the Holocaust use questionable cinematic devices which result in a production that is melodramatic and vulgar. Among these devices are overly dramatic or emotionally manipulative soundtracks, melodramatic dialogue, and an abundance of close-up shots for dramatic effect. They also have a propensity for developing melodramatic or sentimental plots that inaccurately portray history.

It is worth noting that at least one of the "Hollywood" tele-films (*Holocaust*) that has been widely castigated as being vulgar, inaccurate, and a distortion of the real events, seemingly had a tremendous impact on people in terms of informing them about the atrocities of the Holocaust or raising their concern about that tragic event. This seems to say more about the ignorance of the viewers or the power of the medium that the quality of the film, *per se. Holocaust* was televised in the United States and Europe in the late 1970s, and it basically tells the story of the fate of one Jewish family during the Nazi period in Germany. The film was embroiled in controversy from the start. Many Holocaust survivors and film critics decried the film for trivializing the Holocaust. Elie Wiesel said that the tele-film "was one that pretended to tell the truth" (Dupont, 1980, p. 11). Insdorf (1983), however, was more ambivalent about it: "It must be appreciated for its stimulation of concern, both in America and Europe, but questioned for its matter of presentation" (p. 4).

The impact of the show, however, especially on the German audience, was quite remarkable. As critic Irving Howe (1980) noted: "An amazing number of Germans confessed that the film had awakened them to the full extent of Hitler's destruction of European Jewry. They were now less disposed than before to retain the statue of limitations on the punishable crimes of Nazi officials" (p. 9).

Numerous filmmakers from various nations have made use of the archival footage shot by the Nazis. There is an inherent danger in such use, particularly in the areas of stereotyping and historical accuracy since many of these films were made for propaganda purposes.

The themes and plots of films about the Holocaust are extremely diverse, though not to as great an extent as found in literary works on the Holocaust. While many of the films do include dreadful images of the mounds of dead bodies or scenes of emaciated prisoners, most focus on other areas of the Holocaust.

There are also numerous areas that filmmakers have either not addressed at all or only to a minimal extent. Among these are the following: the limited role the United States played in preventing the slaughter of the Jews by Hitler; the political role and moral stance of the church during the Holocaust years; "the ambiguous political resistance of rightists who applauded (silently) the extermination of Jews while fighting against Nazi invaders of their homeland" (Insdorf, 1983, p. 125); the role of Jews in the resistance against the Nazis; and the harboring of former Nazis by certain nations during the war years.

Art

Certain specialists on Holocaust-related art note that there is a major distinction between the "Holocaust in art" and the "art of the Holocaust" (Blatter, 1981, p. 21). The former category is concerned with any piece of art whose focus is the Holocaust, whether created by victims or nonvictims, and either during or following the war. The "art of the Holocaust" refers to that art created by the victims of the Holocaust during the years 1939–45.

It is estimated that over one hundred thousand pieces of art were created by the victims of the Nazis during the Holocaust years. This is astounding in light of the fact that the Nazis forbade the creation of most art by the victims, except that commissioned by them. Of that number over thirty thousand pieces of art have survived. Some of the rest were lost when artists destroyed their own work out of fear of being detected by the SS or were destroyed by the Nazis. Other pieces were hidden and never recovered after the artist's death. Moreover, the material on which the art was created was extremely fragile and did not last. Artwork on paper was also used for fuel and as toilet paper. Finally some art was destroyed by the Allied bombings.

In light of the conditions under which the art was created, it is miraculous that so many pieces did survive. Again, there are numerous means by which the art was saved. Hundreds of works were smuggled out from the ghettos, transit and concentration camps by various means. Artists concealed their works in double walls in the ghettos or placed them in containers such as milk cans, jars, or boxes, and buried them until they could be dug up later. Ironically, the Nazis were also in part responsible for preserving some of this art; they stored over 100,000 Jewish artistic and historical objects which they planned to display in a "museum of an extinct race."

This art was created both by professional and nonprofessional artists on an eclectic array of topics, in diverse mediums and styles, and under many different conditions. The victims, in fact, created art whenever and wherever they possibly could: the ghettos, the transit camps, the concentration camps, the death camps, and the urban and forest hideouts. They also created it on almost any surface they could find: the walls of their barracks, margins of stamps, posters, flour bags, matchbook covers, unused postcards, medical reports, potato sacks, wrapping paper, camp flyers, scraps of newspaper, toilet paper, and even high-quality drawing paper and canvas. Furthermore, the artistic tools they used were also of an extremely diverse nature: pencils; chips of wood; charcoal; fingers in place of brushes; burnt tree twigs; and brushes made from human hair, feathers, straw or blades of grass. Colors for paints were also obtained in very ingenious ways: some artists pressed colors from vegetables and other foods as well as pieces of clothing. Many also used milk as a fixative for their paints.

All types of art—drawings, prints, lithographs, photographs, paintings, sculpture, collages, and montages—were created during this period. Most abundant, however, were drawings, for several reasons: 'In this medium, improvisation was more possible, statements could be made more rapidly (no drying time, as demanded by other media, was required), the works could be done on smaller and more surfaces, and could be more easily concealed" (Constanza, 1982, p. 128). Pencils were also more readily available since the Nazis had such a propensity for keeping statistical charts.

Constanza (1982) has noted: "The artwork produced in the camps and ghettos of Europe between 1939 and 1945 falls into three categories: work assigned by the Nazis and referred to by many scholars and historians as 'legal' or official art; clandestine art, the humanistic work that depicted the awful truths of camp existence; and work by a few that was seemingly unrelated to the experiences in the camps" (p. 21).

In the category of official art, the artists were required to work on numerous projects such as propaganda pieces, signs, emblems, maps, postcards, landscapes, portraits of prisoners, portraits of Nazis, the idealized German family, and the infamous Nazi "medical experiments."

The "clandestine art" covers such areas as pre-Holocaust Jewish life in Eastern Europe; the roundups; life in the ghettos, transit camps, and forests; the deportations; the "selections"; the degrading and brutal conditions and events in the concentration and death camps; and the victims' desperate attempts to retain their own humanity and dignity in such horrific conditions. Other works, though these are much rarer, include satire, gallows humor, or caricatures of both camp guards and prisoners. These served as a catharsis for some artists as well as a weapon with which to strike out at the horror in which they were enmeshed.

While most of the art displays basic realism, many other styles are evident: Expressionism, Surrealism and even Dadaism. Numerous works display the influence of such artists as Goya, Grosz, Brueghel, and Picasso.

Among the most touching art is that by the children who were in the concentration camps. While this work is not very sophisticated, it speaks volumes to the horrors suffered by the young as well as the old.

Numerous photographers (most notably Mendel Grossman and Roman Vishniac) captured a wide range of Jewish life in Eastern Europe prior to its obliteration by the Nazis as well as life in the ghettos on flim. They took such photographs at grave risk to themselves, and their massive collections stand as monuments to the dead.

Following the liberation of the concentration and death camps, many of the survivors continued to create artworks about the events they had experienced, including the liberation and the time spent in the displaced persons camps. Interestingly and significantly, the iconography of the art done following the war is in sharp contrast to that created during the war. As art critic Janet Blatter (1981, p. 35) points out: "Work done after the war more closely resembles the stereotype of war art. The postwar artists, painting from memory, depict grotesque distortions, broken bodies, screaming faces; grisly symbolism, such as death heads and walking skeletons, abounds. Nazis appear often in postwar work, rarely in work done in the camp. This work is harsher, more gruesome, and more macabre than that done between 1939 and 1945. Even those artists whose work was done in other styles during the war switched to more violent forms after they were liberated.

". . . During the war, artists had to put some distance between themselves and their circumstances. They used an almost muted style as a buffer, as if to dilute the horror of their circumstances. On the other hand, they refused to accept the Nazi-approved sentimental realism, preferring a style more conducive to telling the truth. Moreover, not all artists registered indignation at their conditions; their responses were often compassionate. Once removed to more secure conditions, however, they could safely express the full force of their pain and rage in works of fury and damning satire."

Many works of art about the Holocaust have been created by artists other than survivors since the end of World War II. While some of it is admirable work, much of it undermines the significance of the Holocaust. This is true even of those works in which it is obvious that the artist had the best of intentions. Much of this work is either so abstract that it clouds its own message, or is so mundane as to be virtually messageless. Also, like certain pieces of contemporary literature, some of the contemporary art uses the Holocaust as a metaphor for other atrocities for personal suffering. Again, in light of the tragic dimensions and ineffable nature of the Holocaust such usage is unconscionable.

Illustrative of well-intentioned but weak uses of art are the numerous photographs that have been taken either of the long-empty concentration and death camps or the countenances of aged survivors. Most of this photography is bereft of the immediacy and power of the works by the survivors of the Holocaust. In fact, such artwork seems to corroborate critic Susan Sontag's contention that "seeing through photographs . . . promotes emotional detachment" (Grundberg, 1982, p. D31).

There are still areas that need to be addressed vis-à-vis art of the Holocaust. Sybil Milton (1981, pp. 42–43) notes that: "Despite the plethora of available sources, there are still serious gaps in documentation of art produced between 1933 and 1945. Few museums or institutions have systemically collected information about the emigrant artists of this period; the refugee artists became the victim artists when the Nazi occupation of adjacent countries brought them once again into the web or terror and persecution. Virtually nothing has been found from the ruins of Belzec or Chelmno (Kulmhof), where there were virtually no survivors. There are no depositories for Holocaust art created in Italy, Rumania, Hungary, and Belgium. No existing collection identifies art by Gypsies, homosexuals or Jehovah's Witnesses." Furthermore, other than critical essays and reviews in newspapers, magazines, and certain art journals, there has been little written on either the quantity or value of the art that has been created in the last several decades by artists who either were not direct witnesses of the Holocaust or were not alive during that period. This area is rich in possibilities for critical examination.

Music

The role of music was extremely significant in the ghettos, forests, and the concentration and death camps. The singing of songs by the victims and the partisans not only connected them with their past, which had been terminated so abruptly and brutally, but also served as a method of retaining their strength, resilience, hope, values, and beliefs. In relation to the latter points, Shmerke Kaczerginski, a poet who was a partisan fighter of the Vilna ghetto, has written that "The song, the proverb, the joke accompanied the Jew always and everywhere: when he went to work, when he stood in line for a bowl of soup, when he was led to slaughter and when he rose up in battle" (Gordon-Mlotek, 1983, p. 2).

Many professional song writers (Kaczerginski, Abraham Sutzkever, Mordecai Gebirtig, and Isiah Shpigl to name but a few) continued to create songs in the ghettos, forests, and concentration camps. Others, who had never written songs, became composers as they forged music from the crucible in which they were forced to live. Older and popular Yiddish songs were also altered so that they commented on the plight of the Jews in the ghettos and concentration camps. These songs were not intended to be sung by professionals nor were they created for the purpose of entertaining an audience; rather they became a part of the daily life of the incarcerated Jews.

The subject matter of these songs was quite diverse, and included the injustices that were forced upon the Jews, a longing to be back home, calls to fight the Nazis, the plight of relatives in death camps, the fate of children and orphans, the executions, and the need for those who would survive to serve as witnesses to the horrors that the victims suffered. About three hundred of these songs have been published thus far.

Many outstanding composers also continued to compose, both in "official" and unofficial capacities, chamber, orchestral and vocal music. Many of these compositions have survived, and have been compiled and analyzed in various works.

Finally, as is now well known, many composers and performers were forced by the Nazis to create and perform in the concentration and death camps. Not only were they made to play in front of Nazi officials and camp commandants, but also while people were driven into the gas chambers.

Conclusion

When all is said and done, the magnitude of the horror of the Holocaust remains unfathomable. The serious artists who have wrestled with its ineffable dimensions readily acknowledge that. And yet, paradoxically, many of these artists have felt compelled to attempt, time and time again, to penetrate its darkness, its mystery. At the very least, the result of such efforts often explore "the possibilities of human behavior in inhuman circumstances" (Alvarez, 1964, p. 69). Concomitantly, and maybe most significantly, such endeavors often translate into remembrance—remembrance of the victims of one of the most heinous crimes against humanity the world has ever witnessed.

References

Alvarez, A. (1964). The literature of the Holocaust. *Commentary*, 38 (November), 69.

Blatter, Janet (1981). Art from the whirlwind. In Blatter, J., and Milton, S. (Eds.), *Art of the Holocaust*. New York: The Rutledge Press.

Constanza, Mary S. (1982). *The Living Witness: Art in the Concentration Camps and Ghettos*. New York: The Free Press.

Dupont, Joan (1980). Elie Wiesel: the man who will not let others forget. *International Herald Tribune*, 9 April.

Ezrachi, Sidra Dekoven (1980). *By Words Alone: The Holocaust in Literature*. Chicago: University of Chicago Press. 262 pp.

Gordon-Mlotek, Eleanor (1983). A bequest of Holocaust songs. In Gordon-Mlotek, E., and Gottlieb, M. (Eds.), *We Are Here: Songs of the Holocaust*. New York: Education Department of the Workman's Circle.

Grundberg, Andy (1982). Why the Holocaust defies pictorialization. *The New York Times*, 2 May.

Howe, Irving (1980). Foreword to Ezrachi, S.D. *By Words Alone: The Holocaust in Literature*. Chicago: University of Chicago Press.

Howe, Irving (1981). Preface to Blatter, J. and Milton, S. (Eds.), *Art of the Holocaust*. New York: The Rutledge Press.

Insdorf, Annette (1983). *Indelible Shadows: Film and the Holocaust*. New York: Random House. 234 pp.

Milton, Sybil (1981). The legacy of Holocaust art. In Blatter, J. and Milton, S. (Eds.), *Art of the Holocaust*. New York: The Rutledge Press.

Wiesel, Elie (1978). *A Jew Today*. New York: Random House.

Wiesel, Elie (1983). Does the Holocaust lie beyond the reach of art? *The New York Times*, 17 April.

Wiesel, Elie (1986). Welcoming 1986. *The New York Times*, 5 January.

Zvielli, Alexander (1979). Review of Hashoa Betiudi documents on the Holocaust. *The Jerusalem Post*, September 28.

Bibliography

General

Szonyi, David M. (Ed.). *The Holocaust: An Annotated Bibliography and Resource Guide*. New York: KTAV Publishing House. 396 pp.
> One of the most comprehensive listings ever published on the Holocaust. It includes extensive annotated bibliographies of works of fiction and imaginative literature (novels, short stories, drama, poetry), books for younger children, and nonfiction on the Holocaust. It also includes a filmography and a guide to musical resources. Its main weaknesses are that many of the annotations are bereft of key information, and numerous items are not annotated.

Novels

Appelfeld, Aharon (1981). *Tzili: The Story of a Life*. Translated from the Hebrew by Dalya Bilu. New York: E.P. Dutton. 185 pp.
> The story of this poetic novel revolves around a slow and simple Jewish girl who uses her simplicity and tenacious drive for endurance in order to survive the Holocaust. Abandoned by her family when the war breaks out, she is subjected to repeated brutality as well as horrible acts of anti-Semitism. The low-key tone of the novel heightens its power.

Arieti, Silvano (1980). *The Parnas*. New York: Basic Books. 165 pp.
> This novel, by an eminent psychiatrist, is a mixture of fiction and history about the efforts of a Sephardic chief elder's efforts to save the lives of his congregation in Pisa during the Holocaust. Through the novel the author attempts to probe the reality of evil.

Berger, Zdena (1961). *Tell Me Another Morning*. New York: Harper Brothers. 243 pp.
> In this noted novel, Tania, the protagonist, fights with all of her being to retain her own sense of identity as a form of resistance against the horrors she is made to face and undergo in Auschwitz.

Böll, Heinrich (1965). *Billiards at Half-Past Nine*. Translated from the German by Lelia Vennewitz. New York: Signet. 285 pp.
> This is a powerful novel that keys in on the fate or guilt of the German population following the Holocaust. The novel covers part of the eightieth birthday of the head of the Faehmel family, 6 September 1958. The three dominant figures (grandfather,

son, and grandson) are all architects, and architecture, with its concern for stress and strain as well as the creation of beauty versus the destruction of beauty, is the major metaphor of the novel.

Bor, Josef (1963). *The Terezin Requiem*. Translated from the Czech by Edith Pargeter. New York: Knopf. 112 pp.

This Czech novel is a semifictionalized account of the performance of Verdi's Requiem by Jewish prisoners in Theresienstadt for Nazi officers, including Eichmann. The conductor changes the finale of the libretto so that it is transformed into a cry of protest.

Cohen, Arthur A. (1973). *In the Days of Simon Stern*. New York: Random House. 404 pp.

This novel, which is ostensibly "written" by Nathan Gaza, a Jewish scribe who is blind as a result of an injury suffered in Nazi Germany, is about a modern messiah named Simon Stern, who founds the Society for the Rescue and Resurrection of Jewish Survivors of the Holocaust in New York City in the mid-1940s. Cohen makes fascinating use of eclectic sources such as the Bible, Talmudic myths and the Kabbala.

Delbo, Charlotte (1978). *None of Us Will Return*. Translated from the French by John Githens. Boston: Beacon. 128 pp.

A mix between a memoir and fiction, this is the story of a member of the French resistance who was captured in 1942 and incarcerated in Auschwitz.

Fuks, Ladislav (1968). *Mr. Theodore Mundstock*. Translated from the Czech by Iris Unwin. New York: The Orion Press. 214 pp.

The protagonist, who is "split in two" when the Nazis occupy his town of Prague, is faced with the problem of how, as a Jew, to cope with the fact that he will sooner or later be shipped off to a death factory. In the course of the novel, he becomes a messiah figure to other Jews, attempts suicide, and then begins planning a "logical" method to help himself survive. But the "logical" quickly descends into the absurd.

Gascar, Pierre (1960). *The Season of the Dead*. In *Beasts and Men and the Seed*. Translated from the French by Jean Stewart and Merloyd Lawrence. New York: Meridian Books.

This novella about the Holocaust is ostensibly based on the experiences Gascar (a French soldier, but not a Jew) faced while interned in various concentration camps over a period of five years. It is about a group of grave-diggers whose world is turned upside down when they discover a mass grave of half-decayed Jewish bodies. The stench of the bodies, which permeates everything, along with the grisly scenes, serves as a metaphor for the decay of what has previously been known as "civilization."

Grass, Günter (1962). *The Tin Drum*. Translated from the German by Ralph Manheim. New York: Pantheon. 591 pp.

In this powerful novel, which is a scathing indictment of the crimes of Nazism, the reader is supposedly reading the autobiographical novel of Oskar Matzerath, a mad German dwarf who is incarcerated in an institution and is fond of pounding on a drum. At the age of three, after examining the state of the world, Oskar decides to quit growing; and from this point on, he becomes the nemesis of those he despises. His subsequent actions serve as a parody of German history from 1899 to 1954, particularly the brutal period controlled by the Nazis.

Grass, Günter (1965). *Dog Years*. Translated from the German by Ralph Manheim. New York: Harcourt, Brace & World. 570 pp.

This novel is a powerful denunciation of Nazism and of German propensity to suppress that horrible period in history. The title suggests "dog days" when dogs are popularly thought to go mad. The madness suggests Nazism.

Kaniuk, Yoram (1971). *Adam Resurrected*. Translated from the Hebrew by Seymour Simckes. New York: Atheneum. 370 pp.

This psychological novel portrays the fight of a Holocaust survivor to purge himself of the horror and guilt that have engulfed him owing to his experiences in a concentration camp where he used his abilities as a professional clown to lead Jewish victims to death—including his wife and older sister. A richly inventive fable, which has strains of Swift- and Kafka-like satire and humor, this novel examines a number of very serious concerns: God's relation to the Holocaust, Israel's relationship with Holocaust survivors, and the apocalyptic nature of the Holocaust vis-à-vis world history.

Ka-Tzetnik 135633 (1963). *Atrocity*. New York: Lyle Stuart. 287 pp.

This is a stunning novel by a survivor of the Holocaust who writes under the name of Ka-Tzetnik (a pseudonym that means "concentration camp survivor"). It tells the story of the sexual abuse of a young Jewish boy in Auschwitz who becomes a homosexual prostitute in order to survive. Despite the degradation forced upon him, he retains his moral integrity.

Kosinski, Jerzy (1965). *The Painted Bird*. New York: Pocket Books. 272 pp.

This powerful and terrifying novel presents the story of a young boy who, upon separation from his parents, wanders through peasant villages in Holocaust-plagued Europe. Inexorably, he moves from being a victim of abuse and hatred to being a victimizer. The overriding theme of the novel is the evil of the Holocaust.

Kuznetsov, Anatoli (1970). *Babi Yar: A Documentary Novel*. Translated from the Russian by Jacob Guralsky; uncensored edition. New York: Farrar, Straus & Giroux. 477 pp.

A documentary novel based on the notes the author took as a teenager while the Nazi atrocities were being carried out in the ravine near his village. The first edition of this novel was published in Russia, with sections deleted. The chapters that were censored deal with NKVD-provoked outbursts in Kiev, with the intent of provoking a German response.

Lind, Jakov (1966). *Landscape in Concrete*. New York: Grove Press. 190 pp.

This novel, by a Jew who survived the Holocaust working as a laborer under an assumed identity in Germany, parodies man's quest for knowledge and the notion of "civilized society." It uses as its epigram the statement, "There is a plague called man." The protagonist is a sergeant in the Nazi army who has been told that he is temporarily unfit for military service. He journeys across Europe, whose landscape is bereft of all spiritual and human values, in search of his regiment, and slowly but surely reverts from being "civilized" to increasingly barbaric.

Neumann, Robert (1940). *By the Waters of Babylon*. New York: Simon & Schuster. 356 pp.

While this novel is not a great literary work, it is worth noting because of its early depiction of the plight of the Jewish refugees from Nazi-occupied Europe.

Schaffer, Susan F. (1974). *Anya*. New York: Macmillan.

This historical novel tells the story of a survivor of the Holocaust, and her struggle to save her own and her daughter's lives. Especially moving is the agony that Jewish mothers go through in regard to being forced to choose between their life or that of their children.

Schwarz-Bart, André (1960). *Last of the Just*. New York: Atheneum. 374 pp.
This novel provides an account of the Levy family of "Just Men" who follow a tradition of self-sacrifice that originated in the year 1185 during a pogrom against the Jews in York, and culminates in the martyrdom of Ernie Levy in Auschwitz, where he voluntarily goes in order to save the world.

Steiner, Jean François (1967). *Treblinka*. Translated from the French by Helen Weaver. New York: Simon & Schuster. 415 pp.
This novel chronicles how Treblinka—one of the first Nazi concentration camps specifically set up to kill Jews in large numbers—was organized, operated, and how its Jewish slave-laborers rose up and destroyed the camp on 2 August, 1943.

Styron, William (1979). *Sophie's Choice*. New York: Random House. 515 pp.
This novel is set in 1947 in Brooklyn, and is narrated by a young Southern writer who becomes friends with a Polish Catholic survivor of Auschwitz and her boyfriend, a manic-depressive American Jew. Ostensibly these three characters represent concepts of American inaction during the Holocaust, European ambivalence, and Jewish suffering. This novel has been roundly criticized by critics for sensationalism, vulgarity, poor humor, a weak plot, and for trivializing the magnitude of the Holocaust.

Uris, Leon (1961). *Mila 18*. Garden City, NY: Doubleday. 539 pp.
This popular novel is about the uprising of the Warsaw Ghetto.

Wiesel, Elie (1960). *Night*. Translated from the French by Stella Rodway. New York: Hill & Wang. 116 pp.
In this extremely powerful book—which seems to defy categorization in that it has been alternately described by critics as a fictionalized autobiography, nonfiction novel, and memoir—the reader is presented with a stark and graphic first-hand account of the horrors of the deportation and slaughter of the Jews by the Nazis. It is told by Eliezer, a fifteen-year-old survivor, who is ripped from his family home in Transylvania and transported to Auschwitz where he loses his mother, younger sister, father, and his faith in God. A subtly powerful examination of the ramifications of the Holocaust: "the relationships between man and God, man and man, and man and himself."

Wiesel, Elie (1962). *The Accident*. Translated from the French by Anne Borchardt. New York: Hill & Wang. 120 pp.
A novel about a survivor of the Holocaust who is so burdened with his searing memories that he has lost the will to live and wants to die so he can join his loved ones. He has also lost his faith in God, whom he blames for the tragedy of the Holocaust. When he is injured in an accident, he fights against those who try to save him; but slowly comes to understand that, for various reasons, he has an obligation to remain alive.

Wiesel, Elie (1966). *The Gates of the Forest*. Translated from the French by Frances Frenayne. New York: Holt, Rinehart & Winston. 226 pp.
This novel depicts the life of a Hungarian Jew through various facets of his life: as a young survivor of the Holocaust who hides in the woods; as a member of a band of Jewish partisans; and his "return" to God in a Brooklyn prayer hall among pious Hasidim.

Wiesel, Elie (1970). *A Beggar in Jerusalem*. Translated from the French by Lily Edelman and Elie Wiesel. New York: Random House. 211 pp.

> David, a survivor of the Holocaust and now a soldier in the Israeli army, is in a platoon that is sent to liberate the Wailing Wall during the 1967 War. David's best friend disappears just as the platoon accomplishes its goal. In his search for his friend, he sits and talks with a group of beggars. As the beggars relate talmudic legends and tales, David recalls his childhood when he lost everything to the Nazis. David wishes he had not survived but realizes he must go on because of his duty to relate the stories only he knows, so the past will not be forgotten.

Wiesel, Elie (1985). *The Fifth Son*. Translated from the French by Marion Wiesel. New York: Summit Books. 220 pp.

> This novel revolves around a stepson's attempt to break through his father's wall of silence which is a result of his experiences at Auschwitz and his involvement in the attempted murder of an SS officer after the war. The young man discovers that the SS officer is still alive in West Germany, and decides to locate and execute him. A main theme is about revenge and whether it is justified or not, and under what circumstances.

Wiesenthal, Simon (1976). *Sunflower*. New York: Shocken. 216 pp.

> In this allegorical novel, a young Jew is taken from a death camp to a makeshift army hospital and placed next to a dying Nazi who extends his hand towards the Jew. The novel forms the basis for a symposium on various facets of the Holocaust; and the symposium, which includes such participants as Abraham J. Heschel, Cynthia Ozick, Herbert Marcuse as well as others, forms the second part of this volume.

Short-story Collections

Borowski, Tadeusz (1967). *This Way to the Gas, Ladies and Gentlemen*. New York: Viking Press. 180 pp.

> The haunting short stories in this collection are based on Borowski's experiences in Auschwitz. Each story presents life in the concentration camp in all of its "brutal and naked reality."

Gascar, Pierre (1956). *Beasts and Men*. Translated from the French by Jean Stewart. London: Methuen. 227 pp.

> While the allegorical short stories in this collection are Kafkaesque in style, they are supposedly based on actual events that took place to Jewish Poles during the Holocaust years. They are all written from the perspective of a French prisoner-of-war.

Lind, Jakov (1964). *Soul of Wood and Other Stories*. New York: Grove Press. 190 pp.

> This collection of short stories portrays the evil and insanity that were so prevalent while the Nazis carried out their atrocities. Many of the stories are surrealistic in tone while others constitute allegories of sadism.

Lustig, Arnost (1976). *Night and Hope*. Translated from the Czech by George Theiner. New York: Aven.

> This book of powerful short stories "explores the nightmarish interaction between Jews and the meticulous efficency of the Nazis program for extermination."

Rudnicki, Adolf (1951). *Ascent to Heaven*. Translated from the Polish by H.C. Stevens. London: Dennis Dobson. 204 pp.

This collection of short stories by Rudnicki, who is considered to be one of the foremost Polish-language writers on the Holocaust, keys in on the horrors experienced by Poland's Jewish population.

Drama

Hochhuth, Rolf (1964). *The Deputy*. Translated from the German by Richard and Clara Winston: Preface by Albert Schweitzer. New York: Grove. 352 pp.
This morality play, which ignited a heated controversy, is basically an indictment of Pope Pius XII's silence in the face of the Nazis' mass killing of the Jews.

Shaw, Robert (1968). *The Man in the Glass Booth*. New York: Grove Press. 74 pp.
This play is about the trial of Adolf Eichmann during which he was tried in Israel for the crimes he committed during the Holocaust.

Weiss, Peter (1966). *The Investigation*. Translated from the German by Jon Swan and Ulu Grosbard. New York: Atheneum. 270 pp.
This controversial play is a condensed version of the trial, held in Frankfurt from 20 December 1963 through 20 August 1965, of twenty-one of the people who were responsible for the running of Auschwitz. The play is presented in the form of eleven cantos, each of which is concerned with a particular aspect of torture at Auschwitz. Critics have questioned the historical accuracy of the play and criticized its polemical nature.

Wiesel, Elie (1979). *The Trial of God: (As It Was Held on February 25, 1649 in Shamgorod)*. Translated from the French by Marion Wiesel. New York: Random House. 161 pp.
This play deals with the most complex of theological problems: that of theodicy, or the justification of the divine in the presence of evil. The play is set in 1649 as three entertainers wander into the village of Shamgorod on the anniversary of a terrible pogrom to celebrate Purim. Instead of the usual holiday entertainment, the actors agree, upon the insistence of a survivor, to hold a mock trial. The innkeeper plays the part of a prosecutor, the players act as judges, and the defendant is God, who is held responsible for the atrocities inflicted on the Jewish people.

Drama Anthology

Skloot, Robert (1983). *The Theater of the Holocaust*. Madison: University of Wisconsin. 416 pp.
This anthology comprises several plays that deal with various aspects of the Holocaust. Among the plays are Charlotte Delbo's *Who Will Carry the Word*? (a poetic work about life in the concentration camps); George Tabori's *The Cannibals* (which addresses the moral question of choosing between death and cannibalism in a concentration camp); and Simon Wincelberg's *Resort 76* (which is based on Bryk's *A Cat in the Ghetto*).

Books on Art, Photographs and Sculpture

Blatter, Janet, and Milton, Sybil (1981). *Art of the Holocaust*. New York: Rutledge-Layla. 272 pp.
This book contains over 350 reproductions of art created in concentration camps by 150 artists. It also includes essays on Holocaust art by Milton and Blatter as well as a historical overview of the Holocaust by Henry Friedlander. The text is reportedly "the first survey of the artistic record left by the victims of the Nazi terror."

Constanza, Mary S. (1982). *The Living Witness: Art in the Concentration Camps and Ghettos*. New York: Macmillan. 185 pp.
This outstanding text includes over one hundred paintings and drawings as well as succinct but powerful essays on the works and artists. This is among one of the first systematic efforts to reproduce and record the work of the Holocaust artists.

Green, Gerald (1969). *Artists of Terezin*. New York: Hawthorne. 191 pp.
This book comprises one hundred drawings and paintings that were produced by prisoners (Karel Fleischman, Bedrich Fritter, Leo Haas, and others) in the Nazi concentration camp of Terezin.

Grossman, Mendel (1978). *With a Camera in the Ghetto*. Edited by Zvi Szer and Alexander Sened. New York: Shocken Books.
A record of the everyday activities in the Lodz Ghetto during the years 1941–42.

Hellman, Peter (Ed.) (1981). *The Auschwitz Album*. New York: Random House. 180 pp.
This book contains some two hundred photographs, presumably taken by an official German photographer, which shows the "processing" of a group of Hungarian Jews on their arrival at Birkenau, Auschwitz's killing facility, in the summer of 1944. This book reportedly constitutes the "only known visual record of the arrival of a convoy to Auschwitz."

Novitch, Miriam; Dawidowicz, Lucy; and Freudenheim, Tom L. (1981). *Spiritual Resistance: Art from Concentration Camps, 1940–1945*. Philadelphia: The Jewish Publication Society of America. 237 pp.
Based on a selection of drawings and paintings from the collection of Kibbutz Lohamei Haghetaot in Israel, this text contains about eighty reproductions of works completed in the Nazi concentration camps, and outstanding essays by Novitch, Dawidowicz, and Freudenheim.

Rieth, Adolf (1969). *Monuments to the Victims of Tyranny*. New York: Frederick A. Praeger, Publishers. 134 pp.
This book comprises photographs and texts on a wide range of monuments (including many sculptures) to the victims of the Holocaust.

Toll, Nelly (1978). *Without Surrender: Art of the Holocaust*. Philadelphia: Running Press. 109 pp.
Toll, a survivor and artist, has collected approximately eighty paintings and drawings by a dozen artists (Toll, Per Ulrich, Felix Nussbaum, Liesel Felsentha, etc.), almost all of which were done in the camps and ghettos. Information about many of the artists as well as an essay on art of the Holocaust is included.

Vishniac, Roman (1983). *A Vanished World*. New York: Farrar, Straus & Giroux. 192 pp.
This book of photographs provides a gripping record of Jewish life and culture in Eastern Europe before it was obliterated by the Holocaust.

Collections and Volumes of Poetry

Gillon, Adam (Ed.) (1980). *Poems of the Ghetto: A Testament of Lost Men*. New York: Twayne Publishers. 96 pp.
This is a collection of very powerful poems about hope and despair and life and death in the Nazi-organized ghettos.

Kovner, Abba (1972). *A Canopy in the Desert*. Pittsburgh: University of Pittsburgh Press. 222 pp.

> This collection of poems, by a survivor, is about numerous aspects of the Holocaust. The title poem is concerned, in part, with the problem of how one should live in an inhuman world where such atrocities as those committed by the Nazis are perpetrated.

Leftwich, Joseph (Ed.) (1961). *The Golden Peacock: A Worldwide Treasury of Yiddish Poetry*. New York: Thomas Yoseloff. 722 pp.

> This collection contains much of the best Yiddish poetry about the Holocaust. It includes poems by Itzik Feffer, Mordecai Gebirtig, Hirsh Glick, Binem Heller, Leib Olitzky, and Simcha Shayevitch.

Levi, Primo (1976). *Shema: Collected Poems of Primo Levi*. Translated from the Italian by Ruth Feldman and Brian Swann. London: The Menard Press. 56 pp.

> These poems by the noted Jewish Italian author who fought with a band of partisans until he was captured and sent to Buna present vivid images of life and death in Nazi-occupied Europe.

Sachs, Nelly (1967). *O The Chimneys*. New York: Farrar, Straus & Giroux. 387 pp.

> This outstanding collection includes a wealth of poetry whose focus and theme is the Holocaust. The chimney of the title refers to the smokestacks of the crematoriums.

Sachs, Nelly (1970). *The Seeker and Other Poems*. New York: Farrar, Straus & Giroux. 399 pp.

> These poems by Nelly Sachs, who fled Germany in 1940 and later won the Nobel Prize for Literature, are about the Jewish flight from Nazi terror as well as other aspects of the Holocaust.

Sutzkever, Abraham (1981). *Burnt Pearls: Ghetto Poems of Abraham Sutzkever*. Translated from the Yiddish by Seymour Mayne. Available only from the publisher at: Mosaic Press/Valley Editions, P.O. Box 10321, Oakville, Ontario, Canada L6J 5E9.

> This is the first English collection of Sutzkever, a major Yiddish poet of the Holocaust.

Wiesel, Elie (1973). *Ani Maamin: A Song Lost and Found Again*. Translated from the French by Marion Wiesel: Music for the Cantata composed by Darius Milhaud. New York: Random House. 107 pp.

> The title of this poem begins one of the thirteen Articles of Faith set forth by Maimonides, which opens with "I believe in the coming of the Messiah." The poem describes the encounter between the patriarchs (who have witnessed the horrors of the Holocaust) and God over the plight of the Jews.

Books on Music

Bor, Josef (1963). *The Terezin Requiem*. Translated from the Czech by Edith Pargeter. New York: Knopf. 112 pp.

> A survivor tells of the performance of the Verdi Requiem before Eichmann and other Nazis in 1944 by five hundred Jewish prisoners. All of them were subsequently sent to the gas chamber.

Gordon-Mlotek, Eleanor, and Gottlieb, Malka (Eds.) (1983). *We Are Here: Songs of the Holocaust*. New York: Education Department of the Workmen's Circle. With a Foreword by Elie Wiesel and illustrations by Tsirl Waletzky.

> An important collection of ghetto and partisan songs.

Kalisch, Shoshana, and Meister, Barbara (1985). *Yes, We Sang: Songs of the Ghettos and Concentration Camps*. New York: Harper & Row. 160 pp.

    Included in this text are the music and words (with piano accompaniment) of twenty-five songs of the Holocaust, as they were sung in the Nazi concentration camps and ghettos. The texts are given both in transliterated Yiddish and in English translations.

Karas, Joza (1985). *Music in Terezin*. New York: Beaufort Books. 240 pp.

    Karas examines why the quality of creativity among the Jewish composers and performers was so high in the Terezin concentration camp. In essence, it is a provocative, critical study of the creative process itself.

Books on Holocaust Films

Grobman, Alex; Landes, Daniel; and Milton, Sybil (Eds.) (1983) *Genocide: Critical Issues of the Holocaust: A Companion to the Film "Genocide."* Los Angeles: The Simon Wiesenthal Center, and Chappaqua, NY: Rossel Books. 512 pp.

    In addition to serving as a companion volume to the film *Genocide*, this text also includes a discussion of how the Holocaust is portrayed through film, an examination of aspects of modern anti-Semitism, and implications of the Holocaust.

Insdorf, Annette (1983). *Indelible Shadows: Film and the Holocaust*. New York: Random House. 234 pp.

    Richly illustrated, this book is a valuable introduction to the ways in which film-makers have dealt with the subject of the Holocaust. It critically examines seventy-five fictional and documentary films, and includes a list of over one hundred films, along with the addresses of distributors.

Lanzmann, Claude (1985). *Shoah: An Oral History of the Holocaust. The Text of the Film*. New York: Pantheon. 200 pp.

    This is the complete text of Lanzmann's 9½-hour movie in which witnesses—survivors, former SS officers, and Polish villagers—speak about their experiences and insights into the Holocaust.

Films

Act of Faith. (28 min., b & w. Available from the Anti-Defamation League of B'nai B'rith, 823 United Nations Plaza, New York, NY 10017.)

    Presents a first-hand account of the role played by the Danish people in saving their Jewish countrymen from the Nazis.

As if It Were Yesterday. (85 min., b & w. Available from Cinema Five, 1500 Broadway, New York, NY 10036.)

    This film retraces the efforts of an underground network of courageous Belgian citizens who helped four thousand Jewish children evade deportation and extermination during the Nazi occupation.

The Avenue of the Just. (55 min., color. Available from the Anti-Defamation League of B'nai B'rith, 823 United Nations Plaza, New York, NY 10017.)

    In Jerusalem, at the Yad Vashem memorial, there is a garden surrounded by a tree-lined walk which commemorates heroism and life. Each tree on the Avenue of the Just bears the name of a Christian who saved Jewish lives during the Hitler years. Ten of these individuals recount their personal experiences in this extraordinary film.

To Bear Witness. (41 min., color and b & w, videocassette. Available from Zenger Video, 10 000 Culver Blvd., Room 9, P.O. Box 802, Culver City, CA 90232-0802.)

A powerful film about Holocaust survivors and liberators who gathered at the First International Liberators Conference in 1981 to testify about their experiences during the Holocaust. Interspersed with captured Nazi footage and official U.S. Army films, the testimony of witnesses provides an authentic account of myriad aspects of the Holocaust.

Camps of the Dead. (19 min., b & w. Available from Canadian Jewish Congress, 1590 Avenue of Docteur Penfield, Montreal, Quebec, Canada H3G 1C5.)

This extremely powerful film was made from original footage photographed by French and Allied cameramen during the liberation of several concentration camps.

Chaim Rumkowski and the Jews of Lodz. (55 min., b & w, 16 mm. Available from The Cinema Guild, 1697 Broadway, New York, NY 10019.)

The focus is on Chaim Rumkowski, appointed by the Nazis as the Chairman of the Lodz Jewish Council, and his doomed plan to save the Jews by making them indispensable to the industry of the German war effort.

The Eighty-First Blow. (120 min., b & w, in Hebrew with English subtitles. Available from Alden Films, 7820 20th Ave., Brooklyn, NY 11204.)

A chronological documentary of the Holocaust made up of footage and stills shot by the Nazis as well as a compilation of quotes and stories from the Eichmann trial. It covers numerous events, including Kristallnacht, life and death in the Warsaw Ghetto, the deportations, and the acts of genocide. Meticulous in its documentation and painfully explicit.

The Final Solution—Auschwitz (208 min., color, video. Available from The Media Guild, 11722 Sorrento Valley Rd., Suite E., San Diego, CA 92121-9990.)

This is an extremely powerful film about the Nazis' systematic murder of Jews in the death factories.

From the Ashes. (27 min. Available from the Canadian Jewish Congress, 1590 Avenue of Docteur Penfield, Montreal, Quebec, Canada H3G 1C5).

This is a television interview with Elie Wiesel.

The Great Dictator. (78 min., b & w. Available from Libra Cinema 5 Films, 1585 Broadway, Third Floor, New York, NY 10019.)

This classic feature film, directed by and starring Charlie Chaplin, is about a barber and his Jewish girlfriend who are persecuted in the "country" of Tomania. Playing both the barber and a Hitler-like dictator, Chaplin uses satire to present a powerful condemnation of the Nazis.

Holocaust. (120 min., color. Available from the Learning Corporaion of America, 1350 Avenue of the Americas, New York, NY 10019.)

This television film, which was reportedly seen by over 220 million people, focuses on the lives of the Weiss family, wealthy Berlin Jews, as they are torn from their home and killed by the Nazis. The movie has been castigated for its melodramatic and romantic tone, and its superficial presentation of history.

In Dark Places. (58 min., color. Available from Phoenix Films, 470 Park Avenue South, New York, NY 10016.)

A thought-provoking film that focuses on the children of the Holocaust survivors and also includes personal stories of survivors as well as a discussion of how the media exploits the event of the Holocaust.

Joseph Schultz. (14 min., color. Available from the Anti-Defamation League of B'nai B'rith, 823 United Nations Plaza, New York, NY 10017.)
This film is based on an actual incident that occurred during World War II in which a Nazi soldier refused to participate in the execution of a group of villagers and was killed along with them by his fellow soldiers.

Judgment at Nuremberg. (186 min., b & w, 16 mm. Available from Jewish Media Services, Jewish Welfare Board, 15 E. 26th St., New York, NY 10010.)
This feature film is about the Nuremberg trials of the Nazis for the crimes they committed against the Jews. Though this is a "Hollywood" movie made for mass appeal, it does address issues such as freedom, obedience to authority and individual responsibility.

Kamal. (150 min., color, 16 mm. Available from Films Inc., 440 Park Avenue South, New York, NY 10016.)
This feature film made in Poland presents a harrowing view of the last days of the Warsaw Ghetto uprising as the fighters struggle in a losing battle. Brutally real, the film serves as a commemoration to the members of the Polish resistance.

The Last Stop. (120 min., b & w. Polish, Russian, German, and French with English subtitles. There is one print of this film at the Museum of Modern Art in New York City.)
Produced in 1948 and directed by Wanda Jakubowska, a survivor of Auschwitz, this film has been called "one of the most powerful and historically accurate feature films made about (and in) Auschwitz." The film is basically about how the females in Auschwitz supported and nurtured one another even under and in spite of the horrific conditions they were faced with.

The Life That Disappeared. (16 min., b & w, 80 slides with accompanying cassette. Available from the Jewish Media Service, Jewish Welfare Board, 15 East 26th St., New York, NY 10010.)
Photographed and narrated by Roman Vishniac, this slide show provides an overview of what life was like for the Polish Jews under the Nazis.

Night and Fog. (31 min., color and b & w, French with English subtitles. Available from Contemporary Films—McGraw-Hill, 1221 Sixth Ave., New York, NY 10020.)
Directed by Alain Resnais, this outstanding and powerful film documents the Nazis' racial policy from the first deportations in 1933 through the "final solution."

The Precious Legacy. (29 min., color, 16 mm. Available from Modern Talking Pictures, 45 Rockefeller Plaza, New York, NY 10110.)
This documentary is about how the Nazis planned to create a "museum of an extinct race" in Prague and how, ironically, the collected materials now serve as the world's greatest collection of Judaica.

Shoah (9½ hours. Available in video from the Simon Wiesenthal Center, 9760 West Pico Blvd., Los Angeles, CA 90035.)
Completed in 1985, *Shoah* is a monumental documentary about the Holocaust by Claude Lanzmann. Condensed from 350 hours of footage into a 9½-hour film, "its goal is unique, selective and single-minded: to describe in ruthless detail the inhuman bureauratic machinery of the Final Solution during the years 1942–1944." This film has been called "haunting," "hallucinatory," "a terrifying epic poem."

Sophie's Choice. (157 min., color, 16 mm. Available from Films Inc. 7333 Green Bay Road, Wilmette, IL 60091.)

This feature movie, which is based on William Styron's novel of the same title, is about three people, an American Southerner, a Polish Catholic survivor of Auschwitz, and a manic-depressive American Jew, and the impact that the Holocaust has on their interrelationships. The movie has been castigated for trivializing the significance and magnitude of the horror of the Holocaust.

The Sorrow and the Pity. (260 min., b & w, French with English subtitles. Available from Cinema Film, 1500 Broadway, New York, NY 10036.)

This is an unrelenting film, by Marcel Ophuls, about collaboration and resistance during the German occupation of France. The film focuses on the citizens of Clermont-Ferrand: the collaborators, the apathetic, and the resisters.

Voyage of the Damned. (158 min., color. Available from Films Inc., 733 Green Bay Road, Wilmette, IL 60091.)

This is the story of the 937 German-Jewish refugees aboard the luxury liner *St. Louis* who sailed to Cuba in 1939 but were forcibly returned to Europe as World War II was about to begin. While it is melodramatic in parts, it is factually accurate, heartbreaking and enraging.

Warsaw Ghetto. (51 min., b & w. Available from the Anti-Defamation League of B'nai B'rith, 823 United Nations Plaza, New York, NY 10017.)

The footage in this film was taken from 1940 to 1943 by cameramen of the German army, the SS, and the Gestapo, much of it for the private albums of Heinrich Himmler, the Gestapo chief. The documentary shows the frightened and bewildered Jews entering the Ghetto area, the horrors of disease, and the systematic destruction.

Who Shall Live and Who Shall Die. (90 min., color. Available from Kino International, 250 West 57th St., New York, NY 10019.)

This is a controversial film that presents an examination of the role that the U.S. government and the American Jewish community took in relation to protecting European Jews from Hitler's policies and atrocities. Despite its weaknesses, the film does raise a host of issues worthy of examination.

12

The Literature, Art, and Film of Genocide

Samuel Totten

Numerous acts of genocide have been committed during the twentieth century by various peoples across the globe, including genocidal atrocities by U.S. troops while fighting an insurrection in the Philippines in 1900; the slaughter of the Herero in 1904 by the German rulers of South West Africa; the Turkish slaughter of the Armenians; the Soviet genocide of the Ukrainian people by creating an artificial famine; the purges and mass deportations perpetrated by Stalin; the rash of massacres in Burundi, Indonesia, Bangladesh, Nigeria, and Uganda; the slaughter of the Aché Indians in Paraguay; and the mass killings of the Cambodian people by the Khmer Rouge government of Pol Pot. This list is not comprehensive. Yet many otherwise informed individuals are not even cognizant of many of these acts.

Many of these genocidal or near-genocidal acts have never been the subject of fiction, poetry or artworks. Of the works that have appeared, many have never been published in English, and they are nowhere near as numerous as works on the Holocaust. There is clearly a dearth of literature and art concerned with genocide.

Among the possible reasons for this situation may be these: certain populations that were the victims of genocidal acts were more or less illiterate, and as a result the survivors did not have the ability to write pieces of literature; censorship may have been so pervasive as to stifle any attempts to create literature or artwork about genocidal acts carried out within a country; those few works that were created may have met with such lack of interest as to it discourage others from pursuing such activities; and it may well be that neither authors, artists, nor the general public had an interest in such atrocities. Finally, the killing may have been so encompassing that there was no one left to create works of art. As for those genocidal acts committed within the past fifteen to twenty years, time could be a major factor for the lack of works concerning these acts. In this regard it is significant to note that not until almost sixteen years after the Jewish victims of the Holocaust were liberated from the death camps, at which time Eichmann was brought to trial in Israel, was there a great outpouring of literature on the subject of the Holocaust.

In relation to the point about censorship, it is generally acknowledged that numerous authors in the Soviet Union have written works (novels, short stories, poetry, and to a lesser extent, drama) on various facets of the genocidal acts committed by the Soviet government, but they are in *samizdat* (unofficial or self-published works) form. Very few of these works have been published in the West in English.

Interestingly, there are many more films on genocidal acts than there is art or literature, largely because many international human rights organizations have taken it upon themselves to produce films.

Finally, while a plethora of artwork has been created over the past several centuries on various aspects of the horrors of war, very little has been created on genocidal acts other than the Holocaust and the atomic bombings of Hiroshima and Nagasaki. This is an area of concern that merits serious examination.

Literature

Relatively few of the genocidal acts committed during the twentieth century have been the subject of matter of literature, and the literature that does depict such acts is small. Those acts that have been depicted in literary works include the Turkish slaughter of the Armenians between 1915 and 1923, the Stalinist purges in the 1930s, 1940s, and 1950s, the Soviet-contrived famine of the Ukrainian people in 1932–33, and the slaughter of the Cambodian people by the Khmer Rouge in the mid-1970s. Not only are few genocidal acts depicted in literary works, but the styles found in this writing are primarily limited to realism and satire.

Works whose focus is the Turkish slaughter of the Armenians address the following areas: the Armenian way of life prior to, during, and following the mass murder; the story of how and why the large Armenian community in Turkey became the victim of genocide; the heroic attempt by a group of Armenians to stave off the Turks; and the impact that the tragedy has had on both the survivors and the subsequent generations of Armenians.

In comparison with the small number of short stories and novels on the genocide of the Armenians, there has been a virtual outpouring of poetry. Many of these poems are by the most famous Armenian poets of this century—Aharonian, Tekeyan, Dadourian, Zaroukian, Tautian, among others—and a substantial amount is of extremely high quality.

Much more literature, particularly novels, has been written on and about the genocidal acts committed by Stalin and his henchmen. Many of these works are of high quality, particularly those by Bulgakov, Shalamov, Solzhenitsyn and

Wiesel. This body of literature deals with topics such as the pervasive fear that was endemic to Russia during the Stalinist years, the paranoia of the State, and those who served as its loyal dupes (often the subject of scathing satire). The events covered include the collectivization and show trials of the late 1930s and Stalin's genocidal creation of an artificial famine in Ukraine. Writers have dealt with the persecution suffered by both the religious and national minorities, life and death in the prison camps, the way in which millions were swallowed up by the purges, and the mass slaughter of the Jewish writers in 1952.

Very few works have been published thus far in English on the Khmer Rouge regime's slaughter of the Cambodians between 1975 and 1979. One of the most notable is Edmund Keeley's novel, *A Wilderness Called Peace*. It chronicles one woman's life during the slaughter of the Cambodian people as well as numerous other events. While its portrayal of the protagonist is weak, it powerfully delineates the horror of genocide.

Overall, the dearth of literature on genocide is highly disturbing. In light of that dearth, it seems that literary critics, historians, philosophers and others need to examine critically why so many catastrophic events have not been addressed by writers and artists. Such studies may provide important insights into various aspects of the problems arising from genocidal acts, including that of humanity's ostensible indifference to such atrocities.

Films

There are numerous films about various genocidal acts, and many of these are quite outstanding. They are still, however, far fewer in number than those that address either the Holocaust or the threat of nuclear war or nuclear omnicide.

The genocidal acts that are addressed in these films are of both a cultural and physical nature. They include the near-absolute extermination of the people of Tierra del Fuego, the genocide of the Tasmanian aborigines in Australia, the Turkish slaughter of the Armenians, the forced exile of the Estonian people from the U.S.S.R. since 1939, the purges in the Soviet Union under Stalin, the cultural genocide committed against the tribal Igorot people of the northern Philippines by the Marcos government, the genocidal acts committed by the Guatemalan government against its indigenous Indians, the mass killing of the Cuiva people in Colombia, the cultural genocide of the Indians of the Amazon region, and the genocidal acts committed by the Khmer Rouge against the Cambodian people.

Only one of the movies listed in the accompanying bibliography was made as a feature film, namely *The Killing Fields*. It is an outstanding film that tells the true story of one man's struggle to hold on to life during the period when the Pol Pot government slaughtered up to 3 million Cambodian people, and his friend's frantic attempts to save him. All of the other films are documentaries, and only one of these, *Year Zero*, another film about the slaughter of the Cambodians, was specifically made for television.

Notwithstanding, the fact remains that many other incidents of genocide have not been addressed by filmmakers. The exact reason is unclear. Filmmakers may not be cognizant of some genocidal acts or may prefer to key in on the better-known atrocities; and there may be monetary reasons concerning the salability of such films.

Conclusions

It seems as if there will always be questions as to the exact impact or effect that writers, artists, and filmmakers have on humanity via their works of art that address such issues as genocide. Hopefully, though, in the end such works will become "a possible source of wisdom about man's increasingly troubled relationship to the kinds of death which face him" (Lifton, 1967, p. 478).

Reference

Lifton, Robert Jay (1967). *Death in Life: Survivors of Hiroshima*. New York: Basic Books. 594 pp.

Bibliography

Novels

Bulgakov, Mikhail (1967). *The Master and Margarita*. Translated from the Russian by Michael Glenny. New York: Signet. 384 pp.
  This is an outstanding novel in which the "real" world of Stalinist Russia in the 1930s experiences an upheaval due to the "unreal" appearance of the Devil. Much of the power of this satire comes from the inability of "rational" people to accept events that are ostensibly "irrational," even if the irrational (genocidal acts) is the norm in their everyday world. This was first circulated in *samizdat* form; that is, unofficially or secretly self-published.

Chukovskaia, Lydia (1967). *The Deserted House*. Translated from the Russian by Aline B. Werth. New York: Dutton, 144 pp.
  Written in Russia during 1939–40 during the "Terror," this novel depicts what happened to the millions of simple people who optimistically believed Stalin's promise of a happy future. Olga Petrovna, the protagonist, and her son, Kolia, are such believers who turn away from that faith when other people begin to be swallowed up by the purges. This was first circulated in samizdat.

Chukovskaia, Lydia (1976). *Going Under*. Translated from the Russian by Peter M. Weston. New York: Quadrangle/New York Times. 144 pp.
  This novel is set in the 1940s in the Soviet Union. The protagonist suffers greatly owing to the unknown fate of her husband who was arrested during the purges in the 1930s. The novel, which is autobiographical, also touches on the new wave of terror of the 1940s as well as the anti-Semitism that arose at this time. This was first published in *samizdat*.

Groseclose, Elgin (1939). *Ararat*. New York: Carrick & Evans. 482 pp.

This novel presents a vivid picture of the Armenian way of life prior to, during, and following the genocidal acts committed by the Turks in 1915.

Keeley, Edmund (1985). *A Wilderness Called Peace*. New York: Simon & Schuster. 315 pp.

This novel, which takes the form of a diary, tells the story of a woman (Sameth) of European–Chinese–Khmer ancestry who is caught up in and witnesses the cataclysmic events that have torn asunder Cambodia (Kampuchea) since the 1970s. It chronicles the woman's life—her decision whether to remain in the country or to escape—as well as the slaughter of up to 3 million out of 7 million Cambodians by the Pol Pot regime from 1975 to 1979, the Vietnamese invasion of the country, the guerrilla warfare that has continued ever since, and the plight of the refugees along the Thailand–Cambodian borders. The novel has been praised for powerfully delineating "the cynical international politics of our era," but criticized for the weaknesses of its portrayal of the protagonist, who seems more Western than Eastern in her actions and thoughts.

Solzhenitsyn, Aleksandr (1963). *One Day in the Life of Ivan Denisovich*. Translated from the Russian by Ralph Parker. New York: Dutton. 160 pp.

While this novel does not specifically deal with genocidal acts, it does key in on how Stalin rounded up entire bodies of people and sent them to prison camps in Siberia, where the conditions were harsh and cruel if not deadly. This story is about a "lucky day" in the life of one prisoner in the Soviet gulag. The make up of the prisoners in the camp accurately depicts the terrible treatment suffered by the smaller nations under the rule of Stalin.

Solzhenitsyn, Aleksandr (1968a). *Cancer Ward*. Translated from the Russian by Rebecca Frank. New York: Dial. 616 pp.

Set in the cancer ward of a hospital in Soviet Central Asia, this novel portrays the lives of numerous Soviet personalities thrown together under extreme conditions. Significantly, the roles of many of the patients in the hospital reflect the treatment that the smaller nations in the Soviet Union were subjected to under Stalin. Throughout the novel there are direct and indirect allusions to the genocidal acts committed by Stalin's lackeys.

Solzhenitsyn, Aleksandr (1968b). *The First Circle*. Translated from the Russian by Thomas P. Whitney. New York: Harper & Row. 580 pp.

This powerful novel, which takes place in a prison camp for political prisoners, provides a panoramic view of the terror that people lived under in Stalinist Russia. It is rife with allusions to Stalin's collectivization and the show trials of the 1930s.

Vladimov, Georgii (1978). *Faithful Ruslan: The Story of a Guard Dog*. Translated from the Russian by Michael Glenny. New York: Simon & Schuster. 220 pp.

This satirical novel is about a guard dog in a gulag camp who is out of a job as the camp is torn down. It depicts what a loyal servant of the State has had to do during its period of service.

Voinovich, Vladimir (1978). *Pretender to the Throne: The Further Adventures of Private Ivan Chonkin*. Translated from the Russian by Richard Lourie. New York: Farrar, Straus & Giroux. 358 pp.

In this satirical novel, the protagonist languishes in jail while all the petty bureaucrats do everything to prevent themselves from being liquidated. Both Stalin and Hitler are characters in this book.

Werfel, Franz (1934). *The Forty Days of Musa Dagh*. New York: Viking. 800 pp.
This epic novel tells the story of how and why the large Armenian community in Turkey (in 1915) became the object of genocide. Integral to the novel is the heroic story of an attempt by a group of Armenians to hold out on a mountain top against the Turks.

Wiesel, Elie (1981). *The Testament*. Translated from the French by Marion Wiesel. New York: Summit Books. 346 pp.
This novel, whose background is Stalin's mass slaughter of Jewish writers in 1952, is about the life of Paltiel Kossover, who fought as a Marxist intellectual against the Nazis in Germany, served as a Communist agent in France and Palestine, worked as a burier of the dead on the Eastern Front, wrote tracts for the Party in Russia, and is now faced with a death sentence in Russia. Before he dies he composes a testament in order that his life not be totally forgotten. Composed of memoirs, letters, poems, and the words that are spoken at his interrogation, it becomes a celebration because a spirit has survived a pogrom.

Short Stories

Daniel, Iulli (1964). This is Moscow Speaking. In Blake, Patricia, and Hayward, Max (Eds.), *Dissonant Voices in Soviet Literature*, pp. 262–306. Translated from the Russian by John Richardson. New York: Harper & Row.
This bitterly satiric story is about an official proclamation announcing "Public Murder Day," during which all Soviet citizens over the age of sixteen are given the right to kill any other Soviet, except policemen and soldiers. This was first published in *samizdat*.

Shalamov, Varlam (1980). *Kolyma Tales*. Translated from the Russian by John Glad. New York: W.W. Norton. 220 pp.
The powerful short stories in this collection, based on first-hand experience, devastatingly portray life and death in the Stalinist prison camps from 1929 through 1949. Shalamov was incarcerated for nearly twenty years.

Poetry

Akhmatova, Anna (1976). Requiem. In *Requiem and Poem without a Hero*, pp. 22–32. Translated from the Russian by D.M. Thomas. London: Elek.
"Requiem" is a cycle of poems that was written as a memorial to the poet's own suffering and the suffering of millions of others during Stalin's reign of terror. Its intensity derives from its understatement and themes of love, parting, and suffering. This poem has been published in full only in the West.

Balakian, Peter (1983). *Sad Days of Light*. New York: The Sheep Meadow Press. 79 pp.
Many of the poems in this collection are concerned with the impact that the Armenian massacres by the Turks had on the author's Armenian relatives. Among the most powerful poems are "Road to Alepp, 1915," "First Nervous Breakdown, Newark 1941," "In the Turkish War," and "The Claim."

Basmakjian, Garig (Ed.) (1976). *Armenian-American Poets: A Bilingual Anthology*. Translated from the Armenian by Garig Basmakjian. Detroit: The Alex Manougian Cultural Fund of the Armenian General Benevolent Union. 140 pp.
Many of the poems assembled in this book of outstanding poetry are about some aspect of the Armenian massacres by the Turkish in 1915. There are poems by Leon

Srabian Herald, Archie Minasian, Diana Der Hovanessian, David Kherdian, Hagop Missak Merjan, and Harold Bond.

Der Hovanessian, Diana, and Margossian, Marzbed (Eds.) (1978). *Anthology of Armenian Poetry*. Translated from the Armenian by Der Hovanessian and Margossian. New York: Columbia University Press. 357 pp.

Included in this collection, which spans more than twenty centuries of Armenian poetry, is a 200-page section entitled "Post-Holocaust Poetry of the Diaspora and Soviet Armenia." (Note: The "holocaust" in this case refers to the Turkish massacre of the Armenians.) This section includes dozens upon dozens of poems by the most famous Armenian poets: Aharonian, Tekeyan, Zarian, Dadourian, Zaroukian, Tautian, among others of this century.

Art

"Cambodia Witness." (For more information about this exhibit write to: Amnesty International U.S.A. 322 Eighth Ave., New York, NY 10001.)

"Cambodia Witness" is an exhibit of photographs which documents the genocidal acts committed by the government of Pol Pot in Cambodia. Taken by David Hawk during two trips to Cambodia in March 1981 and April 1982, the gruesome photographs provide stark evidence of the bloodbath perpetrated by the Khmer Rouge in which members of many ethnic minorities (Chinese, Vietnamese, Lao and Thai) and religious groups (the Cham and Buddhist monkhood) were victims of repeated massacres.

UNESCO (1980). *Kampuchean Chronicles: Narrated by Refugee Children in Words and Pictures*. Tokyo: National Federation of UNESCO in Japan.

In April 1980, the National Federation of UNESCO Associates in Japan, in cooperation with the U.N. High Commissioner for Refugees and UNESCO, held a drawing competition for children in two of the most crowded holding centers for exiled Kampucheans. More than five hundred children between the ages of five and fifteen submitted drawings. The best of these drawings are included in this slim but powerful volume, which speaks to the horrors these children experienced when all of Kampuchea was a bloodbath.

Films

The Armenian Case. (43 min., color. Available from Atlantis Films, 1252 La Granda Dr., Thousand Oaks, CA 91360.)

In this film the survivors of Turkish atrocities, and European and American eye witnesses, recall the historical events that were to shape the destiny of the Armenian people. It includes documentary sequences on World War I, and the establishment of the Republic of Armenia and Soviet Armenia.

Back to Kampuchea. (57 min., color, 16 mm. Available from First Run Features, 153 Waverly Place, New York, NY 10014.)

This film reports on the attempts of the Cambodians to rebuild the country following the Vietnam War and the genocidal acts committed by the Khmer Rouge. It keys in on a Khmer taxi driver who tells of his family's plight under the Pol Pot regime.

Camino Triste. (30 min., color, ¾-inch, VHS, Beta videotape. Available from Icarus Films, 200 Park Avenue South, #1319, New York, NY 10003.)

This documentary tells the story of 125,000 Guatemalan Indians who fled their country owing to "an alleged counter-insurgency campaign" that killed or exiled thousands of Indians.

Desert People. (51 min., b & w, 16 mm. Available from McGraw-Hill Films, P.O. Box 641, Del Mar, CA 92014.)
   This film is about how one segment of aboriginal people in Australia, whose ancestry dates back to Paleolithic times and who recently lived in the Central Australian desert, were destroyed by the encroachment of "civilization."

Diary for All My Children. (106 min., color, 16 mm. Hungarian with English subtitles. Available from New Yorker Films, 16 W. 61st St., New York, NY 10023.)
   This is a semiautobiographical account by Marta Mezaros (who moved from the Soviet Union to Hungary in the 1950s), and her story of her search for her parents. It includes documentary and newsreel footage from the Stalinist purge trials.

The Estonians: For the Record. (29 min., color, 16 mm. Available from Esto Film/ Canada, 314 Jarvis, Toronto, Ontario, Canada.)
   This film tells the story of the Estonian people who have been in exile since their country was taken over by the U.S.S.R. in 1939.

The Forgotten Genocide. (28 min., color, 16 mm. Available from Atlantis Productions, 1252 LaGranada Drive, Thousand Oaks, CA 91360.)
   This film presents the story of the genocide of the Armenian people which was committed by the Turks in 1915.

Guatemala: Personal Testimonies. (20 min., color, 16 mm. Available from Icarus Films, 200 Park Avenue South, Suite 1319, New York, NY 10003.)
   This series of testimonies from Guatemalan Indians clearly bears witness to the widespread abuse of human rights under the government of General Rios Montt. In interviews survivors of massacres describe army attacks and the role of civil patrols in the military campaign.

Kampuchea: After Pol Pot. (48 min., color, 16 mm. Available from Icarus Films, 200 Park Avenue South, Suite 1319, New York, NY 10003.)
   This film keys in on the international emergency aid campaign that was organized to help the people of Kampuchea rebuild their shattered lives following the collapse of the Pol Pot regime, which was responsible for the murder of over 3 million people.

The Killing Fields. (137 min., color, 16 mm. Available from Swank Film Programmer, 6767 Forest Lawn Dr., Hollywood, CA 90068.)
   This moving film tells the horrific and true story of a man's (Dith Pran, an interpreter for *New York Times* reporter Sydney Schanberg) traumatic escape from Cambodia during the 1970s when that country had 3 million out of its 7 million people slaughtered by the Khmer Rouge. A truly outstanding film.

The Last of the Cuiva. (67 min., color, 16 mm. Available from Michigan Media, 400 Fourth St., Ann Arbor, MI 48103.)
   This film presents the story of the remaining six hundred Cuiva, an indigenous people and now dying people of Colombia, who have been killed off by ranchers and robbed of their land.

The Last Tasmanian: Extinction. (60 min., color, 16 mm. Available from McGraw-Hill Films, P.O. Box 641, Del Mar, CA 92014.)

This documentary examines the act of genocide committed against the Tasmanian Aborgines in Australia after the colonization by the British.

Listen Carcas. (19 min., color, 16 mm. Available from Cinema Guild, 1697 Broadway, New York, NY 10019.)
This documentary focuses on the cultural genocide to which the Indians of the Amazon region are being subjected.

The Ona People. (55 min., color, 16 mm. Available from Documentary Educational Resources, 5 Bridge St., Watertown, MA 02177.)
This film presents the story of the nearly absolute extermination of the Ona people of Tierra del Fuego, first initiated in the 1800s when European settlement led directly to genocide.

Personal Testimonies. (20 min., color, ¾-inch videotape. Available from Icarus Films, 200 Park Avenue South, #1319, New York, NY 10003.)
This film presents the testimonies of Guatemalan Indian villagers concerning the murder of their people by the Guatemalan military.

Political Killings by Governments. (20 min., color, slide show. Available from Film and Human Rights Library, Facets Multimedia, 1517 West Fullerton Ave., Chicago, IL 60614.)
Produced by the Dutch section of Amnesty International, the human rights organization that was the 1978 recipient of the Nobel Prize for Peace, this film discusses numerous aspects of political killings, including genocide, carried out by governments. Suggestions are provided on how viewers can become involved in a campaign against political killings.

Seasons of Thunder. (59 min., color, 16 mm. Available from Philippine Resource Center, Box 4000D, Berkeley, CA 94704.)
This film tells the story of the cultural genocide that was committed against the tribal Igorot people of the northern Philippines by the Marcos government. Slowly but surely the Igorot people lost their land and tradition as the government took away both their land and resources.

When the Mountains Tremble. (83 min., color, 16 mm. Available from New Yorker Films, 16 W. 61st St., New York, NY 10023.)
This film tells the story of a Guatemalan Indian woman who is the only person in her family to survive the genocidal acts committed by the Guatemalan government against its indigenous Indians.

Year Zero. (53 min., color, 16 mm. Available from American Friends Service, Pacific Southwest Region, 980 N. Fair Oaks Ave., Pasadena, CA 91103.)
Made in Cambodia in September 1979 for Britain's Associated Television, this film presents gruesome evidence of the genocidal acts committed between 1975 and 1979 when over 3 million people were slaughtered.

13

The Literature, Art, and Film of Nuclear And Other Futuristic Destruction

Samuel Totten

From the earliest years of the twentieth century, writers of science fiction have created works that depict either horrible genocidal acts or the demise of the Earth through the use of various types of exotic weapon of immense power. Such predictions and depictions more often than not were looked upon as nothing more than the wild imaginings of writers on the fringe. The atomic bombings of Hiroshima and Nagasaki in 1945 by the United States radically altered such views. The change arose primarily from the fact that the single atomic bomb dropped on Hiroshima killed over 138,000 people, and the single atomic bomb dropped on Nagasaki instantly killed over 50,000 people. Thus for a time, one nation had the power virtually to wipe out an entire city of people with a single bomb.

In the ensuing years the magnitude of the problem has dramatically increased. The United States and the Soviet Union immediately became involved in a nuclear weapons race, and each developed the much more powerful hydrogen bomb. Not only is it now openly acknowledged that the United States and the Soviet Union possess the destructive power to annihilate the people of this planet many times over, but there has been speculation by noted scientists that the "use" of a certain megatonnage (about 5,700 MT) of nuclear weapons could cause a "nuclear winter" that could spell the death not only of humanity, but of the entire planet. Equally disconcerting is the fact that a United States intelligence survey in 1983 reported that thirty-one countries will be able to produce nuclear weapons by the year 2,000.

In addition, research into other deadly weapons is under way. Included among these are the areas of laser and particle-beam warfare. Over the past several decades scientists and military researchers have also been stockpiling chemical and biological arsenals, including nerve gases and organisms capable of being used for germ warfare.

All of the aforementioned concerns have become the subject of a large quantity of fiction and film, and to a much lesser extent, art. While much of it is speculative in nature, a great deal of it (particularly that which depicts the atomic bombings of Hiroshima and Nagasaki) is also based on actual events. Interestingly, a large quantity of the work was ostensibly written to warn humanity to be wary of any government's buildup and use of such weapons.

Literature

Over the past forty to sixty years there has been a tremendous outpouring of literature on myriad aspects of nuclear and other futuristic destruction, and it can be divided into three categories: science fiction, which addresses many different types of futuristic destruction, including nuclear; works on various aspects of the atomic bombings of Hiroshima and Nagasaki; and works not in the science fiction genre about possible future nuclear wars.

The threat of nuclear and other kinds of futuristic destruction was first depicted in works of science fiction. In fact, in 1914 H.G. Wells published a novel entitled *The World Set Free*, which is about how civilization is destroyed by atomic warfare. The critic H. Bruce Franklin has pointed out that *"The World Set Free* may be considered the beginning, in imagination, of the atomic age"* (Franklin, 1984, p. 13). Franklin also points out that for approximately forty years, from 1900 to 1940, nuclear weapons and nuclear war "existed nowhere but in science fiction" (*ibid*., p. 12). From the 1940s onward nuclear weapons, nuclear warfare, and biological and chemical warfare have become major themes in science fiction.

Science fiction short stories and novels have explored or depicted, sometimes in a disturbingly prophetic manner, more scenarios and topics than any other genre that addresses such concerns. Among them are the invention of atomic weapons; the dropping of atomic bombs by airplanes; the invention of new weapons systems, including strategic and tactical nuclear weapons, the hydrogen and neutron bombs, and new types of chemical and biological weapon; the concept of nuclear deterrence; accidental nuclear war arising either from computer malfunction or human error; the escalation of a conventional war into a nuclear war; a preemptive first strike; nuclear terrorism; nuclear disarmament; space-based nuclear weapons; the total devastation of civilization by nuclear warfare; and the extinction of all human consciousness by nuclear war.

Most of the fiction in this category ranges from mediocre to good. There are only a few pieces that could be deemed outstanding. In the poorest works the authors have used the subject of nuclear war as a "thrilling fantasy for the indulgence of escapist heroics," says Franklin (*ibid*, p. 13). At the other end of the scale, two-time Nobel Prize winner Linus Pauling has stated that a science fiction novel entitled *Level 7* by Mordecai Roshwald was "the most realistic picture of nuclear war that I have ever read" (*ibid*, p. 25).

Science fiction that addresses the subject of nuclear war may have entertainment as its main purpose, but science fiction writers have warned of the devastation that could be wrought by either a limited or all-out nuclear war, and have explored the profoundly dangerous situation in which a small segment of the world's population has placed all of humanity. However, while science fiction has addressed many topics concerning nuclear war, few works have attempted to come up with solutions or preventive measures.

Among the most poignant, powerful, and significant works are those that address some aspect of the atomic bombings of Hiroshima and Nagasaki. However, as when using the Holocaust as subject matter, artists are faced with profound problems when they attempt to create "art" out of a catastrophe of such magnitude. On the one hand, as a Japanese critic noted, "If you describe the A-bomb in an ordinary way, from a standpoint of personal relationships, your description differs very little from that of other disasters—such as ordinary bombings or earthquakes" (Lifton, 1967, p. 400). On another note, the late Yoko Ota, a survivor of the atomic bombing of Hiroshima and a highly respected writer, once stated that creative writing about the atomic bombing is "outside literature . . . With ordinary fiction, there are patterns and categories—children's literature, romantic stories, and so on. But there is no pattern and no category for the atomic bomb experience. The experience was so strong, so great, so powerful, that one can find no words to describe it" (Lifton, 1967, p. 404).

In another striking parallel between the insights of Holocaust survivors/-writers and the atomic bomb survivors/writers, the latter group has repeatedly questioned and wrestled with the dilemma of whether writers and artists have any right to depict the tragedies of the victims of Hiroshima and Nagasaki. Ota was disturbed by such questions as: "Do I have the right to imagination?" and "Can what I say about the dead ever be authentic?" (*ibid*, p. 405). Another Japanese writer has said, "If you . . . are immature as a writer, and you write about the A-bomb—then you are abusing the souls of the dead" (*ibid*, p. 409). The same could be said, of course, of those who trivialize the significance of the atomic bombings in any way.

In regard to why certain survivors/writers create works about the atomic bombings, there are yet other parallels between themselves and the survivors/ writers of the Holocaust. Many wrote, and continue to write, for three primary reasons: to inform the world as to what happened in Hiroshima and Nagasaki; to warn humanity about the cataclysmic destruction that nuclear weapons are capable of; and out of a "sense of responsibility to the dead" (*ibid*. p. 409). (For an outstanding discussion of the different points of view and themes of *hibakusha* (survivors of the atomic bombings) and non-*hibakusha* writers, *see* the chapter entitled "A-bomb literature" in Lifton (*ibid*).

A vast quantity of literature has been written by Japanese writers about the atomic bombings, most of which is not yet available in English. Each year, though, an increasing amount is translated and published, and most of it is considered to be among the most outstanding work by the so-called "A-bomb" writers. The subject matter of the translated works not only focuses on the horror faced by the victims and survivors in the immediate aftermath of the atomic bombings but many other areas as well, including the long-term effects of being exposed to a heavy dose of radiation, the stigma of being a *hibakusha*, the fears that survivors harbor regarding marriage and child-bearing owing to possible genetic defects, the longing for loved ones who perished in the atomic bombings, and the overwhelming fear of an outbreak of nuclear war.

All of these works hold especial significance for humanity in light of the fact that the people of Hiroshima and Nagasaki are the only ones who have experienced the horrible fate of a nuclear war. Though they are not didactic, inherent in each of them is a profoundly significant message to humanity concerning what it means to live in the nuclear age.

Many highly regarded poets, including Denise Levertov, Lucien Stryk, and John Wain from the United States and England, have written powerful and haunting poems about the tragedy of the atomic bombings. They focus on either the fate of the victims, the role of the pilots whose planes dropped the atomic bombs, or the significance that the atomic bombings have for humanity.

It is both curious and disturbing that so few novelists, short-story writers and poets from the United States have created works about the atomic bombings in light of the fact that the United States not only dropped those bombs, but was the first country in history to use such weapons. Also, with the exception of certain poems, the works that have been written about the atomic bombings have been of inferior quality both in plot and style.

A plethora of novels, short stories, and poetry not in the science fiction genre have been written about the threat or the results of nuclear war. Numerous works, but to a much lesser extent than those on nuclear war, have also been written about the genocidal effects of chemical and biological warfare.

The subject matter of these works is equally diverse and includes the following: an accidental nuclear war caused by a computer error; a preemptive nuclear strike which results in a nuclear war in which hundreds of millions are killed; the devastation caused by a so-called "limited" nuclear war; how a conventional war escalates into nuclear war; the total devastation caused by an all-out nuclear war; slow and agonizing death by radiation; various geopolitical factors that lead different countries to engage in nuclear war; the efforts of the survivors of a nuclear holocaust to resume life in a devastated and primitive world; the long-term cultural and psychological effects that a nuclear apocalypse has on the survivors; humanity's inability to avoid one nuclear holocaust after another; the tension faced by humanity as a result of being forced to live with ever-present nuclear threat; the last generation on Earth waiting to die from the effects of a nuclear war; the destruction of an entire city's population by a neutron bomb; nuclear war fought in space; and wars involving both nuclear and biological weapons and biological warfare.

The quality of the novels and short stories in this category primarily range from good to poor: very few of even the best works in this category approach the quality of the finest novels on the Holocaust. There seem to be several important reasons for this situation. First of all, in light of the fact that neither an all-out nuclear war nor an all-out biological or chemical war has occurred, the works are speculative, a factor that undoubtedly has a tremendous bearing on the verisimilitude of the works, and may explain, in part, why so many of these literary efforts are substandard. Secondly, much of the writing is hackneyed, and the plots and characterizations are weak. Thirdly, far too often the works suffer from a lack of correct information concerning weapons systems, including the power and effects of such weapons.

Several very significant topics still have not been addressed in creative works, and foremost among these are the issues of nuclear weapons proliferation, the concept of "nuclear winter," and the most efficacious ways to avoid a nuclear holocaust. In regard to proliferation there are two concerns worthy of examination: one is the fact that many of the materials and facilities involved in the civil use of nuclear energy are directly or indirectly useful for the manufacture of nuclear explosives, and, secondly, as more and more nations manufacture and accumulate nuclear weapons, the more likely it is that such weapons will be used in a war. The concept of "nuclear winter" reminds us that an all-out nuclear war could very likely result in not only the death of the human species, but also the planet Earth.

Undoubtedly, as the nuclear arms race continues to result in the development and deployment of ever more devastating weapons (not to mention increasingly complex geopolitical situations), and as additional nations join the so-called "nuclear club," writers will have an ever-increasing amount of subject matter to address in their literary works.

When all is said and done, even the best science fiction works, let alone other genres of literature, have great difficulty in "grasping a dead planet without human consciousness" (Franklin, 1984, p. 12).

Films

Dozens upon dozens of films (archival footage of the devastation wrought by the atomic bombings of Hiroshima and Nagasaki, documentaries, Hollywood-made dramas and other feature films, and science fiction movies) have been made about the atomic bombings of Hiroshima and Nagasaki, various aspects of nuclear war, and biological warfare. Most of those available in English have been made in the United States. While numerous feature films and documentaries about the atomic bombings have been made in Japan, very few are available in the United States.

A vast number of documentaries have been produced in the United States about various aspects of the atomic bombings, and many are outstanding. Many of these films use stock footage of the aftermath of the atomic bomb or include interviews with survivors. Among the subject matter covered in such films is the reasons behind the decision by the United States to drop the atomic bombs; the suffering of the victims in the immediate aftermath of the bombings; the long-term impact, psychological and physical, of the atomic bombings on the survivors; the insights, feelings, and memories of the survivors; the effects of the atomic bombings on buildings as well as vegetation; art created by the survivors; and the comments of survivors about their fears that the leaders of the world will not heed their warnings about the horror of nuclear war.

There have been far fewer feature (fiction) films about nuclear war. There are numerous reasons for this. First, during the 1950s, the activities of Joseph McCarthy and the House Un-American Activities Committee virtually put a halt to the production of controversial films. Thus, for "much of the 1950s nuclear war went untreated in Hollywood with the exception of films . . . that closely resembled official government positions" (Musil, 1981, p. 8). Once the McCarthy period was on the wane, numerous feature films were made. However, the "Bomb" and the subject of nuclear war often served merely as a plot situation for poorly written and easily forgettable movies. This was particularly true of a profusion of science fiction films. Then in the 1980s, following huge antinuclear rallies both in Europe and the United States, numerous feature films and television movies were made about nuclear war. While many of these were either thought-provoking or controversial, they were also criticized for either having weak plots, being melodramatic, or being incorrect technically with regard to nuclear technology or the effects of nuclear weapons. Still, it must be acknowledged that several of these films provoked national debate in the United States between politicians, military personnel, and members of the public.

Altogether, through the years many filmmakers have shied away from making movies about nuclear war. There are fewer than a half dozen notable feature films, and the fact remains that "even when Hollywood makes a serious movie about nuclear war . . . it's still built on one fantasy or another" (Lindberg, 1985, p. 3).

Of the numerous documentaries produced, many are quite outstanding. Among the topics covered in these films are the following: all-out nuclear war scenarios; an examination of the possible ways that nuclear war might erupt; the devastation that would be caused by a nuclear war; the power of the hydrogen bomb in comparison with the atomic bombs that were dropped on Hiroshima and Nagasaki; the United States's preparation for nuclear war; the possibility and consequences of a Soviet preemptive nuclear strike against the United States; the impact of a single nuclear bomb on a city; the problem of nuclear proliferation; the pros and cons of a space-based Strategic Defense Initiative; the efficacy of civil defense in the event of nuclear war; the medical problems that would be incurred in a nuclear war; the psychological effects of the threat of nuclear war on U.S. citizens; children's fears of the threat of nuclear war; points of views of both Russian and U.S. citizens in regard to the threat of nuclear war; views of nuclear critics; and antinuclear protests.

However, numerous areas still need to be addressed: the direct link between nuclear power plants and the development of nuclear weapons; a much more thorough examination of the problem of nuclear proliferation and its concomitant dangers; the actual cases in which the United States or the Soviet Union went on nuclear alert or contemplated the use of nuclear weapons; an examination of the dozens upon dozens of solutions that have been explored over the past forty years in regard to lessening the threat of nuclear war; and an examination of the concept of "nuclear winter," as well as its numerous and highly significant ramifications for humanity and the planet.

Numerous movies have been produced about other futuristic destruction but most are in the categories of horror or science fiction. A great many of the films are poorly written and made in a sensationalistic style. Other than sheer entertainment (which is often dubious), the redeeming value of such movies is negligible. An infinitesimal number of documentary films have been made on this subject matter; but most are educative in that they present accurate information, and are thorough in its coverage of the key issues.

Art

Over the past forty years artists from around the world, but especially Japan, the United States, the U.S.S.R., and Europe, have created works whose focus has either been the atomic bombings of Hiroshima and Nagasaki, "the Bomb," or future nuclear destruction. Very little art has been created about other types of possible futuristic genocidal acts.

Most of the best artwork about the atomic bombings of Hiroshima and Nagasaki is either by *hibakusha* (most of whom were not professional artists) or non-*hibakusha* artists in Japan. Such work depicts various aspects of the atomic bombings with an emphasis on the destruction witnessed and the suffering experienced by the victims. These artists, of course, were faced with the same constraints as others who have attempted to depict the horror of genocidal acts, and that is the conundrum as to how to do justice to the horror of the actual event. The truth of the matter is, while many of these works are raw with power, many do not begin to approach that "reality" depicted in the written works or films. Only a tiny fraction of this work has been made available, either in books or exhibits, for viewing outside of Japan.

A large portion of the art whose subject matter is either "the Bomb" or possible future nuclear destruction is antiwar art "in which war is overtly depicted as dreadful" (Heller, 1984, p. 7). Other artwork on this subject often depicts the artist's own perception of the "nuclear nightmare." The predominant images found are: mushroom clouds, rockets, fire, and distorted or anguished countenances. Other images have been appropriated from antiwar artwork that has appeared throughout history: the grim reaper, the death's head, and skeletons. Biblical images, especially from the Book of Revelations, are also quite common in the artwork of artists from the United States and Europe.

This art, like that of the Holocaust, is represented in many different media: painting, illustration, posters, cartoons, prints, sculpture, and photography. The styles are equally eclectic: realism, social realism, expressionism, surrealism, and abstract art. As for the quality of the work, the span is very broad in that it ranges from superb to mundane. The problem with a large quantity of it, and not only those works from the Soviet Union, is that it is quite didactic.

Conclusion

Soon after Hiroshima and Nagasaki were destroyed by atomic bombs, Albert Einstein observed that "everything has now changed except our way of thinking. Because of that, we drift toward unparalleled disaster. We shall require a substantially new manner of thinking if mankind is to survive." In light of the ever-increasing nuclear arsenals, it would be naïve to assert that art about nuclear and other futuristic destruction has been a catalyst for change in the thinking of humanity. However, in its own inimitable way, it is quite possible that such art is currently planting the seeds for such a change. Time will tell.

References

Franklin, H. Bruce (1984). Nuclear war and science fiction. In Franklin, H. Bruce (Ed.). *Countdown to Midnight: Twelve Memorable Stories About Nuclear Warfare*. New York: DAW Books.

Heller, Steven (1984). Preface. In Bruckner, D.J.R.; Chwast, Seymour; and Heller, Steven (Eds.), *Art Against War: 400 Years of Protest in Art*. New York: Abbeville Press.

Lifton, Robert Jay (1967). *Death in Life: Survivors of Hiroshima*. New York: Basic Books. 594 pp.

Lindberg, Tod (4 August 1985). Weapons of entertainment. *Los Angeles Times*, p. 3.

Musil, Robert K. (1981). *Shadows of the Nuclear Age: The Study and Discussion Guide*. Philadelphia: The SANE Education Fund.

Bibliography

Reference Work

Newman, John, and Unsworth, Michael (1984). *Future War Novels: An Annotated Bibliography of Works in English Published Since 1946*. Phoenix, AZ: Oryx Press. 100 pp.
    This text contains over one hundred annotations of novels whose plots and themes are concerned with future wars of various types, including nuclear war and germ warfare. The "emphasis is on realistic novels that focus on military events."

Novels

Anderson, Poul (1961). *Twilight World*. New York: Dodd, Mead. 181 pp.
This science fiction novel explores what the world might be like after World War III. It is a grim story of ruin, famine, barbarism, but also hope.

Braddon, Russell (1965). *The Year of the Angry Rabbit*. New York: Norton. 181 pp.
This is a wild and powerful satiric novel about Australian biological warfare at the end of the twentieth century. Australian scientists develop a biological poison in order to control the rampant rabbit population, but discover it is also lethal to humans. The Australian prime minister decides to use the threat of the poison to force nations around the world to disarm by placing vials around the world that can be set off by remote control. The subsequent results are devastating.

Briggs, Raymond (1982). *When the Wind Blows*. New York: Shocken Books. 40 pp.
This slim volume, told in the form of a comic strip, is a mordant satire of an "average" English couple preparing and muddling through a nuclear war, from fixing up a fallout shelter on through radiation poisoning.

Burdick, Eugene, and Wheeler, Harvey (1963). *Fail-Safe*. New York: Dell Publishing Co. 255 pp.
In this novel a mechanical breakdown in a computer sends a group of U.S. nuclear bombers toward the Soviet Union with no chance of recalling them.

Collins, Larry, and LaPierre, Dominique (1981). *The Fifth Horseman*. New York: Avon. 478 pp.
In this well conceived novel, the President of the United States receives a nuclear ultimatum from Qaddafi: either the U.S.A. surrenders to absurd demands or a major city will be obliterated.

Coon, Horace (1958). *43,000 Years Later*. New York: New American Library. 143 pp.
An epistolary novel, this is the story of extraterrestrial archeologists engaged in exploring the Earth 43,000 years after a devastating war has wiped out everything but insects. They discover that the war was between the East and the West and that 240 hydrogen bombs were used. The insights of the explorers provide a satirical comment on the nature of humanity, nationalities, and political organizations.

Farki, Moris (1983). *The Last of Days*. New York: Crown. 538 pp.
In this well wrought novel, a self-proclaimed Islamic messiah and leader of a terrorist organization believes he has been chosen by Allah to crush Israel. To do that he is bent on unleashing a nuclear holocaust, but Jews and Muslims unite to stop him.

Hoban, Russel (1980). *Riddley Walker*. New York: Pocket Books. 240 pp.
This novel is about a primitive civilization in England, about 2,300 years after a nuclear holocaust, and the growing pains it is going through. It is ostensibly pursuing the same course that led to the demise of the previous "advanced" society.

Ibuse, Masuji (1985). *Black Rain*. New York: Bantam Books. 304 pp.
Written by an elderly and highly respected Japanese writer, this acclaimed novel is about the impact that the atomic bombing had on Hiroshima and its people. It is richly textured, and one of the finest pieces of literature on nuclear war.

Johnson, Denis (1985). *Fiskadoro*. New York: Alfred A. Knopf. 221 pp.

This well wrought novel keys in on some of the many long-term cultural and psychological effects that a nuclear apocalypse has had on a city near Key West, Florida. Sixty years after a nuclear war, most of the U.S.A. is still barren wasteland, and the towns that do exist are on a par with Third World villages. A further problem met by the inhabitants of this world is that while artifacts (or debris) from the twentieth century are in their midst, a sense of history seems to have "deceased."

Jones, Merwyn (1958). *On the Last Day*. London: Jonathan Cape. 266 pp.
An erudite and outstanding literary work, this novel is about a world war between communists and anticommunists in which both nuclear weapons and conventional weapons are being used. It centers around the interrivalry of anticommunist factions over the issue of whether to explode hydrogen bombs on Soviet missile stations.

Kirst, Han Helmet (1959). *The Seventh Day*. Garden City, NY: Doubleday, 383 pp.
A frightening and well written novel, this story is about World War III and how the globe becomes a nuclear battlefield. A battle between Polish and Russian troops erupts into an all-out nuclear war in which the Soviets battle the United States and NATO forces.

Merle, Robert (1972). *Malevil*. New York: Simon & Schuster. 575 pp.
In this well written novel, survivors of a nuclear war (which took place in 1977) in rural France begin life over again in a world comparable to the way it was during the Middle Ages. Ironically, the first industry set up by the survivors is one of manufacturing gunpowder.

Miller, Walter M. (1969). *A Canticle for Leibowitz*. Philadelphia, PA: J.B. Lippincott. 320 pp.
Originally a short story, this Hugo-winning novel is divided into three sections (Fiat Lux, Fiat Homo, and Fiat Voluntar Tua) and tells about a world plagued by nuclear war.

O'Brian, Tim (1985). *The Nuclear Age*. New York: Alfred A. Knopf. 312 pp.
This novel deals with one man's fear of the growing nuclear arsenals in the world. Finally, he decides to dig a bomb shelter—or is it a grave? Numerous themes run throughout this novel, including the devastation of the world by nuclear war, survival and madness.

Rinehart, Luke (1983). *Long Voyage Back*. New York: Dell Publishing Company.
In this novel, a group of people are on a sea voyage when a nuclear war breaks out. The book is both an adventure story and a modern morality tale.

Roshwald, Mordecai (1959). *Level 7*. New York: McGraw-Hill. 186 pp.
This thought-provoking science fiction novel depicts the complete extermination of the human race by nuclear holocaust. Years ago, two-time Nobel Prize winner Dr. Linus Pauling called this novel "the most realistic picture of nuclear war that I have read in any work of fiction."

Shute, Nevil (1979). *On the Beach*. New York: Ballantine Books.
This novel is about the last generation of people on Earth living out their last days prior to the day when the effects—radioactive fallout—of an accidental nuclear war reach them.

Strieber, Whitley, & Kunetka, James (1984). *Warday*. New York: Holt, Rinehart, Winston. 375 pp.

This novel combines scientific and technological data with a traditional science fiction strand to tell the story of a limited nuclear war and the ensuing postwar chaos and devastation of American society. In doing so, it addresses numerous concerns that are not addressed in other novels about the nuclear arms race, particularly the question of whether a limited nuclear war can be fought and won.

Vonnegut, Kurt, Jr. (1963). *Cat's Cradle*. New York: Holt, Rinehart & Winston. 233 pp.
In this wild satire, Vonnegut takes aim at the role of atomic scientists in society as well as the way people "live" their lives while having to face the fact that their very species could be wiped out at any time by a horrendous weapon.

Vonnegut, Kurt, Jr. (1982). *Dead-Eye Dick*. New York: Dell Publishing Co. 240 pp.
This is a biting satire in which an entire city is wiped out by a "friendly" neutron bomb. Vonnegut castigates mankind's stupidities and public disasters with his rapier wit.

Wells, H.G. (1956). *The World Set Free*. London: Collins. 255 pp.
In this classic novel, first published in 1914, a world war erupts and the major cities of the world are destroyed by small "atomic bombs" which are dropped from planes. Civilization collapses as the crazed survivors, sick from radiation, crawl across the face of the earth. This novel has been called "the beginning, in imagination, of the atomic age."

Wongar, B. (1985). *Karan*. New York: Dodd, Mead. 248 pp.
The basis for this provocative novel is that in the 1950s and 1960s the British secretly tested nuclear weapons in South Australia, and these experiments have "a lethal effect on Aboriginal tribal man and his culture." A scathing indictment of modern technological society and its callous production of genocidal weapons.

Short-story Volumes and Collections

Franklin, H. Bruce (Ed.) (1984). *Countdown to Midnight*. New York: DAW Books, 287 pp.
This is a collection of twelve short stories about nuclear "doomsday" by such distinguished science fiction writers as Harland Ellison, Theodore Spurgeon, Joe Haldeman, and others.

Oe, Kenzaburo (Ed.) (1985). *The Crazy Iris and Other Short Stories of the Atomic Aftermath*. New York: Grove Press. 214 pp.
Edited by one of Japan's leading and internationally acclaimed writers, this collection of short stories marks the fortieth anniversary of the atomic bombings of Hiroshima and Nagasaki. Seven of Japan's most noted writers—Masuji Ibuse, Tamiki Hara, Katsuzo Oda, Yoku Ota, Ineko Sata, Kyoko Hayashi, and others—chronicle and recreate the impact of this tragedy on the daily lives of peasants, city professionals, artists, children, families, and others. While the stories are bereft of rhetoric as well as moralizing, the authors make a point of describing in excruciating detail the wounds and injuries suffered by the victims.

Poetry Volumes and Collections

Berlandt, Herman, and Cherkovski, Neeli (Eds.) (1983). *Peace or Perish: A Crisis Anthology*. San Francisco: Poets for Peace. 122 pp.
This anthology, which has been referred to as "the poets" mobilization against the

nuclear holocaust," contains a number of powerful poems concerned with the nuclear arms race and nuclear war by such eminent poets as Robert Creeley, Diane De Prima, William Everson, Lawrence Ferlinghetti, Carolyn Forche, Allen Ginsberg, Bob Kaufman, Denise Levertov, Kenneth Patchen, and many others.

Kaminsky, Marc (1984). *The Road from Hiroshima*. New York: Simon & Schuster. 119 pp.

This book of outstanding poems is based on the testimony of the survivors of the atomic bombings of Hiroshima. The author asserts, however, that "most of the poems . . . are neither versions of the actual or reinventions of the real; they are collages in which the actual and the imaginary freely mix, to give a vision of reality." The poems present a story of Hiroshima and its people in three different stages: life prior to the atomic bombing, during the atomic bombing, and following it.

Ohara, Miyao (Ed.) (1976). *The Sons of Hiroshima: An Anthology*. Translated from the Japanese by Miyao Ohara. Wilmington, OH: Wilmington College Peace Resource Center. 75 pp.

Written by survivors of the atomic bombing of Hiroshima, this anthology comprises poems about that tragedy as well as a world in which nuclear war is possible.

Sklar, Morty (Ed.) (1984). *Nuke-Rebuke: Writers and Artists against Nuclear Energy and Weapons*. Iowa City, IA: The Spirit That Moves US Press. 208 pp.

This collection of poetry, fiction, essays and artwork by sixty-five contributors (among them Gary Snyder, Robert Creeley, Daniel Berrigan, Dennis Brutus, William Stafford, Jacques Prevert) contains a number of very moving works that deal with the atomic bombings of Hiroshima and Nagasaki as well as other aspects of life and death in the nuclear age.

Drama

Kopit, Arthur (1984). *End of the World*. New York: Hill & Wang. 128 pp.

This unique and fascinating play is about a playwright who is commissioned by a wealthy man to write a play about nuclear proliferation and the catastrophic nature of nuclear war. As the playwright becomes more and more immersed in his research, he becomes increasingly depressed. Interestingly, the play is based on the trials and tribulations that Kopit himself experienced while writing it.

Somerville, John (1980). *Crisis: True Story about How the World Almost Ended*. [To order this play, write to the author at: 1426 Merritt Drive, El Cajon, CA 92020.]

This play is about how certain U.S. officials (the president, U.S. ambassador to the United Nations, and various presidential advisors) handled the Cuban missile crisis.

Art and Music

Bruckner, D.J.R.; Chwast, Seymour; and Heller, Steven (1984). *Art against War: 400 Years of Protest in Art*. New York: Abbeville Press, 128 pp.

Included in this text is a succinct survey of artwork (paintings, woodcuts, drawings, posters, sculpture, lithographs, photomontage, etc.) whose subject matter is nuclear war. Many of the prints are in color, and the accompanying text provides an excellent description of key works and the history behind them.

Heller, Steven (1983). *Warheads: Cartoonists Draw the Line*. New York; Penguin Books, 1983.

This book is a collection of political cartoons that are critical of various aspects of the nuclear arms race. There are contributions from many of the top political cartoonists in the United States, including Jules Feiffer, Gary Trudeau, and Pat Oliphant.

Japan Broadasting Corporation (Ed.) (1982). *Unforgettable Fire: Pictures Drawn by Atomic Bomb Survivors*. New York: Pantheon.
In this text of original drawings, survivors of the atomic bombing recreate the scenes of human suffering that took place on 6 August 1945. The vivid color drawings and graphic descriptions/captions make this a very powerful collection. It contains over one hundred color plates.

McEwan, Ian (1983). *Or Shall We Die? Words for an Oratorio Set to Music by Michael Berkeley*. London: Jonathan Cape. 32 pp.
This short but moving oratorio is concerned with the tension between the beauty of life and the life-threatening nature of the nuclear arms race and nuclear war. Its power comes both from its evocative images and its use of stirring allusions: the bombing of Hiroshima, William Blake's poetry, and the Newtonian and Einsteinian concepts of the universe.

Film Guides

Dowling, John (1983). *War Peace Film Guide*. Chicago: World Without War Publications.
This guide lists nearly three hundred films, many of which deal with the issue of nuclear war, and provides both descriptive and evaluative information on them.

Films

American Military Strength: Second to None. (51 min., b/w. Available from ABC Wide World of Learning, 1330 Avenue of the Americas, New York, NY 10019.)
In this film, ABC newsman Ted Koppel leads viewers through an all-out nuclear war scenario at the North America Air Defense Command (NORAD). He also interviews military and political leaders on the main issues surrounding nuclear war.

The Atomic Cafe. (92 min., color & b/w, videocassette. Available from Zenger Video, 10,000 Culver Blvd., Room 9, P.O. Box 802, Culver City, CA 90232-0802.)
This is a fascinating movie in which clips from documentary footage, military training films, television shows and newsreels that deal with "the Bomb," and how U.S. citizens perceived and misperceived "the Bomb" in the 1940s and 1950s are juxtaposed in a purposely ironic manner.

Dark Circle. (82 min., color, 16 mm. Available from Independent Documentary Group, 394 Elizabeth St., San Francisco, CA 94114.)
This film focuses on human costs of the first atomic bombing. It includes previously classified footage of nuclear tests involving seven hundred live pigs dressed in military uniforms to simulate human beings, as well as interviews with survivors of Nagasaki and Hiroshima.

The Day After. (150 min., color, BETA videocassette or VHS videocassette. Available from Social Studies Service, 10,000 Culver Blvd., Dept A4, P.O. Box 802, Culver City, CA 90232-0802.)
This made-for-television movie is about the aftereffects of nuclear war as Kansas citizens attempt to cope with myriad horrors. Some critics have asserted that the

movie presents a hysterical view of a complex situation, while others contend that the horrors it portrays are limited and less than those that would result should a nuclear war occur.

Dr. Strangelove, or How I Learned to Stop Worrying and Love the Bomb (93 min., b/w, 16 mm. Available from Columbia Cinematheque, 711 Fifth Ave., New York, NY 10022.)
    This scathing satire and feature film submits that the mechanism the U.S. and U.S.S.R. rely on to prevent war—nuclear deterrence, technological advances, etc.—are the very things that could lead to nuclear destruction.

Eight Minutes to Midnight. (60 min., color, 16 mm. Available from Direct Cinema, P.O. Box 315, Franklin Lakes, NJ 07417.)
    This 1981 Academy Award nominee features pediatrician Helen Caldicott speaking out against the nuclear arms race as well as about the threat of nuclear war.

Fail Safe. (111 min., b/w, 16 mm. Available from Audio/Brandon, 34 MacQuestion Parkway, South, Mt. Vernon, NY 10550.)
    This feature film, based on the novel of the same title, is about the accidental, irreversible launch of a nuclear attack on Moscow by the United States owing to a computer error.

First Strike. (59 min., color. Available from Chronicle Productions, 1001 Van Ness Avenue, San Francisco, CA 94109.)
    This film examines the possibility and consequences of a Soviet preemptive nuclear strike against the United States as well as the horrific consequences.

Ground Zero. (52 min., b/w. Available from CBS News, 524 West 57th St., New York, NY 10019.)
    This initial section of the CBS series, entitled "The Defense of the United States," examines the prospects, preparations, and consequences of a nuclear war. It includes a detailed description of the effects of a 15-megaton nuclear bomb on the Strategic Air Command headquarters in Omaha.

Hiroshima/Nagasaki, August 1945. (17 min., b/w, 16 mm. Available from Circle Film Programs, 11 West 53rd St., New York, NY 10019.)
    This graphic but outstanding film presents actual footage of the aftermath of the atomic bombings of Hiroshima and Nagasaki as well as comments by numerous survivors.

The Last Epidemic. (35 min., color, 16 mm. Available from Physicians for Social Responsibility, 639 Massachusetts Ave., Cambridge, MA 02139.)
    This is a filmed presentation of a symposium held in San Francisco in 1979 by Physicians for Social Responsibility and the Council for a Livable World. The speakers, prominent physicians and others concerned with the nuclear arms race, describe what would happen if a modern atomic bomb were dropped on San Francisco, including the global ecological catastrophes that would follow a nuclear war. They also discuss the impracticalities of civil defense and the destructive nature of the nuclear weapons that are now deployed.

Legacy of Hiroshima. (60 min., color, 16 mm. Available from Wilmington College Peace Resource Center, Hiroshima/Nagasaki Memorial Collection, Pyle Center, Box 1183, Wilmington, OH 45177.)

This documentary presents the insights, feelings, and memories of survivors of the atomic bombing of Hiroshima.

Missiles of October. (155 min., color, 16 mm. Available from Audio/Brandon Films, 34 MacQuestion Parkway, South, Mt. Vernon, NY 10550.)
This is a feature-length dramatization of the Cuban missile crisis. It attempts to portray the inner workings of government at the brink of nuclear conflict.

No More Hiroshimas. (55 min., color, 16 mm. Available from Icarus Films, 200 Park Avenue South, Suite 1319, New York, NY 10003.)
This film comprises stirring personal testimonies by survivors of the atomic bombings of Hiroshima and Nagasaki. Instead of focusing on the physical suffering of the victims, this documentary reveals the mental anguish of the *hibakusha* (survivors) and their deep-rooted fear that the leaders of the world will ignore their warnings about the horrors inflicted by nuclear war.

The Nuclear Battlefield. (52 min., color, 16 mm. Available from CBS News, 524 West 57th St., New York, NY 10019.)
One of a series of films in CBS's "The Defense of the United States," this show examines the efforts of the superpowers to develop tactics for fighting nuclear war. It also includes a discussion of what would happen to Europe should it become a nuclear battlefield.

Nuclear Nightmares. (90 min., b/w, videocassette. Available from Corinth Films, 410 East 62nd St., New York, NY 10021.)
Peter Ustinov examines four possible ways that nuclear war might erupt: escalation, proliferation, accident, and preemptive first strike. Each sequence culminates in a fallout shelter where Ustinov reveals what happened. It has been called irreverent and cynical.

Nuclear Power in World Politics. (20 min., color. Available from Lifelong Learning, University Extension-Media Center, University of California, Berkeley, CA 94720.)
This film presents a global view of nuclear proliferation: "nuclear club" countries, the attitudes of numerous nations toward nuclear weapons and the concept of a nuclear balance of power, and the possibility of an accidental nuclear war.

On the Beach. (110 min., b/w, 16 mm. Available from Audio/Brandon Films, 34 MacQuestion Parkway, South, Mt. Vernon, NY 10550.)
This feature film, based on the novel of the same title, keys in on a group of people in Australia who all face certain death from fallout poisoning following a nuclear war.

Seven Days in May. (118 min., b/w, BETA videocassette, VHS videocassette. Available from Social Studies School Service, 10,000 Culver Blvd., Culver City, CA 90232-0802.)
This drama, written by Rod Serling, is about the story of why and how an ambitious five-star general plots to overthrow the U.S. government by military coup after the president signs a nuclear disarmament pact with the U.S.S.R. It verges on the melodramatic.

To Die, To Live. (65 min., b/w, 16 mm. Available from Films, Inc., 1144 Wilmette Ave., Wilmette, IL 60091.)
This film cuts back and forth between 1945 and 1975 in order to probe the psychological and physical impact, including genetic damage, on the survivors of the atomic bombing of Hiroshima. It is based on Dr. Robert Jay Lifton's *Death in Life: Survivors of Hiroshima*, a National Book Award winner.

The War Game. (50 min., 16 mm. Available from Films, Inc., 1144 Wilmette Ave., Wilmette, IL 60091.)

This BBC film simulates the effect of a nuclear attack on a town in Kent, England, in which a large proportion of the population is killed. It shows the survivors trying to evacuate while experiencing widespread chaos. The film, which is extremely graphic, is reportedly based on information supplied by experts in the areas of nuclear defense, economics, and medicine. It is one of the most powerful and devastating films on the effects of nuclear war.

War Games. (114 min., color, BETA videocassette, VHS videocassette. Available from the Social Studies School Service, 10,000 Culver Blvd., Dept. A4, P.O. Box 802, Culver City, CA 90232-0802.)

In this far-fetched feature film, a young computer wizard trying to break the codes of video games not yet on the market unwittingly taps into the Defense Department's war games system. He inadvertently sets in motion the countdown for World War III.

Index

Bold-face page numbers following an author's name refer to an annotated bibliographic entry for that author. (In the case of a chapter from a larger work, only the annotated entry relating to that chapter is distinguished by the use of bold face, not the entry for the larger work itself.) The occurrence of more than one annotated bibliographic entry for a particular author on the same page is indicated by a numeral in parentheses following the page number.